ROYAL SPECTACLE: THE 1860 VISIT OF THE PRINCE OF WALES TO CANADA AND THE UNITED STATES

In 1860 Queen Victoria sent her eighteen-year-old son, Albert Edward, Prince of Wales, on a goodwill mission to Canada and the United States. The young heir apparent (later King Edward VII) had not yet gained his reputation as a fashion setter and rake, but he nevertheless attracted enormous crowds both in Canada, where it was the first royal visit, and in the United States. Civic leaders hosted the visitor in princely style, decorating their towns with triumphal arches and organizing royal entries, public processions, openings, and grand balls.

In *Royal Spectacle*, Ian Radforth recreates these displays of civic pride by making use of the many public and private accounts of them and analyses the heated controversies the visit provoked. When communities rushed to honour the prince and put themselves on display, social divisions inadvertently became part of the spectacle seen by the prince and described by visiting journalists. Street theatre reached a climax in Kingston, where the Prince of Wales could not disembark from his steamer because of the defiance of thousands of Orangemen dressed in their brilliant regalia and waving their banners.

Contemporary depictions of the tour provide an opportunity to interpret the cultural values and social differences that shaped Canada during the confederation decade and the United States on the eve of the Civil War. Topics explored include the Orange-Green conflict, First Nations and the politics of public display, contested representations of race and gender, the 'tourist gaze,' and the meanings of crown and empire. An original and erudite study, *Royal Spectacle* contributes greatly to historical research on public spectacle, colonial and national identities, Britishness in the Atlantic world, and the history of the monarchy.

IAN RADFORTH is an associate professor in the Department of History at the University of Toronto.

Royal Spectacle

The 1860 Visit of the Prince of Wales to Canada and the United States

Ian Radforth

UNIVERSITY OF TORONTO PRESS
Toronto Buffalo London

Toronto Buffalo London
utorontopress.com

Reprinted 2012, 2019

ISBN 978-0-8020-8699-0 (cloth)
ISBN 978-0-8020-8665-5 (paper)

Library and Archives Canada Cataloguing in Publication

Radforth, Ian Walter, 1952–
Royal spectacle : the 1860 visit of the Prince of Wales to Canada and the United States / Ian Radforth.

Includes bibliographical references and index.
ISBN 0-8020-8699-3 (bound) ISBN 0-8020-8665-9 (pbk.)

1. Edward VIII, King of Great Britain, 1841–1910 – Travel – Canada. 2. Visits of state – Canada – 1860. 3. Visits of state – United States. I. Title.

FC223.R6 1860 R32 2004 971.04′2 C2004-902520-1

University of Toronto Press acknowledges the financial assistance to its publishing program of the Canada Council for the Arts and the Ontario Arts Council.

University of Toronto Press acknowledges the financial support for its publishing activities of the Government of Canada through the Book Publishing Industry Development Program (BPIDP).

This book has been published with the help of a grant from the Canadian Federation for the Humanities and Social Sciences, through the Aid to Scholarly Publications Programme, using funds provided by the Social Sciences and Humanities Research Council of Canada.

To the memory of my parents,
Margaret Elizabeth (Thomson) Radforth and
Sydney Edwin Radforth

Contents

Acknowledgments

For several months during the summer and autumn of 1860, the visit to Canada and the United States made by Albert Edward, Prince of Wales, captured the imagination of newspaper readers in England and North America. Lavish public spectacles honouring the eighteen-year-old prince (the future King Edward VII) prompted an outpouring of commentary as people pondered their fascination with royalty, gave expression to their gender, ethnic, regional, and class identities, and laid claims to public space and royal recognition. A few years ago, the young prince's celebrated tour caught my attention as a historian, and fortunately for me it has held my interest even though I have been with the tour for many more months than it took young Bertie to make the trip in the first place. While following the perambulations of His Royal Highness, I have incurred a number of debts, which I am pleased to acknowledge here.

By gracious permission of Her Majesty Queen Elizabeth II, I have been able to make use of material from the Royal Archives at Windsor. Archivists and librarians have given me the benefit of their professional assistance at a number of institutions: the British Library; the British Library Newspaper Library; the National Archives of Canada; the Archives of Ontario; the Toronto Reference Library; the City of Toronto Archives; the New York Public Library; the Chicago Public Library; the Bodleian Library, Oxford University; Robarts Library, University of Toronto; the Harriet Irving Library, University of New Brunswick; and Wayne State University Library. At the Royal Archives, Windsor Castle, the registrar, Lady Sheila de Ballaigue, and her staff were wonderfully patient and knowledgeable when answering my questions and accommodating my research needs. The meticulous work of Jill Kelsey, the deputy registrar of the Royal Archives, has saved me from making a number of errors. In Ottawa, Martha Marleau of the Art Acquisition and Research Section, National Archives, was extraordinarily helpful in assisting my research in the Henry W. Acland Collection. Here at home, Carolyn Murray, librarian of the Laidlaw Library, University College, University of Toronto, gave me expert help on several occasions.

It is a pleasure to acknowledge the many historians and friends who have encouraged and cajoled me along the way. For their advice and support I want to thank my Toronto colleagues Carl Benn, Allan Greer, Sean Hawkins, Lori Loeb, Mark McGowan, Cecilia Morgan, Arthur Silver, Barbara Todd, Mariana Valverde, and Sylvia Van Kirk. Allan Greer generously helped me with the French translations. Scholars elsewhere have been equally generous in assisting and encouraging me: Phillip Buckner, Gail Campbell, Adam Crerar, Nancy Christie, Christina Harzig, Elsbeth Heaman, Dirk Hoerder, Jim Miller, Ruth Phillips, and Wendy Mitchinson. My good friends Judith Wilson and Stephen Trumper gave much-appreciated advice on the title.

Two small grants from the (alas now defunct) Research Initiatives Fund, University of Toronto, helped fund the project. Mélanie Brunet and David Goutor obligingly provided first-rate research assistance. At the University of Toronto Press, my colleague and editor, Len Husband, gave me good advice and adroitly steered the manuscript through the review process. Frances Mundy has overseen its production with admirable professionalism. Curtis Fahey, as copy editor, has smoothed my prose and saved me from making a number of mistakes. I am truly grateful for his care and expertise.

My arguments have been sharpened by feedback given by students and colleagues. The undergraduates in my seminar 'Spectacles, Crowds, and Parades' have helped me more than they know. Colleagues asked stimulating questions when I gave papers on various occasions: the Conference on Spectacle, Monument, and Memory held at York University; the Canadian Historical Association meeting at Memorial University of Newfoundland; the Conference on Boundaries hosted by the Centre of Canadian Studies, University of Edinburgh; the Conference on Recasting Canadian History organized by the Research Centre in Canadian Studies, the University of Genoa; the 2000 meeting of the Gesellshaft für Kanada-Studien in Grainau, Germany; the 2003 conference of the Canadian Ethnic Studies Association held in Banff, Alberta. I appreciate the penetrating questions that I was asked when I gave guest lectures at the University of New Brunswick, the University of Manitoba, and Brandon University. On two occasions, I greatly benefited from comments made by members of the Early Canada History Group at the University of Toronto. And I particularly appreciate the advice given by my friends and colleagues in the Labour Studies Research Group who indulged me when I turned to a topic outside our usual fare.

Last but by no means least, I want to thank my partner, Franca Iacovetta. I have benefited enormously from her advice as a historian, and she gave me a much-needed push at a moment when I despaired that the tour would never end. Hosting a royal visitor in our midst was hardly what Franca expected when she first took up with a labour historian more than two decades ago. Yet she put up with Bertie as he intruded into our daily lives in Toronto, our summers on Keewaydin Island, our sojourns in Molise and Abruzzo. Here is my opportunity to acknowledge publicly her unflagging support and love.

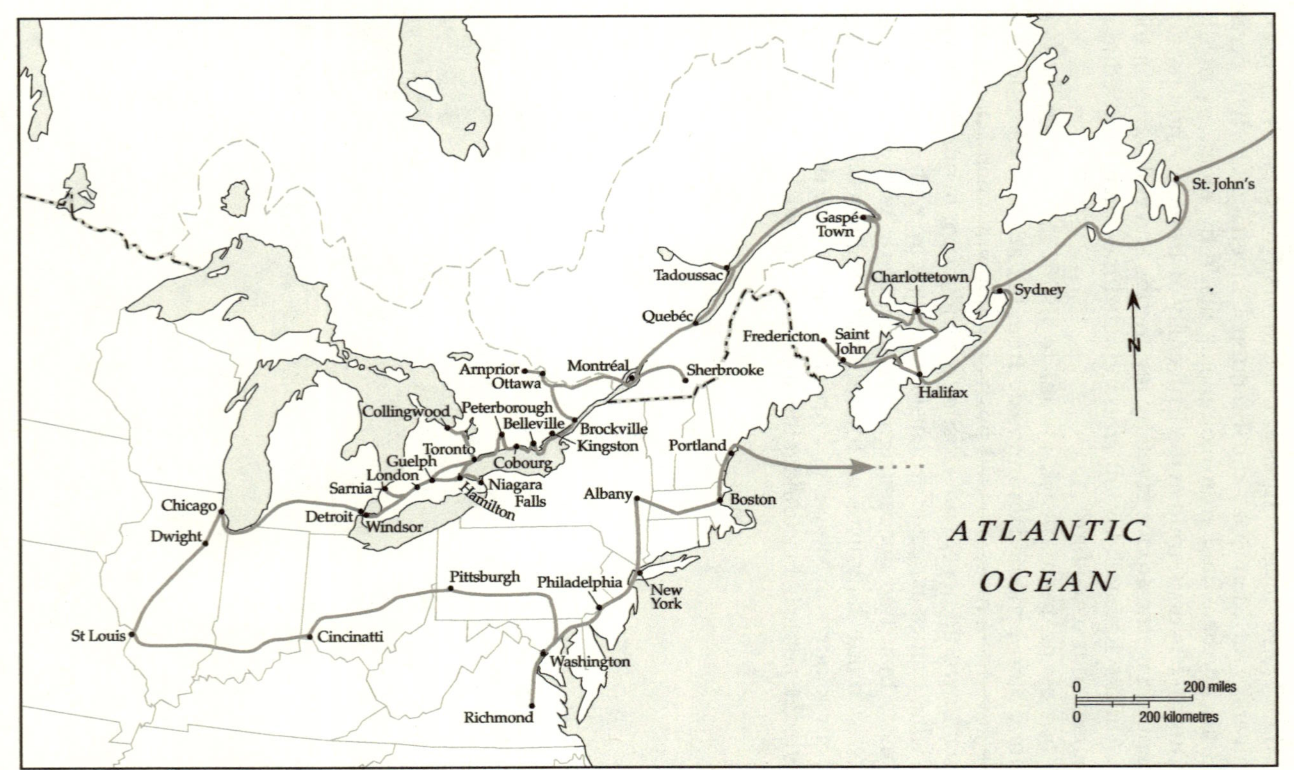

The tour route of the Prince of Wales, 1860

ROYAL SPECTACLE

Introduction

At 9:30 on the morning of Saturday, 25 August 1860, Albert Edward, the eighteen-year-old Prince of Wales, stepped smartly down from the steamer *Kingston* onto the wharf at Bonsecours Market in Montreal. As church bells rang across the city and a salute thundered from the canon of the volunteer artillery, the St Helen's battery, and the guns of the men-of-war anchored in the harbour, the crowd of 40,000 to 50,000 spectators roared their welcome. The cheering in French about equalled the volume of cheers in English. 'Howard,' the reporter from the New York *Times*, told readers that in 'the square behind, on the immense market, on the decks of all the steamboats and the roofs of the neighboring and distant houses, were crowds of people, who, by their numbers, made the whole space ... black and dark.'[1] Brightening the scene were the vast swaths of red-white-and-blue bunting and the thousands of white handkerchiefs waived by the jubilant onlookers. In a cordoned-off space, the lady guests in their hoop skirts and crinolines made as pretty a show as possible, given that the heavy rain had only just stopped and mud clung to everything save for the church steeples.

At the centre of the scene, close to the handsome red and white pavilion where the welcome ceremonies were to take place, stood the dignitaries and members of the press. While some of these men – they were all men – appeared in sombre broadcloth or the black robes of judges, lawyers, and Protestant clergy, others added colour to the scene: the Roman Catholic bishops in their purple soutanes, and various uniformed officers of the British army, the Royal Navy, the Canadian volunteer forces, and the visiting band of the Boston Fusiliers. Even the co-premiers of Canada, George-Étienne Cartier and John A. Macdonald, along with the other cabinet ministers, wore smart blue

The landing of the Prince of Wales at Bonsecours Market Wharf, Montreal. This illustration highlights the order and formality of the arrangements, the predominance of steam power, and the two working languages of the city. The mottoes on the arch read 'WELCOME TO MONTREAL' and 'VIVE LA REINE.' (*Frank Leslie's Illustrated Newspaper*, 8 September 1860)

and silver court uniforms, complete with cocked hats, white kid gloves, and swords. No one, however, outdid Charles-Séraphin Rodier, the mayor of Montreal, who for this special occasion, which meant much to him personally,[2] chose to cloak his immense, rotund figure in a newly made outfit modelled on that of London's lord mayor: a scarlet gown, trimmed with martin fur, lined with white satin, and fastened by gold clasps; a large black hat over a black wig; lilac-coloured gloves and a sword. Needless to say, the journalists, and especially visiting ones, could not resist poking fun at the mayor, whose appearance nearly overshadowed that of the long-awaited prince.

The privilege of greeting the Prince of Wales fell to Mayor Rodier. 'With mincing step and swinging tail,' wrote Howard, the mayor came up to the prince, 'outstretched his arm stiffly, waved it dignifiedly, and pompously signified to the Prince to follow.' Having ushered the royal visitor to his throne chair, Rodier then 'diddled down the steps, put on his specs, pulled down his ruffles, threw open his scarlet robe to display the satin lining, kicked his sword from between his legs, hemmed, hawed, and cleared his throat, preparatory to reading the municipal address.' Reading first in English and then in French, the mayor formally welcomed Queen Victoria's son, the heir apparent to the British throne. At each allusion to the queen or the prince, Rodier would bow low, 'his wig touching the upper step and the end of his sword pointing upwards towards the sky,' and the giant gold seal of office that hung from his neck 'jingled against the toes of his boots.' The address assured the prince that his mother had no more devoted and loyal subjects than the people of Montreal. The address referred as well to the Victoria Bridge, the new railway link spanning the broad St Lawrence at Montreal, which the prince was scheduled to open later in the day. It was, said the mayor, a 'magnificent monument to enterprise and skill with which the fame and prosperity of this city will evermore be intimately connected and most permanently identified.' Reading his reply in English, the prince acknowledged the civic officials' expression of loyalty to the British crown, thanked them for their kind words, and praised Montreal as 'a great emporium of the Trade of Canada ... whose growing prosperity offers so striking an example of what may be effected by energy and enterprise, under the influence of free institutions.'[3]

These ceremonies concluded, the prince then rode in the carriage of the governor general, Sir Edmund Head, at the head of a procession that wound through the city. In behind marched the dignitaries, various volunteer militia units, including cavalry on chargers, and the members of a great many fraternal societies, each one proudly identified by badges and banners. Taking a place near the head of the procession were some Iroquois from Caughnwaga (Kanawake), dressed specially in buckskin and feathers and with faces painted for a ceremonial occasion.[4] Everyone marching was male, but the crowds that lined the streets and cheered from windows and rooftops were made up of women and girls, as well as men and boys. The press represented the female spectators as being particularly enraptured by the romantic figure of a real-live prince – who knew, he might choose a Canadian girl as his bride, and she would one day become queen of England and the empire! Passing under eight grand, triumphal arches which had been specially built for the occasion, the procession eventually reached the new crystal palace on the campus of McGill University where a 'Great Exhibition' had been organized by the Lower Canada Board of Arts and Manufactures.[5] After more ceremonies and addresses, the prince declared the exhibition open, and then he examined the displays of industrial goods, natural products, handicrafts, and art works. Later in the day, there were yet more ceremonies, when the prince drove the last spike in Victoria Bridge, and in connection with the lavish banquet that followed. In the evening, crowds milled about the streets of Montreal, admiring the illuminations and enjoying the festive feeling. The prince tried to join in the fun by disguising himself in a slouch hat drawn low on his brow, but he and his chaperone were soon discovered, and so they rode off through the cheering, pressing throng.

So ended the first day of a busy week that the prince spent based in Montreal. While staying there, he would worship at Christ Church Cathedral, attend a display of 'Indian Games,' dance at 'one of the grandest balls ever given on the continent,' run the rapids in the St Lawrence River above the city, listen to a specially composed cantata at a musical festival, review the volunteer militia of Montreal and district, journey by canoe to pretty Île Dorval, tour the Eastern Townships, and gasp in wonder at a spectacular fireworks display. The jam-packed visit to Montreal came mid-way through the prince's tour of British North America – the first royal visit to 'Canada.'[6] Immediately following this tour, the prince made a six-week, unofficial trip through the United States. Everywhere he went, the prince was met by large crowds of curious onlookers, welcomed by civic and other officials, shown the local sights, and entertained in fine style. In British North America, where the tour had the status of an official state visit, local communities went out of their way to put themselves on display in ways that they hoped would redound to their credit, mustering all the pomp and circumstance they could for this once-in-a-lifetime occasion.

This book tells the story of the prince's 1860 tour from its beginning as a proposal coming from the Province of Canada legislature through to His Royal Highness's return to England. It is in part an exercise in historical recovery: the visit passed from public memory long ago and even in histories of the period it gets scarcely a mention.[7] Yet the coming of the Prince of Wales to British North America and to the United States appeared tremendously important to contemporaries who poured money, talent, and time into staging spectacles and entertainments for the pleasure and profit of the prince and other visitors. Civic promoters of the tour went to great lengths to represent local places and people in ways they imagined to be appropriate for the occasion. Everyone knew that the intensive international press coverage of the royal tour would draw attention to the North America's cities and countryside, and residents could only hope that reports would be flattering. As intended by Queen Victoria and her advisers, the visit provoked much public enthusiasm for the monarchy among Her Majesty's subjects living in North America, and many public expressions of appreciation for the freedom and self-government possible under the British crown – a theme echoed in many subsequent royal visits to Canada and other dominions and colonies.[8] During the 1860 visit to the United States, huge, curious crowds greeted Albert Edward, and various prominent figures spoke warmly of the good relations between the United States and Great Britain. At the same time, the prince's coming prompted considerable soul-searching about the meaning of the English crown for people living in former colonies that were now states of a great republic.

While touching on a range of matters relating to the visit, this book focuses on the ceremonies and spectacles of the sort the prince encountered in Montreal. I examine how civic programs of welcome were devised: who got a say, how people and social groups went about exercising their right to make decisions on behalf of their communities, and the means for legitimating their choices. The ensuing debates and struggles expose the political cultures and the power relations at work in the cities of mid-Victorian Canada and the United States. Similarly, I assess the attempts made by various groups that sought public and royal recognition and that claimed a right to public space. It comes as no surprise that these were highly contested matters; more significant and intriguing is what the contests reveal about the fault lines in civic cultures, the tensions between metropole and colony, and the meaning of monarchy for various groups.

As we will see, when putting on a show for the prince, residents ended up showing off much more than they intended about themselves and their communities. Differences of gender, class, religion, and race came into play, however much the supporters of the tour sought to convey the impression of harmonious, progressive New World communities. Various Aboriginal people called attention to their presence and their concerns by performing in buckskin and feathers. The Roman Catholic hierarchy in Quebec assumed a prominent place on public platforms, making clear the church's strength in French Canada. Orangemen in Kingston and Belleville sought equal recognition from the prince and took to the streets in a vain effort to get it, a move that provoked such a public controversy that it nearly derailed the tour. Though women of every racial and religious group found themselves excluded from centre stage during civic ceremonies, women were there throughout: as enthusiastic spectators, as workers behind the scenes, and as crinolined dancers momentarily caught in the limelight at the many public balls enjoyed by the prince during his tour. In these and many other ways, the actual public performances, and the journalists' representations of them, complicated the simple images of harmonious communities that civic reception committees so assiduously crafted. The 1860 visit would highlight colonial loyalty and American goodwill towards England, but it would reveal much more as well.

This study is based mainly on contemporary newspaper sources. Local newspapers reported on preparations for the prince's visit to their towns, relating discussions held by civic reception committees, detailing the decorations prepared for the special occasion, and advertising goods and services available for participants or spectators. And, of course, they described the local visit, almost always in triumphal terms. The great metropolitan dailies, however, are an even more significant source because they could afford to provide extensive coverage of events both in their home towns and as the prince moved from place to place. Some of these papers, such as the Toronto *Globe* and the Montreal *Gazette,* contracted with journalists on the spot or they sent their own reporters to cover visits to particular places. Even more extensive was the coverage in New York and London newspapers that assigned their own 'special correspondents' to travel with the prince for the entire tour. 'Howard' of the New York *Times* was the pen name for one such journalist (Arthur Harvey), and he had his equivalents in other leading New York papers: the New York *Herald* and the *Daily Tribune*. Nathaniel Woods, the special correspondent covering the tour for the *Times* of London, became a familiar figure in his own right in 1860, as newspapers everywhere reproduced his locally controversial 'letters.' These journalists, assigned because of their descriptive powers and flair for storytelling, sent in lively reports aimed at building readership and circulation. Quite new at the time, such human-interest reporting of distant events became feasible only with the emergence of well-financed, big-circulation dailies and the expansion of telegraphic and railway networks in the 1850s. The transatlantic cable, laid shortly before the visit, ought to have made transmissions to London just as rapid, but in fact the cable was not in good working order at the time of the visit. Mail steamers carried reports across the Atlantic in about two weeks.[9]

The 1860 visit became a media sensation. British North American newspapers, which had always been preoccupied with politics, now dwelt on matters of protocol, dress, and street decorations. In American and Canadian newspapers, French-Canadian journals included,[10] the coverage of wrangling over local arrangements and elaborate celebrations everywhere filled column after column packed with tiny Victorian type. So popular and controversial did the story become that in the New York newspapers it threatened to crowd out other contemporary news concerning such matters as the presidential election campaign that brought Abraham Lincoln to the White House and the military struggle of Giuseppe Garibaldi that resulted in the unification of Italy. The illustrated newspapers of New York and London also lavished attention on the festivities, providing readers with hundreds of images based on sketches by artists on the scene or by members of their own staffs on special assignment with the tour.[11] In the months following the prince's return to England, no less than six 'instant books' were published to commemorate the tour and take advantage of public interest.[12]

This fascination with the young prince, and with the receptions given him, had to do with such matters as the novelty of the occasion – the arrival in North America of a real-life prince, the heir to the world's most powerful nation and empire – and the widespread admiration for Victoria and her domestic circle, but it resulted as well from the vitality of the journalism of the day. The press conveyed a keen sense of the

Fireworks punctuate the celebrations for the opening of the Victoria Bridge, Montreal. (*Harper's Weekly*, 1 September 1860)

drama of the occasion – the uncommonly brilliant spectacles, the extraordinarily large and motley crowds, the passions of those who came into conflict as a result of the visit. Best of all, the journalists of 1860 had fun narrating the visit. It was a happy break from the squabbling of provincial politicians and from the bitter fights in the United States over secession and slavery that would shortly lead to the outbreak of civil war. Journalists used humour, mockery, and hyperbole to enliven their stories of the tour. In this book I have, in turn, relied on the irreverence of much of the journalism of 1860 to enhance my retelling of the story. In places, the nature of the humour reminds me of our distance from the culture of the mid-Victorian period, but elsewhere I find myself chuckling right along with the original readers.

The journalists' accounts and assessments of what they saw during the tour lend themselves to close reading for meaning, that is to say, for insights into both the social relations and the cultural values of the period. Particularly interesting are the international conversations that took place as local commentators responded to the accounts penned by visiting journalists. At a time when residents knew that their town was in full public view for all the world to see, they were interested – and often horrified – to learn what others thought of them. In the process, civic and other identities were presented, re-presented, and reassessed.

In addition to scrutinizing these public records of the tour, I have turned where possible to private sources that shed light on the events. Where such sources have survived at all, they are generally less extensive and less consistent in their coverage of the tour than the public ones. Precious indeed is the diary of George Templeton Strong, a wealthy New Yorker who planned and participated in his city's reception for the prince and who daily recorded his impressions in a manner that was frank and acerbic.[13] I have been fortunate, too, in having access to some fine collections of letters written by the prince and members of his 'suite' – the entourage that travelled with him. The prince himself wrote frequently to his parents, giving them brief and guarded indications of what he saw and thought about his trip.[14] His personal governor, General Robert Bruce, kept the young prince's father apprised of how the tour was going and how its main attraction was handling the public attention.[15] Reports also went back to England from the fifth Duke of Newcastle – the colonial secretary and the prince's political adviser and travelling companion during the tour. He penned some formal letters to Queen Victoria and more frank ones to the prime minister, Lord Palmerston.[16] The richest letters written by a member of the royal entourage were the work of Dr Henry Wentworth Acland, Regius professor of medicine at Oxford University and the prince's physician during the tour.[17] Acland kept in frequent touch with his own family, and he sent home many long 'journal letters,' which commented on the sites and celebrations as well as on relations among members of the suite. In addition, Acland was an accomplished artist who sketched and painted hundreds of scenes during the trip, and these are available today in the National Archives at Ottawa in the same pristine condition as when the doctor presented them as a Christmas gift to his wife in December 1860.[18]

In making sense of these primary sources, both public and private, I have drawn on insights gleaned from reading a range of secondary sources, especially the recent literature that explores public spectacles in the past. Scholars of early-modern Europe have done outstanding work on the period's exceptionally rich civic pageantry, which drew from classical models to express contemporary concerns.[19] In a curious yet obvious way, the royal entry of the Prince of Wales at Montreal in 1860 bears a connection to both the Renaissance and the classical precedents. More relevant still is a growing literature on street rituals in nineteenth-century cities, most notably studies by American historians interested in the parading tradition and the many civic celebrations of the period. Theatre historian Brooks McNamara has studied state visits to New York – including that by the Prince of Wales in 1860 – as staged performances. Susan G. Davis has explored the ways in which parades put on display the social order of the nineteenth-century American city. With a keen appreciation of gender dynamics, Mary P. Ryan has perceptively examined nineteenth-century public-holiday celebrations in three American cities and shown how a public was constructed even as the festivities engendered 'civic wars' among conflicting social groups.[20]

Equally helpful have been recent works on the rituals of monarchy, particularly those of Victoria's reign. Eric Hobsbawm and David Cannadine revived interest in this field in 1983 with their contributions in the influential collection *The Invention of Tradition*.[21] Cannadine drew attention to the fact that, over time, the forms and significance of royal ritual in Britain have been far from unchanging, and he contrasted the early- and mid-Victorian periods, when a utilitarian outlook held pageantry in low esteem, with the late nineteenth century, when imperialism fostered the extravagant pageantry of the queen's jubilees. For the past two decades, scholars have refined our knowledge of such rituals, qualified Cannadine's periodization, and cast doubt on the validity of the term 'invention' in this context.[22] William M. Kuhn, in his 1996 book *Democratic Royalism*,[23] analyses 'the high politics of symbolic representation' by showing how leading figures in English public life during the period 1861–1911 devised ceremonies of monarchy that reinforced class hierarchies *and* a sense of national community at the same time. Kuhn argues that these ceremonies helped to make monarchy relevant in an increasingly urban, industrial, and democratic polity, a theme taken up by other scholars too.[24] In *The Contentious Crown* (1997), Richard Williams examines the two strands of commentary on the monarchy in Victorian England, one critical, the other reverential, and shows how support for pomp and circumstance grew over time. Even in the first phase of Victoria's reign, the so-called utilitarian decades, there was tremendous enthusiasm for royal spectacles and a popular feeling that Victoria and her court could do more to gratify the public.[25]

More recently still, John Plunkett, in *Queen Victoria: First Media Monarch*, acknowledges that elaborate royal ceremony was less characteristic of the first third of Victoria reign than it would later become, but he shows that in the earlier period, before Victoria's widowhood (which began in December 1861), the queen and her consort became hugely popular as a result of their frequent public engagements and the intense media coverage of them. The press cast the royal family's many tours and visits throughout England and Scotland 'as a recognition of Victoria's reliance on the approval of her subjects, a celebration of the inclusivity and participation of the People in the political nation.'[26] These media reports, argues Plunkett, were expressed in 'the discourse of popular constitutionalism,' and they gave expression to 'royal populism.'[27] As we will see, the 1860 tour of British North America was part and parcel of this phenomenon. The prince's endless round of public engagements dominated the public sphere in the colonies that summer and gained wide press attention in the United States and Great Britain as well. Moreover, many reports from Canada represented the prince's popularity as being a happy sign of the people's public participation in the political life of the British nation writ large. Thus, while Plunket confines his analysis to England, it can usefully be extended to parts of the wider empire. The 1860 tour is an illustration par excellence of the interconnectedness of cultural developments in the metropole and in the colonies.

Some of the scholarship on public spectacle explicitly focuses on the formation of national identity. In the British case, of course, royal rituals were one of the important means for expressing nationality, as Linda Colley explains in her magisterial book, *Britons*.[28] And even in the case of the United States, royal rituals provided ready models for certain spectacles in the large repertoire of public celebrations that helped shaped American nationalism during the formative years of the republic. A wide-ranging study of this topic by David Waldstreicher, *In the Midst of Perpetual Fetes*, shows, for example, how George Washington's presidential tours featured civic receptions, complete with formal entry ceremonies, militia reviews, triumphal arches, and public addresses that hailed him as a war hero, founder of the nation, and father of the republic.[29] The story of a particular Canadian spectacle of nationalism/s has been brilliantly told by H.V. Nelles in *The Art of Nation-Building*, which studies the pageantry performed on the occasion of Quebec's tercentenary in 1908 before a large audience that included another Prince of Wales.[30] As Nelles shows, in 1908 a civic reception grew into a commemorative event that used romantic notions of the Canadian past as a medium for advancing contemporary political struggles and nation building. Nelles's study graces a small but ever-growing list of books on commemoration in Canada.[31] In this connection I want to stress at the outset that, while the 1860 visit had its commemorative aspects, the tour was not mainly about looking to the past nor about using history for nationalistic purposes. In the spirit of the mid-Victorian decades, the 1860 visit looked resolutely *ahead* to further commercial expansion, industrial transformation, moral and social progress, and nation building. The two significant commemorative ceremonies performed by the prince – his opening of Montreal's Victoria Bridge and his laying of the foundation stone of the Ottawa legislature – were rituals that focused on new beginnings, on a promising future.

National identity was, of course, no straightforward matter in the British North American colonies of 1860. Local identities were strong, and the idea of a confederated state was as yet ill-defined. Old ties to France, England, Scotland, Ireland, and Wales fractured the population as well. People wondered whether a Canadian national identity were possible in a society where French Canadians had a sense of nationality that was distinct from, and in many ways at odds with, the national sentiment then stirring among English Canadians. Everyone – French Canadians, Irish Catholics, English Protestants, African Canadians, and others – was supposed to be proudly British, in the sense of being part of an globe-encircling empire and linked by a sovereign who demanded allegiance but not cultural conformity. But in Canada West especially, the tidal wave of British immigration in the forty years before 1860 had reinforced notions of Britishness rooted in a cultural chauvinism that saw people from the cultural mainstream of the British Isles – its white, Protestant, and English-speaking core – as having a superior if not exclusive claim to a British identity. The 1860 tour brought both forms of Britishness into play and occasionally into conflict. Some British North Americans saw the young prince as the personification of British ethnic nationality and his visit as a confirmation of the dominance of the British ethnic fact in Canada. Other people of diverse origins latched onto the idea that they were all subjects of the queen, equal in their allegiance to her; the prince's visit was a reminder of the cultural diversity of the peoples of the empire. In sorting out these complex notions of identity, I have been influenced by the insights of Benedict Anderson's *Imagined Communities* and some of the further studies and critiques it has engendered.[32] Because of the colonial status of British North America in 1860, works in the new imperial history have also informed my study.[33] Catherine Hall has wisely insisted on the need to locate the racial and gender components of Englishness in the encounter between the metropole and the colonial empire.[34] In the white settler societies of British North America, Britishness was shaped as much by ongoing encounters with the metropole as by interactions with indigenous peoples and other residents of North America.

In organizing this account, I have parted company with the authors of the 'instant books' on the 1860 visit who followed the prince's movements from his landing at St John's, Newfoundland, to his departure from Portland, Maine. My rendition of the tour is organized topically with a bow towards chronology. The book begins with a chapter that provides background about the visit's origins, the itinerary, the division of responsibilities for the arrangements, and the leading players; it ends with the story of the prince's departure from England and transatlantic voyage. Chapter 2 turns to the preparations made in the Province of Canada and the other colonies for the prince's reception. The bulk of the book deals with the tour through British North America. Two chapters on the celebrations in colonial cities are followed by three chapters that focus on identity and inclusion. The section on British North America ends with a chapter on the prince as tourist. The last part of the book deals with the tour through the United States: one chapter provides an overview of the American progress and the other a close look at the visit to New York City, a highpoint of the U.S. tour and indeed of the entire journey. In the book's conclusion, the prince sails home to England, the bills come in, and assessments are made of this royal spectacle.

Finally, an editorial note. Throughout this book I have used the terminology of the period to denote places. Thus, 'Canada' is sometimes used to refer to all the colonies or 'provinces' that made up what was more accurately known as 'British North America': Newfoundland, Nova Scotia, New Brunswick, Prince Edward Island, and the United Province of Canada. The United Province had two sections: Canada East and Canada West. In 1860 the former section, which would become the Province of Quebec in 1867, was often referred to as 'Lower Canada,' its name prior to the union of 1841, while the latter section, which became the province of Ontario in 1867, was often called by its previous name, 'Upper Canada.' In this book I use the names Lower Canada and Upper Canada interchangeably with Canada East and Canada West.

1

Proposal, Planning, and Players

The 1860 visit by the Prince of Wales came at the initiative of the legislature of the Province of Canada, whose members reflected the then-current admiration of the monarchy and British connection in their society. British power and prestige ran high in 1860, even though there had been some troubling recent developments: the sobering disasters of the Crimean War, the humiliating Indian Mutiny, and the outbreak of military conflict in China. Just a hint of defensiveness now lay behind the boasts of British imperialists that England was 'the workshop of the world,' that the Royal Navy ruled the waves, and that, whereas other nations and some former colonies had been wracked by revolution, Britain's constitutional monarchy had endured. British North Americans were proud of the way responsible government – introduced under Victoria's sceptre – had enabled the white settler colonies of the British empire to grow and prosper without their severing imperial ties or disclaiming monarchical traditions. Here was something to celebrate! Moreover, the comparative calm in social relations that was evident both in Great Britain and in its North American colonies by 1860 made it a propitious time for a visit.[1]

'May It please Your Majesty'

The 1859 invitation that brought the Prince of Wales to Canada came after a lengthy period of negotiations around the idea of a royal visit. Prior to 1859, Canadians had put forward various proposals for a royal visit, and though the queen turned them all down, in the mid-1850s, she had given encouragement to the notion that one day such a visit might take place. According to the official biographer of the Prince of

Wales, the queen wanted to express her appreciation for the imperial sentiment demonstrated by Canada during the Crimean War (1854–6). When approached immediately after the conflict by a delegation from Canada inviting her to visit, she had said that while she could not go herself, the Prince of Wales might make the trip once old enough to do so.[2]

The 1850s also saw some noisy critics of imperial policy – the so-called Little Englanders – gain attention by publicly expressing doubts about the value of colonies.[3] In response, British imperialists wanted to reassure the colonists that they were indeed valued: a royal visit would serve that purpose well. Moreover, in Canada, the rebellious days of 1837–8 and of the 1849 Annexation Manifesto had passed. Canadian politicians of nearly every stripe were content to work within British institutions and the framework of monarchy and empire. The advent of responsible government in the colonies had worked wonders – not least among the French Canadians who had posed the biggest threat to British authority in 1837–8.[4] Hostile and insulting remarks about the young Queen Victoria, uttered in some quarters in both Lower and Upper Canada in the rebellion era, were seldom heard twenty years later.[5] There was little doubt that, overwhelmingly, Canadians would be gratified by a visit from the Prince of Wales and that he would be welcomed with loyal fervour.

The 1859 invitation from the Canadian legislature grew directly out of a botched proposal of the previous year. In the summer of 1858, John Gustavus Norris, a resident of Toronto with Reform party connections but no official position, got up a petition inviting the queen to send the Prince of Wales to Canada to open the new crystal palace exhibition hall in Toronto that October.[6] Although the petition was presented to the queen, there was no hope of approval because Norris had failed to go through proper channels by submitting it to the governor general, and in any case it had arrived too late in the year for serious consideration of an autumn visit. Back in Canada, the Conservative newspapers ridiculed Norris,[7] but Reformers were pleased that the petition had at least reached the queen. The Toronto city council (and its Reform mayor) formally thanked Norris for his mission and expressed the 'fervent hope' that a royal visit to the city might soon take place.[8]

Norris's petition gained a great deal of press attention in Great Britain, where various journals praised this colonial expression of loyalty and endorsed the idea of a royal visit. The London *Morning Post* observed that the timing of the request for a visit was 'singularly opportune.' Technological advances, such as the Atlantic cable, trunk railways, and steam shipping, were linking the continents more closely. Moreover, Canadians were prospering and loyal. A royal visitor to Canada would see not only 'what the enterprise of Britain in Canada has already accomplished' but also 'that English institutions, English liberty, English self-reliance, and English loyalty are plants which do not deteriorate in the soil of Canada.' Some newspapers urged that a tour of the United States be appended to the visit to Canada. The *Leinster Express* of Belfast, for instance, argued that a tour of the States would be 'evidence of kindred feeling between communities derived from one common stock.' For Canadians, the most reassuring news came from the gossipy London *Court Journal*, which reported that in court circles there was 'a hope, and a well-grounded hope too, that in the course of the next summer the people of our great American dependencies will have their feelings gratified by a visit from some prominent member of the Royal Family, such as the Prince of Wales.'[9]

Shortly after the queen had seen Norris's petition, she invited the Canadian premier, George-Étienne Cartier, who happened to be visiting London, to Windsor Castle for the weekend. Cartier's visit with the royal couple was bound to go off well. The charming French Canadian from Montreal was an Anglophile and monarchist; indeed, he had even named a daughter 'Reine-Victoria'![10] It was in the course of this visit to Windsor that Cartier said that 'an inhabitant of Lower Canada was an Englishman who spoke French.'[11] When the queen and Cartier talked about a royal visit to Canada,[12] he would have been enthusiastic and reassuring, dispelling any qualms there might have been about French Canada's response.[13] As the single most powerful politician in Canada East, Cartier worked closely both with the Roman Catholic hierarchy in French Canada and with the Anglo-dominated business community of Montreal. After returning to Canada, Cartier backed the legislature's initiative that came at the end of the session in May 1859. In the assembly he moved the address to the queen.[14]

The address to Victoria gained the support of both chambers of the legislature without a single dissenting vote. In the 1850s, complete agreement was seldom reached in the Canadian legislature, where partisan differences were keenly felt and where the government majority was always in doubt. The Liberal-Conservative government in power in the Province of Canada in 1859–60 was headed not just by Cartier but also by his co-premier from Kingston, Canada West, John A. Macdonald. As one of his biographers has put it, John A. was 'British to the core' and 'intensely proud of his lifelong commitment to the British monarchy and Canada's ties to the motherland.'[15] Yet, although Macdonald came from a different background than Cartier – John A. was Scottish-born, Upper-Canada reared, and a Protestant – he found that he could work effectively with Cartier by making judicious trade-offs and cleverly balancing conflicting interests. Macdonald's nemesis was George Brown, the editor of the Toronto *Globe* and a Reform politician who claimed with some justification to speak for the majority of Upper Canadians. Brown, a Free Kirk and Scottish immigrant who believed fervently in the separation of church and state, never tired of railing against the machinations of the Roman Catholic bishops and the political domination of English-speaking and Protestant Canada West by the French-speaking Catholics of Canada East. Notwithstanding their many differences, when it came to proposing a royal visit, Brown and other members of the opposition happily allied themselves with the Cartier-Macdonald government.[16]

The joint address of the legislature expressed the hope that the queen would honour her subjects in British North America with her presence and 'receive the personal tribute of [their] unwavering attachment to [her] rule.' The people would be gratified if she were 'to witness the progress and prosperity of this distant part of [her] dominions,' and to that end it was proposed that she be present on the occasion of the opening of the Victoria Bridge, 'the most gigantic work of modern days.' An invitation was extended, as well, to the prince consort and other members of the royal family who might accompany her on the trip.[17] The address was included in the official dispatch of the governor general, which was taken specially to England and presented to the queen by Henry Smith, a senior Conservative politician and the speaker of the assembly. In London, Smith and the address were handled by the colonial secretary, Henry Pelham, fifth Duke of Newcastle, a minister in the new, Liberal government of Lord Palmerston and a man committed, as he said, to strengthening imperial 'bonds of mutual sympathy and of mutual obligation.'[18]

A reply to the legislature's invitation was slow in coming even though by August the queen had signalled to Newcastle her willingness not to go to Canada herself but to send the Prince of Wales. (It is likely that no one, including the Canadians, had expected a visit by Victoria herself, but etiquette required that the invitation go first to her.) That summer, Palmerston's cabinet agreed on the 'desirability of the visit and ... that the Prince of Wales would represent the Queen at the ceremony of the opening of the Bridge, [that] he should go with a certain amount of state and that any necessary expenditure would be authorized.'[19] Newcastle, however, had consulted with John Rose, a respected Canadian cabinet minister, who had some misgivings about the visit, perhaps in connection with the financial problems of the company responsible for building the bridge, the Grand Trunk Railway.[20] Newcastle double-checked with the governor general of British North America, Sir Edmund Head, and the invitation was formally accepted on 30 January 1860.

Newcastle informed the governor general that the address of the Canadian legislature had been presented to the queen, and that she valued the attachment to her and the loyalty to the crown that lay behind the address. It was her hope that, when the time came for the opening of the Victoria Bridge, the Prince of Wales would attend the ceremony in her name and 'become acquainted with a people, in whose rapid progress towards greatness, Her Majesty, in common with Her subjects in Great Britain, feels a lively and enduring sympathy.' It was anticipated that the visit would take place that summer.[21]

The bridge opening made a fitting focus for the tour. 'Everyone' in Britain and North America knew about the Victoria Bridge: its great length (9,144 feet), its innovative tubular structure, its staggering cost ($6,600,000), its defiance of nature's challenges, most notably the massive ice floes that annually attacked its stone piers, the brilliance of its designers, Robert Stephenson, Alexander Ross, and Thomas Keefer, and the Herculean powers of the workforce, organized by James Hodges and the contractors Peto, Brassey, and Betts.[22] Hailed at the time as the 'Eighth Wonder of the World,' it was also a symbol of British imperial achievement: British capital, engineering, and contractors had marshalled the strength and skills of colonial workers to span Canada's grandest river. More particularly, the bridge signified Montreal's commercial prowess, with its long reach into the hinterland of North America and its new, ready access to an ice-free winter port on the Atlantic at Portland, Maine. Surely the entrepreneurs behind the Grand Trunk Railway and its audacious project deserved the attention and legitimacy that royal recognition would bring! In the new, industrial era, the royal family had taken on such a role, conferring its approval on the class of men who built such tangible symbols of progress.[23] Industrialists basked 'in a warm royal glow' while they bolstered the monarchy by publicly acknowledging its continued importance.[24]

By the time the governor general read the queen's reply to the Canadian legislature,[25] the item was scarcely newsworthy because the acceptance had been long expected, but the *Times* of London published two editorials endorsing the tour.[26] The visit, the *Times* maintained, would break a long-standing tradition: the immobility of royalty. In the case of past kings, that immobility had reinforced the monarch's narrowness and despotic tendencies, and so by implication the *Times* linked the prince's tour with broader horizons and the liberalism of the mid-Victorian period. The newspaper speculated that the visit would make travel on the American continent more popular and that it would bring Canada more public attention – which was only fitting. After all, during the period of Victoria's reign, 'what may be called a nation' had grown 'upon the banks of the St. Lawrence and Lake Ontario.' Moreover, it was a nation content to remain within the empire – 'as long as the mother country rules with kindness and moderation.' The *Times* urged that the prince's tour be extended to include the United States, a recommendation that prompted further discussion among Americans about the possibility of the prince's touring the republic. It was not until June 1860, however, when invitations reached England from James Buchanan, the president of the United States, and from the mayor and city of New York, that the prince's U.S. tour was formally announced and the details worked out.

As for the Atlantic colonies, each of the legislatures petitioned for a visit once news of the Canadian tour reached them. In the diplomatic language of the day, Newcastle had as much as told the lieutenant governors to arrange petitions from Newfoundland, Nova Scotia, New Brunswick, and Prince Edward Island.[27] On 19 March, when it was moved in the New Brunswick assembly that the province invite the Prince of Wales to pay a visit, some members of the government, as well as of the opposition, objected to the proposal, complaining variously that there was no money to pay for the welcome, that constituencies off the tour route would fail to benefit directly, or that just a few individuals would stand to gain (by acquiring honours) while everyone would have to pay for the visit. The next day the newspapers howled at the behaviour of these critics of the tour, and, as one historian has put it, 'overpowered by a sense of shame for the province before the bar of posterity,' the assembly agreed both to expunge the grumbling from the official record and to invite the prince to New Brunswick.[28] Newspapers in the province were soon hailing the practical benefits of the visit.[29] It appears that New Brunswick was the only place where there was any open opposition to the idea of inviting the prince to visit British North America.

Planning an Imperial Progress

The prince's itinerary was firmed up quite quickly after only a little consultation within a small circle. On 17 February, Newcastle wrote to Governor General Head sketching in barest outline the plan, the essentials of which changed little in the end. The prince would leave England on about 10 July and pay short visits to the Atlantic colonies before arriving in Canada where he would formally represent the queen at the opening of the Victoria Bridge in Montreal. It would be a state visit, so he would therefore have a naval escort for the Atlantic crossing and be accompanied on his travels with certain 'Functionaries of State.' If, upon leaving Canada, he were to travel in the United States, he would do so 'in a strictly private capacity.' Newcastle then asked the governor general to suggest a program for the visit, with proposals as to how the prince would spend his time. The duke explained that, while the queen wished the program to reflect the preferences of the people of Canada, she would nevertheless need to consider and approve all suggestions.[30] The ball was now in the governor general's court.

Sir Edmund laid out a program for the tour that Newcastle and the queen soon approved with only minor amendments. It appears that Head himself set the itinerary, although he mentioned to Newcastle that it had the approval of the principal members of his Executive Council. Head recommended flying visits to the capitals of the Atlantic colonies and longer stays in Canada at Quebec, Montreal, Ottawa, Kingston, Toronto, Hamilton, Niagara Falls, followed by visits to Detroit, Chicago, western Illinois, St Louis, Cincinnati, Washington, Philadelphia, New York, and Boston. The governor general worried that Her Majesty 'may think it is too much,' but he believed that even the whirlwind tour of the United States could be 'easily performed and without much fatigue.'[31] (As it turned out, members of the royal party would disagree with this latter point as they raced through the eastern United States.) The itinerary included visits to all the cities of British North America and to many of the largest cities in the United States. (See table 1.1.) In palace circles there was concern to prevent the visit to the United States – with its population ten times that of British North America – from overwhelming the visit to the more modest colonies.[32]

The schedule was both tight and rigid up to the visit to Montreal because the bridge opening was intended to be the centrepiece of the tour and it had to occur on a set date so that all the people involved could make their arrangements. Afterwards, more flexibility was possible. There was a chance that the program could include a two-day canoe trip up the Ottawa River, which the Hudson's Bay Company proposed, and a three- or four-day excursion to the Prairies beyond Chicago for shooting. Newcastle and the prince were interested in both these excursions. Although there had been concerns that the queen might not want the risk of a canoe trip for the heir apparent, she approved it.[33]

The royal parents worked closely with senior officials in making plans for the visit. Though the queen acted as final arbiter, it was the prince consort who corresponded with officials and oversaw arrangements, a role where his indefatigable energy and attention to detail were decided assets. Early in March 1860 the Duke of Somerset wrote Prince Albert from the Admiralty, requesting the queen's approval for the naval arrangements for the young prince's trip. The prince would travel aboard a ninety-gun ship from the Channel or Mediterranean fleet, with two smaller escort vessels to do double duty where coastal and river waters were too shallow for the ship. Even so, Prince Albert thought that a local river steamer would be needed for travel up the St Lawrence River above Quebec. He liked the idea of using 'one of the fine large Canadian River Steamers, which are built expressly for that service & are said to be very good and very fast.' The Admiralty gave Prince Albert a list of three ships to choose from for the main duty but recommended the *Hero*.[34]

On the Canadian end there were queries and worries about a number of matters, which the colonial secretary did his best to answer reassuringly. Newcastle told Head that he would not be troubled with many visitors from England besides those in the official party, which was expected to number only seven or eight men. No special royal mount would be necessary when the prince rode out on a saddle-horse. Uniforms would be optional for anyone presented to the prince at a levee, where the ceremonies should be kept relatively simple and in line with those familiar to people who had attended New Year's levees hosted by colonial governors. The governor general could decide for himself as to where and when the prince should lodge while at Quebec, both the governor's residence or quarters in town being acceptable.[35]

The duke and Sir Edmund together decided on the distribution

Table 1.1
Reported population, 1860–1

Selected cities of British North America, 1861	
St John's	24,851*
Halifax	25,026
Saint John	27,317
Quebec	59,990
Montreal	90,323
Ottawa	14,669
Toronto	44,821
Hamilton	19,096
Provinces of British North America, 1861	
Newfoundland	124,000
Nova Scotia	331,000
New Brunswick	252,000
Prince Edward Island	80,000
Canada East	1,112,000
Canada West	1,396,000
Total	3,295,000
Selected cities in the United States, 1860	
Albany	62,367
Baltimore	212,418
Boston	177,840
Chicago	112,172
Cincinnati	161,044
Detroit	45,619
New York	1,174,779
Philadelphia	565,529
Richmond	37,910
St Louis	160,773
Washington	61,122
(United States	31,443,321)

*Population in 1857.
Source: George A. Nader, *Cities of Canada*, 2 vols. (Toronto: Macmillan 1976), vol. 2; Census of Canada; Donald B. Dodd, comp., *Historical Statistics of the States of the United States: Two Centuries of the Census, 1790–1990* (Westport, Conn.: Greenwood 1993), 443–63.

of honours. Newcastle had been advised by a Mr Fraser, a prominent merchant at Quebec, that it would please French Canada were a French-Canadian member of the 100th Regiment of the colony to be appointed aide-de-camp to the prince during the Canadian tour.

Everyone realized that that would mean having to appoint a second aide-de-camp from among the officers of the volunteer force of Upper Canada. Head recommended two men, who were duly appointed: Étienne Taché and Sir Allan MacNab. Both had had long careers in public service and were strong supporters of the militia.[36] Head and Newcastle decided as well that it would be best if the queen were to honour the Canadian legislature, which had made the invitation, by the conferring of knighthoods on the speakers of the lower and upper chambers, Henry Smith and Narcisse Belleau, who, conveniently, happened to be an English-speaking Upper Canadian and a French-speaking Lower Canadian. The queen readily agreed that the honours should be given, and it was only left to decide whether the knighthoods would be conferred in the usual way by the queen or whether special arrangements would be made so that the prince might knight Smith and Belleau while in Canada.[37]

Another delicate matter concerned the role that the consulate officer of France would play while the prince visited French Canada. The consul, Charles-Henri-Philippe Gauldrée-Boilleau, was eager to augment his own role in Canadian affairs,[38] an ambition that fit well with France's interest in French Canada, recently rekindled by the goodwill visit of the French corvette *la Capricieuse* to Canada in 1855.[39] For the enhancement of the 1860 ceremonies at Quebec, Boilleau offered his 'services' to Head. 'I think you had better find a good excuse for declining his invitation,' Newcastle wrote Head. 'He has no real standing in the Queen's Colony in respect of the Prince, and if he wishes to appear as representing the French Canadians such interlocutions between the Prince and them should be discountenanced.' The duke added that the refusal would need to be handled with care because 'of course it will not be desirable to appear to suspect him of such intention.' Head must have done his job well because there is no indication in the papers of the French consul at Quebec that Boilleau took offence, and indeed his reports to Paris are strongly enthusiastic about the reception given the prince at Quebec.[40] Though relations between France and England were strained in 1860, the French government paid the prince an honour by having a naval vessel or two follow his movements from port to port as far as Quebec. The escort reminded everyone – in a diplomatically acceptable way – of France's interest in the colonies that she had founded.

The early months of 1860 also saw authorities in Britain sorting out the financial arrangements for the visit. The lords of the Treasury started from the premise that, while the prince would use his own income (from the revenues of the Duchy of Cornwall) to defray his private expenses, the British government would cover most of the costs of the trip because the government had recognized it to be 'a Mission undertaken with a view to a great Public Object,' and it wanted to ensure that the proceedings were conducted 'in a manner befitting the occasion.'[41] The Treasury planned to reimburse the Admiralty for the cost of transporting the prince and his suite by sea. The British government would also pay for land transportation in the colonies, public receptions and levees hosted by the prince, and donations made by the prince to charitable or educational institutions. (Such donations were described as being the means for commemorating the visit.) Gifts that the prince would give to hosts and others who provided services, and who were not in a position to be paid for them, would similarly be paid for by the government. The expenses associated with 'the maintenance' of the travellers were to be mostly covered by the government, but the prince was to defray his own expenses and those of the members of his immediate household. He also, of course, would pay for any private expenditures and for any donations he wished to make to private charities or individuals. Since the trip through the United States was not a state visit, the prince would pay all the expenses incurred there, including those of his suite.[42]

Altogether it was estimated that the Treasury would be faced with a bill of about £10 000, a sum that officials considered 'not very large.' Initially the plan was to take the estimates to Parliament, but in the end Newcastle's advice was followed and the expenses were lumped with others and put down to 'Civil Contingencies,' as had been done in similar situations in the past. Newcastle said that he was reluctant to take to Parliament estimates that were 'necessarily imperfect,' but the dodge was a way of avoiding close scrutiny and embarrassing questions in the House of Commons. It appears to have worked because, on this occasion, there was no public outcry – in contrast with the later tour of India taken by the Prince of Wales, which drew howls about excess and provoked attacks on the monarchy.[43] As for practical matters in 1860 – obtaining cash in each of the colonies, making necessary payments while en route, and keeping accounts for the Treasury Board – these were assigned to the colonial secretary's private secretary for the period when the prince was touring the Atlantic colonies. For the longer trip through the Canadas, an official was to be attached to the suite to handle finances.[44]

Provincial Preparations

Across the Atlantic, the Canadian government was similarly engaged in a flurry of planning and preparing. The opposition in the assembly had proposed that, since the invitation had come from the legislature rather than the government, a joint committee of both chambers and all parties arrange the visit, but the government of the day had flatly rejected the idea.[45] The Cartier-Macdonald ministry had a responsibility to take charge – and thus to assume whatever glory or blame fell their way as a result. The governor general, as both the representative of the queen in the province and the government's chief executive officer, had a role to play especially in conferring with London, but the administrative duties associated with the preparations fell to the ministry and more particularly to one of the ministers, the chief commissioner of public works, John Rose.

John Rose had a flair for business and administration that served the Canadian government well, and not only at the time of the royal visit. Rose had emigrated from Scotland as an adolescent along with his family, and they settled in Lower Canada. After building a thriving law practice serving the Anglo elite of Montreal, Rose was persuaded to enter politics in 1857 by his old friend, John A. Macdonald, who appointed him to his cabinet as solicitor general, Canada East. In January 1859 Rose moved to Public Works, an important portfolio at the time, given the disputes over the construction of the Parliament Buildings in Ottawa. His position was made more onerous, though probably more appealing too, once he took on the job of planning for the prince's visit.[46]

Effective administrator that he was, Rose sought the assistance of a talented subordinate, Thomas Wily, a young officer in the Canadian militia, who made many of the necessary arrangements and who – fortunately for the historian – wrote an account of his role in the visit some twenty-three years later.[47] The assignment stood out in Wily's memory as a challenging and exciting time when his manhood and mettle were tested, what with all the tasks that needed to be accomplished in short order and the negotiating he had to do with dozens of people from many walks of life.

Early in May 1860 Wily was summoned by Rose and informed that the government had decided to second him from the military and attach him to Public Works, where he was to make arrangements for the transportation, accommodation, and other needs of the royal party

John Rose, as chief commissioner of public works for the Province of Canada, carried the main responsibility for arranging the tour of Canada. The text accompanying this sketch attributed much of the success of the visit 'to the abilities and exertions of the Hon. John Rose.' (*Illustrated London News*, 6 April 1861)

and for the large number of people who were expected to follow alongside the visitors. Most of the entertainments – the public processions, ceremonies, touring, balls, and so on – would fall to the municipalities or particular individuals to organize, but getting the prince and his following from city to city and finding them places to stay and food to eat would be the responsibility of the Canadian government.

Arranging for transportation involved negotiations with various railway companies, steamship owners, and liverymen. Since the prince would travel long distances up the St Lawrence River and Lake Ontario, it was decided to hire one vessel for the entire run. Wily chartered the *Kingston*, one of the Upper Canada Mail steamers, and it was refitted and embellished for the occasion. Negotiations took place with a great many railway companies, which agreed to have special train services available when and where needed. Such commitments set in motion a competition among the railway companies to improve their facilities for the event and to prepare luxurious cars for royal use. A contract was made with W. Kirwin, 'a noted Livery Stable Keeper at Quebec,' to supply eighteen horses for the use of members of the royal party wherever they were visiting. An especially fine charge, 'Lady Franklin,' was kept for the exclusive use of the prince.[48]

Wily also travelled throughout Canada to arrange accommodation for the visitors. At Quebec, he set in motion a major refit of the neglected and unoccupied Parliament Buildings, where the prince and his suite could stay and where official receptions could be held. Governor Head planned to host the visitors for part of their stay at Quebec, but since his official residence, Spencer Wood, was only partially rebuilt following a fire in 1859, it was decided that only some of the less important members of the suite would be accommodated there and that improvements would be made to Head's temporary home, Cataraqui, for the comfort of the distinguished guests. In Montreal, Rose's own fine house on Mount Royal (rented to General Fenwick Williams, commander of the British forces in Canada) was selected as a fit residence for the prince, but, because it lacked sufficient bedrooms even for the core party, the construction of a new wing was begun. (One member of the royal party highly approved of the house: 'a good library, a splendid view, and some nice pictures – a place altogether in good taste.'[49]) In Montreal the overflow of visitors attached to the prince was housed in St Lawrence Hall, a large hotel on Craig Street. In Ottawa, Wily leased the entire Victoria Hotel, which could accommodate everyone; he was able to do so because the hotel had only just been completed and had not yet taken any reservations. Wily oversaw preparations in Kingston of the former government house, known as Alwington House, and in Toronto the old Government House was similarly made ready for the prince and his inner suite, with additional rooms reserved at the Rossin House, the city's only luxury hotel. For the reception in London, Wily made arrangements with the proprietor of the Tecumseh Hotel, while in Niagara Falls, Emmeline Zimmerman, the widow of businessman Samuel Zimmerman, leased her fine house for the use of the prince and a few of the visitors, with the rest to be accommodated at the prestigious Clifton House. Similarly, at Hamilton, a fine residence owned by Richard Juson, who would be away in Europe, was to provide a comfortable home for the appreciative visitors, while the Royal Hotel looked after the overflow.[50] The Canadian cabinet approved these arrangements at its meeting of 22 May.[51]

Only a little controversy swirled in Canada around the decisions made with respect to the prince's accommodations. Isaac Buchanan, a prominent Hamilton merchant closely connected to the Great Western Railway, publicly accused Rose and the government of showing a preference for spending money lavishly in places on the route of the Grand Trunk Railway (the railway closely associated with the Conservatives), to the neglect of rival places without Grand Trunk connections. Rose denied the allegation, insisting that it was wise to select a few main stopping places (Quebec, Montreal, Ottawa, and Toronto), where full services would be set up for the prince and his retinue, while simpler arrangements would be sufficient at other places where the prince was staying only briefly.[52]

Local newspapers filled in the details about the refurbishing of particular buildings for the use of the prince, in the process reassuring the public that he would be treated royally. The Toronto *Globe*, for instance, carefully described the apartments being fitted up at Government House in Toronto. A little wallpapering was necessary to freshen the rooms, which were in good repair, but, since the building was empty, the commissioner of public works had to have it carpeted and he placed large orders for furniture with Jacques and Hay, the city's largest and most prestigious furniture-making firm. Craftsmen rushed to complete top-quality suites, with custom carving that featured Prince-of-Wales plumes and maple leaves. The prince was given a large apartment in the building's southeast corner with a view both of the well-kept garden ('supplied with a variety of choice and fragrant flowers') and of the lake.[53]

Officials also had to make arrangements for feeding the visitors. Hotels would provide meals for the parties they accommodated, but catering arrangements – and splendid ones – would be needed for the prince and others when staying in private homes or government buildings. Wily credits Rose with securing the talents of I.M. Sanderson, the impresario at one of New York's large hotels (the New York Hotel). He was judged to have the requisite skills both in overseeing the complexities of the mobile food operations and in acting as head chef. During the tour, some of his menus gained the attention of the press, which praised their elegance, and Wily reports that the distinguished visitors 'became quite enthusiastic over them.' Sanderson had ambitions for himself and for American cuisine. 'I am a gastronomer by taste, by profession, and by science,' he boasted to one member of the prince's suite. 'I hope to live to prove that in my hands the school of cookery in France, England, and Russia or Germany is inferior to the school of America.'[54] If the diners had praise for the catering arrangements, the opposition press found fault with them on nationalist grounds. The Toronto *Globe*, always ready to pounce on a Conservative minister, criticized Rose for his 'unpatriotic mission' to New York to select 'a cook for the Prince from Yankeeland, as if no Canadian *maître de cuisine* was competent to tickle a princely palate.'[55]

As part of the preparations for the entertainment of the royal party and their guests, the Canadian government also placed orders for fine glassware, plate, and dinner sets with firms in England that customized them for the occasion. The tableware, for instance, displayed the prince's crest, surrounded by wreathes of maple leaves, and it was, according to Wily, 'extremely handsome, very costly, & much admired.' Two complete sets of everything were ordered so that, while one set was in use, the other could be shipped to the next place on the prince's itinerary. A London purveyor that often supplied the royal household offered to ship candelabras to Canada, but Rose decided that they would not be needed because there was gas in all the houses where the prince was to stay.[56] It was Wily's job to order considerable quantities of wine, spirits, and beer, which he had distributed to various points along the route of the tour. The wines were imported, except for a few cases of a rare Canadian wine, which Wily identifies as 'Catawba' and which he says he procured only with some difficulty. Predictably, the visitors found the Canadian wine unpleasing and drank little of it. Ironically, when the leftover cases were sold at auction, they fetched quadruple their original price because, says Wily, for 'connoisseurs' the wine now had 'the imprimatur of the Prince!'

Wily also had to make arrangements with the military and police. The prince would be escorted by three officers and 100 men of the Royal Canadian Rifles, who, with their brass band, accompanied the visitors from place to place. In most locales they provided an honour guard for state ceremonies. Providing the soldiers with accommodations was easily done, since they camped wherever the prince stopped, but the transportation of the men and their considerable amount of equipment had to be arranged. Wily says that the soldiers enjoyed themselves, for the detail was a pleasant change 'from the dreary monotony of barrack life.' Their duties were light, they got to see all the sights, and they had a field allowance that enabled them to make 'a jolly time of it.' According to press reports, these men in their smart tunics drew the attention of admiring spectators, many of them young ladies. By contrast, the police that accompanied the prince for security purposes drew little comment at the time and have left scarcely a trace in the historical record. Wily notes in passing only that 'several clever & experienced detectives accompanied us from first to last,' and that for the visit to Ottawa, where tour organizers still feared violence from the Shiners who had once terrorized the town, a detachment of twelve men and a sergeant from the Montreal Harbour Police were taken up to the frontier capital.[57]

The onerous responsibilities of Wily notwithstanding, the Canadian government, like the imperial one, took a back seat to the municipalities in the planning of the tour. During the prince's progress through British North America, civic receptions dominated the public sphere. In an era when the administrative state was not yet full-blown, it was, of course, convenient for the higher levels of government to delegate the job to local committees, which would raise the funds and do the job. Yet delegating the responsibilities also accomplished important political and cultural goals. In this regard, there are parallels with Queen Victoria and Prince Albert's visits throughout England and Scotland in the 1840s and 1850s. For these visits pageantry was not imposed from the centre or top down onto the localities. Local committees made the arrangements and, in the process, notes British historian John Plunkett, the visits 'helped to forge a local consensus around the crown.'[58] Such was the idea in British North America in 1860. And it actually worked out that way – much of the time.

The Prince and His Suite

Who was this young man, the Prince of Wales, and who were the members of his entourage? On the eve of the royal visit of 1860, the public knew precious little about Albert Edward, or 'Bertie,' as he was commonly known. Newspapers had given the prince attention on only a few occasions, notably, at the time of his birth on 9 November 1841, his christening several weeks later, and when he turned eighteen in 1859.[59] His personality and interests were so little understood by the public in 1860 that commentators could graft onto his name whatever qualities they chose. Certainly, his future reputation as womanizer and bon vivant had not yet been established. To the extent that he personally had any public image at all before his 1860 tour, it was as one of the nine children who clustered around Victoria and Albert in royal family portraits. Visual and verbal representations of Victoria, her husband, and the family (as a unit) were everywhere in the mid-Victorian years, and the people who planned, observed, and read about the prince's tour would have fit the images projected in the course of the tour into a wider knowledge of the royal family. By 1860, Victoria had been on the throne for twenty-three years; she was a mature (but not yet elderly) woman, best known – because the image was endlessly reinforced by media reports – as a hard-working monarch ever serving the public at openings, dedications, charity events, and the like.[60] In England, the press she received during the decade before the tour was overwhelmingly positive, though there was always a critical voice directed at the institution if not the woman.[61] Victoria's service to the people, and their support for her, were reinforced by images of her as a good wife to an equally industrious husband and as a model mother to an ever-growing family. She was the mother to the nation, and the nation's most potent and ubiquitous symbol. According to the middle-class press, notes historian Richard Williams, 'the qualities which she and the Royal Family ... exemplified were those prized as the foundations of Victorian society – hard work, thrift, probity and the sanctity of the home and family.'[62]

The public knew little about the Prince of Wales before the tour not only because, prior to his eighteenth birthday, he was officially not permitted a public role on account of his youth, but also because his parents placed tight constraints on him.[63] The prince consort in particular worked tirelessly at supervising Bertie's schooling in the hope of rearing a son fully capable of one day assuming the burden of rule. Tutored

Albert Edward, Prince of Wales, as photographed in Boston, 19 October 1860, by J. Gurney and Son of New York. Though young-looking for his age (he was about to turn nineteen), the prince appears self-assured in his smart clothes. (National Archives of Canada, PA 127299)

privately until he started at Oxford in October 1859, Bertie, a social extrovert, was a reluctant and lacklustre solitary scholar, and he got little positive reinforcement from his tutors and parents, who continually nagged him and found fault with his performance. The royal couple's parenting might well have been disastrous, and it is something of a miracle that the young prince who visited North America was not an utter misfit.

Before coming to North America, Albert Edward had had some experience with travel, and it was during his travels that he had been allowed a few pleasures. At fourteen he accompanied his parents and elder sister, Vicky, the princess royal, on a state visit to Paris, where Bertie charmed the court of Emperor Napoleon III and gained considerable attention. Later he travelled unofficially on the continent, and when he visited the court in Berlin, Albert Edward was 'a brilliant success.'[64] Several balls were given at which he danced well and with enthusiasm, foreshadowing his success in North America. About the same time, the prince consort complained that his eldest son took 'no interest in anything but clothes, and again clothes. Even when out shooting he is more occupied with his trousers than with the game!'[65] Perhaps he would benefit from a trip to North America, where he might gain focus and maturity by assuming some state responsibilities.

On the 1860 tour of British North America and the United States, the members of the prince's suite supported him in his duties and protected him on his travels. Moreover, the gentlemen who made up this retinue added weight and lustre to the grandeur of the tour.

The leading figure of the prince's suite was the Duke of Newcastle, member of the cabinet at Westminster, who was entrusted by the queen with giving her young son political advice during the 1860 tour and who, as colonial secretary, bore official responsibility for the state visit to the colonies. Born Henry Pelham, and titled Lord Lincoln at his birth in 1811, the prince's political adviser became the fifth Duke of Newcastle upon the death of his father in 1851. Lincoln had been elected to the House of Commons in 1832 and soon became a follower of Sir Robert Peel, the Conservative leader.[66] By the time he came to Canada in 1860, the Duke of Newcastle was best known to the public for his embarrassments, notably his humiliating divorce, which had exposed his wife's sexual adventures in England and on the continent, and the bad press he got for the part he played in the mishandling Britain's military campaign in the Crimea. When British setbacks in the field and the appalling condition of the troops became a cause célèbre

The fifth Duke of Newcastle, as photographed in Boston, 19 October 1860, by J. Gurney and Son of New York. On Newcastle's shoulders rested the burden of advising the prince, the effects of which are evident in this image taken near the end of the tour. (National Archives of Canada, PA 127301)

of the nation and empire, the duke was compelled to resign as minister of war. But he was soon back in government. In 1859 the new prime minister, Lord Palmerston, made him secretary of state for the colonies, a position that enabled him to restore at least partially his damaged reputation. In tune with the mainstream of English public opinion, Newcastle was a committed imperialist who defended the retention of the colonies. Moreover, in the colonies he gained praise as a liberal imperialist who advocated responsible government for the settler colonies and encouraged the process of colonial nation-building within the framework of the British empire.[67]

Newcastle was a complex character. Publicly, he had a commanding presence. 'The duke stands very erect, and has an air and manner which instantly announce the high-born gentleman,' commented one journalist in 1860. 'The firm, independent, honest, open character of the man inspires his whole form.' In private, Newcastle could appear like a different person entirely. One member of the prince's suite was touched by the man's openness about his private troubles: 'The poor duke burst into tears yesterday with reference to his domestic life ... What a tale it is!' Only to a small circle was it known that the duke suffered from severe headaches that occasionally debilitated him during the tour.[68]

Next in rank among members of the suite travelling with the prince was Major-General Robert Bruce. On the tour, the middle-aged governor to the prince fulfilled the role of guardian in the absence of Victoria and Albert. It was his job to keep an eye on the young prince's behaviour in both public and private, to do everything possible to ensure that the trip was an educational experience for the youth, and to report back regularly to the queen and her consort, who trusted Bruce completely. The stern general was well prepared for the role, since it amounted to a continuation of the duties he had performed since 1858, including while the prince was studying at Oxford. A fellow member of the prince's suite in 1860 found that Bruce ran hot and cold, sometimes sharing his innermost thoughts and sometimes being 'wrapped in the profoundest grandeur.' Bruce had an advantage over other members of the suite insofar as he knew British North America, having served as military secretary to his elder brother, Lord Elgin, when Elgin was governor general in the 1840s.[69]

Adding yet more distinction to the prince's retinue was the Earl of St Germains, a former lord lieutenant of Ireland and in 1860 lord high steward of Her Majesty's household. Born Edward Granville Eliot in

The prince and some members of his suite, as photographed by William Notman outside the mansion of John Rose, where the prince and some of his party stayed in Montreal. From left to right: Sir Edmund Head, governor general; Major Christopher Teesdale, equerry; the Prince of Wales; General Robert Bruce, the prince's governor; the Duke of Newcastle, colonial secretary. (National Archives of Canada, C 18140)

1798, the earl came from an aristocratic family long associated with public service. During the North American tour, St Germains provided expertise on royal etiquette and made certain that everything ran smoothly, both during public ceremonials and behind-the-scenes among the members of the suite and their eight servants. Always charming and always correct, St Germains, it seems, was both liked and respected by everyone who met him. 'With his handsome form,' wrote one commentator, 'set off by the best made of frock coats, or the full dress uniform of the members of Her Majesty's household, his hat jauntily set on one side, his cane lightly held or tapping his brightly polished boot, St Germains looks every inch the Earl.'[70]

Dr Henry Wentworth Acland served as physician to the prince and his suite during their travels in North America, continuing in a role that the Regius professor of medicine had performed during the prince's stay in Oxford during the 1859–60 academic year. Though Acland was a little intimidated at the prospect of taking responsibility for the health of England's princely heir throughout his travels, the duties proved to be light since none of the distinguished visitors required much treatment during the tour. Acland remained in the background, free to pursue his own interests, which he did with great gusto – visiting people and places, writing about everything he saw, and sketching scenes of natural beauty and human interest both as a hobby and for posterity. Because he left an extensive and valuable record of the tour in the form of letters home to his family in England and drawings and paintings made while travelling, he plays a more prominent role in the history of the tour than would otherwise have been the case.[71]

The nearest thing the prince had for companions among the members of his suite were his two equerries, young men a few years older than himself. The handsome Major Christopher Teesdale, a hero of the defence of Kars in the Crimean War and the holder of a Victoria Cross, had been in attendance on Bertie in Oxford, where, among other duties, he played tennis with the prince (and to the latter's frustration, always beat him). Captain Charles Grey, another decorated young army officer, was also said to be good-looking. Young ladies in North America would pay both equerries much attention when given the opportunity at public balls and on other occasions during the tour.[72] The lowest-ranking member of the suite was John Gardner Dillman Englehart, the private secretary to the Duke of Newcastle, who kept in the background throughout the visit. As with Acland, Englehart's role was enhanced by the record he kept of the tour. Soon after returning from America, his travel journal was published, accompanied by many engravings of sketches he had made during his travels.[73]

Several other individuals followed alongside the royal suite for all or part of the tour. A few young gentlemen attached themselves for periods of time to the royal suite. Charles George Eliot, the youngest son of the Earl St Germains, accompanied his father for most of the trip. He was a friend of the prince's, as was the twenty-one-year-old Viscount Hinchingbrooke (later the Earl of Sandwich), who joined the prince's tour at Montreal and stayed the run.[74] British authorities granted semi-official status to two members of England's journalistic community who were to cover the tour: Nicholas Augustus Woods, special correspondent for the London *Times*,[75] and George Henry Andrews, an artist working for the *Illustrated London News*. On ships, steamers, and trains, they were free to travel everywhere with the royal party.[76] Although Woods and Andrews were part of a group of special correspondents and artists who pursued the prince during his tour, they got favoured treatment because their papers, which were unusually influential London publications, had by 1860 earned the trust of Queen Victoria.[77] Her confidence was well placed. Woods's reports of the tour could be acerbic when describing local arrangements, but they were as flattering of the prince as the etchings and commentary in the *Illustrated London News*.[78]

The Departure of the *Hero*

Just before the departure of the prince from England, the queen invited members of the prince's suite to stay with the royal family at Osborne House on the Isle of Wight, the elegant mansion purchased and improved by Victoria and Albert as a comfortable residence for their young, growing family. Located near Plymouth, the port of departure for the royal squadron, it made a handy assembly place for the members of the party as they came down from London, Oxford, Windsor, and elsewhere. Dr Acland, not being used to such company, was at first intimidated by the gathering, but the queen soon put him at ease. 'After dinner she came herself to me and talked quite as merrily & freely as my dear mother in her merriest mood would have done,' Acland excitedly explained to his wife in a letter he penned that same evening. When she asked 'to begin with, "Are you a good sailor?"' Acland had replied, 'Pretty well, Madam.' '"Pretty well, is that all?"

and she laughed ... and chatted away.' He reported as well, however, that the spirits of the 'Little Prince seemed dull.'[79]

The next morning the royal family and the prince's suite were driven by carriages the short distance from Osborne House down to Trinity Pier at East Cowes, where Bertie said farewell to his mother and four of his younger siblings. The sentimental Dr Acland was touched by the scene, as he recorded later in the day. The queen had bid farewell to her son 'just like a simple English Mother parting with her child – we not altogether unmoved as she wished him good bye.' '"Come safe back,"' the queen said to Acland when he himself stepped from the wharf. The tender pulled away, making for the royal yacht, *Victoria and Albert*, and the queen, said Acland, 'stood with her bare head ... waving her handkerchief as my mother would have done.'[80] The prince consort accompanied his son and the other travellers to Plymouth, where the royal squadron awaited the departure for America.[81]

In fine weather, and with thousands of inhabitants watching from the heights above Plymouth, the Channel squadron – eleven vessels under full canvas in a smart breeze – formed two lines outside the breakwater to receive the royal yacht, which hove into sight at 7 o'clock in the evening. The yards of the *Hero* and certain other ships were manned and a salute was fired in homage. The Prince of Wales then received the first of hundreds of addresses presented during the tour, when the mayor and corporation of Davenport wished him a safe and happy voyage. Alluding to former colonizers from the county – Raleigh, Drake, and Gilbert – the address situated the prince's trip in a tradition of great colonial expeditions that had sailed from the port.[82] That evening the Prince of Wales boarded the *Hero*, where he and his father dined together before Prince Albert took leave of his son, no doubt proffering some fatherly advice as he did so.[83] That night, the overtaxed Duke of Newcastle slaved at his desk until 4:00 in the morning, tying up as many loose ends as possible, but he was up at 7:00 all the same to see the ship get under weigh.[84]

The *Hero*, the ship that was to carry the prince across the Atlantic, was a steam/sailing ship of ninety-one guns, under the command of Captain George H. Seymour of the royal squadron. She was accompanied by the steam frigate *Ariadne*, with twenty-six guns, under Captain Edward W. Vansittart. Accounts of the day were quick to stress the appropriateness of these vessels for the august purpose; they were said to the 'the finest and fastest ships in the navy.' A third vessel, the sloop *Flying Fish* of six guns, under Commander Hope, had left for Newfoundland a week prior to the prince's departure because, though well suited to manoeuvring in tight harbours and shallow waters, she was slower than the other two vessels and thus needed a head start.

The press took the trouble to describe the quarters aboard the *Hero*, highlighting their modesty. Newcastle and St Germains divided the ward room between them, while the other members of the royal suite had temporary cabins built for them along the main deck. The prince took the quarters that were normally the captain's. Cornwallis reports that the Admiralty had planned to decorate the prince's quarters 'in regal splendour' but his mother had not permitted it and indeed insisted that any personal accommodation made for her son should be 'of the plainest kind.'[85] The image is of a wise mother, concerned that her son not be weakened by pampering. In fact, the captain's quarters were quite comfortable. There was a large room, with a mahogany dining table, two card tables, and seating for twenty-two. Gilt lines decorated the panelling, and over a mahogany sideboard were suspended four silver candleholders, once the property of Lord Nelson and used by him aboard the *Victory*. Off that main saloon was a comfortable sitting cabin with a large table and leather sofas and chairs, and another cabin for sleeping, complete with cot, mahogany washstand, brass shelves, and a speaking tube with which the prince could summon his manservant from adjoining quarters.

On the morning of 10 July, the pair of ships departed Plymouth, accompanied by the Channel fleet formed into two lines. In the fine weather, thousands of spectators watched from the heights as the tall ships sailed westwards. The impressive escort continued until mid-afternoon. Since it was the last chance for sending letters back to England before crossing the Atlantic, the prince and members of the suite took the opportunity to dash off a few lines that afternoon. 'The Prince of Wales is very well, and so far seems to enjoy the voyage,' Newcastle wrote reassuringly to the queen. General Bruce informed the prince consort that his son had 'made no difficulties or complaints,' but there had been rumblings from the servants about all the work. 'They promised beforehand to make themselves useful,' he harrumphed, '& I intend to hold them to it.' There was little as yet to report, but the prince dutifully wrote to his mother. Already sounding like an old hand, he told her that rather than relying on steam power, the *Hero* had been 'under sail the greater part of the day, as the wind is a fair one, & we are anxious to save coal.'[86]

The voyage to Newfoundland proved largely uneventful. The seas occasionally got rough, but that caused only a little discomfort among the royal party. Proud of his sea legs, the prince was quick to point out to his mother that he had been sick only on the third and fourth days out. For much of the trip, Newcastle talked a good deal in the main saloon about politics and colonial affairs, past and present, not only because he enjoyed doing so but also in a deliberate attempt to educate the prince. General Bruce thought it a useful exercise, and Dr Acland appreciated the duke's frankness about his reverses in political life. Before leaving for Canada, Newcastle had assembled a collection of almanacs, tourist guidebooks, and maps of North America, so that members of the party, and the prince in particular, could study them during the voyage. According to Bruce, the prince pored over these materials, familiarizing himself with the places he would soon be visiting, and he took 'a lively interest' in the running of the ship and navigation, in the process 'acquiring much really useful knowledge.' Acland, too, took the opportunity to read from the collection on British North America and the United States, consulting such volumes as the *Elements of Canadian History.* In a letter to his wife, the doctor joked that he was 'beginning to understand a good deal more about colonies than I ever expected – or dreamed of.' He was 'pretty well up now in the generalities of St John's 1, 2 & 3, of Halifax, Pictou, Anticosti, the French Fisheries, and Canadians, Quebec, Montreal, Toronto, Hotels, Cars ... and I know not what all.'[87]

The young prince spent most, but not all, of his time aboard the *Hero* with middle-aged men. General Bruce smugly reported to the prince consort that, as directed, he had kept H.R.H. from engaging in 'any undue familiarity with the Junior Officers of the ship.' But, in the same breath, Bruce added that they were a 'very well disposed set of youths.' A few of them had been asked to dine with the prince and his party by the commodore, who presided at the table and made up the guest list for meals.[88] One day the prince accepted an invitation from the young midshipmen to have lunch with them, an occasion that became part of the folklore of the tour. The seas at the time were running so high that a wave poured through the cabin window, dowsing the prince and the 'middies' and sweeping them from the table. The story was recounted by various sailors and passengers, along with other accounts of the youthful prince's behaviour aboard the *Hero*.[89] According to the reporter for the New York *Herald*, the prince 'used to sit cross-legged, with telescope in hand, signalling the other ships of the squadron, alternately asking humorous questions, and returning all sorts of jocular replies.'[90] Private accounts noted the prince's subterfuges in escaping the watchful eyes of his elders. 'The Sailors say,' wrote one man who talked to them in New Brunswick, 'that the prince would come forward and listen to the singing and watch their dancing and appear to enjoy it first rate. That the Duke of Newcastle would allow him only a certain number of cigars a day but that he would steal the smoking of more, and that when the Duke was below he would haul out a little black pipe, wink to the crowd around, and pull away. When he saw the Duke coming, he would stow the pipe in his pocket and be much amused by the dodge.'[91]

So it was, then, that twelve days were passed in traversing the Atlantic. All things considered, it was an enjoyable and problem-free start to a long and possibly momentous imperial progress.

British newspapers not only covered the spectacle of the prince's sailing from Plymouth, they also took the departure as a cue to reflect on the meaning of this first royal visit to British North America. Imperial grandeur and imperial purpose sprang immediately to mind. The visit, declared the *Times*, 'will illustrate not only the loyalty of these prosperous Provinces, but the immense extent of British dominion and the deep-laid foundations of British power.' During the ocean crossing, the prince would daily see the fleets of British ships. Upon reaching St John's, he would observe the Union Jack flying, as he had seen it ten days before in England. Travelling through the mainland colonies, everywhere he would view the results of industry, largely the work of emigrants, 'the pure stock of the English race.' Even along the St Lawrence River, where there dwelled 'a people strange ... in race, religion and language,' he would find subjects living 'contentedly and loyally under the sceptre of Victoria.' To the northwest could be imagined the boundless territory that stretched to the Pacific, a fit home for nearly 'the whole present population of Europe.' And this was but *one* country in a world-encircling system of colonies over which the prince would one day rule![92]

The prince's trip also provided monarchists with a rationale for the royal family that fit with the times. As symbols of Britishness and as goodwill ambassadors, members of the royal family enhanced England's links to its colonies and to other states. 'Surely princes perform one of their noblest functions,' argued the London *Chronicle* on the occasion of the *Hero*'s departure, 'when they become bearers of good intelligence and cordial feeling between great States.' It was pointed out that, at the very same time as the Prince of Wales would be opening the bridge at Montreal, his younger brother, Prince Alfred, would be inaugurating a breakwater at Cape Town, South Africa. This same thought delighted the boys' father, who wrote privately: 'What a cheering picture is here of the progress and expansion of the British race and of the co-operation of the royal family in the civilisation which England has developed and advanced.'[93]

The prince's departure also prompted editorial writers in Britain to make a case for the educational advantages that he would derive from his travels in America. The London *Herald* expected that 'by developing his mind and enlarging his experience,' the tour would 'prepare the young Prince himself for the task of government.' Along the same lines, the London *Chronicle* referred to the tour as the prince's 'great course in the study of kingship.'[94] Presumably, what the *Chronicle* had in mind was a training in public ceremony because, in the mid-Victorian period, the public generally imagined the monarch to be removed from partisan politics and to have a vital but largely symbolic role in constitutional affairs.[95] After the prince had seen America first hand, argued the Liverpool *Post*, 'it will be his own fault if he fails to know that it [the crown] is an emblem of power to be used for the preservation of constitutional liberty and the advancement of civilization.' Moreover, the frontier experience could prove beneficial for the prince; the future 'head of the most complicated artificial system of Europe should confront nature in her wildest aspect, and see what human energy can do where it is less restrained and most vigorous.'[96]

For Victorian commentators, educational opportunities blended into character-building ones. With evangelical sternness, the London *Saturday Review* commented on the advantages of taking on duties at an early age. 'Public action is probably the best antidote to those corrupting and degrading influences which beset the youth of Princes,' pronounced the *Saturday Review.* They were subject to great moral temptations because honours and wealth had come without effort on their part. 'It is indolence, joined to passion and opportunity, that has too often made the history of an heir apparent one of family misery and personal disgrace.' By taking on a public role during the tour, however, the Prince of Wales would learn about duty, take his academic studies more seriously, and begin to establish a reputation that would win him public support, a necessity for a monarch in the nineteenth century. 'The Prince must see how it fares in the present age with royalty unsupported with personal merit.' There was the risk, however, that Albert Edward would get a swelled head from all the attention he would receive on his tour. The *Saturday Review* insisted that the prince 'must remember that the Sovereign whom he represents is the principal object of the enthusiasm which will attend his progress.'[97]

Time would tell whether the prince's head could handle the adoration shown him – or, rather, the queen. Meantime, people in towns and cities across British North America had much to accomplish before they would be ready to welcome Victoria's heir. The prince's departure from England signalled that it was time for everyone in the provinces to be up and doing.

2

Fit for a Prince

Sound the trumpets! Beat the drums!
The Princely heir of England comes! ...

Write the letters! Sweep the halls!
Erect the arches! Deck the Walls!
Charge all the guns! Subscribe for *balls*!
Polish the engines! Clean the hose!
Pipe-clay the belts for soldiers' clothes!
Burnish the bayonets! Buy new dresses!
Drill the children! Write Addresses! ...
Adjourn the Courts! Postpone the Sessions!
Buy Roman candles! Form processions!
For hark, the trumpets! hark, the drums!
The Princely Heir of England comes! ...

R.J. de Cordova, *The Prince's Visit: A Humorous Description* (1861)

'Canada is preparing, – like a bride putting on her robes, – to meet her future sovereign and invited guest,' declared the Ottawa *Citizen* on 24 July 1860. In the weeks preceding the prince's arrival in each of the places on his itinerary, civic reception committees and residents busied themselves planning events for the visit and decorating streets, public buildings, businesses, and homes for the occasion. Public bodies swung into action, holding meetings to decide how best to welcome His Royal Highness. Evergreen boughs and floral wreaths, red-white-and-blue bunting and flags, patriotic banners and triumphal arches – all these and more needed to be prepared so that drab streets might become magnificent thoroughfares. It was no accident that in this context the *Citizen* represented Canada as female: according to predominant Victorian mores, all this primping and attention to appearance was behaviour suitable only for a woman. The analogy of the bride fit the occasion especially well because, according to script, she is supposed to take care and pride in 'putting on her robes' both to please her groom and to mark her and her wedding day as special. Several weeks later, just before the prince appeared in Ottawa, the *Citizen* reported that the preparations had been completed and the desired effect achieved in the young capital. 'Ottawa,' the newspaper boasted, 'appeared lovely and anxious as a bride awaiting the arrival of the bridegroom to complete the joy.'[1]

While the *Citizen* represented Canada and her capital as female, the newspaper coverage of the preparations for the prince described virtually all the related public activity in masculine terms. As we shall see, journalists gave much attention to the declarations and activities of the men of office and other civic patriarchs who sat on the reception committees and directed the planning for the visit. The members of these committees were carefully watched as well by the ratepayers – men with a stake in the town – who attended public meetings called to monitor the committees' work. According to the newspapers, the execution of the plans of the reception committees was also the work of men – men of many talents and stations: the architects who designed the triumphal arches, the construction crews that built them, and the well-heeled gentlemen and members of voluntary societies who helped to pay for them; the artists who painted the transparencies and the gas fitters that illuminated them; the eloquent men of letters who composed the public addresses and the rank-and-file members of organizations that authorized them. According to the press, making Canada 'fit for a prince' was an inclusive yet manly endeavour.

The colonial cities of British North America had not been designed for ceremonial purposes. Their layouts and architectural features had been formed haphazardly over time, the outcome of countless decisions resulting from the thinking of military strategists, the whims of officials on the scene at the start, the commercial tactics of merchants and manufacturers, the preferences of clergy and their congregations, the tastes of home builders, and the desperation of poor tenants and squatters. Grand avenues and parade grounds, civic monuments, and triumphal marble arches, which define the ceremonial spaces of the world's great cities, were conspicuously absent in these British provinces. Even in the provincial capitals and bigger centres, where the prince would spend most of his time, the public buildings, substantial churches, and larger commercial establishments could only hint at the aspirations and pretensions of the colonials of 1860. Detracting from their grandeur were the muddy streets on which they rose and the jumble of commercial, industrial, residential, and even agricultural structures that crowded round them.

Nevertheless, the cities of mid-Victorian Canada had features that made the ceremonial festivities of 1860 work reasonably well. Even the largest urban places were walking cities, where people could move easily from event to event, site to site, unencumbered by heavy vehicular traffic. Processions could move through all the main thoroughfares, giving a sense of inclusion. Spectators were contained in town-centre streets by buildings that did not dwarf the people but confined them so as to create the excitement of being in a crowd. Moreover, in this early industrial era, natural features were clearly visible and lent charm and even a striking majesty to towns and cities with only small populations. St John's, Halifax, Quebec, Montreal, and Ottawa all won praise from visitors in 1860 who were impressed with their magnificent natural settings. Nearly every town on the prince's itinerary nestled on the banks of a river, lake, or seacoast. Harbours everywhere were enhanced by the beauty of the sailing vessels that plied their waters. On the horizon of most towns and cities, the lofty spires of churches were not yet challenged for position by a forest of belching smokestacks.

Residents must have gone about decorating their towns in honour of the prince with the confidence that their handiwork could have an impact. Flags and bunting in red, white, and blue, masses of evergreen boughs, handsome, if temporary, triumphal arches in wood and plaster, Bengal lights, and Chinese lanterns would show up well and transform dull, quotidian places into cheery, festive sites where royalty could be welcomed with pomp and pride.

Civic Planning

To every city on the prince's itinerary fell the tasks of devising a local program and making arrangements for the prince's visit. Usually the municipal corporation assumed responsibility for setting up a reception committee to oversee preparations, but there were many local variations. At St John's, the governor, Sir Alexander Bannerman, took charge of appointing a reception committee because the city was not incorporated and thus lacked a mayor and council. At Halifax, where the military presence loomed large, the civil and the military authorities shared in the planning and preparations. Rear-Admiral Alexander Milne, the commander of the naval base, arranged for the prince's ceremonial landing at the dockyard, Major-General Trollope, of the British army, oversaw the military reviews, and the civil authorities took responsibility for everything else.[2] Toronto, however, is a more typical case, insofar as the municipal authorities there had sole authority for planning the prince's visit. How Toronto went about laying its plans is a study in participatory democracy at work on the civic level.

Preparations began in Toronto at a meeting called by Mayor Adam Wilson for the morning of 1 June. By means of a circular, he had invited local citizens to a public meeting that about fifty residents attended at St Lawrence Hall, the city's largest and most commodious meeting place near the centre of town. The *Globe* judged those in attendance to be 'a fair representation of all classes of citizens,' although it did not explain its criteria for doing so. Modern readers might well doubt whether women and various minorities were at all represented, and certainly the press made no mention of them. Men of weight, that is, white men of property, individuals who had a record of civic involvement, took the lead by speaking out publicly and were invited by the mayor to take part in the committee culture that thrived in the realm of civic affairs. Presumably, what the *Globe* was really saying was that those interests that usually shared in such public discussions were represented, and that some balance was evident in that members of the various religious groups and political parties were included on the committee. Thus, at this public meeting, the presence of the Reverend Dr John McCaul, an Anglican clergyman and the president of University College, was mentioned along with the Reverend Dr Michael Willis, principal of Knox College, the Presbyterian divinity school, William Henry Boulton, a Tory stalwart, and Malcolm 'Coon' Cameron, a Clear Grit radical. In this book I refer to the men of prominence who backed the local visits as 'the civic promoters.'

Those attending this first Toronto meeting were perplexed by the dearth of basic information about the timing of the prince's visit, the length of his stay, and the extent of the city's responsibilities. George Brown, speaking as an opposition MPP holding a Toronto seat, reported that 'nothing' was yet known even by the provincial authorities. The meeting nevertheless struck a committee to correspond with the office of the provincial secretary to procure what information could be had. Sheriff William Jarvis, a prominent and well-connected resident, explained that he had talked to the commissioner of public works, John Rose, and learnt that the provincial government would take care of the costs of accommodating the prince, but that otherwise local events would have to be paid for locally. The meeting briefly discussed various ideas for filling out the program, including an official reception, an illumination, a levee, a dinner hosted by the bench and bar, the formal opening of University (later Queen's) Park, and a ball. Just how the program should be financed was touched upon, some commentators urging that tax revenues be used and others that a public subscription be made.

The meeting resolved to form a 'General Committee of Arrangements' responsible for drafting a program and beginning the preparations. There was much discussion about the composition of the committee; personal prestige and substantial expenditures were at stake, after all. In the end a large committee was struck, one chaired by the mayor and with a membership composed of a great many office-holders and prominent men. The list, which reads like a who's who of mid-Victorian Toronto society, included all locally elected politicians in municipal as well as provincial affairs, various appointed officials from the police, the sheriff's office, and the judiciary, the elected presidents of the societies of St George, St Andrew, and St Patrick, and grandees such as Casimer Gzowski, William Cumberland, and Sanford Fleming.[3]

The general committee met a few days later. Because it was so large and cumbersome, several more manageable subcommittees were formed: one to draft the city's address, one to work out a program, one to consider finances, and one to plan the decorations. The thorny issue turned out to be how to pay for the local events – by a special tax assessment, by private subscription, or by some combination of the two. Some speakers expressed confidence in the ability of fund-raisers to get hold of the necessary money soon enough, while others doubted that it was possible. Precedents were cited, including both the fund-raising experiences of the rival cities of Montreal and Hamilton for their royal receptions and past experience in Toronto, when subscriptions had been used to pay for the celebrations for the opening of the Great Western Railway, for the 1855 reception for the popular singer Jenny Lind, and for the support of the daughter of a boxer recently incapacitated. Sheriff Jarvis declared that, if 100 guineas could be raised in the city during past weeks for the 'pugilistic hero,' Tom Sayers, then 'surely £5,000 could be raised to get up a fitting reception to our future sovereign.' Conflicting views were expressed about the willingness or ability of humble 'mechanics' to foot the bill through extra taxes. Alderman William B. McMurrick, who claimed familiarity with that class, thought that the mechanics would object, but W.H. Boulton, the owner of the Grange, one of the city's finest houses, opined that Toronto's keenly loyal workingmen would want the prince to have a proper reception and would gladly pay a tax increase of 37 and ½ cents. Indeed, he did not think that 'there was a single working man in Toronto who would be opposed to paying such a paltry sum, a sum that the mechanic was in the habit of spending every Saturday night for his own amusement.' Mayor Wilson argued that, since the city would host 50,000 to 60,000 visitors for the duration of the prince's stay, taxpayers had a duty to make a proper reception, but that additional expenditures would be better covered by means of private subscription or by those invited to the particular event. It was decided that the general committee should reconvene a week later, when a program would be proposed and expenditures estimated in readiness for a meeting of the public.[4]

When the general committee met on 20 June, Mayor Wilson read a letter from the provincial secretary who explained that the visit to Toronto would most likely occur at the end of August and last three or four days. The committee announced a proposed program for the Toronto visit, which included the events they had already discussed as well as plans for a regatta, a floral fête, and the construction of triumphal arches. Speakers at the meeting debated the length of the procession route, some of them insisting that the whole public must have ample opportunity to see the prince, while at least one speaker objected to excessive parading. As for costs, the committee on finances put a price tag of $15,000 on the reception. It was hoped that $3,000 would be raised privately and that there would also be some income from the sale of tickets for seats in the civic viewing stands and for other events, such as the public ball. The private subscription was needed for certain costs that the taxpayers might object to covering. An example was a trophy, costing £25, which the committee planned to present to the Royal [Canadian] Yacht Club for the yacht race to be held during the prince's visit to the city.[5]

On the evening of 28 June, all of Toronto had the opportunity of considering the program. The *Globe* said that the dense crowd at St

Lawrence Hall afforded 'abundant proof of the deep interest taken by the people of Toronto in the arrangements for giving a worthy reception to the eldest son of our Sovereign.' The mayor explained that all previous committees had been preliminary, and that this public meeting would establish the actual working committees and approve all plans. It was a time for rhetoric and puffery as prominent citizens read prepared resolutions to the cheering crowd. The Reverend Dr McCaul, a member of the subcommittee on the city's address to the prince, led off by moving that the citizens of Toronto, in response to the honour of the prince's visit, 'gladly avail themselves of the occasion ... to manifest their high appreciation of the distinguished honour thus conferred upon them by a reception suitable to the exalted station of his Royal Highness as Heir Apparent of the British Crown, and worthy of their city as the capital of Upper Canada.' In his own remarks, McCaul waxed eloquent about the deep roots of loyalty in the community, roots that reached back to 'the gallant band of U.E. Loyalists' who had found liberty 'in the bosom of the wild woods of Canada.' The second resolution, read by Oliver Mowat, the prominent lawyer and Reform politician, sketched the proposed program for the visit. Mowat then digressed on the way liberty and loyalty ran together under the British crown and ended by saying that, although the people of Toronto had 'their different political cries,' on this occasion they would unite 'in the cry, "Long live the Prince."' Other prominent members of the community, including H.J. Boulton and George Brown, read additional resolutions and made comments.

Whipped up by the patriotic fervour of the occasion, the crowd at St Lawrence Hall passed the various resolutions enthusiastically. However, heads were cool enough to insist on a qualifying amendment to the motion on finances, which had placed no constraints on the spending of the general committee. It was now agreed that the committee would be limited to a budget of $12,000 from the city treasury. A debate occurred, too, on the matter of the appropriateness of immediately reading and approving the address of the city prepared by the subcommittee. Some speakers maintained that it was important for the public, and not just a committee acting behind closed doors, to know what would be said on its behalf. Others argued that, by reading it publicly now, the prince would end up with a 'second-hand address.' A compromise was struck. The address was read and approved by the meeting, but it was agreed that it would not be published in the local papers until actually presented to the prince. With the bulk of the finances in place and a program outlined, the various committees were prepared to get down to business and carry out the plans during the following two months.[6]

In the case of Toronto, then, the planning process was represented by the newspapers as one of extensive public involvement. The press kept the public abreast of plans by reporting in detail on the composition of committees and discussions at their meetings. The usual cast of prominent public figures moved into the limelight to take positions of responsibility and power. Included among the civic promoters were public representatives – the mayor, aldermen, city councillors, and local MPPs who sat on the various reception committees and, in theory at least, looked out for the public interest. The mayor managed the planning process and invited members of the public, representing the various recognized interests or 'classes,' to share in decision making. Meetings were conducted with some formality, measures being moved, seconded, debated, and voted up or down. Final approval of plans rested with the public itself, or more precisely the ratepayers, who took in the heady rhetoric but voted with their pocketbooks firmly in mind. Reporters' detailed accounts of all the meetings – public, committee, and subcommittee – served as an accessible record of the debates and of the decisions reached. Civic debate and decision making were impressive examples of participatory democracy at work. Who could argue that, by the exacting standards of the day, the public had not had an opportunity to scrutinize, modify, and ratify the plans for the royal visit? The notion that Toronto welcomed the prince had real substance. The colonial secretary had wanted to avoid the appearance of a contrived show of colonial loyalty, and now the public record showed that the residents of Toronto had done their utmost to make the prince's welcome in their community a civic affair that had the full support of the people.

Once the plans were outlined and approved, Toronto's municipal authorities swung into action to make a host of improvements intended to beautify the city for the visit. In the park to the east of the University of Toronto, which the prince would inaugurate as 'Queen's Park,' new carriage roads and paths were laid out and gravelled, some five hundred additional trees planted, and the banks of the stream passing through it trimmed and sodded. The old gates to the park were removed and 'new, elegant, and substantial' substitutes were put in place, and the Russian guns, presented by Queen Victoria to the city at the end of the Crimean War, were placed on new stone pedestals and the grounds around them improved. Throughout the city, various roads were freshly macadamized and sidewalks replanked. In an attempt to make the city centre appear more attractive, a new by-law was introduced to compel owners of vacant lots to fence them. A lot at Yonge and Front streets in the heart of town needed a special fence to screen from view 'the unsightly Shanties.'[7] Micro-management was the order of the day. A Mr Austin, whose awning in front of his store at the market was in poor repair, was ordered to appear before a meeting of the Toronto Board of Works, where he promised to cover the problem with spruce boughs in time for the prince's arrival. City council by-law no. 327, passed on the eve of the visit, made 'some special provision for the safety of life, the protection of property, and the preservation of order.' Its twenty-one clauses attempted to exclude nuisances, including dogs, geese, pigs, sheep, and goats, from public streets; to create a core pedestrian zone, where horses, cattle, and unauthorized vehicles were not permitted; and to banish unlicensed fireworks and bonfires.[8] Were civic officials overdoing things? Time would tell.

Sprucing Up

'Halifax did not know itself on the 30th of July,' wrote Nathaniel Woods, the special correspondent of the London *Times*. 'It was completely buried in green leaves and flowers, and metamorphosed into a gigantic bouquet.'[9] Every place on the prince's itinerary sought to undergo a similar metamorphosis by 'sprucing up.' Spruce and other evergreen boughs provided a ready means to alter the appearance of a town and set the stage for the festivities. No matter how small, no matter how poor, each hamlet and town could adorn itself in nature's best dress. At the other extreme, Montreal, with its extravagant, formal decorations, also turned green on the urging of the local press. Residents were encouraged to plant evergreens 'profusely' in front of their houses because, though the civic arches looked 'well,' they were 'stiff and formal.'[10]

In British North American towns and cities, a supply of evergreen branches and small trees was never far away, and they were brought into town by train and cart and used lavishly. Haligonians smothered their houses in them. 'Every building was decorated with evergreens; not shamly spread in patches, here and there, but completely covering many of them, hiding much of all.'[11] Civic committeemen authorized the 'planting' of evergreen trees (minus their roots) to hide ugly gaps in the street-scape caused by vacant lots. The steamers plying the St Lawrence near Trois-Rivières were ornamented with spruce trees, and in Lake St Peter 'the very buoys were decorated.'[12]

Extensive evergreen displays did not always have the intended effect. From Quebec it was reported that, because of the heavy rain, branches drooped low, soaking passers-by, blocking traffic, and making the muddy streets appear like a swamp. Woods of the *Times* complained: 'People groped their devious ways through the streets under the branches of small wet fir trees, that rendered an umbrella doubly necessary at the time they utterly prevented its use.'[13]

There is nothing like news of the coming of a visitor to prompt people to clean and polish, paint and decorate. The press troubled to report precisely who was taking part in the refit for the prince. In Fredericton, the public buildings and grounds around them were beautified, Mr Watts being in charge of the painting and decorating of the legislative building, and Mr Barry of the improvements to the lawn and gardens outside the prince's rooms at Government House. In Saint John the courthouse was refurbished for a levee, with the ceiling given a special paint treatment by by George F. Thompson, assisted by Mr Swift. On the main street of town, an artist in Wiley's employment rushed to complete a large painting of the coat of arms of the Prince of Wales that adorned the corner of the brick building owned by his boss. At Canada's leading furniture maker, Jacques and Hay, the top carvers busily completed renderings of Prince-of-Wales' plumes, maple leaves, and the like so as to embellish the six bedroom suites commissioned for the prince's rooms in various Canadian cities. By the time of the visit to Halifax, the *Acadian Reporter* proudly declared that no one had neglected to decorate their premises: 'Even the poorest classes – the tenants of single rooms, hung out something from their walls – a little flag, an evergreen wreath, or a garland of flowers – as an evidence of their feeling in the matter.'[14]

No aspect of the decorations gained as much press attention as the ceremonial arches, which were raised in honour of the prince in every town he visited. 'Arches seemed to spring up everywhere the Prince would, could, or might pass,' declared Woods. Even the smallest hamlets, passed through by the royal party in a flash, welcomed him with at least one evergreen arch. Cities vied to outdo their rivals by constructing either more arches or bigger, more impressive ones. Journalists reported on the results of these civic rivalries, providing many details about the design, execution, size, and number of arches in each place and judging the extent of civic pride, local talent, and loyal enthusiasm accordingly.

Arches were raised by three means. First, most municipalities commissioned at least one civic arch, the funds coming from local (or county) rates and the arrangements being made by the local decorations committee, a subcommittee of the reception committee. Secondly, local voluntary societies built arches, a committee taking charge of the project and drawing on funds from dues-paying members. Thirdly, arches were erected by private individuals – perhaps a group of neighbours, men in the same line of business, or merchants with shops located on the same block. It was possible to raise an arch on the cheap by relying on volunteer labour and by using a few poles, evergreen boughs, and flowers. Many arches in small towns, as well as those raised by city-dwellers of modest means, were built this way. At the other extreme, the most elaborate arches in the largest centres were designed by top architects, built by leading contractors, illuminated with costly gas fixtures, and decorated by talented commercial artists.

Because the civic arches involved the expenditure of public funds, controversies swirled around their construction. In Barrie, for instance, a public meeting aired some of the differences between town residents and the members of the rural-dominated county council, which authorized a mere $50 for arch building in the county town. In the end, the dispute was put aside, those present agreeing that as 'it was no ordinary occasion,' preparations should be 'carried out with the utmost good feeling.'[15] A more serious dispute at Toronto led to the resignation of all the members of the decorations committee after it was alleged that contracts associated with arch building were going to favourites, or even to members of the committee, rather than being put to tender. Here, too, the matter was resolved fairly quickly in order to ensure that the work got done in time.[16]

Journalists whipped up excitement about the visit by reporting, in some cases daily, on the progress of the arch building. During the lead-up to the prince's arrival in Toronto, the *Globe* related every advance made in the decoration of the city. On 15 August it was reported that, during construction, the civic arch on John Street – 'the finest arch in the city' – would be enclosed by a high board fence, whose purpose was twofold: to keep back gawking members of the public, who might impede the workmen, and to enhance both the sense of anticipation and the surprise on the day of the prince's arrival when the arch would at last be unveiled. With fanfare, the *Globe* announced when construction actually began on each large arch, and it mentioned the contractors by name and noted the hammering of 'hundreds of workmen.' The people themselves were said to be fascinated by the work: 'The streets of the city yesterday were densely crowded with pedestrians, all watching eagerly the work of constructing and decorating the arches, platforms, and balconies.' These were attentive gazers, not afraid to exercise their own judgment as to the merits of the fantastic structures. 'Crowds were assembled at the base of each arch criticising each shield or flag as it was hoisted to its place,' reported the *Globe*. In the evening, once the hustle and bustle of construction had halted, it was the turn of 'the ladies' to turn out 'in large numbers to admire the preparations.' Note that their role was *to admire*; it would not have been ladylike to shout publicly, much less to criticize openly the efforts of their menfolk.

In Ottawa, the festive spirit was said to have infected even the workmen building the arches. Soaring above the giant arch at the government works (the site of the new Parliament Buildings) was a flagpole designed to bear the royal standard. The Ottawa *Citizen* reported that 'a man, who must have been well accustomed to such work, swarmed the pole to adjust some ropes, and when at the top lay flat on the button, hands and feet free, as a professional acrobat might have done.' His feat 'was hailed with hearty cheers by his fellow workmen.'[17] For the workers, as well as for spectators, then, arch building was presented in the press as standing apart from the humdrum routines of the workaday world.

In the pages of the London *Times*, Woods heaped praise on the people of Halifax because they had entered into arch building with such enthusiasm, even as he feigned annoyance at the racket they made. 'All these preparations were not got through without a terrific din of hammering and sawing,' he reported. Because the work had not been completed, Sunday provided a break only in the morning. At twelve o'clock, 'the hammering was renewed with conscientious accuracy and redoubled vigour, and a lively night was the result to all who lived within hearing (as who did not?) of some monstrous hollow drumming arch. One would have thought from the sound, that each leaf on the structure required a tenpenny nail to secure it.'[18]

Journalist had fun describing the flurry of building at Port Hope, which had only four days' notice of the prince's visit. (The royal itinerary had been changed at the last minute because of Orange troubles at Kingston and Belleville.) Notwithstanding the short notice, the local decorations committee decided that no less than four impressive arches needed to be built 'in keeping with the occasion.' It was a scramble to get ready. 'Every man in town who could handle a saw, or drive a nail, or wield a pick, was at once pressed into service.' The streets came alive with traffic. 'Carts were hurrying hither and thither, hauling boards, scantling, poles, nails, etc; and trains on the Port Hope, Lindsay and Beaverton Railway came in at frequent intervals bringing whole forests of evergreens – hemlock, spruce, cedar, and pine trees.'[19]

Every city on the tour route had some large arches in formal architectural styles, the better executed of which were indistinguishable at a glance from the kinds of permanent, stone structures they imitated. The London *Times*, when commenting on Montreal's grand arches, observed that they were decorated wooden arches, similar to the kind erected in England on such occasions, 'the great object in the design of which is generally to make them as granite-looking as possible, and deprive them, in fact, of all appearances which could show what they really were: decorations specially erected in honour of the Prince.'[20] Illustrations of them, which appeared in periodicals such as the *Illustrated London News* and *Harper's Weekly*, confirm this impression of permanency and formalism.

The formal arches were decorated lavishly. In Toronto the John Street arch stood on main piers that had 'foliated capitals, composed of lotus leaves tastefully gilt.' There were cornices with 'roman mouldings decorated in fresco.' On either side of a portrait of the prince stood 'figures emblematical of the arts, science, literature, and commerce.' Such detailing gave visual interest to the structures and added to their impressive formalism, lending an appearance of grandeur to the colonial city. Many of the arches, even the more formal ones, were also decorated with flags, mottoes, and artwork that spoke directly to the occasion. Trophies of red, white, and blue ensigns not only added colour to the structures but forcefully signified the British patriotism of the arch builders and community. Mottoes such as 'Long Live the Queen,' 'Rule Britannia' and 'Old England Forever' similarly made straightforward statements.

The artwork and illustrations were frequently in the form of 'transparencies.' Amateur and commercial artists painted scenes in black-and-white or colour, using charcoal or paints, on cotton sheeting. At night these were lit from behind with oil lanterns or gas jets, making them glow impressively. On some of the larger arches, transparencies might be as large as three feet by six feet, and there could be many on a

One of several formal arches raised in Montreal. This one, built in Saint Jacques Square, mimics the triumphal arches of ancient Rome. (*Frank Leslie's Illustrated News*, 8 September 1860)

single arch. Those building modest arches outside their homes or businesses could turn to the services of commercial artists who advertised in the daily press. More often than not, the journalists praised the artists and the impressions they skilfully created. Some transparencies were singled out for their poor craftsmanship, such as one at Charlottetown showing Britannia on a seahorse, which the *New Brunswick Reporter* judged to be 'gaudily painted.' The New York *Tribune* dealt harshly with the arches at Quebec, which it said were 'disfigured by cheap pictures of the Royal family, inscriptions forcible in color and feeble in sense, glaring blotches of paint signifying nothing, and reducing everything to the most tawdry effect in the world.'[21]

At the other extreme from the formal arches in traditional styles were the simple evergreen ones erected in small towns or in the backstreets of the larger centres. Over and again, the journalists praised the patriotism and especially the good taste of ordinary folk who made these special efforts. On the carriage road leading to Pictou, Nova Scotia, in any place that had even two or three houses, there would be an arch, 'sometimes a simple one of sweet spruce fir, sometimes a more ambitious effort in which half the wild flowers of the woods were woven in rich confusion.'[22] In Simcoe County, Canada West, the village of Angus had 'a handsome arch,' little Sunnidale 'a neat arch,' Nottawasaga 'two arches,' and the town of Collingwood no less than twelve, 'some of them quite handsome.'[23]

In between the grand, formal arches and the modest evergreen arches were the many built to represent particular groups within the community or aspects of local life. For instance, the maritime and New World traditions of Halifax were alluded to on an arch at the dockyard. Over the opening was 'an Indian canoe (with paddles), moored by two anchors.' Incorporating objects into the design was by no means unusual. At St Catharines, then a port made lively by the wheat trade of Canada West, an arch was composed entirely of flour barrels. The inscription read 'Our Staple Production.' One commentator thought it 'handsome and well proportioned,' though of 'rather unstable appearance.'[24] The Volunteer Artillery Company at Halifax put a gun carriage on top of its arch along with 'other warlike paraphernalia,' which the Halifax *Constitutionalist* thought had 'a fine effect.' In the same city, the Union Engine Company decorated its arch not only with flowers and transparencies saying 'Welcome' but also with fire buckets and caps.[25] Near Port Hope, workers in the flourishing lumber trade constructed an arch of rough boards, which they decorated with themselves. 'On

Spruce Arch, bearing the motto, 'GOD SAVE THE QUEEN,' photographed at the time of the prince's visit to Aylmer, Canada East. (National Archives of Canada, C 29335)

the crest of the arch,' explained one observer, '200 red-shirted, stalwart lumbermen' were to stand and shout, "Welcome to the Prince."' At Brantford, an arch had been built in the form of 'HRH,' and 'a bevy of young ladies were arrayed upon the crosses of the letters.'[26] Such novelties were both attention-grabbing and inexpensive.

Merchants and mechanics similarly made use of materials at hand to declare their presence and honour the royal visitor in a distinctive way. At Quebec, the mechanics built an arch on top of which there stood 'a number of sewing and other machines set in motion.'[27] Two millers at Belleville erected an arch surmounted by a threshing machine, a fanning mill, a mechanical reaper, and two cultivators. Farther along the street, G.J. Brown, a local foundryman, had built an arch with pillars made of potash kettles, stacked one above the other. These supported a pair of scales and 'a Scotch plough.' Mid-Victorians, proud of tools and equipment that spelled prosperity and progress, were not backward in showing them off.

Two arches stand out as extraordinary attempts to make statements about the local scene: the harvest arch at Toronto and the lumbermen's arch at Ottawa. Sandford Fleming designed the enormous, quadruple arch, or harvest arch, at King and York streets in Toronto. It was a complex structure made up of sixteen small arches and two large ones, with an immense crown on top almost large enough 'to accommodate a dinner party inside it.' The main pillars were made up of logs with the bark left on, giving it a rustic look. Several of the supports were thatched with oats and the borders were done in 'rustic work.' Gold and silver maple leaves on a blue field symbolized Canada, while Union Jacks and mottoes underscored the Britishness of the place and occasion. At the corners of the arches 'sprang tall, waving plants of Indian corn, with large open-work baskets' filled full of pumpkins, squashes, melons, apples, peaches, and grapes. The arch underscored the importance of agriculture to the prosperity of mid-Victorian Toronto, while also bearing signifiers of both the high-cultural traditions of the old country and the rougher ones of the frontier.

No arch gained more attention than the lumbermen's arch at the suspension bridge near the Chaudière Falls in Ottawa. It was built entirely of lumber – 180,000 lineal feet of planking of uniform thickness. 'A magnificent sample of the staple trade of the Province,' declared the Ottawa *Union*. The planks were stacked, and the curve of the arch made 'by the simple and ingenious process of *corbelling*.' Despite is massive size, it did not appear heavy because the planks had been laid

The 'Letter Arch' at Brantford, Canada West: '10,000 WELCOMES TO H.R.H.' Prettily dressed young ladies posed on the cross of each H. (*Frank Leslie's Illustrated News*, 29 September 1860)

traversely to allow light to pass through the structure, 'producing a peculiar and pleasing effect.' Decorations were kept to a minimum, with the intention of enhancing the arch's gracefulness and stunning simplicity. In Woods's opinion: 'It was *the* arch of all the arches the Prince had had erected to his honour; and it was almost a pity that a monument so strong, so beautiful, and so characteristic of the country should be removed.'[28] The concept had been that of James Skead, a local lumber baron responsible for various ambitious displays prepared for the prince's visit to Ottawa, and three prominent lumber companies contributed materials and labour. Its construction took the skills of expert workers, long accustomed to making great, tidy piles of lumber. For all their efforts at display, the manufacturers behind the project proved their worth as businessmen. Because no fasteners had been used in its construction, not a plank was spoiled for future sale!

Especially when boasting about their own community's arches, journalists must have reached for their thesauruses to find alternatives to 'immense,' 'gigantic,' 'enormous,' 'gargantuan,' 'stupendous,' as they tried to convey an impression of the colossal size of what they, in all innocence, referred to as 'erections.' The civic 'arche de triomphe' on Fabrique Hill at Quebec stood 'some 50 feet high.' At Toronto, the Yonge Street arch, the tallest of the big nine, reached sixty-four feet high, with forty-eight-foot-high piers. The Lumbermen's Arch at Ottawa was eighty-two-feet in length and sixty-five feet high. General Trollope's erection at Halifax outshot the rest, however, thrusting upwards a full seventy-one feet. It is hardly necessary to comment on the masculine perspective and competitiveness of both the arch builders and the journalists!

The local newspapers identified closely with their own communities and sometimes engaged in spirited attacks on the displays in rival centres. The Fredericton *New Brunswick Reporter* judged the arches in Charlottetown to be 'neat and tasteful enough' but continued dismissively, saying that they 'were of a style which could be got up in a day.' The Barrie *Northern Advance* found the arches at Hamilton 'not up to the mark in quality,' mostly being 'shockingly plain, and of the character that adorned the lesser Stations on the Northern Railway.' In its biased view, even one arch of the quality of those at Barrie 'would have preserved the credit of Hamilton in this respect.'[29] 'Comparisons are said to be odious,' the Toronto *Globe* disingenuously remarked before boasting that the Toronto arches were 'higher and consequently more imposing than those of Montreal and Quebec, and of more artistic

The Lumbermen's Arch, Ottawa, as photographed by Elihu Spencer. Everyone, including the distinguished visitors, marvelled at this immense arch, so skilfully constructed of piled lumber, the city's principal product. (National Archives of Canada, PA 99734)

design.' The arch outside the old parliament house at Quebec was judged by the *Globe* to be 'very large and very ugly,' the spruce branches belying their name, 'instead of being ever-green, they are brown – and of the dirtiest, nastiest brown too.'

Why arches, rather than some other form of decorating? No one at the time reflected on the matter, as far as I have been able to discover. Building arches was so much associated with civic festivities, so deeply embedded in the culture, that it was one of those many things that goes without saying. Canadians had customarily built arches to honour the visits of governors to their towns.[30] Arches defined ceremonial space by creating an entry point and markers along the routes. Moreover, it was well understood, at least by those Victorians who thumbed the illustrated newspapers, that arches – whether permanent or temporary – figured prominently in scenes of royal progresses in the British Isles and on the continent. In the United States, republicans had adopted the tradition when fêting heroes such as George Washington and General Lafayette.[31] Civic arch building had a long history, with roots extending back at least to medieval times in England[32] and a flourishing past in Renaissance Italy[33] and early modern France.[34] Ceremonial arches were traditionally built in connection with the grand entry celebrations and processions got up for visiting princes and other royal figures. And these arches, in turn, harked back further still, to ancient Rome, where victorious emperors built triumphal arches to celebrate military achievements and to humiliate conquered peoples.[35] Temporary arches of wood and plaster were thrown up immediately after the victories, providing symbolic focal points where the heroic soldiers could march past admiring spectators and captured enemies could be forced to acknowledge their enslavement by passing through the triumphal arch of their conquerors.

The cultural significance of ceremonial arches has had little attention from historians of the nineteenth century, notwithstanding their ubiquity on royal occasions, but it has been a topic of great interest for students of Europe and Britain in early periods. Scholars influenced by the cultural anthropology of Victor Turner have interpreted the ceremonial arches as structures that create a liminal space. Arches are gateways through which honoured visitors move, leaving one status behind and taking on another. When civic authorities in Renaissance Italy fêted a visiting prince from another state, they built an arch and organized a procession. The visitor arrived a stranger and hence one with a limited status locally, but, as he passed through the arch, he was welcomed into the city, made a part of it. Associated ceremonies often involved a local authority presenting the visitor with the keys to the city, another tradition that lives on. For the Renaissance prince, passing through the arch was transformative; the outsider became insider, a stranger in the community became an honoured member of it. The visitor no longer represented a potential rival or threat. He was integrated into the city. Such ceremonies have been interpreted not just as ones of diplomatic significance, that is, opportunities for promoting good external relations, but rather as deeply significant cultural moments for the host city, when the bonds of community are ceremonially affirmed, internal civic tensions are eased, and the city made whole again.

We cannot know the extent to which mid-Victorian residents of Canada were aware of these sorts of cultural meanings. What we do know is that, when confronted with the opportunity of welcoming a royal visitor, civic officials, members of organizations of various sorts, and many individuals threw themselves into the job of raising arches of welcome for a prince who had travelled far to visit their communities. Similarly, they rushed to prepare something to say to the prince upon his arrival in town.

Addresses

'It would be cruel,' observed the Toronto *Leader*, 'to curtail the time which our Royal visitor can spend with us by a weary round of meaningless addresses.' The trouble was that men of every description wanted to present an address: officials connected with city, county, and provincial governments, militia officers, judges, clergy, officers of voluntary societies of every description, and even spokesmen for occupational groups. Editors expressed strong reservations about subjecting the honoured guest to such a tiresome outpouring of loyal effusions, no matter how well intentioned. In their coverage of the tour, however, the newspapers reproduced dozens of addresses for the scrutiny of readers. The instant books written about the visit similarly printed large numbers of them. And to commemorate the royal progress, the Duke of Newcastle himself oversaw a substantial volume that contained nothing but these addresses. 'The weary round of meaningless addresses,' then, assumes a surprisingly prominent place in the texts of the visit.[36]

Public addresses of the sort prepared for the Prince of Wales in 1860 were a form of state ceremonial familiar to the colonists. Residents would have been well aware of the tradition in England, where members of the royal family had long been formally addressed during their visits to provincial towns or on important public occasions. Closer to home, when a new governor arrived or made a public tour of a colony, addresses had been routinely prepared by local authorities and corporate bodies. And the official replies equally were an established part of these state ceremonials.[37]

In 1860 the addresses and replies assumed a standard from. Carefully prepared in advance, an address welcomed the prince to the community, rejoiced in the visit, assured His Royal Highness of the group's loyalty and devotion to the crown and British connection, expressed appreciation for the good government enjoyed under the sovereign, wished the prince enjoyment during his travels, and offered best wishes to his mother and the other members of the royal family. Averaging about two hundred words, the addresses were intended to be impressive both in their formal language and in their physical form, the ponderous texts having been elegantly inscribed on parchment or sheep skin. Sometimes they were read to the prince by a delegated individual, such as the mayor, in the case of municipal addresses, or the chief officer of a voluntary association. Otherwise, the addresses were simply handed to the prince at a levee.

The prince replied to many of the addresses. (Nathaniel Woods reported that the prince received upwards of 390 addresses, a number he thought enormous, and that the prince honoured about 100 of them with a reply.) If the address had been read aloud, then the prince replied similarly, following a text written by the Duke of Newcastle. If the addresses had simply been handed to his highness, then the royal reply was mailed. Briefer than the addresses, the replies also followed a pattern, expressing thanks for the loyal display and warm welcome, promising to report to the queen on the attachment of her subjects, and sometimes referring to a local matter. At Halifax, for example, the prince's reply mentioned the imperial presence in the form of the Royal Navy and the commercial prosperity it helped to foster locally.

Newcastle himself prepared ahead of time for what he saw as the weighty responsibility of crafting the prince's replies. The prince consort had impressed upon the duke the importance of this task, in which Prince Albert took a special interest no doubt because the nature of the replies could shape public perceptions of his son and the royal family. For the benefit of the ghost writer, the prince consort made suggestions on how best to proceed. 'They will be of the greatest use to me,' Newcastle wrote the prince consort, 'not only as furnishing new ideas for documents which from the frequency of their repetition must unavoidably have the fault of sameness when proceeding from one pen, but as informing me of the tone and character which will be most in accordance with the Queen's and Your Royal Highness's wishes.'[38]

Before departing for North America, Newcastle took the trouble to write to the provincial governors explaining how he wanted to manage the matter of the addresses and replies. The duke wanted duplicates of important addresses in advance so that he would have the time to prepare appropriate replies. The timetable was tight. Newcastle asked that Governor Head send the addresses from Canada to either Halifax or Gaspé in order to allow time to draft replies. In the case of Newfoundland, the duke wanted the addresses brought by pilot boat to him as soon as the *Hero* entered the harbour. The provincial secretaries were expected to inform the public that only addresses that had been submitted ahead of time to the governor's office and approved could be read aloud to the prince. Spontaneity and its attendant risks would be avoided.

Address writing was a product of the same committee culture that was responsible for making the rest of the preparations for the prince's reception. As but one example, consider the address drawn up on behalf of the surviving Upper Canadian militiamen from the War of 1812. At a public meeting held at the fashionable Rossin House in Toronto, it was agreed that a three-man committee, consisting of John Beverley Robinson, Archibald McLean, and Allan MacNab, all prominent figures, would do the job.[39] By contrast, the address of the Legislative Assembly of the Province of Canada was actually written by one individuals, Thomas D'Arcy McGee, an assemblyman more recognized for his eloquence than for his outspoken affection for the royal family.[40] Generally speaking, the body getting up the address would lend authority to the document by meeting publicly to approve it. The opposition press in Nova Scotia made much of the fact that the government had not asked the lieutenant governor to call the legislature into session so that it could approve the address the government had adopted on its behalf. The criticism was part of a larger campaign to discredit the government for the way it usurped the role of host, cutting the opposition members in the process.[41]

In the summer of 1860 a great many people were engaged in writing addresses. Clergy and laymen from the churches of nearly every Christian denomination busied themselves preparing them. Included, as well, among many other addresses sent ahead of time to the provincial secretary at Quebec were ones from the following diverse organizations: the Highland Society of Hamilton and Canada West; the Working Man's Temperance Association; the Homeopathic Medical Board of Canada, the Boards of the Canadian and American Suspension Bridge Companies; the Agricultural Society of the South Riding of the County of Hastings; Welshmen and Their Descendants at London, C.W.; Survivors of the War of 1812; La Société Saint-Jean-Baptiste de Québec; the British Chiefs at St Regis; the Natural History Society of Montreal; the Faculty of Saint Frances College, Richmond. For whatever reason, few addresses came from businesses, just as only a few trade unions and other organizations of workingmen took up the opportunity.[42]

In the weeks leading up to the royal visit, several colonial newspaper editors crafted editorials outlining their concerns about the excessive number of addresses in preparation.[43] The popularity of the topic and the humorous approach of the editorials had something to do with the fact that, at this early stage, news regarding the tour was slow. Addresses were being 'manufactured by the car load,' complained the Toronto *Globe*, adding that it would cause 'a rise in the price of sheepskins.' 'When we think that hundreds are forthcoming, we tremble for the safety of the illustrious visitor.' The Toronto *Daily Leader* similarly focused on the plight of the poor prince, who was about to be pestered with at least one address in every single place on his itinerary, and he would 'be lucky indeed when he gets off so easily.' The problem was that everyone wanted into the act. Addresses were 'coming from village, and town, and city, and township; and county councils,' exclaimed the Toronto *Globe*. 'The magistrates are meeting in consultation; the clergy will soon be racking their brains for fitting terms in which to proclaim their loyalty. Then we have the universities, the learned societies, the mechanics' institutes, the St George's, the St Patrick's, the St Andrew's Societies of each individual town, city, or village, militia companies, the Boards of Trade – all of whom will want to present addresses.' The Saint John *Morning News* complained of this outpouring from 'every mushroom society in the Province, or even ... those who claim existence to a date anterior to Solomon.' And why were the societies so active? Because, explained the *Morning News*, 'human nature is weak. The desire of the leading minds of these Associations to stand forth before Royalty, to be enabled ever after to say that when the Bunkum Association presented an Address to the Prince of Wales, they had the honour of reading it.' Pity the prince and his staff who would have to bear the work of replying to these addresses. The *Globe* correspondent thought that the Duke of Newcastle, 'who had the management of this department of literature, had better get some stereotyped replies ready.'[44] On its part, the *Morning News* simply called for a halt: 'Above all, let us avoid all kinds of vapid nonsense engrossed in illegible hieroglyphics upon the skins of defunct sheep.'

Silenced

The preparation of addresses raised a serious and important matter concerning the desire of African Canadians to present addresses to the prince. At stake were issues of recognition, power, and inclusion/exclusion.

In the 1850s, the number of people of African descent living in Canada West had risen sharply as a result of the influx from the United States not only of fugitive slaves but also of free Blacks who, in response to congress's passage in 1850 of the Fugitive Slave Act, were fleeing a new assault on their rights. About 21,000 African Canadians lived in Canada West at the time of the visit.[45] A political elite among the African Canadians tackled both the racial discrimination that Blacks faced daily in the Canadas and the even worse situation in the United States, where slavery and related oppressions prevailed. These anti-slavery activists saw the prince's visit to the province as an opportunity to stand on public platforms where they would bring attention to their cause by praising the fundamental liberties enjoyed by Blacks who lived under the British crown and by opposing the cruel injustices and human degradation suffered by Blacks living in the United States.

African-Canadian organizations publicly asserted their support for the visit and their commitment to taking a full part in welcoming His Royal Highness. 'As a free people escaped from slavery,' declared a Toronto convention of 'colored people,' we want 'to show all classes in this noble Province, that we will not be behind them in coming forward to show our Queen's Representative, the Prince of Wales, all the loyalty we can possibly bestow.' The people of the Elgin Settlement at Buxton, Canada West, the recently established all-Black experiment in rural self-help, petitioned authorities in the hope that the prince would visit them and judge for himself 'whether we are capable of appreciating that Liberty which the true Philanthropists of the British Empire have labored so long and arduously that we should have.'[46]

The drafts of addresses sent by African Canadians to the governor general's office heaped praise on British institutions in the Canadas and condemned, either directly or otherwise, the presence of slavery in the United States. The address of 'Her Majesty's subjects of African descent residing in the Western portion of Canada' asserted that 'the large majority of us were once slaves in another land; the victims of a cruel oppression.' However, they were now free and thankful to be living in Canada: 'Blessed be God, there still remains a country on the North American continent where the poor outcast slave can find a refuge from persecution.' The address of the 'Colored Inhabitants of this Province residing in Chatham, Oxford, Toronto, Galt' referred to themselves 'as freemen many of whom have escaped from a land of cruel injustice and oppression.'[47] Another of the addresses alluded to all that had been done in the United States 'to destroy our manhood' and 'to obliterate our rights to liberty and the pursuit of happiness.'

Astonishingly, the governor general denied African Canadians the right to address the prince, either in person or in writing. In response to the polite requests of African Canadians who asked to present their flattering addresses to the prince, Sir Edmund Head said that it would not be possible. A.R. Green, who had written on behalf of 'the colored people of Windsor and Sandwich,' was told: 'His Royal Highness learns with pleasure the expressions of loyalty contained in your address. He is, however, desirous to recognize no distinctions of race among Her Majesty's subjects residing in Canada, and he is therefore advised to accept no address which owes its origin to such a difference on these grounds.' Much the same point was made in a reply to Sam Gale, who had sent in an address adopted by 'the colored population of Lower Canada': 'While conveying His Royal Highness's thanks for the good wishes expressed in the address, I have to inform you that the address itself cannot be received. His Royal Highness desires to view all British subjects residing in Canada in but one light, owing equal allegiance to the British crown, and enjoying equally the privileges arising from such allegiance. The address, therefore, of the coloured inhabitants of Canada representing themselves in an isolated position places them in a point of view which His Royal Highness declines to recognize.' Such a response carried liberal notions of the equality of all subjects to the point of absurdity, with the result that African Canadians were effectively silenced.[48]

It is difficult to know why the governor general responded this way. I have found no trace of any justification for the policy other than what appears in the replies cited, nor have I seen any papers that shed light on how the governor general came to his decision and with whom, if anyone, he consulted. Perhaps Sir Edmund's explanation should be taken at face value; British law made no distinction on the ground of colour, and the same principle was simply being asserted by the prince. It is possible, however, that the authorities acted as they did because they feared that the criticisms of the United States contained in the addresses of African Canadians would antagonize Americans and jeopardize the goal of the prince's U.S. tour. Certainly, slavery was a red-hot issue at the time, just a few months before the outbreak of the Civil War. The U.S. government and American public opinion were powerful factors in the decision making of imperial authorities such as the governor general and the colonial secretary. By contrast, authorities regarded the organizations and opinions of African Canadians as being much less significant.

The relative powerlessness of African Canadians in 1860 was made clear by the fact that the newspapers scarcely mentioned any complaints from the African-Canadian groups that were denied the right to present addresses to the prince. Contrast that with the uproar over the denial of 'Orangemen's rights!' From the local (white) newspaper in Chatham to the Toronto *Globe* and the metropolitan dailies of New York and London, there was only silence on the matter of the prince's refusal to hear African-Canadian addresses. The Toronto *Leader* did at least report that the governor general had 'pointedly refused' the addresses of African Canadians, and it observed that the African Canadians were 'too weak to complain.' A contrary view came from 'A Subscriber' (possibly an African Canadian), who, in a letter-to-the-editor of the *Leader*, objected to the characterization of African Canadians as politically weak and maintained that Black votes had swayed the election results in at least one seat in the Chatham area. The writer said as well that some leaders among the African Canadians had argued all along that Blacks should not present themselves as a separate class, and that these leaders were pleased by the frankness of the prince's explanation.[49] Be that as it may, it is striking how little publicity the whole issue gained. The press was owned and operated by whites. In 1860 there was no newspaper published by an African Canadian, the province's two such newspapers having recently expired for lack of financial resources and support.[50] Without such a vehicle, African

Canadians had less opportunity to air their concerns or to assert themselves on this occasion. By silencing the attempts of African Canadians to address the prince, imperial authorities effectively excluded African Canadians from an important part of the festivities.

Cashing In

Entrepreneurs who hoped to profit from of the prince's tour busied themselves in the days and weeks leading up to the local visits by ordering products specially for the occasion and by advertising goods and services. Woods of the *Times* was struck by the commercial acumen shown by various businessmen in British North America on the eve of the prince's arrival: 'No advertisement ever appeared without some adroit allusion to his expected arrival to rivet the attention of readers to the puff. His name and titles were somehow mysteriously associated by advertisers with cheap pork, old patents, ladies' dresses, sales of timber – everything in fact from a waterproof coat to a barrel of mild cider. You could not sit down to dinner but his portrait loomed dimly from beneath the gravy in the centre of the plate. It was Prince's hats, Prince's boots, Prince's umbrellas, Prince's coats, Prince' cigars.'[51] Woods was exaggerating for effect, of course, and yet there was some truth in what he said, even if by today's standards the extent of the commercialization appears modest.

Advertisements – heavy on text and lacking illustrations – appearing in daily newspapers prior to the prince's arrival illustrate the kind of entrepreneurship that Woods describes. John Nasmith advertised in the Toronto *Globe* a 'new and delicious article,' the 'Prince of Wales Biscuit.' Cut in the shape of the prince, the biscuit made a nice companion piece to others Nasmith had on hand for sale, among them: 'Victoria and Albert, Sir Edmund Head, the Hon. J.A. Macdonald, and George Brown.' A great many newspaper ads had eye-catching headings designed to draw attention to products that consumers would want to purchase for the festivities. Under the heading 'The Prince of Wales is Coming!' Isaac Campbell of Saint John advertised to readers of the *Morning Freeman*: 'the finest article of Champagne ever offered in this City, and just what is wanted on the present occasion.' An advertisement for the St Lawrence Hall, the large Montreal hotel, boasted of its 'airy rooms' opposite Notre Dame Cathedral and added: 'We think the fact of the Government having taken a part of our Establishment for the suite of His Royal Highness, the Prince of Wales; and for the Prince's Levees, is a sufficient guarantee of its respectability.'[52]

A great many businesses advertised commodities and services that they had made ready for the occasion. Owners of steamers everywhere in the provinces offered tickets to passengers wishing to go out to meet the prince. Costly cabins aboard the *Bowmanville* were available for patrons having the time and means to travel from Toronto to Gaspé to greet the prince upon his arrival in Canada. For just one dollar a head, the *Peerless* offered standing room to people wanting to spend part of the day of the prince's arrival in Toronto travelling alongside him on his approach to the city.[53] Various firms advertised anything from bunting and flags to shoes and fancy-dress clothing. One haberdasher tried to shame people with only a '*Shabby*' hat or cap into purchasing a better one so as to 'present a respectable appearance.' 'Feeling anxious that *all* should look well at the Reception of the Prince of Wales,' declared C.D. Everett and Son of Saint John, 'we have made up a splendid assortment of satin hats and cloth caps.' Food and drink were also on offer in extraordinary quantities for the celebrations. A. Thomas McColgan of Saint John advertised fresh oysters, of exceptional quality, which he had 'imported expressly for His Royal Highness, the Prince of Wales and all his loyal subjects [sic].'[54]

Special commemorative items also were prepared for consumers, but, if the newspapers can be trusted, then the range of items was much more limited than it would be for later royal occasions, such as the Queen Victoria's Diamond Jubilee, when plates, mugs, spoons, jewellery, clocks, and medals with images of Her Majesty were manufactured.[55] In 1860 only two commemorative products got play in the press. First, images of the prince and of his tour were offered by booksellers, photographers, and the illustrated newspapers. The *Illustrated London News* and *Frank Leslie's Illustrated Newspaper* took out large display ads in leading newspapers to remind readers that their regular issues would provide ample visual coverage of the tour. The recent portrait of the prince by Franz Xaver Winterhalter, the original of which was in the royal collection, was widely reproduced as an engraving and offered for sale in the provinces.[56] Second, medals were designed and produced for use both as presentation items and as souvenirs.

According to one authority, more than twenty medals were struck commemorating the visit to Montreal alone. 'No sooner was it known that the Prince was to visit Canada,' explains Alfred Sandham, 'than several enterprising speculators devised schemes where by two objects might be accomplished; the one – to furnish some lasting memento of the event; the other (doubtless of most importance to them) to make money by the transaction.' For example, a Mr Hoffnung, a Montreal dealer in fancy goods, issued a prospectus stating that, if there was sufficient support, he would issue a medal commemorating the opening of the Victoria Bridge. Interest proved to be keen, and so he ordered, from a firm in Birmingham, dies based on his own designs. Medals were struck and sold: $100 for the gold (one of which was presented to the queen), $10 for the silver, $3 for the bronze, and $1 for the white. Sales were brisk, especially of the cheaper ones. Medals commemorating the visit to the city were also struck by institutions such as the Board of Arts, McGill College, and the normal schools in Lower Canada, which used them to honour scholastic achievement.[57]

All this commercial activity broadened the public that participated in the preparations for the visit. Businessmen who had no role on the civic reception committees nevertheless found a place in the stream of events. By producing their goods and services, they were drawing on a long tradition of commercial production for British royal ceremonials, a tradition that would expand along with the wider consumer culture. Historian Tori Smith has shown that, by the time of Victoria's Diamond Jubilee in 1897, this sort of commercial activity had become so central to royal ceremony that it helped to create its meanings. And furthermore, she argues, as these spectacles became more commercial, new forms of public participation became possible: royal spectacles were not only viewed by an audience but consumed by the public. Consumers of the Diamond Jubilee purchased souvenirs, went to jubilee shows, saw advertisements, bought jubilee clothing, and took snapshots of the events. In 1860, by contrast, the consuming public in British North America had more limited options in connection with the royal visit, but consumption was nevertheless a part of the experience for many people. Moreover, businessmen, for their own reasons, helped popularize the prince and put his image 'everywhere.' As Woods summed it up, 'the whole colony nodded, in fact, with Prince's coronets and feathers.'[58]

Lighting Up

On at least one night of the prince's stay, each city planned to add to the festivities with a 'general illumination.' Reception committees urged residents to light candles, oil lanterns, gas jets, and special decorations on their homes and businesses. Public buildings and ships were similarly fitted up so that they might shine with unusual brilliance during the prince's visit to town. Illuminating a town, a cultural practice with deep roots,[59] enabled the day's celebrations to continue into the night and marked it as a special evening, with a bright, playful gleam that cut through the gloom that generally prevailed at night in mid-Victorian cities. Undoubtedly festive, illuminations gestured towards the carnivalesque by inverting the natural order, making night into day.[60] In 1860 British North Americans hoped to please the prince with their evening celebrations, but the illuminations were even more about bringing pleasure to the residents and encouraging a vigorous competitiveness among them.

The local reception committees played only a limited role in directing the illuminations, leaving to citizens the actual arrangements and to newspapers the job of advising about how best to prepare. Reception committees announced the date of the night when the illumination would take place, and they oversaw the lighting of a few structures, such as the city hall and the triumphal arches that the committee had raised. They approved the firemen's torchlight procession, making it an official part of the program, and they contracted with an individual or firm for the fireworks display, which could cost $1,000 or more.[61] But most of the preparations were made by the people themselves. Journalists insisted that this was *the* merit of civic illuminations. 'Among the many modes that exist for public rejoicing,' declared the Quebec *Mercury*, 'we know of none to equal a general illumination of a large city.' After all, 'parties of every species, stingy, seedy, shaky, poor, rich, good, bad and indifferent, all find themselves invested with a duty and responsibility when a general illumination is the *mot d'ordre*.'[62]

In preparing to illuminate, residents had the assistance of businesses eager to profit from the festivities. The Quebec *Mercury*, for instance, carried the ads of various entrepreneurs in this line. Thomas Andrews offered 15,000 'Variegated Illumination Lamps' in a range of sizes and colours, as well as 'novelties in stained glass.' John Traffe announced that his shop had 'just received 25 boxes of sperm and Belmont sperm candles for the Illumination.' Kerr and Son advertised ornamental gas jets, 'adapted for windows, outside decorations, triumphal arches, etc.' Two firms of artists at Quebec competed for contracts to design and execute transparencies, which could be backlit at night.

In 1860 gas-lit decorations figured prominently in the illuminations. More costly than candles or oil lights, gas jets provided the brightest available lighting and the opportunity to create elaborate decorations, although their heat and high risk of fire necessitated special safety measures.[63] Gas fitters enjoyed a booming business. On the outside walls of buildings, they wound tubes in patterns, thus linking individual gas jets that together formed brilliant 'devices.' It was a straightforward task to outline significant letters of the alphabet, such as 'A.E.' (for Albert Edward), but the effect was said to be impressive. Plumes, crowns, stars, and crosses also proved to be popular and were also much admired. However, portraits and profiles overtaxed the artistic abilities of most gas fitters, and the results were often ridiculed in the press.[64]

Gas illuminations could be quite expensive. The correspondent for the Ottawa *Citizen*, writing from Quebec, exclaimed that he had 'just seen the apparatus for illuminating two private houses outside, which cannot have cost much less than £100.'[65] The reception committee at Toronto voted $250 to light up city hall, and the Law Society of Upper Canada paid $1,111 to have Osgoode Hall illuminated.[66] When the (possibly padded) bills came in for lighting particular government offices at Quebec, the amounts were substantial: the office of the civil secretary, $1,751; that of the receiver general, $1,261; the Quebec court house, $1,028; and so on.[67] Hamiltonians were fortunate in being saved a little expense because, being one of the last cities visited, they were able to reuse some of the gas fittings dismantled from cities downstream.[68] According to the Toronto *Globe*, merchants were 'vying with each other in a manner which is highly commendable, who is to make the best display.'[69] Commentators of the day valued competition in and of itself, but the rivalry among residents who illuminated homes and businesses was especially welcome because it increased the town's chances of being judged more dazzling than rival towns.

Newspapers gave exceedingly detailed coverage of the illuminations in their own cities, their descriptions referring to every illuminated building no matter how conventional the display. Here was the pay-off for participation: public acknowledgment in the daily press, a permanent record of individual and civic achievement. Moreover, the sheer accumulation of details about the community's display added weight to a city's claim that its citizens had done themselves proud and surpassed their rivals. In one issue of the Ottawa *Citizen*, the account of the illumination ran for many columns, but the next issue contained several more columns of descriptions, informing readers that, for instance, John McCarthy 'exhibited a view of the Chaudiere

Falls and other transparencies, which appeared well,' Mr. Clow's residence showed 'a picture of the settlers' life,' and Dolly's Chop House 'was one glow of light and displayed beautiful transparencies.'[70]

All the mottoes and iconography reported in Toronto were declarations of loyalty, and many proudly identified Canada as being British and part of the empire.[71] 'Our glorious empire,' was the preferred motto, but Owen's coach factory chose instead 'British supremacy.' R. Davis and Company had a large transparency in which 'Britannia with her feet placed on a globe formed the central figure, a railroad bridge, vessels, etc. filling up the background.' One of the transparencies at Hugh Miller's showed, according to the *Globe*, 'the battlements of Windsor [Castle] with a figure of Neptune on the one side and Britannia on the other,' while a second transparency featured Niagara Falls and Indians. Mr Ridout's three transparencies similarly depicted Canada in an imperial context: in the first, a female representing Canada carried a sickle and a handful of grain, with a cornucopia and scythe on the ground beside her; in the second, a figure of Britannia was accompanied by representations of ships and a railway; the third depicted the heroic death of Wolfe on the Plains of Abraham.

Representations of females figured extensively in the iconography of the illuminations, even though the press attributed the designs to men (where attribution was given at all) and the great majority of the decorated properties were described as being the premises of men. A predictably narrow range of female figures was represented. Britannia was, of course, the most ubiquitous. Canada, too, was sometimes pictured as a female: either a white woman symbolic of the country's fertility and wealth of natural endowments, or a Native woman who signified the distinctiveness of Canada within the empire and/or its natural beauty and resources. There was one transparency depicting woman as teacher and nurturer. Insofar as we can tell from the descriptions of these images provided in the newspapers, all the representations of females were respectful, as befitted the occasion; ridicule is not evident.

These depictions of female figures are part of a much wider phenomenon in the civic ceremonies of the mid-nineteenth-century. Though women were much overshadowed by men in public celebrations, representations of the female figured prominently in the iconography of civic display. In her studies of American parades of the mid-nineteenth century, Mary Ryan has noted the way men used icons of women to depict abstract values such as the nation, truth, justice, and so on. Because actual women were excluded from the realm of legislative politics, representations of them worked all the more effectively to convey such abstractions.[72]

A reading of the press coverage of the preparations for the 1860 visit to Canada nearly makes it appear as though only men, and not women, had any role in the actual work undertaken to make the provinces 'fit for a prince.' It stands to reason, however, that nothing could be further from the truth. Men excluded women from their committees and the public meetings (or never thought of including them) that set out the plans for celebrations. But when it came to carrying out the plans, women must have been involved. Who sewed the miles of bunting and innumerable flags? Who prepared the floral tributes, filled the cornucopia, and decked the halls? Who painted the transparencies and copied the addresses in beautiful script? Who prepared the food for the receptions, made up spare beds for visitors from out of town, and purchased candles for illuminating front windows? Surely it could not always have been men!

There are just a few traces in the record that hint at women's substantial role in executing the plans set out by the program committees. The day of the ball at Quebec, the New York *Daily Herald* said that the streets were 'thronged with tailors, hairdressers, milliners, etc., who have been running about from customer to customer fixing them up for the grand ball of the evening.' At least some of the milliners, and possibly some of the hairdressers, were women. An account based on a Cobourg *Star* report notes that, among the various preparations made for the ball at Cobourg's new town hall, Mrs Weller brought luxurious furnishings from her home to fit up retiring rooms for the honoured guests, and Mrs Cockburn provided some of the flowers that lent grace to the ballroom.[73] A similar passing remark was made in the Port Hope *Guide*, as it described the frantic, last-minute attempts to get the town ready in time for the prince's arrival: 'The ladies worked night and day in the market building, making wreaths of evergreens and festoons of flowers.' And the newspaper gallantly complemented them: 'To their industry and skill the fine appearance of the decorations is in a great measure owed.'[74]

The contributions of these very same Port Hope women are confirmed by a private source, one of the precious few, extant diaries containing comments on the preparations for the visit. In September 1860 Sarah Hill, an immigrant from England, lived as a widow with her two children on a farm outside Port Hope, Canada West. In her diary entry for Wednesday, 5 September, she observed that on that day she visited town, where she found everyone occupied in preparing for the prince's visit. 'The Ladies are all busy decorating the Town Hall,' she said. The next day she herself was occupied part of the day helping her nineteen-year-old daughter, Margaret, 'do her frock' so that it would be ready to wear for the festivities. Later in the day, Margaret went to the town hall 'to help to decorate it,' while her seventeen-year-old brother ventured into the country by train 'to get evergreens.' These private notations and public acknowledgments of the preparations made by 'the ladies' at Port Hope and the milliners of Quebec underline all the more the silence that otherwise runs through the press coverage of the tour. When white men of property controlled the press and access to public office, there was generally little acknowledgment of women's contributions, however extensive they may have been behind the scenes.

Notwithstanding the great amount of planning and work that communities undertook so as to ensure a successful welcome, inevitably there was a last-minute rush to complete the plans. Journalists liked to amuse their readers with depictions of the antics of locals as they struggled to meet the deadline. It was a way to dramatize the period of waiting and to convey a sense of the anxious anticipation that made the eventual arrival all the more cathartic.

Take the case of St John's, where the tour began. There was near panic because the prince arrived in the harbour two days before expected and so much remained to be done. The voluntary societies called emergency meetings to ready themselves for the procession. The newly raised volunteers were just then being sworn in and outfitted in smart uniforms. Matters of protocol had yet to be sorted out. Outport folk were still pouring into the capital, dressed in their holiday best and seeking accommodations, if not at the hotels, which were fast filling up, then with the householders of St John's.[75] Business had been suspended everywhere 'except in the calico shops,' said the correspondent for the Toronto *Globe*, and the cod were 'left for a time to roam the seas in peace.' High officials, anxious that everything be ready, were compelled to exert themselves in unfamiliar ways. The attorney general was seen erecting his own flag staff 'by the aid of his own arms,' no less, and rumour had it that another 'high functionary' had been seen washing a Union Jack with soap and water! It was a world turned topsy-turvy, or, to put it in the language of ethnic stereotypes, as one reporter did: 'The natural staid and sober character of British-blooded folk is quite lost – a French excitability of temperament has taken its place.'[76] Until they saw the *Hero* arrive, many members of the public could not believe that the prince would land early. 'Why our windows are not washed yet, and the arches are not completed – and the candles are not cut – and our flags are not up – and a thousand reasons of equal importance render it impossible that the Prince should land to-night! But still, – has the Prince come? Yes, – most decidedly.'[77] The time for preparations had run out; the anxiety of anticipation was nearly over.

Neither the people of St John's nor the journalists knew that aboard the *Hero* the members of the royal party were equally apprehensive as they anticipated their landing on the morning following their entry into the harbour. 'You may imagine,' wrote Dr Henry Acland to his wife, Sarah, 'that we had no small expectations as we went to bed later than usual of what would happen on the morrow – the first day that the new duties of the Prince of Wales would be entered upon – or the feelings and opinions of these important Colonies.'[78] The next morning would at last bring to the anxious bride her long-awaited and equally nervous groom.

3

Right Royal Welcome

The Prince of Wales entered St John's, Newfoundland, in two stages: on the evening of Monday, 23 July, when the *Hero* arrived in the harbour, and on the following day, when he first set foot on the soil of the New World.

On the Monday afternoon, lookouts on Signal Hill at St John's sighted the royal squadron just off the coast. The intrepid correspondent for the Toronto *Globe* said that he hired a cab and, with the aid 'of a reckless Irish driver, full of loyalty – and whiskey,' succeeded in reaching the heights above the entrance to the harbour. He described the breathtaking view, as well as the sight of the *Hero* and the *Ariadne* as they grew more and more distinct. Meantime, a pilot boat steamed out to meet the prince's ship, bringing some officials and not one but two pilots because they could not agree on which of them would have the honour of guiding the *Hero* to a safe anchorage. On the batteries, the gunners at the fort on Signal Hill waited until the prince's ship passed through the narrows and entered the harbour, and then they fired a royal – twenty-one-gun – salute.[1]

A great number of Newfoundlanders stood outdoors enjoying the fine weather and waiting in anticipation of the squadron's arrival. But when the guns fired, the remainder of the people rushed from their homes and lodgings to witness the spectacle. Nearly everyone had a good view, thanks to the layout of the city, with its streets tiered steeply one above the other 'in amphitheatrical form,' as one reporter put it. The correspondent for the New York *Herald* was struck by the prevalence of women in town, and not just among visiting spectators. Because the menfolk were at the fisheries, women had 'take[n] the places of men in stores, in the markets, and as waiters in the hotels.'[2]

As the *Hero* drew close, the sailors aboard climbed her yards 'until every spar ha[d] its complement of blue jackets.' The tars on other vessels, including those aboard the *Sesostris*, a French man-of-war, did likewise, and everywhere flags were run up and fluttered in the pleasant breeze. At 7:10 in the evening, the *Hero* dropped anchor. From the shrouds, the sailors shouted jubilantly, and their cries were answered by the thousands of spectators looking down on them. The cheer, gushed the *Globe* correspondent, 'commenced in the west and travelled east; it was wafted through the air by the evening breeze, and was echoed loudly from the opposite shore. It was such a cheer as can only be given by a people who render a free and sincere homage to the son of a much-loved and venerated Queen. Money could not purchase it; hypocrisy could not have uttered it. It was the heartfelt tribute of a grateful and a contented people.' Even a reporter from New York, who had sneered at St John's – its houses 'confusedly jumbled together, as if some players had been using them for dice,' its streets which did 'not pretend to sidewalks for pedestrians,' and its 'immense number of liquor stores' – enthused about the spectacle of the royal squadron's arrival, saying 'nothing could be grander.'[3]

Soon after the *Hero* had anchored, it was announced that the prince would land the next day, at 10 A.M. But the excited crowds were not ready to call it a night, and during the evening thousands more people found their way to town from the outports. A festive feeling prevailed. Various buildings were colourfully illuminated, and the bells of the Catholic cathedral continued to ring out a welcome. According to the reporter for the *Globe*, the people 'hung about the streets and sang songs and fired crackers, and drank healths and gave themselves up to a general unmitigated "spree."' 'Imagine,' gasped the Toronto reporter, 'the celebrating of ten thousand Queen's birthdays concentrated into one, and you will have an idea of the amount of crackers, squibs, serpents, wheels, back-rapers, and rockets fired off.' It was hours before the populace settled down for the night.

By the next morning the fine weather had gone and the rain came down, as the *Globe* reporter quipped, 'with as little hesitation as it would have done had the Prince not been there.' Crestfallen ladies, who had laid out their pretty summer frocks and bonnets the night before, reluctantly donned clothing suitable for the wet and cold. Conditions were so bad that the entry was postponed until noon. Although it was still raining at 11:30, 'the ladies were determined to have the celebration,' reported the New York *Herald*, 'and, with umbrellas,

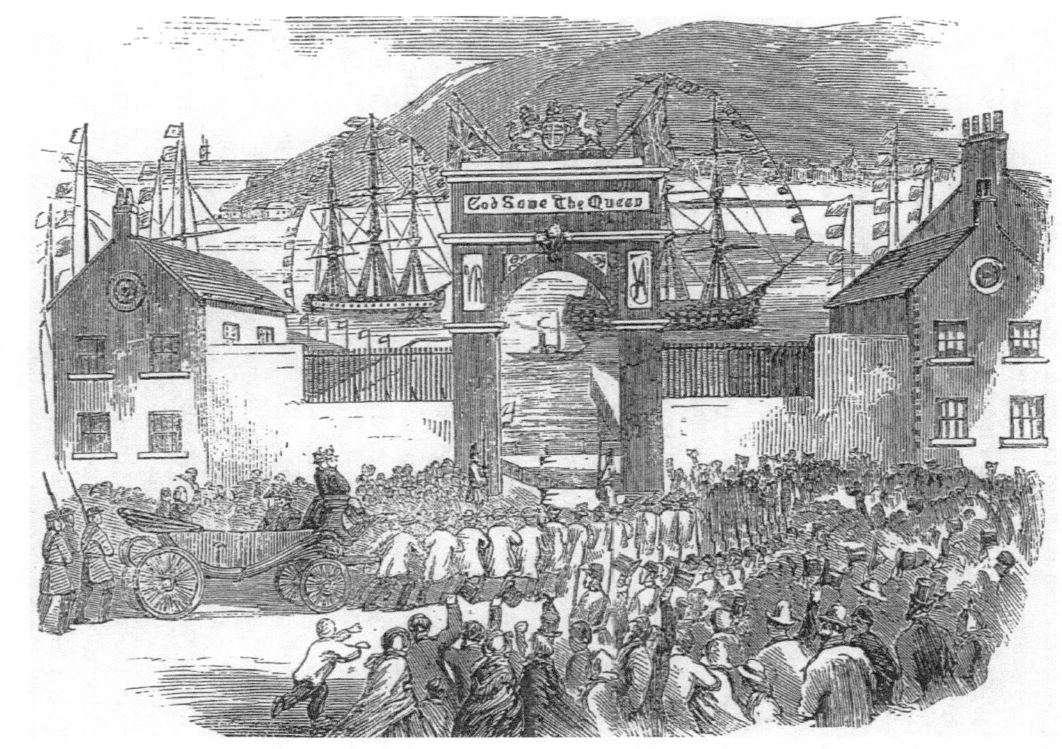

The *Illustrated London News* chose to feature the prince's departure from St John's, Newfoundland, but the scene closely resembled descriptions of his royal entry to the city. (*Illustrated London News*, 15 August 1860)

overcoats, and pattens, trooped down to the Queen's wharf, and filled the tiers of seats erected for their accommodation.' From this area, which was cordoned off for ticket-holding ladies, a fine view could be had both of the three royal ships at anchor in a semi-circle off the wharf and of the landing area with its large arch of evergreens, topped with the royal arms and the inscriptions 'Welcome' and 'God Save the Queen.' Standing on the landing place were the male dignitaries – the clergy, the judiciary, Newfoundland government officials, and the resident foreign consuls – along with neat rows of the men of the Newfoundland Corps, the honour guard for the occasion. A nearby gallery provided almost as good a vantage point for a few hundred more spectators – men, women, and children. Thousands more spectators looked on from wherever they could: any window overlooking the scene, the rooftops of nearby warehouses and homes, the spectator vessels, which were tied to a giant hawser running out from the wharf, and the rigging of every vessel in the harbour. Crowd control was managed by the companies of volunteer riflemen who stood guard at the approaches to the landing site and by the entire sixteen-man police force of St John's. Fortunately for everyone, the rain finally stopped shortly before noon, though the fog hung in patches here and there.

At precisely noon the *Ariadne* and the *Flying Fish* thundered a twenty-one-gun salute, and the prince descended from the *Hero* into the royal barge, Royal Navy oarsmen powering him towards the wharf. Once the salute had finished, the multitude began cheering, the noise mounting in a deafening crescendo, and the prince, standing on the barge, bowed repeatedly in recognition. In only a few moments, the barge pulled up to the wharf, the prince ascended the red-carpeted steps, and the governor, Sir Alexander Bannerman, welcomed him to the capital of Newfoundland. Once the members of the prince's suite had come ashore, the band of the Royal Newfoundland Company struck up 'God Save the Queen.' The cheers then redoubled and, according to the New York *Herald*, 'the demonstrations of enthusiasm became almost frantic.'

The all-male platform party at the landing was a mix of the sombrely and the colourfully clad. The governor appeared in blue and silver court dress, but he was outdone by the French captain of the *Sesostris*, as well as by the consul of Spain, described by the Toronto *Globe* as being 'dressed in an excessively showey [*sic*] uniform,' with cream-coloured trousers and scarlet dress coat with buff facings. By contrast, the U.S. consul appeared in a simple black coat and white shirt. Most of the clergy of the various Protestant denominations were also dressed in black and could barely be distinguished from the lawyers and judges present. Not so the members of the Catholic hierarchy. 'There was no mistaking them,' said the *Globe* reporter disapprovingly; they appeared 'in their pink stockings, buckled shoes, knee-breeches, and canonical drapery,' and 'round the neck of each was suspended a massive gold chain, supporting large crosses of the same valuable metal.' The prince himself wore the uniform of a colonel of the British army: a scarlet tunic with a blue sash, black trousers with a thin, red stripe down each leg, patent leather boots, white gloves, a black cocked hat with a tuft of white plumes, and a regimental sword.

The prince did not linger long to take in this scene but instead walked purposefully along the scarlet runner to his waiting carriage, which he entered along with the Duke of Newcastle and the governor. The royal cortège then set out at a moderate pace in the direction of Government House, as members of the platform party followed behind on foot. Lining both sides of the route were members of the various voluntary societies, dressed appropriately. The men of the Benevolent Irish Society, for instance, wore green scarfs, with the harp of Erin embroidered on them. As the procession passed each of the societies in turn, the members fell in behind, joining the procession themselves. The cortège passed through the various arches raised along the route, and the prince had a chance to admire the abundance of patriotic banners, flags, and bunting that decorated the town. As he passed, the crowds lining the route cheered, and then the people rushed through the back streets and up the hill so they would have a chance to see him again.

When the prince's carriage reached the gates of Government House, the officials stepped down and walked through the grounds. On the front lawn stood 250 children from the city's Sunday schools, the girls appearing in white with wreaths of flowers while each boy had a blue or scarlet scarf. There was also a company of 100 boys from the volunteer corps dressed in uniform. The boys and girls shouted a welcome and then sang the national anthem. Amid cheers from the children and the multitude beyond, the prince disappeared into the handsome stone building.

The entry of the Prince of Wales to the first town on his lengthy itinerary had gone off rather well, everyone agreed. After the visit was over, one of the local newspapers, the *Newfoundland Express*, praised the work of the reception committee and its chairman, Sir Francis

Brady, who said that the prince and members of his suite were 'highly satisfied with the reception given them.'[4] The wife of the Anglican archdeacon wrote privately to a friend saying that at St John's the prince had 'taken the place by storm and won all hearts.'[5] The bishop of the Church of England gave a first-hand report to the people of St John's in which he extolled the prince's performance – his first-ever experience receiving and replying to addresses. Albert Edward had listened 'with a demeanour that was grave, dignified, patient and considerate,' and he had replied in a voice that was 'clear and melodious.' The whole spectacle had been 'a beautiful sight, – none the less interesting and affecting for being shorn of the usual adjuncts and appendages of royal Courts.'[6] And, in their own reports, the distinguished visitors, too, were fulsome in their praise. General Bruce, the prince's governor, wrote to the prince consort reassuring him that his son had 'entered cordially into the spirit of the thing and was evidently gratified and moved by the warmth of the welcome.' He was more frank when writing to friend at home in Windsor, to whom he reported that all had 'gone well' and that the young prince had 'acquitted himself admirably and seems pleased with everything, himself included.'[7] The prince consort was delighted to learn of the enthusiasm of the crowds at St John's, but in a private letter he admitted that, because he (a 'German Philistine'!) knew almost nothing about the place except for its famous Newfoundland dogs, all he could picture was 'the Prince of Wales ... surrounded by these animals, and their taking an animated part in the prevailing enthusiasm.'[8]

There had been some disappointments and glitches at St John's, which foretold developments later in the tour. The weather had behaved badly, but that was hardly unusual for the place and, as it turned out, downpours would follow the prince nearly everywhere he travelled that summer. There had also been some local skirmishes over matters of precedent, and these, too, foreshadowed what would happen elsewhere. Prior to the prince's arrival, the *Royal Gazette*, the official publication of the governor, had given notice that the Anglican and Roman Catholic bishops were to greet the prince at the landing. The clergy of other churches had reacted in anger at their exclusion, compelling the governor to issue a *Royal Gazette Extraordinary* in which he stated that he would be pleased to see the other clergymen 'if they chose to be present.' Because he had not specified the order or precedence among them, the Toronto *Globe* asked facetiously, 'Will the Episcopalian [bishop] walk *pari passu* with his brother of Rome? Will the disciples of John Knox, John Wesley, and John Whitfield settle the matter between them, without the aid of ecclesiastical blows and knocks?' In addition, the foreign consuls had complained that they had been placed too near the bottom of the list of dignitaries at the landing. Scrapping over the order of precedence would bedevil reception committees throughout the tour.

In many ways, the entry ceremonies at St John's set the script for many that would follow. Everywhere the prince went, communities mustered all the pomp they could in order to dramatize his arrival; the grandeur and enthusiasm of the welcome reflected the loyalty and prosperity of the place. Reputations were at stake. Not every town had St John's advantages: its magnificent harbour and the entry of a ninety-gun battleship-of-war. Yet, the same basic components could be found in every entry: the ceremonious landing by water or railway, the official welcome by top officials, the gallery of admiring ladies, the cheering crowds, the singing of the national anthem, the public addresses and princely replies.

Royal entries and civic processions together made up the principal means by which communities welcomed the royal visitor. The entries and processions were carefully planned and executed, but the civic promoters behind them could not completely control the performances. Bad weather or delays that literally left participants in the dark could mar the effect. In the heat of the moment, crowds could grow too frantic, or appear awed and strangely quiet. Religious or French-English conflicts could intrude upon the scene. And there was no telling what the journalists would have to say about an event or how individuals, including the members of the royal suite, would perceive and respond to the performances.

The royal entry, as a ceremonial form in British and European culture, dates back centuries, and there is a vast scholarly literature on the history of civic entries made by royal figures, especially in medieval and Renaissance Europe, because of the elaborateness of the entries, their significance as public events, and the often superb documentation concerning them.[9] Close readings of their iconography and pageantry have highlighted the richness and diversity of meanings conveyed through royal-entry rituals in different times and places. An important theme running through the literature is particularly relevant here. Nearly everywhere, municipalities sought, through ceremony and symbol, to manufacture their own corporate self-image, to convey a message about the place and its people. In 1860, from St John's to

Sarnia, civic promoters similarly used the royal-entry ceremony as a means of telling visitors and the watching world something about their community, its particular self-image. Invariably these images – whatever their particularities – were crafted so as to give a simple but positive impression of a unified, cohesive community.[10]

The processions that followed the prince's entry into each British North American city were also carefully staged events, but they fractured the image of the community, presenting the place in its component parts. Groups were put on display, rather than individuals or the whole. Near centre stage, in the processions themselves, appeared the corporate groupings of men – civic and other government officials and, above all, fraternal orders, militia, companies, volunteer fire brigades, and the like. These groups were composed of residents who, by marching, made a successful claim to what Mary Ryan has aptly called, in an American context, 'ceremonial citizenship.'[11] Nearby, and in close interaction, were other residents and visitors, men who did not belong to such groups or who, on this occasion, did not march, and other spectators who were barred from ceremonial citizenship either because of their outsider status as visitors or because of their gender or age. Women and most of the children took part in these ceremonial events not as processionists but in a subordinate capacity as admirers of the men who exercised their rights of ceremonial citizenship.

Entry upon Entry

In every town where the prince made more than a whistle-stop, residents turned his arrival into a ceremonial event. As the list of entries grew longer, their repetitiveness taxed the journalists' descriptive powers. The repetition gave recognition to local participants everywhere, and it underscored the breadth of the prince's popularity. For our purposes here, it will suffice to examine a few of the grander or more interesting entries.

The entry at Halifax, the next provincial capital on the prince's itinerary after St John's, stood out because of the impressive naval and military presence, which appropriately reflected the history and main significance of the place. No account of the prince's landing failed to mention the city's origins as a naval outpost of empire, founded in 1749, or the might of the naval force stationed there in 1860, itself only a small fragment of the world's most powerful navy. Given the navy's pre-eminence locally, it fell to Rear-Admiral Alexander Milne, the ranking naval officer at Halifax, to take charge of the landing and reception, although some duties were assumed by Major-General Charles Trollope of the British army and by the mayor, Samuel R. Caldwell.

On Monday morning, 30 July, Halagonians were astir before five o'clock, standing about the streets speculating about when the squadron would appear. By seven, when three guns signalled the prince's approach, though rain was coming down in sheets, thousands of eager spectators travelled out to intercept the royal squadron and accompany the ships to their anchorage in the harbour. The people went by sailing yachts and aboard merchant vessels, and two steamers, the *Neptune* and the *Eastern City*, carried large numbers of ticket-holding spectators, including various reporters. When the steamers came up to the *Hero*, still miles out, the passengers cheered wildly and the brass band aboard the *Neptune* struck up 'God Save the Queen.' The sailors of the royal squadron answered the cheers, while spectators peered curiously at the figures on the quarterdeck of the *Hero*: the young prince, dressed in plain black, who acknowledged their cheers, and the naval officers dressed in their black cocked hats, red coats, and white trousers and with spy-glasses in hand, who returned the gaze of the crowd. Meantime, in the streets of Halifax, people anxiously dashed about, alternately assuming good vantage points from which to view ships as they grew closer and seeking shelter from the intermittent downpours.[12]

The approach was judged to be grandly impressive. As the *Hero* passed by each of the batteries positioned along the shore, the gunners fired a twenty-one-gun salute. The thunder of the guns seemed to boom forever, with the echoes from the surrounding hills only amplifying the 'thrilling' effect. Smoke from the guns mingled with the clouds hovering over the bay. Before 10:00 A.M., the *Hero* and its many accompanying vessels drew into the harbour proper, passing close to the great men-of-war ships that were already anchored there. All of the ships were dressed in their ceremonial best, and thousands of red jackets lined the walls of the towering citadel. 'The spectacle was really imposing,' wrote the correspondent for the Toronto *Globe*, 'one well calculated to impress the mind with some sense of the power and greatness of the nation over which rules the Mother of the Prince now visiting these shores. It was a sight over which one might legitimately rejoice; and even those who neither owe nor pay allegiance to the flag of our empire, must see in it a guarantee that the country which in the

Raising the royal standard at the Halifax Dockyard upon the prince's landing. The original caption reads: 'The progress of the Prince of Wales in British North America – His Royal Highness landing at Halifax.' (*Illustrated London News*, 1 September 1860)

old world has so long been the guiding beacon of liberty and the protectress of civilization has still much wherewith to make her position good.'[13] Readers everywhere, as well as the spectators of Halifax, could not help but understand that here was a display of imperial power. Etchings of the scene, which appeared in the illustrated newspapers of the day, vividly underscored the theme.

At noon, His Royal Highness, now dressed in his colonel's uniform, descended from the *Hero* into a white boat. Under brighter skies, people watched from all possible vantage points – sailors from every yard and shroud in the harbour, the honoured ladies from the gallery seating, the general populace from the crammed wharves and rooftops. On his trip to shore, the prince's boat was accompanied by a small flotilla of canoes, decorated with fir boughs and manned by Mi'kmaq. Writing home to his wife, Dr Henry Acland described how 'the glassy waters around were thick with the dancing canoes of the Micmac Indians who with their strange dress and fir trees in every bow came to salute with their cries the son of the Mother Queen.'[14]

When the prince stepped on the wharf, passing through a triumphal arch decorated with two anchors and a canoe, from which sprang Prince-of-Wales plumes, he was welcomed by Admiral Milne and then by the Earl of Mulgrave, the lieutenant governor of Nova Scotia (and formerly a treasurer in the royal household[15]). Standing nearby were many military, clerical, provincial, and civic officials. A detachment of the 62nd Regiment paid the visitor military honours, and a passage to the waiting horses was kept clear by a number of sailors, dressed in blue shirts and white trousers 'and armed with drawn cutlasses.'[16] The recorder read the address of the city, to which the prince replied briefly. He and members of his suite then mounted their horses, and the procession began moving towards Government House, where there would be many more addresses. Even the choir of Sunday school children was mighty at Halifax: no less than 4,000 voices serenaded the visitors. One account carefully noted 'a social feature' of the choir: the inclusion of 'a large number of negro children, and with the exception of some attempt at classification at one end, white and black were generally mixed together.'[17]

The prince's reply to the civic address sounded a note of imperial pride and one of flattery, saying in part: 'In your noble harbour the navies of Britain can ride in safety, whilst you prosecute that commercial activity, which, under their protection, would seem destined to make Halifax one of the most important cities of the Western World.' It was a fitting tribute to the image of the place that Admiral Milne and his assistants had carefully crafted for the occasion.

Not every entry was as well prepared or grand as the one at Halifax, which was backed by naval resources. At Saint John, New Brunswick, by all accounts, including even the local ones, preparations had been left until far too late, and though the city was a thriving commercial centre, there was a hard-headed reluctance to spend money on the reception. Early arriving crowds, which came to town in droves by rail and steamboat, were disappointed to find so few preparations and decorations. People of all sorts, including 'swindlers and monkey grinders,' milled about so that 'Prince William Street resembled Broadway.' Only on the very eve of the prince's reception did a flurry of activity take place. By that time, New Brunswick officials had learned about the elaborate preparations and fine display in rival Halifax.[18]

Because things had been left too late, the Saint John landing was a flop – and this was the main theme of newspaper accounts. As people thronged the harbour to welcome the prince on the morning of 3 August, they discovered that a visiting American steamer, the *Admiral*, had moored in such a way that it blocked both the view from the gallery seating and the prince's access to the wharf. Authorities begged the master to move the *Admiral*, but he refused because his passengers wanted a good vantage point and because he was in the process of making a handsome windfall by selling standing room to yet more spectators. The *Morning Freeman* grumbled that the captain had shown a 'total disregard of all decency.' As a result of his recalcitrance, the reception committee had to alter its plans at the very last minute, and the landing place was moved hurriedly to another location nearby. The timing was tight, as the reporter for the New York *Herald* made clear: 'While the carpenters were still at work on the stage, there arose a general shout of "Here he comes," and true to the words, a boat with the royal standard fluttering at its peak, came bounding towards shore.'[19] Writing in the London *Times*, Nathaniel Woods described the situation:

> It was an exciting moment when the 'Styx' began to man yards and the royal barge pushed off from her side, and still the unfortunate landing-stage was not completed. The good mayor and sheriffs hurried about hither and thither; provincial dignitaries, seizing on tools, began to hammer wildly, dragging a smooth carpet over the inequalities of the woodwork, as if the whole machine was not slippery and dangerous enough already. Nearer and nearer came the barge and louder and louder grew

> the hammering. Everybody said it would be finished though everybody thought it wouldn't, until at last, as the prince disembarked, the professional carpenters were driven away, while the amateurs threw down their tools and stood with a bland smile to receive His Highness, as if everything had been ready, and they in waiting for his landing since midnight.[20]

Woods had found a clever way to rescue his readers from a dull account of the reception.

Journalists faulted the city council at Saint John for putting too much faith in private enterprise. A contractor had taken on the job of building the arch and the seating at the landing place as a speculation, and he charged such a high price for tickets that they remained unsold. Consequently, the first thing the prince saw upon landing at Saint John were rows of empty seats![21] The reporter for the New York *Evening Post* described the arch that the same contractor had built as being 'exceedingly shabby,' so much so that 'the word "Welcome" on the arch did not seem very sincere.' Altogether, it was 'a small transaction for a [civic] corporation of a large seaport city, receiving for the first time the heir apparent of the mother country.'[22]

In a backhanded way, the accounts of the Saint John reception capture something of the place. Life bustled in mid-nineteenth-century Saint John, which helps to explain why the people were reluctant to take time away from their businesses and why, when they did at last set about making preparations, it was with gusto. Private enterprise thrived, if not to the glory of the city, as the empty benches had shown. Authorities in New Brunswick's leading commercial centre could not bring themselves to intervene in the rights of an enterprising neighbour – however disruptive the captain of the *Admiral* had been. The city's economy was in part tied tightly to New England, and the American steamer's dominance of the scene nicely captured that relationship.

One of the American visitors who watched the scene from aboard the *Admiral* gained a fine impression of the city and its celebrations. In his diary, George F. Hill describes how he was one of about four hundred excursionists who had left Calais, Maine, aboard the *Admiral* the evening before the prince's landing at Saint John. The vessel was so crowded that most of the passengers had either to sit up or walk on deck all night, but the trip was nevertheless pleasant, it being 'a splendid moonlight night and the water as smooth as a mill pond.' Hill

Greeting the Prince of Wales upon his landing at Saint John, New Brunswick. The artist, G.H. Andrews, has tidied things up so that the image conforms to the scene as imagined by the local organizers. (*Illustrated London News*, 15 September 1860)

appreciated the superb view of the landing he had from aboard the *Admiral*, and it appears that was oblivious to the criticisms of his captain. Once in the city itself he admired the procession, the main street, 'being lined on each side by the Sons of Sampson – Firemen – Rifle Companies, etc.,' and he thought that 'Queens Square and Prince William Street surpassed in beauty anything [he] had imagined.' All the Americans remarked on the politeness of the crowds, saying that 'everyone seemed to make room for you, and that it was very different from the elbowing and jostling of the American crowd on a similar occasion.' So satisfied were Hill and the others that they returned 'highly pleased with the demonstration and there is one universal voice of commendation from the strangers who visited the city.'[23]

The prince's entry to the Province of Canada was nearly as modest an affair and lacking in newsworthiness as his arrival in New Brunswick. Quebec would have made a fitting entry point to the province, but for some reason the Duke of Newcastle had determined that it would be appropriate for the Canadian cabinet to welcome the prince and his party when they first entered Canadian waters. So it was, then, that the Gaspé coast not far from Percé Rock provided the setting for what turned out to be quite modest official ceremonies. In that remote, thinly populated locale, the tiny number of spectators diminished the event, and so journalists were once again left struggling to find something of interest to report to their readers.

Vessels carrying the royal party, the Canadian officials, members of the press, and visiting spectators converged on the Gaspé basin from several directions. Governor Head and the cabinet, who had left from Quebec aboard the steamship *Victoria*, waited anxiously at Gaspé, along with a number of American fishermen who had been in the vicinity and decided to take in the event. Meantime, the prince and his suite travelled from Prince Edward Island aboard the *Hero*, accompanied as usual by the *Ariadne* and the *Flying-Fish*. Newspapermen covering the royal tour followed in hot pursuit, most of them taking the steamer *Arabian*, which was making a special trip to the Gaspé from Shediac, New Brunswick. A few journalists and spectators ventured from Toronto or Montreal, making the best connections they could by train, steamboat, and schooner.

Getting to the Gaspé became the subject of considerable discussion in the press partly because of the novelty of the trip and partly because at that point there was little else doing. The Toronto *Globe* printed a long account by 'A Correspondent' who travelled from Toronto to the

Gaspé via the north shore of the St Lawrence, crossing the gulf some six hundred miles beyond Quebec and skirting Anticosti Island. The story, following the conventions of contemporary travel literature, was replete with depictions of the rocky, barren coast, of adventures while searching for bears, and of the 'French fishermen,' whom the writer found, much to his surprise, 'remarkably polite, hospitable, and intelligent.'[24] Kinahan Cornwallis of the New York *Herald* whined about the discomforts he endured aboard a steamer travelling to the Gaspé from Shediac. Passengers had been packed 'closer than ... on board an African slaver, and the ventilation [was] less perfect'; the crew 'displayed the grossest incompetence and want of discipline'; the provisions were 'as bad as the cooking'; and the waiters 'disgustingly unclean.' Altogether, it was 'a miserable purgatory.' Woods, comfortably ensconced aboard the *Hero*, entertained his *Times* readers by describing the tricky passage through the rain and fog off Prince Edward Island, as the vessels of the royal squadron crept along, 'stopping, sounding, and signalling,' and the 'bold magnificence' of the Gaspé coast with its huge cliffs of red sandstone lit by the setting sun so as to resemble 'mountains of fire.'[25]

The Toronto *Globe* correspondent sought to maintain his readers' interest by poking fun at the governor general, Sir Edmund Head, always a favourite target of George Brown's newspaper. While awaiting the prince's arrival at the town of Gaspé, His Excellency 'could not sleep, he could not eat, he could not think, he feared so much that the Prince might slip past unnoticed by him.' When at last the royal fleet was sighted, Sir Edmund paced nervously on the deck of the *Victoria*, dressed 'in his official uniform of blue and silver, with his sword girded to his loins, his cocked hat, feathers and all, upon his head.' The *Hero* did not anchor off the Gaspé shore until after dark, and so the governor could do little that night. But first thing the next morning, 'thinking perhaps His Royal Highness was rather dilatory in sending an invitation to breakfast, determined to awaken him to a sense of duty by means of a royal salute.' Because the *Victoria* had only one gun and a less than skilful crew, the salute was both irregular and sounded with a painful slowness. Halfway through the twenty-one firings, it was cut short. 'Why, cannot be told,' declared the correspondent. 'Perhaps the invitation to breakfast had arrived – perhaps the powder had fallen short – perhaps Commodore Seymour had threatened, if the folly were persisted in, to put the whole under hatches.'[26]

The official ceremonies appear to have been so modest that the journalists scarcely mentioned what was supposed to have been the point of this segment of the tour. The people living in the Gaspé basin had whitewashed their houses and decorated the streets in anticipation of the prince's visit, but in fact he never did land there. The reception ceremonies took place aboard the *Hero*, and so it was difficult for even the small number of potential spectators in the area to view the proceedings. There was very little to be said: 'The Canadian ministry, with the exception of Mr. Vankoughnet, proceeded on board the *Hero* and were presented to the Prince by the Duke of Newcastle. They then lunched with him and returned to the *Victoria* with His Excellency, the Governor General.'[27] We learn just a little more from a letter penned by General Bruce, who told the prince consort that the encounter with the Canadians had gone off well. On this occasion the prince had been 'particularly civil to all, and conversed with them individually and collectively more than usual,' and Bruce hoped that the cabinet ministers had gone away 'very favourably impressed.' The prince's governor added that the 'bay and harbour of Gaspé are remarkably commodious and picturesque, being encircled by high wooded hills, and [so] we sailed round ... before taking our departure.'[28]

More interesting to the journalists were the problems the royal fleet had in navigating. In trying to enter the Gaspé basin, the *Hero* ran aground on a sandy shoal. The *Times* provided a detailed account of how the crew of the *Ariadne* succeeded in pulling the *Hero* off the shoal by means of precision manoeuvres and a heavy cable and a bower anchor. During the proceedings, several boats came out from Gaspé town carrying passengers who cheered and waived handkerchiefs, delighted by this impromptu opportunity to get close to His Royal Highness. Meantime, Woods reported, on the quarterdeck of the *Hero* the prince 'sky-larked' with the younger officers, appearing to do so 'with as much good-humour and *sang-froid* as if he visited Gaspé every day in the year, and was rather in the habit than otherwise of getting ashore in a line-of-battle ship.'[29] Altogether, it was a strange introduction to the Canadas, one that could have given the visitors the impression that the country was a pretty wilderness, with hazards lurking beneath its serene surface and populated mainly by uniformed cabinet ministers and an overwrought governor!

Quebec provided the first of several grand civic entries that the prince made in the Canadas, an entry noteworthy because of the immense crowds, the striking beauty of the setting, and the participation of French Canadians. According to all reports, Quebec was bursting at the seams with visitors, including many Americans. The correspondent for the Toronto *Globe* was struck by the predominance among them of southerners, some coming from as far away as Florida and Louisiana. Professional pickpockets had arrived from New York, but the ones whom the police detected were quickly banished. The better hotels, such as Russells' and the Clarendon, raised their daily rates from $2.50 to $4.00; 'those who do not like it may go and lodge in the gutter.'[30] Rooms were so scarce everywhere that many boats along the shore were converted into temporary lodgings. Various ships of the Royal Navy had come up to Quebec and were moored in the harbour, their thousands of sailors briefly adding to the throng on shore. Quebec's notorious crimps quickly set to work among them, and, as a result of the desertions, Admiral Milne cancelled shore leave for all but officers.[31]

On the morning of the prince's landing, the crowds swelled again with the arrival of French Canadians from the surrounding countryside. Heavy clouds moved in, too, and the rain came down in sheets. 'One could not but feel compassion,' wrote the correspondent of the New York *Times*, 'for the pretty Canadian girls who had come from a distance, with their coquettish little hats, their waving white plumes, and their dear little boots, protected in no way from "the little drops of water," which one by one stole their way through the gauzy fabric of their "cut-aways" and wetting the very cuticles of her Majesty's most loyal dames.'[32]

A whole flotilla of excursion boats went down the St Lawrence to meet the royal squadron and accompany it to town. The *Magnet* and the *Saguenay* offered passengers a trip all the way down to the mouth of the Saguenay River. 'Though the fare was four dollars a head,' reported the amazed correspondent for the New York *Herald*, so keen were people that 'several hundred excursionists were taken down in both boats.' Many other vessels, charging excursionists only a dollar, left Quebec early on the day of the reception to join the escort not far beyond the Île d'Orléans, where they crowded round the prince's ship. In the recollections of a naval officer who was aboard the *Hero*, the ship's band 'got up on the poop and ... treated the fair Canadians on board the steamers to all the latest quadrilles and valses. Much amusement was caused by the people on board one of the craft, who promptly got up a quadrille-party and danced away to the notes of our powerful band floating across the water.' According to Cornwallis of the New York *Herald*, the *Jenny Lind* travelled so close alongside the

Landing of the Prince of Wales at Quebec, watercolour by C. Williams, 1860. The artist captures the grandeur of royal entries where the *Hero* and other ships embellished the scene. (McCord Museum of Canadian History, M1131)

Hero that the passengers peered in her portholes, while the many 'pretty girls on board' exchanged 'harmless glances with those on the *Hero*, Albert Edward included.' From the houses lining the shores of the river came cheers, as well as *feus de joie* from guns and small arms. The smoke from these combined with that of the squadron and the steamers so that the St Lawrence, wrote Woods in the *Times*, 'seemed on fire from one end to the other.'[33]

When the royal squadron rounded Point Lévis, coming into sight of those in the harbour of Quebec, a royal salute boomed forth from ships in the harbour, the citadel, and the battery on the Durham Terrace. By 3 P.M., the weather had considerably improved, and some 20,000 spectators watched as the *Hero* anchored off the Champlain Market Wharf, where all was ready for the prince's landing. In the grandstand fronting the wharf, 2,000 ticket-holders, most of them 'ladies,' sat admiring the scene. The reporter for the New York *Times* contrasted the appearance of the ticket-holders, who were 'generally well-dressed and well-behaved,' with the spectators on the ground, who made 'noisy demonstrations, and ... rude muscular displays.' Of 'a very different class, grade and rank', these spectators 'were dressed very much as our commonest laborers are when at work.'[34] Still, humble people had made a point of being there to cheer the prince.

Dominating the site was a pagoda-like pavilion built of wood, covered in evergreens, and decorated with banners, flags, bunting, and flowers. A large number of local, provincial, and visiting dignitaries awaited the prince's arrival inside it. Though they had threatened to boycott the ceremony, representatives of many churches were present. (The Anglican bishops and non-conformist clerics had objected to the fact that the Catholic-dominated civic government had initially invited only the Roman Catholic Church to participate in the welcome at the landing.) Once again, the Catholic clergy fell victim to the poison pens of certain journalists, one of them, for instance, reporting: 'The bishops, in their broad-brimmed hats, black collars, purple velvet gowns, huge gold crosses and massive gold chains, presented a gorgeous and unctuous appearance, though rather unapostolic. Their eyes, not to say bellies, stood out with fatness, and their oily skins seemed bursting with jolly good living and luscious food.'[35] Members of the cabinet were also there, once again dressed in their uniforms, complete with cocked hats and swords – except for Philip M. VanKoughnet, who refused to wear livery. Noticeably absent were the other members of the legislature. Supporters of the government and the opposition had caucused earlier and decided to express their annoyance at the governor general's plans which denied them sufficient contact with the prince.[36]

At 4 o'clock the prince descended from the *Hero* into a barge and was rowed ashore as the guns again boomed a deafening salute, window panes shattered, and the crowd cheered heartily. The usual formalities took place upon his landing, the civic address this time being read by the mayor, Hector Langevin, in French and then English. The prince's reply, given only in English, explained that the queen would 'rejoice to hear from your own lips that all differences of origin, language, and religion are lost in one universal spirit of patriotism, and that all classes are knit to each other and to the mother country by the common ties of equal liberty and free institutions.'[37] On completion of the reply, the crowd gave three cheers.

Members of the prince's suite were pleased with the reception. Newcastle wrote to the queen, saying: 'The landing at Quebec took place in rather unfavourable weather but amidst the cordial greeting of the People and under salutes from six English Ships of War and from the Citadel and all the Battlements.' General Bruce reported to the prince consort that there had been 'great enthusiasm to greet the Prince, French and English vying with each other in their endeavour to do him honor.' And he added: 'The loyal excitement in Canada has been wound up to fever pitch.'[38]

If French and English had joined together in the welcome, the ceremonies were perceived differently by journalistic spokesmen for the two groups. According to the report in the Toronto *Globe*, the landing, with the six men-of-war looking on, drove home the power of the British empire in both the past and the present. 'It tells of that mighty struggle,' declared the Toronto reporter, alluding to the Conquest, 'when the two most powerful nations of the world fought out a contest; it tells of the greatness of the enemy we had to overcome; it tells of stern resistance and of sterner assault.' Everything in the scene 'bore witness to the fact that the nation whose flag waved from the citadel is mistress of the seas and told, too, in unmistakable language that she has the wherewithal to make her position good, contest it who may.' Not surprisingly, in this culturally divided town, the French-Canadian press saw things utterly differently. The ceremony had been one where the Roman Catholic bishops had effectively asserted their presence on behalf of French Canadians and where French had been the first language heard by the prince when he had landed.[39]

The entry at Ottawa was distinguished by an imaginative display designed to convey a sense of the town's historic role as a way station for voyageurs travelling into fur-trade country and its ongoing importance as a base for lumbering. The queen had only recently selected Ottawa as the capital of the Province of Canada, and so its importance as the home of Parliament and the civil service still lay in the future. The entry ceremonies would represent Ottawa as a boomtown on the commercial frontier.

On Friday, 31 August, the prince travelled up the Ottawa River aboard the steamer *Phoenix*. As he approached Ottawa shortly before sunset, he was met by a fleet of 150 birch-bark canoes, manned by 'near a thousand lumbermen.' The local lumber barons, under the leadership of James Skead, had collected the men from 'great distances and at great expense.' The canoes had been painted up for the event, and each had a banner, while the woodsmen, invariably described as 'bronzed,' had been specially costumed in white trousers and red shirts faced with blue. (Dr Acland gasped that £300 had been spent on their dress alone.[40]) Under the direction of Commodore Skead, they floated out to meet the prince, singing boat songs as they paddled in tight formation. 'All was order and precision,' remarked the reporter for the Toronto *Globe*, the men 'manifesting a skill which long practice alone can give.' When the canoeists got close to the *Phoenix*, the crowd on shore gave a great 'hurrah,' which, according to the *Globe* account, came 'from the hearts as well as the throats of a thousand stalwart men as the world may find.' The Prince of Wales was reported to have been 'excited' by the sight. The canoes then accompanied the prince to the landing, racing as fast as the river steamer. As they skimmed along, they would form tight groups, 'like race horses,' and then pull apart, only to repeat the moves. Woods of the *Times* thought that it 'made one of the strangest, wildest, and most beautiful scenes that is possible to imagine.' The Ottawa *Citizen* proclaimed the spectacle 'the most novel, striking, and picturesque incident which His Royal Highness has witnessed in Canada.'[41]

The event was only slightly marred by the lateness of the hour and an unfortunate change in the weather. By the time the *Phoenix* and its escort came within what ought to have been clear sight of the waiting crowds near the landing site, the sun had set and the darkness obscured the full beauty of the entry. And then, once the prince had landed, and just as the mayor, Mr Workman, was unrolling the civic address, the skies opened. Although the prince did not flinch, the crowds rushed for cover. The prince reported to his mother that, while he was reading his reply, 'such torrents of rain came down that I had great difficulty in finishing it.'[42] That evening, Skead and the other lumber barons provided a feast for the canoe crews. 'The men supped by the light of huge bonfires,' reported the Ottawa *Citizen*. 'Several hundreds mustered around the well-spread tables, and enjoyed themselves to their hearts' content.' It was a satisfying conclusion to a ceremony carried out with finesse and one that redounded to the credit of the backwoods capital. Could other Upper Canadian towns match its show?

Toronto was determined to best its rivals. In 1860 the self-proclaimed capital of Canada West was a go-ahead kind of place, rapidly growing in population, commerce, and self-importance. Its elite, loyal to the core, liked to trace the city's roots to the arrival of the Loyalists who fled the American Revolution, and so, for them, the prince's visit was a cause for great excitement. The general populace was no less on edge. 'We are expecting the prince in Toronto in about 3 weeks,' wrote one Torontonian privately, '& the people are well nigh crazy.'[43] Only a grand entry at Toronto would do, notwithstanding the city's natural disadvantages: a low-lying and unprepossessing physical location far upstream and thus beyond the reach of the handsome vessels of the royal squadron. Most worrisome of all was the fear that Orange demonstrations, which had prevented the prince from landing at Kingston and Belleville, would do so in Toronto, too. The mayor worked long and hard with the Orangemen to ensure that they would not cause trouble, but no one could be certain what would actually happen on the fateful day. As it turned out, the tremendous anxieties only served to heighten the drama of the royal entry when it did take place.

Since the Toronto reception committee wanted to stage an entry at the harbour, in the afternoon of Friday, 7 September, the prince ended his travel by train and boarded the government mail steamer, the *Kingston*, at Whitby, a Lake Ontario port several miles east of the city. The usual flotilla of boats carrying excursionists went down to greet the prince and escort him to the city. Delays in the prince's travels meant that instead of arriving mid-afternoon, the *Kingston* did not appear there until nearly sunset. At least 50,000 people waited for him on the shoreline of the city. Looking towards the lake, they squinted into the gloom, the weather being poor and the hour growing late.

At 7 P.M. the *Kingston* pulled up alongside the wharf at the foot of John Street, a few steps across the railway tracks from the site of the reception. Of all the structures built especially for the prince's tour, the amphitheatre, with seating for 20,000, and the grand civic arch at John Street were among the most impressive. On the level ground was mus-

Welcoming the prince near his landing place at the foot of John Street, Toronto. Citizens spent lavishly to build a grand amphitheatre and civic arch specially for the occasion. (*Illustrated London News*, 27 October 1860)

tered the volunteer cavalry, the men under Colonel George Taylor Denison's command dressed smartly in blue and silver. In the front seats squirmed 4,000 children from the schools and Sunday schools ready to serenade the prince, and above them rose the tiers of ticket-holders, a great many of them ladies in summer dresses dampened by the light rain that was falling. On the platform stood the fidgeting officials, the tension showing on their creased, manly faces.

A sailor aboard the *Kingston* threw the landing rope, the gangway was pushed out, and the prince stepped ashore, to the relief and joy of the multitude. The Orangemen, true to their agreement with the mayor, were out of sight. The mayor himself greeted the prince enthusiastically, and, a few moments later, the civic address was read as darkness descended. After the prince's reply, the welcoming roars of the overwrought but relieved crowds were deafening.

Commentators on the scene judged the entry a magnificent sight. Of course, the local newspapers could be expected to enthuse. 'Words cannot describe that vast volume of sound, thrilling, soul-stirring, heart-heaving,' said the *Globe*. 'Never before have we witnessed so imposing a spectacle.' More surprising was the concurrence of the members of the royal suite. Writing from Toronto, General Bruce informed the prince consort that 'the reception here was magnificent – 8 or 10,000 persons were assembled in a sort of semi-amphitheatre opposite the landing place and the enthusiasm as well as all the preparations for H.R.H.'s reception were very gratifying.' Newcastle wrote the queen (formally, in the third person), saying that 'both as an artistic display and as a popular demonstration it was the finest thing He has yet seen, and He likens it to be unsurpassed by any similar spectacle on the continent of Europe or elsewhere.' The prince himself echoed Newcastle's words, saying in a letter to his mother that the entry ceremony had been 'one of the finest sights of the sort I have ever seen.' The members of the Toronto reception committee would have been most gratified had they been privy to these private communications; instead, they satisfied themselves with assurances from members of the suite that Toronto had welcomed the prince in a way that reflected the loyalty and vigour of the young colonial city.[44]

On Display

In every city visited by the prince, a 'grand public procession' immediately followed his reception at the landing. The procession solved the practical problem of getting the honoured visitor from A to B, that is, from the landing place to his lodgings or the site of the next event on the program. Turning the trip into a ceremony made it more interesting for the public and the special guests alike. The procession not only put the prince on display for the enjoyment of the spectators; it put the city on display for the appreciation of the prince and his suite. Moreover, participants in the procession gained status by being included as performers, rather than spectators, and by their proximity to the royal figure. The French consul, for instance, was delighted when the mayor of Quebec placed him and the consular officers of other countries third in rank, immediately behind the bishops and the judges of the Superior Court.[45] People came out by the thousands to see the prince first hand, but the attention in the press focused more on the display put on by the city: the many men marching in the procession, the appearance of the streets, and the responses of spectators.

If the city as a whole welcomed the prince during the royal entry ceremony, the emphasis being on a seamless public, a community, the city on display during the public procession appeared broken into its various parts: what Mary Ryan has called its 'distinctive publics.'[46] There were those on display – the officials, the fraternal orders, and other groups of men who possessed the right of ceremonial citizenship – and then there was the rest, the people who were excluded from exercising such a right but who participated by watching, cheering, clapping, and waving. Because the processions in 1860 were secular, and sharply demarcated the processionists from the spectators, they might better be called 'parades'; but contemporaries used the older term 'procession,' with its long associations with royalty.[47]

When civic reception committees made their plans for the grand procession following the landing, one of their concerns was an appropriate route: it had to be sufficiently long for plenty of people to get a chance to see the prince, and it needed to follow the main thoroughfares so as to show off the character and grandeur of the place, such as it was.[48] Unlike religious processions associated with the Catholic Church, which formed a loop that encircled spiritual space, the routes were free-form. In Halifax, a public debate occurred when the planning committee designated Water Street as forming part of the route. While critics feared that it looked too seedy, defenders maintained that it had the advantage of displaying the wharves and shipping, which had always contributed much to the city's prosperity.[49] In Toronto, too, citizens debated about the procession route. Colonel William

Jarvis, a patriarch of one of the city's grand old families, objected to the excessive length of the proposed route. 'It was too much like making an exhibition of His Royal Highness,' harrumphed the colonel. He did not 'approve of the Prince being taken up one street and down another to gratify public curiosity. It savoured too much of the style of our neighbours across the lakes.' In response, the reception committee maintained that only with the longer route would all the people have a fair chance of seeing the prince, and on this occasion it was important to satisfy 'the multitude.' It was also pointed out that 'great personages' were obliged to undergo public receptions and that so youthful a prince would not be easily tired. The queen herself was accustomed to processions and had shown that she 'was not afraid to be seen by her subjects.' The supporters of the longer route easily won the debate.[50]

Reception committees were responsible for encouraging groups to participate in the processions. Public announcements in local newspapers would invite the 'societies' to indicate their intention to march, and a subsequent notice would list the participants in the order assigned to them. The process by which committees or the mayor's office came to decide on an order of precedence was seldom transparent, and there was just a little suspense to see how things would come out. Would the shamrock precede the thistle, or vice versa? At St John's, where the hosts delighted in trumpeting the 'ancient' origins of their city, precedence was given to age, the local society with the earliest founding coming first. As a result, the Masons went first and thus nearest to the prince's carriage, followed by the Benevolent Irish Society, the Newfoundland British Society, the St Andrew's Society, the St George's Society, the Newfoundland Native Society, the Phoenix Volunteer Fire Company, the Sons of Temperance, the Coopers' Society, and the Total Abstinence Society. In Toronto, the prince was placed almost at the end of the procession, and so the order rose climactically, from least important to most important. The Loyal United Colored Society went first, which gained the group attention even as it put African Canadians in the least prestigious place.

The composition of the processions varied according to the particular groups that were locally active and enthusiastic about the visit, and thus a local procession made a statement about the identity of a community. At Halifax, for instance, the military presence was predictably strong, with representation from the volunteers, the Royal Artillery, the Royal Engineers, the 62nd Regiment, and the Marines. But the African Abolition Society was also there, drawing attention to the city's well-established Black community as well as to a reform cause. At Brantford, on the edge of the Six Nations Reserve, First Nations were a notable presence, but they were given a low-ranked position between the fire companies and the temperance societies. Within the Six Nations' contingent the ranking was also made clear. Their marshall, Chief G.H.M. Johnson, led, with others following behind: 'the Indian [marching] Band; the old Warriors of the Six Nations; the Chiefs of the Six Nations; and the Mohawks, Oneidas, Onondagas, Cayugas, Tuscaroras, Delawares, Chippewas, in full Indian War costume.' At Montreal, no First Nation group appeared on the program for the procession, but, according to Woods of the *Times*, the 'Cawknawaaga Indians' from nearby Lachine '*placed themselves* at the head of the very grand procession.'[51]

Virtually everywhere the three main national societies with connections to the British Isles appeared in the processions: the St George's Society (English), the St Andrew's Society (Scottish), and the St Patrick's Society (Irish). Such groups, which were committed to preserving ethnic ties, had a tradition of claiming recognition by marching on public occasions, such as on the queen's birthday in May. Because the royal visit was seen as being a special occasion, the groups in Toronto raised funds for new, beautiful banners. The *Globe* carefully described these 'works of art,' noting, for instance, that the principal banner of the St George's Society had a wreath of roses, the figure of St George and the dragon, and on the reverse the three lions of England. It was made of fine silk with rich gold trimmings. In Halifax the processionists included the North British Society, the Caledonia Club, and the Highland Society, the latter two in Highland dress and accompanied by pipers.

Other national societies appeared in particular places where their numbers were strong. In Quebec, the Société Saint-Jean-Baptiste, the national association of French Canadians and the impresario of the annual Saint-Jean-Baptiste parades,[52] made a good show. An advertisement in *Le Courrier du Canada* of Quebec invited 'all French Canadians' to attend a general meeting of the Société Saint-Jean-Baptiste in preparation for the city's reception of the prince. It appears, then, that not just members were encouraged to march with the Société. According to one report, 'the young St Jean Baptistes mustered very strong and had many fine banners of white silk.' At Ottawa the Société Saint-Jean-Baptiste led the national societies. Otherwise, the press took no

The prince and the procession halt as they pass the children's gallery at Halifax. (*Illustrated London News*, 1 September 1860)

particular interest in the participation of this society in the processions, only routinely noting the presence of 'the national societies' in the cities and towns of Canada East. In Hamilton, Canada West, the German Society took its position in the procession. In Cobourg and Toronto, the marchers included 'Native Canadians' – men who chose to identify with Canada and wear a maple leaf. (See chapter 7.) Although not strictly speaking a national society, the African Society joined the others in Halifax, where the reporter for the New York *Times* observed gratuitously that its marchers were 'all colored but of varying degrees of duskiness.'[53]

The trade societies turned out in only a few places, Saint John being the city with the best showing. The tradesmen added variety to the scene by bringing with them their tools and banners and wearing distinctive clothing, as was their custom when on parade. Not surprisingly, for a major shipbuilding centre, the marchers included 'a large body of ship carpenters, caulkers, riggers, etc., carrying a banner representing a ship on the stocks.' Their banner declared 'Success to our trade.' Shoemakers also turned out in considerable numbers, wearing 'aprons, sashes, and gilt crowns on their coats, and look[ing] remarkably well.' Foundrymen had their banners, too, as did the mill men and lumberers, the latter two being the largest occupational groups in the city. The *Globe* correspondent objected to the inscription on the lumberers' banner – '"We are the hard workers," an assumed monopoly of labour not altogether justifiable, as there were hundreds of other men before and behind them who work just as hard as they.'[54]

In a great many of the processions honouring the prince, the temperance men appeared by the thousands. In 1860 the temperance movement was thriving and proud to display its numerical strength, which in turn spoke to the moral strength of colonial communities.[55] Some temperance groups, perhaps modelling themselves on the customs of the trades procession, adopted distinctive dress and banners. At Saint John, for instance, the Sons of Temperance wore their special collars and bore 'banners, staves, emblems, such as the wine cups with hissing serpents crawling out of them.' Accompanying the temperance men were the Cadets of Temperance and the St Stephen's Band, altogether about 1,200 to 1,500 in number.[56] In Canada West, the temperance men were so determined to impress that they planned their own special processions at Kingston and Toronto on the day after the main processions. One supporter explained that they not only wanted to show their loyalty and attachment but also 'to exhibit their strength to the

Prince of Wales.' Another earnest soul hoped that their giant procession 'might exercise an influence upon the eminent men who would accompany His Royal Highness.'[57] An advantage of marching at a different time than the civic procession was that it freed many of the temperance men to march in the ranks of other societies to which they belonged. Had they all marched as teetotallers during the main event, these other societies would have had much-reduced ranks and made a poor showing.

Firemen and volunteers added yet more colour to the processions, their uniforms and discipline drawing the attention of journalists and spectators. The volunteer (militia) movement had only just taken off, the uniforms were new, the young men enthusiastic. Similarly, fire companies provided an outlet for adventurous men, eager for comradeship, and, like the volunteer militiamen, they enjoyed strutting in uniform on public occasions.[58] In Halifax's civic procession in honour of the Prince of Wales, members of the Axe Fire Company bore their axes while the Union Engine Company pulled six decorated fire engines. No. 1 engine, the 'Rapid,' was decked out in flowers and accompanied by 'a reel, "Salamander," representing a Bower, with a youthful fireman reposing in the shade.' The message was reassuring: under the care of the firemen, the community was peaceful and idyllic, safe from the ravages of fire. Another company made a more curious display, drawing attention by representing the exotic. The engine of No. 5 fire company was drawn by four horses led by 'four colored men dressed in the garb of Turks,' and its horse cart was pulled 'by two Shetland ponies led by two colored boys, likewise dressed in the garb of Turks.'[59] Possibly they were supposed to resemble the captured slaves of ancient Rome, thus lending power and status to the rest of the (white) firemen in the procession. Members of the local Black community also appeared in 'non-exotic' guise, marching, for instance, as a company of militia volunteers. Even then they drew comment. The reporter for the New York *Herald* referred to the company as 'the Greeley guard,' while the Toronto *Globe* reporter remarked that the men of this company 'did not show anything which would lead one to imagine that they are the "inferior race" they are so often said to be.'[60]

The processions, then, were generally quite inclusive of the fraternal societies active in the life of British North American cities. It is harder to assess who was absent and harder still to know why some groups did not appear. More participation from trade unions might have been expected, given their parading propensities. Were their members expressing opposition to the royal visit by not taking part in the procession? Possibly, but I have found no evidence that sheds light on the matter. It could also be that on this occasion many working men thought first of marching as volunteers or firemen or teetotallers rather than as craftsmen. We do know that in places the Masons absented themselves from the prince's presence, not because of anything smacking of republicanism, but because they were aware that there could be a problem in the queen's heir apparent recognizing a secret society, and they did not want to make an issue of it. Thus, at Halifax the Masons marched but avoided appearing before the prince. The New York *Times* reported that 'a body of colored Free Masons ... stopped at the Masonic Hall and went into the lodge with their white brethren, instead of passing before the Prince.'[61] Lodges of the Orange Order absented themselves entirely from the processions in the Maritime provinces and Lower Canada for similar reasons. As noted earlier, and as will be discussed in greater detail in chapter 5, the decision of many Orangemen in Upper Canada to exercise their right to demonstrate in the public streets would cause the biggest controversy connected with the visit. In Kingston and Belleville the Orangemen's insistence on marching led to the cancellation of the prince's visit, thus depriving all other groups in those towns from exercising their ceremonial citizenship. In Toronto, by contrast, the Orangemen abandoned their plans to march in front of the prince, reluctantly accepting their ceremonial disenfranchisement.

Women, of course, could neither be members of fraternal societies nor serve as public officials, which effectively barred them from marching in the processions. Indeed, their exclusion from the processions proper was nearly total. Societies that encouraged women to join their organizations – many church and temperance groups – either did not join in the processions at all or permitted only their male members to march on the occasion of the visit. I have found no evidence of public debate about the matter, the women's exclusion being expected and carried out without incident or comment. Bonnie Huskins provides a wider context for such exclusion in her study of the ceremonial space of women in Victorian Halifax and Saint John. She argues that, while women would expand their activities in the late Victorian period, the prevailing 'gender ideology' in the mid-nineteenth century 'limited the range of performative roles open to women.'[62]

Journalists and other commentators did, however, make much of an isolated instance of women's intrusion into the ceremonial realm, when a group of ladies at Belleville announced their intention of taking

In Saint John, a chivalrous prince doffs his hat to ladies elegantly posed beneath the motto 'WE HONOR OUR QUEEN.' (*Illustrated Times*, 8 September 1860)

part in the civic procession by providing the prince with an equestrian escort. The Toronto *Leader* accepted their initiative as both an indication of the ladies' loyalty and a 'novel idea.' It reassured readers that the women were 'not Lucy Stones, we presume; they do not mount the rostrum, and argue the rights of women to vote in elections to pitch their husbands – if they have them – overboard, or anything of the sort. They simply desire to take part in welcoming the Prince.' By contrast, the *Hastings Chronicle*, a local Belleville paper, pretended to accept the women's proposal on the grounds that 'the ladies see nothing *outré* in such a performance,' and of course, 'no one else has a right to question the taste of the arrangement.' And then, in the guise of chivalry, the *Chronicle* objected to the ladies' participation for fear of their safety. 'Amidst the firing of cannon, and the cheers of thousands,' said the editor, 'it is not at all impossible that some of the horses may grow restive and throw their fair rides; and once unhorsed in such a crowd, life wound not be worth a minute's purchase.' While not wanting 'to throw cold water on the project,' the editorial urged the men of the Belleville reception committee to 'consider the matter carefully.' Whatever was said or not said by members of the reception committee, the ladies were resolved to ride. On the morning the prince was scheduled to land, they appeared dressed smartly in the riding clothes, with red sashes, mounted (side-saddle) on their horses. For reasons that had nothing to do with them, and everything to do with the Orangemen, the prince never landed at Belleville, and the ladies lost their chance to welcome him.[63]

I have found only one reference to women who actually took part in a procession honouring the prince, and that was in the village of Chippawa, on the Niagara peninsula. The prince and his party arrived there after dark, and so 'the firemen, and many ladies also, lighted up their torches and escorted him to the Pavilion Hotel.'[64] The women got a chance to participate in an impromptu procession because everything had happened on the spur of the moment. The incident went without comment in the press.

In the newspaper coverage of the processions, the ladies were, however, given considerable attention as spectators whose presence counted for a great deal. Their numbers swelled the vast crowds, while their beauty and enthusiasm embellished and enlivened the scene. For the benefit of readers of the *Times*, Woods drew a word picture of the main thoroughfare at Halifax as the procession passed through it: 'the roadway densely crowded and all the windows, roofs, and balconies thronged with hundreds of ladies waving handkerchiefs and throwing down bouquets til the whole place seemed fluttering in the wind.' Proper and prudent ladies removed themselves from the crowds in the streets, finding a safe perch even if it meant paying for the privilege. Though upper windows in buildings lining the procession route through Quebec fetched 'considerable prices,' reported the Ottawa *Citizen*, all were 'filled with anxious gazers.' Those who risked the streets could find themselves in genuine danger, according to press reports. Near the Prescott Gate in Quebec, the narrow street grew so crammed that 'women fainted or screamed out for help, and with damaged bonnets and torn dresses were pushed through the neighbouring houses.' In the crush at Montreal, one person was trampled to death, a gloomy news item that the press preferred to pass over quickly amid all the rejoicing.[65]

Journalists represented the Prince of Wales as a young man who truly appreciated the beauty and attention of the female spectators. Though the Toronto *Globe* panned nearly every aspect of the celebrations at Quebec, the stronghold of French-Canadian nationality so despised by the paper, it admired the presence of the town's ladies, who in their pretty dresses appeared at every window watching the procession. Moreover, it maintained that the prince was 'by no means insensible to the bright eyes which looked down upon him.' So charmed was he that 'it is much to be questioned whether he saw anything of the decorations ... the mottoes or the male creatures.' There could be no doubting the sexual orientation of this prince charming. 'Your dandified little Frenchman curled his moustache in vain,' said the report. 'Albert Edward cared not for him. It was to the fair throng at each window he bowed.'[66]

The Duke of Newcastle, who shared the vantage point of the prince, appears to have been genuinely impressed by the processions and the crowds accompanying them. In describing to the queen the procession at Halifax, he wrote privately: 'Everywhere blazed with flags, streamers, mottoes & pictorial devices, enlivened with branches of the spruce and with flowers, and the whole distance was lined on both sides, first by the different Companies of Volunteer Firemen who form a splendid Corps ... next by the various societies ... many of which have gay costumes and lastly the newly raised companies of Volunteers, numbering on this occasion 1,000 men.' Perhaps because he was writing to a woman, Newcastle made a point of describing the lady spectators: 'Every window was filled with females dressed generally in white.' In

Saint John, Newcastle reported to Victoria, the women were even less restrained: 'Hundreds of well-dressed women not satisfied with such safe points of view lined the streets and braved the clouds of dust and pressure of the multitude.' So many bouquets were thrown that 'the carriage ... was half filled, though not one in fifty reached its aim.'[67]

Men performed, and women watched admiringly – so went the script. According to the journalists' accounts, however, the men's performance in the processions did not always warrant or win the approval of female spectators. In Sherbrooke, the Cookshire Cavalry rode well enough until a band began to play and the cheering commenced, at which point the horses panicked and the riders lost control. 'The unfortunate cavaliers became objects of ridicule to the populace,' reported the *Globe*, 'and Julia Maria, or Mary Jane, looking anxiously from the window up there, expecting to see her "bould sojer boy" conduct himself as became a warrior, was mortified to discover him belabouring his horse with the flat side of his sword, or otherwise endangering the safety of his companions in arms by his ungainly flourishes of the noble weapon.'[68]

Press reports overwhelmingly praised the enthusiasm shown by the crowds as much as they did the displays of the societies that marched in the processions. In the warm glow of the visit, and in the spirit of civic boosterism, the local newspapers seldom found anything to criticize in their home towns. It is unusual to find a comment like that of the Saint John *Morning Freeman*, which judged the number of gangs of sawmill workers marching in the Saint John procession to be 'exceedingly small' compared to the 'great body employed.' Visiting journalists were more apt to note shortcomings. The *Globe* correspondent, covering the same procession, thought the lumberers' banner 'ill executed': 'a bungling attempt ... to depict the various processes through which a tree passes before it is made into timber.' (Was this the frankness of a detached observer, or the bias of an anti-labour writer?)[69]

American reporters could be harsh at times when covering the processions. 'I regret to state,' wrote the New York *Times* correspondent while in Quebec, 'that the "Triumphal Procession" was a humbug, a failure, and a complete non-success. The societies staggered along the line with a portion of their members in uniform and a larger number without it. Some of them carried umbrellas under their arms, and others over their heads, some of them wore hats, some caps, some marched four abreast and others marched or strammed along in single file.' He was used to seeing American parades, the best of which were grand shows of uniformed men skilled in making precision movements, the Americans having by 1860 honed the parade to an art form. In Quebec, by contrast, 'every American' was annoyed beyond all description on seeing 'chaps with banners or instruments of musical torture ... walk listlessly by.' After observing the procession at Montreal, the same reporter wrote: 'If I may judge from those which I have seen, I should say that Canadians are not *au fait* in the getting up of street demonstrations or municipal processions.' He ridiculed especially the militia volunteers: 'Of all the laughable sights that ever we saw, the volunteer force, and its parade was the most so. Their hats were ill-shapen, their coats were either under or over stuffed, some having the padding in the chest, and others at the belly *en famille.*' No doubt the Quebec volunteers were not as impressive as the best-trained and equipped militiamen of the republic, but it appears that the writer's American nationalism also was responsible for his making this slur on the manliness of the volunteers at Quebec.[70]

Musically, the processions certainly fell short of fine American parades of the period. In large cities in the United States, joining marching bands was popular with a great many men who enjoyed showing off their musical talents, dressing up in colourful uniforms, and marching with razor-sharp precision. That pastime had not caught on to the same extent in British North American cities, where the bands of the British garrison did duty, and so there were few good local bands available for the processions honouring the prince.[71] Orangemen had their bands, but they were excluded from participation on this occasion. Military bands provided the best show available in the provinces, and a few of these bands drew highly favourable comment in the press. In the Canadas, the Royal Canadian Rifles – 'the best brass band that was ever in Canada' – travelled everywhere as an escort and honour guard for the prince.[72] Toronto benefited from the talents of the Union Maltese Band and the Poppenberg's Germania Band, brass bands that came up from the United States.[73] At Montreal, the prince was so impressed by a performance by the Germania Band, which accompanied the Boston Fusiliers to Canada, that he asked to be introduced to the band leaders.[74] While in general such sturdy props to spectacle were missed by American correspondents reporting on the processions honouring the prince, British and provincial reporters expressed less interest or concern about band music and marching.

Some commentators were hugely impressed and even deeply moved by the sight of processions in provincial centres, as is evident

The firemen of Saint John drawing the prince's carriage. The original caption identifies the location as Carleton, a Saint John suburb. (*Illustrated London News*, 1 September 1860)

from public and private remarks about a procession in Saint John. The people of Carleton, a working-class suburb, had made known their disappointment that when the prince first visited the city he had not appeared in their neighbourhood, and so it was arranged for him to pass through Carleton as he left the province. The place was thronged with people, and the streets were lined with shipbuilders, fire companies, and militia. Upon the approach of His Royal Highness, the firemen removed the horses from the prince's carriage, attached a grappling hook to it, and themselves pulled the prince for a mile and a half past the cheering crowds. Woods, writing in the *Times*, said that the scene 'forbids description.' People reached up to the carriage to shake the prince's hand, and he kindly obliged them. The multitude took up the cry of one 'old lady,' '"God bless you – God bless your mother!"' And the 'thousands of people assembled cheered almost incessantly; true British cheers. No mincing matters.'[75]

Other uncontrived demonstrations – or rather, performances that lacked the imprimatur of the reception committees – enlivened the receptions by mocking the very forms of public ritual so earnestly engaged in by the rest of the populace. In several places, groups calling themselves 'Calithumpians' or by other extraordinary names staged mock entries and processions, as well as other rituals, when the prince came to town. Their performances added to the carnivalesque atmosphere already present because of the crowding in the streets, the jubilation, the firecrackers, the pickpockets, and the organ grinders.

The Calathumpians of the Maritime provinces were active in both Halifax and Saint John during the royal tour. Taking their name from similar American groups, these performers came together on various public occasions in the mid-nineteenth century, never bothering to organize themselves into formal organizations and resisting the conventions of formal theatre troupes. In 1860 in Halifax, the Calithumpians mocked the pomposity of the prince's entry. The performers – who may have included some of the visiting sailors – got hold of a miserable, half-sinking barge, which they rowed *backwards* in the harbour during the regatta. Crammed to far beyond its safe capacity, it made a ridiculous sight as the Calithumpians replayed the landing of the prince in burlesque fashion. A couple of dozen men were dressed outrageously, with masks or make-up and crazy hats, some resembling crowns, some the cocked hats of naval officers, some the top hats of gentlemen, and still others wore working-class women's kerchiefs. One man in Highland tartans puffed at the bagpipes, another blew on a sort of tuba, a third, in black face, banged a tambourine, while a fellow dressed as a jester danced a jig. People enjoyed the performance, seeing it as good fun – in tune with the antics of the tars who cavorted nearby. The artist from New York covering the tour for *Frank Leslie's Illustrated Newspaper* captured the scene for the amusement of subscribers.[76]

In Saint John, the local Calathumpians mocked the civic procession before it took place. They chose to perform on the morning of the prince's arrival in town, turning out even before sunrise at the firing of a gun, thus rousing the people from their slumbers and getting the day off to an early start. 'They were dressed in every imaginable style,' said the *New Brunswick Reporter*, 'and to make their appearance more ridiculous, had their faces painted red, with very blue noses.' According to the Saint John *Morning Freeman*, their 'extravagant pantomime' depicted 'the volunteer movement in strange fantastic fashion.' They paraded through several of the main streets 'headed by a Scotch Piper,' and then halted at Reeds Point, where 'those who had guns fired a *feu de joi*, shortly after which they dispersed.'[77]

In Canada West, performers came out in the evening, taking advantage of the darkness and torchlights to enhance the effect of their absurd demonstrations. In Ottawa, a group calling themselves the Phisiocarnivalogicalists prepared ahead of time for their appearance during the prince's visit to the city. Well known and well organized locally, the 'Phisiogs' held a fund-raising concert at the Ottawa Theatre on 7 August in the hope that the proceeds would enable them to make a 'Grand Demonstration' upon the arrival of His Royal Highness. (One plan, apparently abandoned, was to hire a boat, go down the river, and escort the prince into town.) The Phisiogs ended up holding a torchlight procession through the central streets which stopped outside the prince's lodgings at the Victoria Hotel. These men mocked the fraternal orders that were so predominant in the official civic procession. They billed themselves as belonging to the 'tribes of the Illustrious Order of the Chloronophthelossossulphuricosso.' Their grand secretary, 'Acribino Ferdinandidido,' ordered all members to be present in full costume and mounted in readiness to present a 'degree of the third order.' 'Ottawa expects every man to do his duty,' he announced, concluding: 'God Save the Queen.' One report notes that the prince, who appeared at his hotel and watched the scene, took 'much interest in the strange "institution."' Dr Acland mentioned in a letter to his wife that, while the royal party was at a dinner party in the hotel, 'a great torch-

Spoofing the prince's entry to Halifax. The original caption reads in part: 'merry band of masqueraders and Calithumpians on a raft.' (*Frank Leslie's Illustrated Newspaper*, 18 August 1860)

light procession' had passed, 'with a Masquerade on horseback.' Included in the procession were 'sailors, cobblers, Indians of all kinds,' and the prince himself.'[78]

Local groups of Phisiogs also appeared in mock procession at Kingston and Belleville. Actually, the Phisiogs of Kingston had planned a ceremony of installation, believing that it was 'fitting that the Crown Prince of Great Britain should be entered on the roll of membership of a society which looks back with pride to "Brother Noah" and "Father Methuselah" in its associations.' No such ceremony was possible because the prince did not land at Kingston, but the disappointed crowds there and in Belleville were kept entertained on the evenings scheduled for his landings by the Phisiogs' processions. One of the local Kingston newspapers, the *British Whig*, feigning seriousness, explained the origins of this organization, which had been resuscitated for the occasion: 'The most Ancient Order of Antediluvian Phisiogs (so their phraseology runs) is an organization said to have had its origin in Normandy, and to have been transplanted to this country by the Norman French settlers of Lower Canada. The old French system of charivaries is considered to have been the primitive source from which the customs of the most Ancient Order were derived.' After dark, the Phisiogs gathered in each of the two towns and provided a substitute procession for the one the people had missed. 'The Phisiog Brass Band headed the cavalcade,' came the report from Kingston, and 'the Ethiopian Harmonists, Vulcan forging the bolts of Jove, sea monsters, and Phisiogs in every variety of indecorous dress made up the procession, which proceeded past Morton Wood and Alwington House, in front of which they described their antics.' Their appearance, said the *British Whig*, 'may be briefly disposed of as being a mixture of the infernal, ludicrous, and ridiculous, with a good share of fun.' A large crowd enjoyed the performance, everything passing off 'peaceably and good naturedly.'[79]

If we are to believe the spin put on these events by the press, there was nothing nasty about these performances. The *British Whig* alluded to the tradition of the charivari, but the cruelty that could be part of that custom is not evident in the reports of these bizarre demonstrations. The mockery was self-mockery, performers directing their barbs at members of their own community and, quite possibly, at themselves. Among the targets were pomposity and the seriousness with which residents were taking their encounter with the royal visitor. Inversion was certainly evident: daytime events transposed to the dark of night, men dressed as women, civilians as soldiers, whites as Ethiopians. Yet it is a stretch to see this behaviour as amounting to a challenge to the authority of the crown or even nose-thumbing at the prince and the monarchy. By appearing silly and being ludicrous, the performances lightened the tone of the events. And who among the civic promoters could object to that? It only enhanced the holiday atmosphere, the jubilation, the joy.

Thus, the royal entries made by the Prince of Wales and the processions following them drew attention to the places he visited in 1860 and made an occasion of his arrival in town. Some of the festive ceremonies came off better than others. The entry into the Province of Canada at Gaspé lacked the excitement of a large crowd and a built environment that structured and enhanced the prince's entries into the cities. Journalists described some of the entries in ways that delighted the civic promoters because their intended messages were conveyed. For example, Halifax was represented as a great outpost of empire, and Quebec as a historic meeting place of French and English. In other cases, impressions were conveyed inadvertently: through some mishaps, Saint John displayed its commercial acumen. Yet, one way or another, each place was tidily labelled, its essence encapsulated in the reports of the entry ceremonies. However repetitive the entry ceremonies became, each place was represented distinctively.

The processions dissected these images, theatrically portraying each locale as an amalgam of social groups. Variations occurred from city to city, depending upon the make-up of the voluntary societies locally. In Saint John the firemen made remarkable displays, in Brantford it was the Six Nations Iroquois, and in Toronto the African-Canadian abolitionists drew attention, though the Toronto Orangemen – by their absence – stood out above all other groups. Those who enjoyed the right to ceremonial citizenship usually dominated the scene everywhere, but, without the spectators and the civic backdrop, the pageantry would have fallen utterly flat. The women especially, by throwing their bouquets and charming glances and by waving their handkerchiefs, played a crucial and complementary role to the ceremonially enfranchised men.

In the United States, the rhetoric of the American parade – including ones got up for the prince (as we will later see) – represented the voluntary societies and militia companies that marched on ceremonial occasions as being superb examples of democracy in action. They were *demos* triumphant, organized, and disciplined. Historians of the American parade have echoed this interpretation. Mary Ryan argues that ceremonial citizenship 'was the work of groups, not individuals; it displayed association as well as differences. The power of people in association will explain much of the vitality and the democracy of civic culture in the antebellum period.'[80] In the British North American provinces, groups likewise demonstrated the vitality of civic culture in 1860. But they did so without commentators referring to democracy. Instead, the displays were about the loyalty of subjects, a fervent, participatory aspect of provincial life under the crown. Ceremonial citizenship – an appropriate label for activities both north and south of the border – was represented differently in the monarchical provinces than it was in the American republic.

4

Princely Duties, Princely Pleasures

What transports the Canadian will evince
When they behold our youthful Prince!
Not ours alone, but also theirs,
Each colony with England shares
In Protestant Sophia's heirs.

How all the bells will ring, the cannons roar!
And they who never saw a Prince before,
Oh, won't they feast him and caress him!
  Waylay him and address him,
  His royal Highness – bless him! –
Their demonstrations possibly may bore.

'Ode on the Departure of the
Prince of Wales,' *Punch* (1860)[1]

In 1860 the civic promoters of the royal tour faced the host's perennial problem: what to do with your guest once a warm welcome has been given and accepted. Reception committees arranged such a busy – and repetitive – round of activities to keep the Prince of Wales occupied that he was in danger of being overworked. 'There is an awful amount of work laid out for the Prince during the coming week,' wrote the correspondent for the New York *Times* from Montreal. 'He is to look at Indians, go on steamboat excursions, hear and deliver addresses, attend musical festivals, open balls, and witness torchlight processions, regattas and firemen's musters. He is to present silver trumpets and gold medals, and award prizes at various races and exhibitions, besides dining on several occasions with big wigs innumerable.' And to make matters worse, there was a worrying sameness to all the civic programs. The Fredericton *Head Quarters* maintained that the repetitive programs amounted to 'one of the most serious conspiracies ... that [had] ever happened beneath the skies of the western hemisphere; it is nothing more or less than a scheme to bore a Prince of the Blood Royal – the heir presumptive to the British Throne – to death!'[2]

These festivities raised issues about recognition, ones that were posed even more acutely, as we will later see, in connection with First Nations and Orangemen. Who would gain royal recognition? In what order of precedence would they be acknowledged? Who would gain special honours? Which individuals, activities, and organizations would meet with royal favour? Such matters were of great interest locally because reputations might be either confirmed or not, and social divisions might be seen to be either meaningful or not. As it happened, the social dividing line that the festivities most emphasized was the one between the sexes. At the levees, the militia reviews, and the sporting events, men took centre stage; only at the dances did women gain the limelight.

Levees and Knighthoods

After the prince was received by civic officials upon his entry to their cities, reciprocity demanded that he host a levee, where people could be formally introduced to him. Residents were familiar with this ceremonial form thanks to the annual levees hosted by the colonial governors on New Year's Day – a tradition that has survived into the twenty-first century. After conferring with the queen, Newcastle informed the governors about the arrangements for the levees to be hosted by the Prince of Wales. The formalities would be the same as those at the levees held by the prince consort in England, where gentlemen passed and bowed and there was no 'kissing of hands.' Because the prince had not reached the age of majority, women could not be presented to him.[3] Court dress would not be required. The colonial secretary saw the levees as an opportunity for as many men as possible to meet the prince, and thus as an important means to enhance popular interest in the visit and strengthen the bonds of empire. In a private letter, Newcastle expressed his delight that the queen had agreed to allow 'great latitude,' which he thought 'very politic' and could 'do the Prince no harm.'[4]

The civic promoters did not necessarily share the colonial secretary's enthusiasm for the inclusive levee. Formal attire at levees added to the pageantry and signalled the polish that colonial cities had acquired, at the same time as it screened out riff-raff who might be an embarrassment. The reporter for the *Times*, when commenting on the levees in New Brunswick, approved of a formal dress code, saying that 'there was no limit to the number of those who wished to go, but there was a decided limit to the number of dress coats in the Province, and the Levees were thus kept down.'[5] Notwithstanding dress requirements, some of the levees were huge. In Montreal the prince greeted 2,000 people, thus demonstrating, it was said, his 'iron constitution.'[6]

Newspapers covered the first few levees closely. The one at St John's was held at Government House. Those 'gentlemen' wishing to be presented had to pass through a series of rooms, each a little less packed and chaotic than the previous one, so that by the time they reached the prince, there was at least a semblance of order. The correspondent of the Toronto *Globe* described the 'very promiscuous crowd': 'Lawyers, doctors, judges, soldiers, bishops, naval officers, editors, volunteers and civilians; long and short, stout and thin, of intelligent looks, of stupid looks, of humble bearing, or of manifestly quiet self-importance. There they were, all wedged together, anxious to render personal homage to the Prince.'[7] In the main reception room, His Royal Highness stood behind a brass rail, with the premier of Newfoundland and the members of his suite ranged to his right. The card of each man wishing to be presented was first handed to the equerry nearest the door, and then passed to the Earl St Germains, who, bowing to the prince, read aloud the name. The prince bowed to each man, who bowed in return and then passed through the exit.

The prince won universal praise for his conduct on these occasions. According to the correspondent of the *Times*, he spoke 'with his royal mother's clear distinctiveness and proper emphasis that made every word as audible as though he spoke in a room to half-a-dozen listeners.'[8] He enhanced his popularity by being considerate and receiving all comers no matter how long the queue. Newcastle had told the queen after the tour of the Atlantic colonies that the prince 'is always kind and amiable to those who are presented to Him though necessarily many of them present few attractions to one of His position. It is impossible that so much state and ceremony should not weary Him, but He does not allow Himself to shew it.' Of course, the prince was freer to express his views in his letters home, and he occasionally did so, as when he commented on the levee in Ottawa, 'to which few people came.' Even they, he added 'were not of a very good stamp.'[9]

Journalists did their best to enliven their accounts of the levees. The special correspondent for the New York *Daily Tribune* struggled to amuse his readers when writing about the levee at Hamilton, where he saw 'officers in uniform, clergymen in gowns, and red Indians in nothing at all but paint.' He told the story, possibly apocryphal, of one of the 'sharp men of business' who, instead of handing over the appropriate card with his name clearly marked, presented a business card bearing 'this strange device: "Try Horning's Mills, where you will find a Varied Assortment of Dry Goods and Groceries, selected expressly for this Market, by ____, sole agent."' His card was rejected.[10]

The presentation of the addresses sparked the odd controversy. In its never-ending campaign to stir up English Canada against French Canada, the Toronto *Globe* strongly objected when at Quebec the mayor, the Roman Catholic bishops, and the authorities of Laval University all read their addresses first in French and only subsequently in English. Meantime, *L'Ordre*, the Montreal Rouge paper, complained about the bad French translation of the Legislative Assembly's address. (The Rouge newspaper blamed the Bleu ministers, Cartier, Cauchon, and Langevin, for butchering the thing.) One shuddered to think what His Royal Highness – who spoke perfect French – would make of such bad French that 'it could pass for Iroquois.'[11]

Levees gave rise to intense conflicts over matters of precedence. Local government officials fussed over who should go first: mayors, wardens of counties, or sheriffs.[12] In Quebec, the lawyers fumed when they learned that the magistrates were to be presented before themselves, and that the magistrates' address was to be read aloud and replied to, while that of the bar was simply to be handed to the prince. The members of the district bar voted to refrain from participating altogether.[13] In response to irritants like these, the colonial secretary wrote to his prime minister, Lord Palmerston, saying in exasperation: 'The labor to keep small jealousies and personal rivalries from interfering with the general good will has been very great.'[14]

The biggest controversies arose over the precedence of clergy of the various denominations. Not only was the status of each denomination at stake, but wounds from old, interdenominational disputes were irritated. Anglican leaders in the provinces saw the royal visit as an opportunity to reclaim momentarily the superior status their church

Gentleman being presented to the prince at the levee held in Government House, Halifax. In this illustration, the colonial setting successfully replicates the lavishness of the imperial court. (*Illustrated London News*, 1 September 1860)

had earlier enjoyed as an established church; the relevant imperial policy, which was based on the status of churches in England, gave the Anglicans precedence.[15]

Quebec provided one flashpoint for religious conflict. When the municipal authorities (who were mostly French Canadians and Roman Catholic) placed the Catholic bishops at the head of the list, Protestant critics, including Governor Head, objected, maintaining that the Anglican bishop should have precedence in a British colony. The Roman Catholic hierarchy was reluctant to concede the precedence given it, claiming rights going back to the Quebec Act of 1774 and pointing out that their church was Quebec's largest. Eventually, the matter was finessed by having the Anglican bishop take a place alongside the prince as though part of the official suite, and assigning the Roman Catholic bishops the top position among those being presented to the prince. The Anglican bishop's address was read and replied to at the levee, while that of the Catholic bishops was presented and replied to when the prince honoured the church by visiting its university, Laval. The Fredericton *Reporter* believed the 'sectarian question' had thus been disposed of by this 'ingenious contrivance.' However, the Anglican clergy remained annoyed because, while their bishop took his place beside the prince, the other Anglican divines had been assigned a place behind the Roman Catholic bishops and clergy. Rather than take that place, they refused to attend the reception.[16]

Developments in Montreal pushed non-conformists into high gear. First, the city authorities neglected to invite the clergy of several dissenting churches to participate in the procession. In response, clergy from the Methodist, Baptist, Presbyterian, and other denominations wrote the governor complaining not only that a wrong had been done to them but that His Royal Highness had been misled as to the 'actual state of religious opinion in the City of Montreal.'[17] Secondly, when the Reverend Dr Mathieson, moderator of the Presbyterian Church, arrived at the Montreal levee and went to read the church's address to the prince, Governor Head stopped him, saying that the moderator could only hand in the address. Mathieson refused to do so, thinking it an insult, especially since he had just heard the Anglicans' address and the reply to it. 'There was no time for Presbyterians,' stormed the *Globe*, 'but ample time for Episcopalians.' Governor Head was practising 'the most reckless tyranny.'[18]

The Quebec levee stood out from the rest because of a special ceremony: the conferring of knighthoods. At the same time that the two houses of the Canadian legislature were to honour the prince with their addresses, he in turn would honour the legislature by knighting the speakers of the two chambers. Not only were these the only knighthoods given during the tour, they were both the first ever knighthoods conferred by the prince and the first ever conferred in Canada. The queen had decided that the prince would do the honours in Quebec,[19] and so letters patent were issued making Albert Edward 'Viceroy of all the North American colonies.'[20]

It was no accident that, in recognizing the two speakers, the prince was honouring a French Canadian from Canada East and an English Canadian from Canada West. By 1860, such political balancing was central to politics under the Union of 1841. Narcisse Belleau, the speaker of the Legislative Council, had first been appointed to that office by the Macdonald-Cartier government in 1857 because the Conservatives had wanted to strengthen their presence in Quebec. Belleau was a prominent lawyer, the president of the city's main railway project (the North Shore Railway), and a reforming mayor of Quebec in the period 1848–53. (At Confederation in 1867 he would become lieutenant–governor of the new Province of Quebec and the first French Canadian to represent the British crown.) Henry Smith, the speaker of the Legislative Assembly, had represented Frontenac County since 1841. A Kingston lawyer, Smith was a close friend and political ally of John A. Macdonald in the 1840s and 1850s. It will be recalled that in 1859 Smith had gone to England with the Canadian legislature's petition that led to the royal visit. Smith had expected to be immediately honoured with a knighthood, and when he was not, he blamed his Conservative colleagues back home, a dispute that eventually took him into the Reform party. For Smith, the knighthood given at Quebec came too late.[21]

In describing the ceremony where the prince did the honours, certain journalists lavishly embroidered their accounts, most notably Walter Harker of the *Globe* and E.H. House of the New York *Times*.[22] Both writers played up the elaborateness of the proceedings, making them appear preposterous. In describing the arrival in the chamber of the speaker and members of the Legislative Council, House wrote: 'The door opened and a queer little man in tight tights, a wig, dress-coat and pumps walked hastily in, holding on his left arm a black wand tipped with gold.' This fellow had been selected to be usher,

Harker joked, because he was 'the only man the Province c[ould] produce who really knows how to make a courtly bow – a bow that cannot be mistaken for a nod; an unmistakable bow paining onlookers, penetrating them with fear lest the little man should overstep his mark and fall prostrate on the floor.' The entry of the speaker of the assembly was announced by another usher who, according to the report of the New York *Times*, 'popped in like a puppet, wiggled his left leg, and squirmed his body like a snake for about half a minute, and then bowing once, advanced a foot, bowing twice, proceeded another twelve inches, and doing it again came to a pause, and announced Mr. Speaker of the Lower House.' In came Henry Smith, walking, said Harker, 'as stately as he could, his long black satin tail dragging behind; his shoe-buckles shining before; his Valenciennes ruffles waving slightly like the comb on the skull of a Cochin China rooster; and his face flushed as though he had been taking an incidental drink – or two.' Then followed the assemblymen. 'Never did any set of men bear with less grace a courtly uniform,' says Harker. 'The Toronto firemen would expel from their brigade any of their members who should look as awkward.'

When it came time for Henry Smith to kneel, writes Howard, 'he dropped upon both knees in a most ridiculous and absurd manner, causing a smile to pass over the face of His Royal Highness and making the scene a painful one for all beholders.' The *Globe* correspondent feigned concern that Smith would ever be able to rise from the floor. 'I thought of Sir John Falstaff's "Have you got any levers to lift me up again?"' Sir Henry – for that was his new designation – managed to rise well enough, but in attempting to back away from the prince, he shuffled awkwardly and tripped repeatedly on his gown. At last the speaker gave up and swept out of the room, 'his stern to the throne.' Everyone breathed a sigh of relief since the manoeuvring had 'not resulted in the catastrophe that all expected.'

Though both newspapers lampooned the ceremonies at Government House, the *Globe*, unlike the New York *Times*, never directly challenged the idea of royalty's conferring titles in Canada. Rather than tackling this monarchical tradition, the Reform *Globe* preferred to spoof, in partisan fashion, the Conservatives being knighted and the Conservative ministry behind the event.[23] For the New York *Times*, however, the very idea of titles was offensive, especially in North America, where they signified a dusty past best left behind in the Old

World. In an editorial entitled 'Rise Sir Cannuck-Cannuck,' the New York *Times* railed at the 'ridiculous erection of an aristocracy through the Prince's granting titles in Canada.' The ceremonies in Quebec were 'truly a curious drama ... to enact in our Democratic Nineteenth century world!'[24] In fact, it would be a half-century more before the conferring of titles on Canadians would be officially discouraged. This particular aspect of monarchy remained a sought-after symbol of recognition in Canada, not least of all by many politicians. Canadian readers of the New York *Times* in 1860 might well have wondered whether its lampooning of 'Sir Cannuck-Cannuck' did not contain an element of envy.

Openings

During his stay in British North America, the Prince of Wales formally inaugurated two parks and one public garden, a waterworks, and a provincial exhibition, in addition to laying the foundation stone of the new Parliament buildings in Ottawa and, of course, opening the Victoria Bridge. The inauguration of the mighty bridge and the other openings turned out to be stiff and dreary ceremonials. Journalists spoke frankly about the dullness of the inaugurations. In an editorial, the Fredericton *Head Quarters* surveyed the programs prepared by reception committees and wondered whether the prince would not be '*inaugurated* to death!' Nathaniel Woods of the London *Times* never stopped griping about the tedium of the inaugurations. 'The ceremony of laying a foundation stone,' he wrote from Ottawa, 'is, of course, like opening a bridge (which has been traversed for months), or inaugurating waterworks, or any other meagre and unsatisfactory State ceremonial which Royalty is occasionally compelled to endure in deference to public feeling.'[25]

Journalists brought some accounts of the inaugurations to life by telling a good story with a punchline. Take, for example, the report filed by Kinahan Cornwallis for the New York *Herald* on the opening of a park in Fredericton. 'The day was very hot,' he began, 'and there was little shelter from the vivid rays of the sun.' In a large viewing stand, several hundred school children 'were anxiously undergoing the baking process.' Thousands of other spectators milled about in the heat, waiting for the prince to appear. Eventually, His Royal Highness arrived and the ceremonies began. According to the script, the events were to climax with the prince turning on the water for a new fountain, the jet of water soaring high into the clear blue sky. When the prince drew the plug, however, a meagre trickle spread onto the ground. Everyone wondered what had gone wrong. 'Lo and behold, it was discovered that the thirsty multitude of spectators had drank nearly all the water out of the tank which supplied the fountain.'[26]

Even the centrepiece of the visit – the inauguration of the Victoria Bridge – strained journalists' powers of description. Woods of the *Times* said that it was a dull event, but he attempted to interest his readers by evoking the eerie scene as the prince and others went by train to the middle of the tubular structure, where the rivet-driving ceremony was to take place. 'The bridge,' he wrote, 'bellowed and rumbled like thunder as the train progressed, and the opening by which it had entered grew smaller and smaller till it only shone faintly in the distance like a pale blue star.' After the passengers scrambled out of the train, they 'stood listening with a feeling almost of awe as the hoarse sustained rumble of the engine moving away went echoing up and down the dark tube, which seemed to sway and vibrate as the noise went rolling on backwards and forwards, striving for escape from its hollow iron prison.'[27] Other journalists opted for a lighter mood when they described the same event. The correspondent of the Saint John *Morning Freeman* poked fun at the elaborate arrangements for screening the spectators: 'There were platform tickets admitting the holders to one place; blue and purple tickets giving the right to a seat on the causeway, under a fierce burning sun; gold tickets admitting to the cars, and to the platform where the prince was to lay the last stone; and other tickets admitting to the dejeuner.' Many of those who thought they had tickets to see all the formalities were sorely disappointed when they were allowed to go no farther. 'There was great order and regularity,' observed the writer, 'and much sweating and mortification.' The special correspondent of the Saint John *Morning News* mocked the antics of 'the ladies' who, while guests were preoccupied with the luncheon, 'stripped bare the site of the bridge inaugural, grabbing at the flowers, evergreens, gold fringe, and other decorations, as memorials of the occasion.'[28]

Controversy could also spice up a story. Journalists had something to talk about in connection with the costly preparations surrounding the laying of the foundation stone of the Parliament Buildings because of the involvement – or rather, non-involvement – of the Freemasons.

The Prince of Wales laying the foundation stone of the Parliament Buildings in Ottawa. Although the props were impressive, the ceremony was simple. (*Illustrated London News*, 13 October 1860)

In Canada it was customary for Masons to open Protestant churches and public buildings and it was expected that they would participate in Ottawa.[29] Then suddenly, on the eve of the event, it was reported that the Duke of Newcastle was refusing to permit the prince to share the platform with Masons dressed in their regalia. The Masons decided that, if they could not fulfil their usual role, dressed in their robes, they would not attend the ceremonies as a group.[30] The Montreal *Pilot* spoke for many when it maintained that the Duke was wisely taking a firm and consistent line against all secret societies in an effort to bolster his position, then just emerging, on the Orangemen. 'Surely after this,' editorialized the *Pilot*, 'the members of the Orange Society cannot find fault with the Duke.' (Wishful thinking, as it turned out!) Meantime, the *Globe* tried to whip up Protestant feeling in Canada West by claiming that the Masons had been grossly insulted by the Roman Catholic Church since it 'permits none of her sons to be Masons, and, as a matter of course, must have objected to the connection of the order with a ceremony in which Catholics were to take part.'[31] The actual ceremony, which was conducted by John Morris, clerk of the works, and Samuel Keefer, the engineer, was a brief affair, as the prince stressed when writing home: 'The ceremony was a very short one and did not last above 20 minutes.'[32] So much for the grandeur and the political complexity of the occasion!

Volunteers and Veterans

From the moment that the idea of the 1860 tour had been broached, military matters had been part of the mix. As we have seen, Queen Victoria had agreed to send her son partly as a way to acknowledge Canadian contributions to British mobilization in the Crimea and at the time of the Indian Mutiny and to encourage more of the same in future. Moreover, the visit provided an opportunity to popularize the volunteer movement, which was just getting off the ground in British North America, as it was in the British Isles. In England, the threat of a French invasion in 1859 prompted nearly 160,000 artisans, clerks, and middle-class young men to join the volunteer movement.[33] Also in 1859, the authorities in the Maritime colonies sought and won approval for creating volunteer forces.[34] In the case of the Province of Canada, the initiative had come a few years earlier, during the Crimean War, when patriotism ran high and British garrisons in the province were seriously stripped of men. The Canadian Militia Act of 1855 introduced a new volunteer force of militia who would be trained through regular drilling.[35] Smart uniforms, parade-ground displays, and a club-like atmosphere would make the volunteer militia units attractive to a better class of men eager to strut their stuff.

From the start, the Duke of Newcastle, in his capacity as colonial secretary, had planned to use the opportunity presented by the royal tour to boost the volunteer movement in the colonies. British taxpayers and successive British governments had long hoped that the burden of colonial defence might be assumed by the colonies, especially where they had demanded and been granted a measure of self-government, as was the case in Canada and the Maritime colonies. Though colonial taxpayers and governments had resisted this particular devolution of power, the writing was on the wall.[36] Shortly before leaving England for St John's, Newcastle had written Governor General Head, and the lieutenant governors in the Atlantic colonies urging that during the tour they 'shew off your volunteers as much as possible.' He reasoned: 'As the real Military defence of the Country must, in case of war, devolve upon them, any compliment which can give an impetus to the spirit of self protection would be well placed.'[37] From Newcastle's perspective, encouraging the volunteer movement was about relieving the imperial treasury of a substantial cost and freeing regular troops for duty elsewhere.

Early in the tour, the prince was made to understand the importance of encouraging the volunteer movement. After leaving Newfoundland, the *Hero* stopped off at Sydney, Nova Scotia, to refuel, taking on a supply of locally mined coal. When the royal suite paid a surprise visit to the town, all the men were working down the mine about one hundred fathoms below the sea. The call went out that the prince would inspect the volunteers, all work stopped, and the men rushed home to change before mustering for inspection. Albert Edward explained to his mother that the review had taken place because 'the Duke is always very anxious that I should see the Volunteers on every occasion so as to give them as much encouragement as possible, because he says it is very important that the inhabitants of the Colonies should understand that they must have some troops for their own defence, which hitherto they have been very slow in comprehending.' While the volunteers at Sydney were disadvantaged because they were new recruits and had been surprised by the royal inspection, they passed muster. The prince gravely told his mother that he thought 'the Volunteers ... looked very well & after more drilling will form a very efficient body.'[38]

British North Americans had their own reasons for wanting to show off their volunteers. By putting on a big display, the provincials just might persuade the British that they had done enough and should not be called upon to spend more. Volunteers jumped at the chance to parade in front of the prince, their officers proved equally eager to hobnob with the distinguished visitors, and the recognition was welcome, too. During the royal tour, newspapers, like the Halifax *Constitutionalist*, presented the local volunteers as 'a body of able, trained and effective men, ready and willing to strike a blow in Nova Scotia's defence; men who have responded with manly ardor to this call upon their patriotism.' On the occasion of the royal celebrations, it was only fitting that these local defenders of empire take a prominent part. Moreover, their bands, uniforms, and artillery would lend colour and pomp to the celebrations. The only catch was that the newly organized troops were insufficiently practised.[39]

Orders from the commanders set out the various duties that volunteers were to play in the festivities during the royal tour. The governor general, who was commander-in-chief of the volunteers, issued an official order from Quebec on 18 August setting out the duties of specific companies. In Montreal, for instance, the Volunteer Field Battery was ordered to fire royal salutes on the prince's landing and departure, as well as at the ceremony at the Victoria Bridge; the city's Volunteer Cavalry were to provide an escort and any orderlies needed. A guard of honour consisting of 100 men was to be formed by taking 'in equal numbers from each company of the 1st Battalion, Volunteer Rifles, Canada.' The remaining volunteers were commanded to 'line the streets at such places as may be deemed most expedient by the Commandant, and ... present arms as His Royal Highness passes.' And, finally, the whole of the volunteer force was told to 'hold themselves in readiness to be inspected during the Prince's visit at Montreal.'[40] In rural areas, volunteers were told to congregate at chief railway stations along the prince's route. Wherever they came out 'in full force,' the prince would inspect them.[41]

The press took note of the volunteers' contributions to the festivities. From Pictou, Nova Scotia, for instance, the correspondent for the Halifax *Constitutionalist* reported that two companies of volunteers from the Albion Mines formed the prince's guard of honour, while the Pictou Artillery Company fired the royal salute.[42] Upon the departure of the prince from Quebec, the Ottawa *Citizen* described the volunteers – their brass bands, firing parties, cavalry brigades, and flying batteries 'with their bright brass six pounders ... coming through St Louis Street.'[43] In Cobourg, security during the ball was provided by the Cobourg Cavalry, 'dressed in their scarlet coats and bright brass helmets, holding drawn swords, ready to "do to the death" any intruder.'[44] Their counterparts at nearby Port Hope did not get as good press. The Ottawa *Union* charged that the Port Hope volunteers had fired 'salutes not only of 21 guns, but of at least twice 21, with the utmost disregard of the ordinary rules of sponging and ramming, and a complete indifference to the consequent peril.'[45]

The volunteers came into their own when the prince reviewed them, and nowhere was this more the case than near the citadel in Halifax, where both the volunteers and the regulars were featured. Some twenty thousand spectators streamed onto the grassy slope and viewing stands. 'Ladies, who dressed in gay summer clothes, much enhanced the brilliancy of the scene.' But most of the attention focused on the 1,100 volunteers from the city of Halifax, 'careful and steady in their discipline, neat and handsome in their uniform and equipments.'[46] As His Royal Highness, mounted on a fine horse, rode past the double line of troops, each volunteer and regular presented arms. According to the *Globe*, the prince examined them 'with great attention and evidently with much pleasure.' Next, the troops were drilled, and the commentators agreed that any difference in precision between the regulars and the volunteers was 'imperceptible.' The companies several times 'charged at imaginary enemies with a vigour which gave earnest to what they would do had they really somebody to fight.' The stirring sight 'spoke of Great Britain's power and ... told of the real strength of the Empire, of the love which is borne to it by the subjects of the Queen, of the determination of all to stand by it in the hour of trial, firmly, faithfully, and bravely.' As an American, Kinahan Cornwallis of the New York *Herald*, was rather less carried away, but he admired both the 'imposing appearance' of the Halifax troops and the 'picturesque effect' of the display. Woods, of the *Times* gave the Halifax volunteers his highest praise, saying: 'Very many of them indeed are equal to the picked companies of the best volunteer regiments in London.'[47] The prince told his mother that the review was 'a very pretty one and went off very successfully.' As in the reports by the journalists covering the event, his account remarked on the presence of a corps of

Blacks: 'One of the Companies was formed of Negroes, which had a very curious effect.'[48]

No other review of volunteers stood up to the splendid show at Halifax. Quebec had no review, though the city boasted some eight hundred volunteers, provoking speculation that Quebec authorities did not want to compete with the Halifax volunteers.[49] At Montreal there was a full-scale review, with drills and charges, but its impact fell short. Woods quipped that members of one company of artillery looked like they had 'escaped from some minor theatre.' The *Globe*'s report was remarkably bland and neutral, given that an event had flopped in rival Montreal. No doubt the Toronto journalists were prudently anticipating what was to come: that the greener troops in their own city would do even less well. Indeed, Woods was dismissive of the display by the troops in Toronto, where the parade ground was 'little better than a dilapidated watercourse,' and 'the spectators under *parapluies* looked as muddy and damp as a group of fungi.'[50]

Notwithstanding the comparative success of the volunteers' display at Halifax, it was there that the local press voiced sharp criticisms concerning neglect and mistreatment of the volunteers by the authorities. In the Halifax *Constitutionalist*, a letter to the editor, signed 'A Volunteer,' complained that during the procession in the Nova Scotian capital, the volunteers, unlike the regulars, had been 'stowed away in the narrowest part of Water Street.' While various officers in the military establishment had been invited and given tickets to the grand ball, the officers of the volunteer companies had had to pay their own way. When ordered to duty at Windsor, the Halifax volunteers found that no one had arranged for refreshments or a resting place for them.[51]

Probably in response to such criticisms, greater efforts were made to recognize the volunteers. After the review at Fredericton, the prince, through the Duke of Newcastle, wrote the volunteer officers not only complimenting them on their performance but also flattering them with the promise that 'he should himself make honorable mention of the troop to his Mother, the Queen.' Major Wilmot, who led a cavalry troop, was honoured by a personal invitation to dine with His Royal Highness on the evening of the review. Moreover, a few days later the lieutenant governor announced that the prince would present a 'Challenge Cup,' to be competed for every year, as a prize for marksmanship among the New Brunswick volunteers, and he committed the government to paying for ammunition used by the volunteers during target practice. The prince specially honoured the Montreal rifles, who had travelled far with him and provided a guard of honour. It was widely reported that, while in London, Canada West, His Royal Highness had given Colonel Wily's First Regiment of the Volunteer Rifles the privilege of calling itself the 'Prince of Wales Regiment,' or the 'Prince's Own.' (The royal name was not only a mark of prestige but also unique among volunteer corps at the time, the Rifles gaining the status of a regiment.) The special correspondent of the New York *Times* observed that the announcement 'had caused great excitement in military circles, and as I write the guard are in front of the prince's window, and their band are serenading him – a compliment which he has graciously acknowledged.'[52]

In the end, the attention that the volunteers expected and got during the tour from the press, the public, and the prince encouraged recruitment in the way that Newcastle had intended. Certainly, enlistments increased in the wake of the visit, although this was also a result of the coming of the Civil War in the United States. A year after the prince's visit, a newspaper commented on the way Toronto's young bloods had been 'seized with a very ardent military fever.' The population as a whole was said to be fascinated by the drilling, and a visit to the parade ground to watch the marching had become a popular summer evening stroll.[53]

The centrepiece of the military display during the prince's visit to Canada West was supposed to be on the Niagara peninsula at Queenston, the 1812 battleground where the very soil had been 'laved and fertilized with the crimson tide of our ancient defenders.' By his presence at Queenston, the prince would lend majesty to a tradition, a particular version of Upper Canadian history – or so the organizers hoped. Their ambitious plans had several components: the presentation to the prince of an address by the surviving veterans of the War of 1812; the completion by the prince of the reconstructed monument commemorating the heroic leadership in 1812 of General (Sir Isaac) Brock; the raising by the prince of an obelisk marking the spot on the heights at Queenston where the general fell in battle; and a review of scores of volunteer and militia companies from across the province. Indeed, supporters hoped that the visit would be the occasion for the province's first giant review of the volunteers, one modelled on recent successful reviews in Great Britain. (The local papers described reviews that summer made by the queen of some 18,000 troops in London and 20,000 Scottish volunteers in Edinburgh.[54]) When the St Catharines *Post* declared that 'the Duke of Newcastle will be gratified with the sight of at least 10,000 uniformed officers and men, horse, foot, and artillery, encamped around the base of Brock's Monument,' it was expressing the hope that a brilliant spectacle would announce, to a watching world Upper Canada's proud militia tradition. What's more, concentrating the military display at Queenston would make it not only bigger but *'national.'*[55]

As it turned out, there was insufficient organization and support for a giant review at Queenston. The fact that towns and cities wanted their own shows, as part of their competitive municipal celebrations, undercut the Queenston review. It is possible, too, that Upper Canadians were not as deeply committed to the Upper Canadian militia tradition as McNab and other old officers imagined them to be. Certainly, practical difficulties stood in the way of participation. For many an ordinary volunteer, the trip to Niagara was too expensive and too time-consuming, especially since it was harvest time. As a result, the show at Queenston fell quite flat.

At the Brock Monument, just two companies of volunteers stood on either side of the platform, and between them were the veterans, about one hundred twenty of them, dressed for the most part in 'a blue uniform with steel epaulettes and glazed caps.'[56] Upon the arrival of the Prince of Wales, the old gentlemen saluted with their swords. The address, which had been prepared by well-known veterans,[57] and signed by as many survivors as possible, trumpeted both the veterans' own role in 'the successful resistance' against 'the invading enemy' and that of 'the lamented hero Brock.' The general's 'gallant and generous heart shrunk not in the darkest hour of the conflict from the most discouraging odds,' and his 'example inspired the few with the ability and spirit to do the work of many.' When the colonial secretary wrote the prince's reply, he was thinking as a politician, his main concern being to ensure that the prince did not offend the Americans. 'Every nation may without offence to its neighbours commemorate its heroic deeds,' the prince declared. 'This is no taunting boast of victory, no revival of long passed animosities – but an honourable tribute to a soldier's fame.' The reply even went so far as to insist that this tribute was 'the more honourable because we readily acknowledge the bravery and chivalry of that people by whose act [Brock] fell.' No newspaper dared to ask how such a reply sat with the veterans. According to the *Globe*, only moments before the address and reply, the veterans in the crowd had been overheard to be indulging in comments 'by no means complimentary to the citizens of the United States,' and the reporter added, 'Your old veteran is no republican.'[58]

One special 'veteran' of 1812 had signed the address along with the men: Laura Secord, the Upper Canadian heroine of the Niagara district. Although advanced in years (she was eighty five in 1860), Secord had made her way to the office of the clerk of the peace at Niagara a month before the prince's arrival; there, she insisted on signing the address, notwithstanding the objections of the clerk. A local newspaper supported her forwardness, saying that after all she had 'done her country more signal service during the war than half the soldiers and militiamen engaged in it.'[59] Secord had also demonstrated wherewithal by sending to Quebec a petition addressed to the prince and informing him about the patriotic wartime service she (and her late husband) had rendered the British army in 1812.[60] After his return to England, the prince sent Mrs Secord £100 in gold, the only financial reward she ever received for her service. The gesture won her benefactor recognition in the press at the time. 'The Prince of Wales is a true, gallant Prince,' declared the Niagara *Mail*, 'with a warm regard for the old ladies as well as for the young ones.'[61] This petition, the prince's gift, and the press reports helped establish a narrative tradition of female heroism that would flourish in later decades.[62]

After His Royal Highness replied to the veterans' address at Queenston, he climbed to the top of the Brock Monument where he raised a flag, 'completing' the rebuilt structure – which had in fact been formally opened a year earlier. On a nearby grassy slope, the prince spread mortar on the pedestal and watched an obelisk descend to mark permanently the spot where Brock fell. To his side, and holding a Union Jack, stood 'Ensign Doyle,' a grandson of a soldier who fell at the battle of Queenston, and 'Adjutant Green,' who carried the banner of the First Battalion, York Volunteers. The event was soon over, the prince immediately sought his carriage, and a few minutes later he boarded the *Zimmerman*, bound for a holiday at Niagara Falls. The *Times* referred to the Queenston display as being a 'rather meagre ceremony,' and the author of a letter-to-the-editor of the *Globe* called it a 'most higgledy-piggledy affair.' The *Globe* poked fun at the 'new, spick and span regiments' that showed up for the event, noting the oversupply of officers and their inexperience.[63] According to the same writer, the veterans themselves were justifiably disappointed and felt slighted. Some elderly gentlemen had travelled as much as three hundred miles, hoping for more 'than a march up the hill, and a march down again.' The Queenston event was a far cry from the volunteer displays of London and Edinburgh and inadvertently demonstrated the Canadians' limited commitment to military preparedness. As such, it accurately conveyed what has proven to be an ongoing tension in Canadian culture: flights of military fancy brought to earth by a tough-minded reluctance to pay.

Games People Play

Sporting events either featured in the official program or were appended to it in several cities visited by the prince. Not central to the official ceremonies, the games and regattas nevertheless enhanced the holiday atmosphere and provided crowds and journalists alike with spectacles to view and make the most of. The prince chose to watch some of the games, apparently enjoying a diversion from the tedious routines of the formal levees and military reviews.

Where there was time in the program, reception committees had their own reasons for promoting sporting events during the prince's stay in town. Responsibility for organizing regattas and games could be conveniently delegated to the executives of existing sporting clubs – reliably upper-middle-class men in the mid-Victorian period. Reception committees only needed to donate cash prizes to attract participants, and it was money well spent. Crowds that had assembled for the royal entry could be kept occupied by more or less structured, respectable activities suitable for large numbers of spectators, men, women, and children alike. With a little luck, the weather would be fine and newspapers would praise the local sporting talent, the splendid arrangements, and the picturesque scene.

On the second day of his North American tour, the prince made an appearance at the regatta held on Quidi Vidi Lake, just outside St John's. Although it occupied the prince only briefly, the regatta was reported to have entertained 10,000 Newfoundlanders, many of them visiting from the outports and looking for something to do. Good times were had in the many colourful booths erected 'to accommodate the multitude' by selling 'eatables and drinkables.' The *Globe* reporter wryly observed that from these booths, later in the day, there came 'sounds of merriment, which proved that His Royal Highness's health had been enthusiastically drunk.'[64] The rowing races were the focus of interest, sturdy rowboats and skilful oarsmen being easy to come by in the vicinity of St John's. There were separate races for whale-boat crews, men from Her Majesty's ships, tradesmen, amateurs, and juveniles, with prizes ranging from $5 to $25. The special correspondent for the New York *Herald* reported that 'the races were not particularly interesting or well contested,' but he admired the pretty scene. 'The lake is small,' he wrote, 'but deep, and is delightfully located. All around the lake were groups of spectators, and booths of gay-colored stuffs flaunting rich flags in the sunshine, which flashed upon the waters of the lake its sunniest smiles.'[65]

The Halifax reception committee organized games on the commons and a regatta in the bay, both of which the prince attended unofficially and incognito, which gave him a chance to observe, as the Toronto *Globe* put it, 'the manners and customs of the Blue Nose in the 19th century.' The sports on the common included foot and sack races, hurdles, putting twenty four-pound shot, sledge throwing, 'greased pole climbings, and expeditions after pigs with anointed tails.' According to the upbeat reports, the events were contested with spirit and immensely enjoyed by the throngs of people who cheered for favourite teams, 'great rivalry' being shown 'between the military and the civilians, and also between different towns in the Province.' Mi'kmaq contestants participated enthusiastically both in races restricted to their own people and in the other competitions. Great hilarity was had during the chase after the greased pig, which got loose in the crowd, causing pandemonium.[66]

The regatta drew high praise from the reporters. 'The finest regattas in the world,' gushed the New York *Times*, 'not excepting even the British Islands, are those of the maritime provinces of British North America.'[67] To view the sailing, rowing, and canoe races, some two thousand spectators were afloat in the harbour, some of them bobbing in dinghies, others lining the rails of Her Majesty's ships.[68] The tars from Her Majesty's fleet cavorted in ways that delighted the crowds. One crew of 'jolly fellows' took over a raft and paddled it with shovels, while another group rowed boats about backwards, or 'stern foremost.' Spectators focused especially on the antics of the sailors who walked a twenty-foot greased pole suspended over the water. Attached to the end was a squealing pig in a barrel. The object was to walk out the length of the pole, open the barrel, and 'cut the brute's throat.' Some contestants inched out cautiously, others rushed along, but their fates were the same. As each sailor fell and swam back to the ladder, 'the crowd would laugh heartily, especially when the catastrophe happened awkwardly.' The prince, who had 'a capital view' of the antics of the contestants, gave every appearance of enjoying himself immensely.[69]

In the Province of Canada, one of the main sporting events was the grand canoe regatta hosted at Ottawa. The event, organized by a special committee, was open to canoes of six or four paddles, but only craft that had participated in the aquatic reception of the prince were eligible for the cash prizes. (The stipulation was made, of course, to get a good turnout for the reception.) Entrants were required to register ahead of time at Dolly's Chop House and to carry a flag in a conspicuous place so that judges could distinguish the competitors. The course was a long one: a mile down the river and back. All the races were hotly contested, at least by the lead canoes. Red-shirted lumbermen outnumbered the rest, their crews identified by the company for which they worked. But Algonquins in 'traditional' dress prevailed in many of the competitions. 'Six Indians of the Allejonquin tribe,' declared the correspondent for the *Times*, 'distanced the best crews and canoes of the lumbermen beyond all chance of doubt.' The Ottawa *Citizen* provided detailed coverage of each race. In the third race, for example, it reported that 'the struggle was mainly between two canoes, and well they contested for the prize. They were stem and stern over a great part of the course, every minute increasing their distance from the others. At the last the canoe of Puck Ne Watick, with an Indian crew, crept ahead and won.'[70]

The many spectators, including the prince, thoroughly enjoyed the Ottawa regatta, though for the reporters the appeal was as much aesthetic as athletic. The prince had a good view of the competition from his seat on a large barge that John Morris, clerk of the works at the Parliament Buildings, had had built and jauntily decorated for the occasion. Around the royal barge, there played about several steamers crammed with some two thousand spectators who were at least as interested in the royal party as they were in the races. (The municipal corporation had chartered some of the steamers to accommodate members of the press and the legislature.) When the prince clapped as the lead canoes approached the finish line, the nearby spectators, observed the *Globe*, 'all participated in his evident delight, and took up the applause in one tremendous chorus.'[71] Their cheers, in turn, triggered those of the 20,000 people observing from the top of the cliffs. This put life into the exhausted contestants, who 'panting and grasping, reached their goal.'

The Crush of Crinoline

The highlight of the festivities in most cities visited by the prince was a splendid ball – if not two. Civic fathers and journalists alike went to great lengths to present the balls as dazzling spectacles, occasions when people could enter a fantasy world where the ordinary and familiar were transformed. Dull buildings and landscapes, some of them the sites of serious state business in the daytime, on the night of the ball became places of make-believe. Inversions were everywhere. Women, whose role had been carefully choreographed as secondary throughout the other festivities, at the ball became the leading players on the spectacular sets, their dresses, their dancing, their speculations about the prince's partners taking on great significance. Even the prince himself took on a new persona at the balls, truly coming to life.

Communities had not expected that the prince would condescend to dance at balls hosted in the colonies. A widely reprinted article from the Montreal *Pilot* reported on plans for a ball at the Champs de Mars, an important public square in Montreal, but it said that the queen would not likely countenance her young son's attendance at such an event, given that the tour was a state visit.[72] Shortly after the prince's arrival in North America, however, the newspapers reported that not only had the Prince of Wales attended the public ball in St John's, but that he had made it a smashing success by dancing with gusto. For the ladies, denied access to the prince during the levee, the ball had provided their opportunity for meeting him, and they had made the most of it, vying for introductions and dances with him. Lady Bannerman, the governor's wife, had been entrusted with the responsibility for choosing his partners, and wisely she had selected not only married women but also young belles, which delighted them and the royal visitor. The prince had obviously enjoyed himself and had not left the ball until nearly three in the morning.[73]

With this exciting news, committees throughout the provinces remade their plans. In Toronto, the Law Society of Upper Canada transformed their Osgoode Hall reception into a ball. In Montreal, the *Times* reported, a committee planned a ball on a scale that could not be matched, 'when it was understood that the Prince preferred balls to any other kind of entertainment that could be offered to him.' The *Globe*, meanwhile, observed that once it was 'understood that the Prince was fond of dancing, the number of balls projected for his amusement are almost numberless.' The suspicion now was that the prince would 'get enough of ball-room amusement while in North America to satisfy him for some years!'[74]

No city made more elaborate preparations for their ball than Montreal, where facilities were built from scratch in order to create a fantasy.

The Montreal ball committee built a grand ballroom set in extensive grounds. 'It literally rose by magic,' exclaimed one writer. A site had been chosen at the foot of Mount Royal, where 'only five weeks before the date fixed for the ball, the cattle were grazing over the ground.' But on that special night, the place 'looked like a fairy land.'[75] The ballroom resembled a castle. The ceiling, which was painted a soft pink with white and gold accents, rose toward the centre of the three hundred yard dance floor and was supported by whitewashed, wooden columns, wreathed with garlands. Around the circumference ran an observation gallery, beneath which were retiring rooms for the prince, dressing rooms for guests, and endless refreshment tables. The fantasy carried through into the surrounding grounds, an 'extemporised Eden,' with coloured lanterns, twisting pathways, ornamental trees, and an artificial lake with water lilies.[76]

Unfortunately for the guests, the weather on the night of the ball was cold and wet, and so few ventured into the elaborate grounds 'and the fairy land had nor elves nor fairies.'[77] But the ball itself was said to have been magnificent. It was reported that a group of prominent New Yorkers in attendance admitted with dismay that even the great metropolis could not match what Montreal had done, especially its ballroom. '"Beats our Academy of Music, hollow,"' they said.[78] The Toronto press was much less generous, saying that Montreal's purpose-built ballroom was not a patch on Osgoode Hall, where the Toronto bar planned to host its ball. 'Your Montreal ball-rooms, your large exhibition buildings were excellent in their way,' sneered the *Globe*, 'but they are to the exquisitely wrought architecture of Osgoode Hall, as the theatre drop scene is to the work of Turner or a Claude.'[79]

Journalists had fun playing with the conversions that public buildings underwent on the night of the ball. In Fredericton, the liveliest part of the ball took place in the chambers of the Legislative Council. Upon entering, instead of finding the male legislators seriously deliberating matters of state, one 'found some hundreds of ladies, who gave to the Prince a most cordial welcome.'[80] The ball supper took place in the adjoining courthouse, where the hungry crowd 'ranged themselves, like prisoners at the bar, at a table spread in front of the judge's seat.'[81] Toronto's Osgoode Hall usually echoed with the 'earnest voice of the barrister pleading or the solemn tones of the judges,' but on the night of the ball 'laughter and merriment reined unchecked by any threat of heavy fine or committal for contempt.'[82]

Gender reversals – of a respectable kind – were made much of by the

Guests arriving at Montreal's fairy-tale ballroom. The temporary structure, which boasted a three-hundred-yard dance floor, was erected expressly for the prince's visit. (*Frank Leslie's Illustrated News*, 15 September 1860)

Globe, as its reporter sought to enliven his account of the ball at Osgoode Hall. He made fun of the lawyers (all of them men, of course), who tripped 'the light fantastic' – in their gowns! 'Why did they not put on hoops?' asked the reporter, with tongue-in-cheek. 'And as it was, did the ladies ask *them* to dance?' Indeed, the ladies had taken over Osgoode Hall: 'Crinoline made itself comfortable in the capacious seats of their Lordships.' The *Globe* continued: 'Imagine what Sir J.B. Robinson must have felt, at seeing a scarlet cloak in his chair, or Chief Justice Draper felt, at finding his desk covered with ladies' shawls; their retiring-rooms filled with looking-glasses, their consulting-chambers bedecked with confused heaps of female frippery. It was enough to try their inmost souls, but ... they bore it well.' As presented by the journalists, these particular reversals were amusing and delightful. Women's entry into male realms, which on other occasions might be regarded as outrageous or threatening, here was welcomed. Everyone knew that the ladies had not really come to occupy the judges' chambers; they had come to dance at a ball. And what would a ball be without them?!

People, as well as places, were transformed by attending a ball where the Prince of Wales was both guest of honour and life of the party. In London, Canada West, for example, the prince danced with such 'great vigour,' reported the Montreal *Pilot*, that his 'example seemed to inspirit afresh the already gratified dancers.'[83] When the prince requested that a lady dance with him, she forgot her nervousness and danced better than usual. (Of course, it helped that, as in Fredericton, everyone had been rehearsing, 'dancing masters' having enjoyed full employment; and many a family party ha[d] been made up for practice.'[84]) Remarkable, too, was the behaviour of the partners of the lucky ladies who danced with the prince. From Halifax, Woods reported that 'the young officers and dandies' were not in the least perturbed when the prince broke through 'in the most ruthless manner' and 'bore away [their partners] in triumph.' Even the party animosities of politicians melted away in the presence of the prince. In Toronto, the Conservative premier from Canada East, George-Étienne Cartier, and his partner shared a set with the Reform leader from Canada West, George Brown, and his partner. 'Who knows what good consequences may result,' one journalist exclaimed.[85] Some commentators worried that belles who had danced with the prince would be spoiled forever and would consider themselves 'fit mates for a Duke at the very least.'[86] Fanny Fern, in a widely reprinted advice column, warned:

Gowns and beauty on display at the grand ball held in Halifax. Civic promoters in the colonies hoped that flattering images like this one would appear in the metropolitan press. (*Illustrated Times*, 1 September 1860)

'Have a care girls!' Her concern was that young women of marriageable age would get such swelled heads after dancing with the prince that they would end up old spinsters. 'Don't carry your heads too high,' she intoned, 'or at least not so high that you may not have the pleasure of telling your children "all about the Prince."'[87]

The Prince of Wales himself was said to be changed by the balls. The reserve and quiet dignity that he showed during levees and entries gave way at the balls to a joviality that brought him closer to the people. 'Albert Edward is in his glory ... and is fond of gayety and excitement,' commented the reporter for the Montreal *Gazette* after witnessing the ball at Halifax.[88] An article in the evangelical press pointedly observed: 'His Royal Highness would rather dance than eat.'[89] From the start, at the ball in St. John's, the prince had entered wholeheartedly into the spirit of the thing. Cornwallis, of the New York *Herald*, snootily described that ball, especially at 'the plebian end of the hall,' as 'equal to the most ridiculous scene that ever Rabelais, Cervantes, Smollett, or Dickens imagined in their merriest moods.' But the reporter admitted that the prince was not in the least put off by the dancers and their *faux pas*. 'The prince,' he said, 'could not avoid laughing outright at the mishaps, but continued to dance, good-naturedly correcting mistakes, and calling out the figures to the awkward squad before him.'[90] The prince's willingness to mingle with the people at the balls and his sheer love of dancing greatly enhanced his image. 'How much his popularity was increased by the way he had mixed with his future subjects, we can scarcely venture to tell,' came a report from St John's. 'His praise was in everybody's mouth.'

Albert Edward's reputation as a prince charming grew mainly from the representations of him at the balls. A report from Halifax, early in the tour, set the tone for what would follow. 'It is amusing,' an onlooker at the ball was reported to have said, 'to observe the eyes of the ladies in the room and gallery watching his every movement and gesture, and casting envious glances at his fortunate partners. I heard more than one whisper "What a beautiful dancer!" as he glided in the dance.' The reporter for the New York *Herald* added: 'Before, we heard of his brilliant hazel eyes; now we are told his "almost Roman nose" is equally fine. Halifax is one grand carnival, so popular is the Prince; and as for the ladies, they are dying about him.'[91]

For most of the balls, the prince donned the uniform of a colonel, which appropriately made him stand out amid the prevailing black clothing of most of the other men. The uniform included spurs, which generally he managed well during the dances, 'so that no crinoline was torn.' On occasion, however, he stumbled and thus drew ridicule from some of the American reporters who liked to bring royalty down a notch.[92] It became a running joke the way the prince's determination to enjoy himself by staying late at the balls exhausted members of his suite. As the dancing at Cobourg wore into the wee hours, according to *Harper's Weekly*, 'the Duke of Newcastle stroked his bushy beard, the Governor General closed, opened, and shut again his pale and weary eyelids, and the players of the band began to flag in their attempts at grinding out in good time the enlivening and spirit-stirring strains.'[93]

In his own correspondence, the prince made special note of several of the balls. He told his mother that the ball in Halifax was 'very full, & the room was beautifully decorated.' Quebec, he said, had 'one of the prettiest I have seen yet, but it was rather too full, and very hot.' He enjoyed himself most in Cobourg, where, he explained, there was less of a crush. The reporter for the New York *Times* had a different explanation for why the prince liked the Cobourg ball: he had been given the rare freedom 'to glide through the maze with one of his own choice.'[94]

Generally, the reporters had remarkably little to say about the musicians and their performances at the balls. This much is clear. At every ball, two bands played, the one spelling off the other. In Newfoundland and the Maritime provinces, the band from the *Hero* did duty for the dancers,[95] and a local band would also play; at St John's, for instance, it was the band of the Royal Newfoundland Rifle Company. In the Canadas, the band of the Royal Canadian Rifles travelled with the prince and played at the dances; at Toronto's Crystal Palace, Poppenberg's Germania Band from Buffalo did duty. Reporters commented only briefly on the type of music played at the balls, seldom noting the name of any particular composition.[96]

Of much greater interest to everyone was the topic of the prince's dance partners. For every ball, the newspapers printed lists of names of the fortunate ladies, and often they specified the particular dance each one had with the prince. Such reporting added to the excitement of the tour, as curious readers looked to see who had had the distinction of being chosen.

One of the prince's young Canadian dance partners, Jessie Anne Hope, nineteen, kept a diary at the time of the prince's visit to London, Canada West, where her father was a politician and dry goods merchant.[97] Her entries for the two days prior to the prince's arrival describe how 'the whole town' was 'in a great state of excitement' receiving the prince and enjoying a festive time. On the day after the ball, she carefully records her experience of the evening before, when the prince asked her to dance:

> The Grand Ball has been & past and I have had the high and distinguished honor of dancing (note it Uncle) with H.R.H. The Prince of Wales, Heir Apparent to the Throne of Great Britain. My dance was 16th, Ever of Thee 'Galop.' The Orchestra sang the words of the song. General Bruce introduced me to H.R.H. who bowed and requested the pleasure of the next dance with me: he then took out his programme & wrote down my name for the Galop; after that, gave me his arm & promenaded me up & down the ball-room and danced when the music began, resting me frequently & giving me his arm while standing: he conversed with me making several remarks about the ball, the music, the dances etc. When the music ceased he led me to the dais bowed & thanked me, leaving me not a little delighted with the high honor he had just conferred in so kind and pleasing a manner. H.R.H. brought one of his suite to me, Capt Grey, & said, Miss Hope, allow me to introduce to you Grey – who asked me to dance the Quadrille with him. He then led me to my place in the same set with H.R.H. & other members of his suite.

Jessie then lists all the prince's other partners and carefully records the details of the ball dresses – her mother's, her friends,' and her own. And she observes proudly that her name had been on the prince's 'list from the first.'

Although a private account, Jessie's rendering of the ball conforms to the published accounts insofar as she expresses much delight in the 'high honor' paid to her, but it differs from the newspaper descriptions by providing many details about the ball dresses. Jessie goes to some lengths to describe the colours, fabrics, patterns, and trims of various dresses, and especially her own gown. By contrast, the male reporters shied away from such matters. Howard, reporting from Montreal for the New York *Times*, said that while he could generally tell whether a lady's dress was acceptable, he was 'no connoisseur' of ballroom attire, and, not knowing the names of the various fabrics, he would chronicle the ladies' attire only in 'an entirely unprofessional way.'[98] Both Jessie Hope and the male journalists, in their contrasting ways, followed a gendered script.

To the deep regret of the ball committees responsible for local arrangements, there were sometimes glitches which cut through the magic of the spectacles, at least partly destroying the illusion. At Quebec, according to the reporter from the London *Times*, the waiters were too drunk to serve the supper, and when at last all was ready and substitute servers found, it was discovered that the tables could not accommodate more than 'a tithe of the guests.'[99] Cornwallis, who in the pages of the New York *Herald* pricked the bubble of every ball, described the Toronto Crystal Palace as being so 'uncomfortably cold' that among the dancers 'blue noses attenuated features, cold hands, and occasional shivers were general.' Hamilton's citizens' ball was worse still. The floor was 'spotted with tobacco juice, like a bar-room,' and throughout the night an offensive odour rose 'in pestiferous puffs' from a sewer, causing the ballroom to stink unbearably by the time the royal party arrived.[100]

The dances generated more serious criticisms and controversies, too. When the evangelical press pondered the civic balls arranged for the prince, it did not conjure up a fantasy world of exotic delights but rather a New World Sodom and Gomorrah. Such widely read newspapers as Toronto's *Christian Guardian* and the Montreal *Witness* fumed about the moral degradation bound to ensue from all the attention and public approval that the prince's dancing gave to that sin. For a start, city fathers across the provinces were corrupting the prince by inviting him to dances – 'not the best way to entertain a Royal youth now only nineteen years of age.'[101] When news of the St John's ball reached Upper Canada, a letter writer to the *Guardian* declared: 'How much better it would have been to hear of his attending the House of God and giving thanks for bringing him safely to our shores.'[102] For another thing, the prince's advisers, by allowing Albert Edward to join in the dancing, were offending the large and loyal evangelical community. 'When so much talk is heard about not offending the prejudices of any part of Her Majesty's subjects,' harrumphed the *Guardian*, 'nothing at all is thought of grieving hundreds of thousands of the very best subjects of Her Majesty's dominions.'[103] Worst of all, explained the Montreal *Witness*, by his setting such a bad example to the youth of the country, the prince threatened to undermine the hard-won achievements of evangelicals: 'Churches, ministers and parents will, we fear, find their difficulties about dancing and late hours greatly increased; and many persons will be led, by high example, into this seductive gaiety, who might otherwise have resisted the temptation.'[104] Keeping young people on the straight-and-narrow path was hard enough without negative interventions by civic fathers and the most prestigious youth in the empire. Still, knowing that God was on their side, the evangelicals remained optimistic. 'A distant future generation may boast that great great grandmother danced with the Prince of Wales,' the *Christian Guardian* speculated. 'Though we hope that by that time dancing will be so out of fashion that they will be ashamed to boast of it.'[105]

Controversies also arose around matters relating to the inclusiveness of balls. For a ball to be successful in the eyes of civic promoters, at least the illusion of splendour had to be achieved, and this required the guests to dress and act the part. But not everyone could afford the appropriate attire – or even a rough approximation – nor could all residents be trusted to conduct themselves respectably. Hence, ball committees announced dress codes and set ticket prices with the intention of screening out the unwanted. Doing so, however, raised questions about access and the use of public funds. After all, the events organized by municipalities were intended to allow the prince to get to know as many of his future colonial subjects as possible, and not just one group of them, the well-to-do. Moreover, because public funds from provincial treasuries and municipal rates were being spent to mount the balls, it was a fine point just where to draw the line on who could attend.

The *Acadian Recorder*, an opposition newspaper, raised several of these matters in criticizing the government of Nova Scotia's preliminary arrangements for the Halifax ball. According to an editorial, the ball had been got up by the wealthy for their own benefit, and while there was nothing wrong with that, 'the Government are going to take a thousand pounds of the people's money out of the Provincial treasury to devote to this purpose.' It was an outrage! In terms of the squandering of public funds, the matter was up there with 'the "spree" at the laying of the cornerstone of the Lunatic Asylum!' The editorial writer predicted that the ball would flop, because the prince would not be permitted to attend and there were too few wealthy people in Halifax to fill the large ballroom being built by the government.[106] As it turned out, the editor of the *Acadian Recorder* had to eat crow, for Halifax's posh ball proved to be a great success.[107]

As journalists' assessments of balls made clear, there was a risk in setting low ticket prices and flexible dress standards. Cornwallis thought that the low admission price at Fredericton had resulted in a poor supper (because 'nothing better could be afforded'), overcrowding, and guests 'of an order less select that at Halifax.'[108] Even journalists writing for more humble newspapers could sometimes be harsh in their criticisms of balls that lacked polish. The correspondent for the *Northern Advance*, a Barrie newspaper, thought that the Hamilton ball 'fell short of the strength and brilliancy of the previous ones to the east of this point.' He judged 'the company ... more promiscuous and [of] a class of gentry whose purse was contracted, and their wits more so.' It was not enough to disparage their intelligence and modest means, he also attacked the masculinity of the male guests: 'In short, the small-salaried men made up the bulk of the party – heroes of starch and dry goods, exquisite fops of the counter, and the effeminate masculines that parade their padded outlines before the fleeting public.'[109] Presumably, wealthier, better dressed male patrons, in the eyes of the *Northern Advance*, would have projected a more pleasing and appropriate male image.

On the other hand, the grand balls looked impressive but were often criticized for being too exclusive. In Montreal the reception committee held a 'Peoples' Ball' a few nights after the main event, as a way both to answer critics of exclusiveness and to make money for paying down debts. Its success was guaranteed once placards in the streets announced that the prince would attend, or, as the writer for the New York *Daily Tribune* put it, 'the one dollar celebrators and unrestricted dressers would be vouchsafed a royal recognition.' The reporter sneered at the crowd of dancers that night because of the 'oddest comminglings': gentlemen in full dress and elegant belles alongside men in overcoats and 'ladies wearing bonnets and aprons,' the 'prevailing fabric [being] calico.'[110]

Class became a matter of intense concern to the Toronto *Globe* when the newspaper learned that the Law Society of Upper Canada had decided to host a lavish and exclusive ball at Toronto's Osgoode Hall. George Brown, the newspaper's editor and publisher, strongly promoted the citizens' ball planned for the Crystal Palace, which the *Globe* billed as being 'by far the most magnificent affair of the kind that ever came off in Upper Canada.'[111] Brown published no fewer than five editorials denouncing the plans of the lawyers and supporting the citizens' ball committee in its efforts to persuade the lawyers to reconsider.[112] 'The lawyers will get the first glass of the bottle; the citizens will be compelled to drink the dregs after the cork has been out some time,' the *Globe* maintained. Considerable money was being spent on preparing for the citizens' ball, and without large ticket sales there would be a substantial loss. Moreover, this 'desire to shut out the vulgar herd' amounted to an unfortunate 'attempt to establish an exclusive class.' In the end, the lawyers had their exclusive ball, which, incidentally, Brown attended and the *Globe* declared 'a great success.' The citizens' ball was not ruined as a result; according to the *Globe*, 'the assembly was brilliant beyond compare.'[113]

Ironically, the Osgoode Hall ball struck the New York reporters present as extraordinarily inclusive, not because of the class of those present but rather on account of the race of one man there. 'Prominent among the hosts,' reported the New York *Times*, 'was a black barrister, named Sutherland, who was rigged out in full court costume, – gown, bands and badge. He mingled freely with the *élite* of the city, and is said to be noted for his talent, humor, and good sense.' Neither the organizers of the ball nor the local journalists had anticipated that such attention would be drawn either to the Society's inclusiveness or to one of their number, the Jamaican-born Robert Sutherland, a graduate of Queen's University in 1852, who practised law in the small town of Walkerton, Canada West.[114]

One price the lawyers of Toronto had to pay for their competitive ball was that it ended up being held on a Saturday evening, which meant that the dancing could not last past midnight, the beginning of the Sabbath. In the midst of dancing the Lancers, the clock chimed twelve and the band struck up 'God Save the Queen.' The crowd soon dispersed. Though schooled to show no disappointment, the prince must have resented his pleasure being curtailed, and, if given the opportunity, no doubt he would have danced for hours more.

Altogether, then, the prince was certainly kept busy during his tour. While some of his duties were just that – duties that had to be done, however tiresome – others he took pleasure in fulfilling, to the great delight of his hosts. No one had expected that he would dance half the night away at various local balls, but the other guests were delighted that he did so. By dancing with particular ladies he had conferred upon them a mark of royal favour every bit as meaningful as when he acknowledged individual gentlemen at the levees, officers in the reviews, or teams of men competing in sporting events. Even ladies at the dances who were not singled out by royalty at least had the chance to participate fully and to be featured in the press – an opportunity largely denied women in connection with the other festivities.

The press portrayal of the prince during these public engagements and performances accomplished significant cultural work: it gave expression to a white-settler, colonial version of 'popular royalism.' The prince appeared at the very centre of the public sphere, his every movement described in reports consumed by people from St John's to Windsor. The heir apparent was made to seem both utterly special – the focus of everyone's gaze – *and* one of the people. The public, as constructed by the press, had given the Prince of Wales its heartiest approval. By gathering in crowds, cheering him everywhere, and reading depictions of the popular demonstrations, Canadians had strengthened the pact between the people and the crown. For Canadians, or so it seemed, the tour had made the monarchy appear less distant, abstract, and awesome, and feel more familiar, approachable, and down-to-earth.

At the conclusion of the Canadian tour, the correspondent for the New York *Daily Tribune* wondered whether members of the royal party could take much more of the strain. (In fact, it was his colleague, Nathaniel Woods of the London *Times*, who collapsed from exhaustion at this point in the trip.) 'It would be bad,' he quipped, 'if any of the royal party should be made to die of a surfeit of sweet popular demonstration.' The journalist continued, voicing his own weariness: 'What long and weary weeks they have been – there is so little to be discerned apart from the mazy vista of garlanded towns and gorgeous halls of reception, and brilliant balls and levees without number, all now inextricably confused.' It was, he said, 'so easy to be surfeited with this pastry work of ceremony and sensation.'[115]

5

Arch Rivals: The Orangemen and the Duke

The biggest controversy of the royal visit of 1860 pitted the militant Protestants from Upper Canada's Orange lodges against, initially, the Roman Catholics of the province and, ultimately, the prince's adviser, the Duke of Newcastle. Sectarian differences that were deeply embedded in Upper Canada – and often displayed in street confrontations on public occasions – fuelled a conflagration that nearly curtailed the prince's visit to the province. At the heart of the dispute were different understandings about the right to demonstrate of a so-called party organization: the Orange Order. Fiercely committed to the British crown (when worn by Protestants), the Orangemen of Upper Canada presented themselves as the prince's staunchest supporters. In Kingston, Belleville, and Toronto, Orangemen built impressive arches of welcome, emblazoned with the talismanic dates and slogans of their brotherhood, and they made arrangements to participate in the civic processions, dressed in their colourful regalia, with banners held high. However, the Roman Catholics of the province took strong exception to these plans, fiercely objecting to royalty's recognition of a rancorous party that had caused so much strife in Ireland and elsewhere and that threatened the Catholics' own rights in Canada. A fierce confrontation then ensued over access to public space, official recognition of the Order, and acceptable forms of public ritual.

The story of what the newspapers of 1860 dubbed 'the Orange difficulty' has never been fully told nor carefully analysed.[1] The authors of the instant books on the prince's visit preferred to describe a triumphal progress, and so they skimmed over this trouble. Yet the newspapers brimmed with news of the events as they unfolded, and their coverage provides the basis for the narrative that follows. As well, private papers are available to supplement the public accounts and shed light on the behind-the-scene manoeuvres and motivations of the major players. Together, these sources allow for a rich, and, I hope, compelling reconstruction of the visit's central dispute – of public ceremony gone completely awry.

Orange and Green

By 1860 both the Orange Order and the Roman Catholic Church had a firm grip on the social landscape of Canada West.[2] Each institution spoke in a strident voice for a substantial part of the population of the towns and the heavily populated agricultural districts. Orangemen preferred to think of themselves as fervent defenders of Protestantism, but that made them, in effect, militant opponents of the Catholic Church. They drew on a heritage of fierce sectarian troubles in Ireland, and in Canada they railed at the Catholics' 'blasphemies'[3] and the church's political power, which in the Province of Canada was greatly strengthened by the French-Canadian clergy of Canada East. In 1860 the Catholic Church in Canada had recently been revitalized and made militant under the influence of ultramontanism. Lay and clerical leaders within the Catholic population were caught up in a struggle to assert political and social influence commensurate with the community's growing numbers, and many of these assertions were inflected with an Irish accent and gained potency through appeals to Irish nationalism.

Kingston, known at the time as 'the Derry of Canada,' was the centre of activities in eastern Upper Canada for both the Catholics and the Orangemen. The patriarch of Upper Canada's Catholics, Bishop Alexander Macdonell, had established key institutions there, including a seminary, the College of Regiopolis, founded in 1838, and St Mary's Cathedral, consecrated in 1848. By 1860, the Catholics, who were mainly Irish immigrants and their descendants, amounted to about 30 per cent of the city's population. Kingston was also the headquarters of the Orange Order's Central District. Orangemen were at the heart of politics in Kingston, their lodge rooms occupying symbolically significant space in the city's commodious city hall. The mayor of Kingston in 1860, Orlando S. Strange, was the brother of the grand master of the Central District of the Orange Order. Certainly, the city's most distinguished provincial politician, John A. Macdonald, understood the Orange Order's influence in his riding, and he himself had been a member of the Order since 1841. At the same time, however, Macdonald proved adept at winning the backing of the local Catholic bishop and the faithful. But, notwithstanding this political modus vivendi, Protestant–Catholic factionalism frequently led to brawls in the streets of town.[4]

Toronto, 'the Belfast of Canada,' was also a home to both Catholic and Orange institutions and to sectarian conflict. The Catholic population, which had swelled with Irish refugees from the great potato famine of the 1840s, made up about one-quarter of the total number of residents in 1860. During the 1850s the Catholic community's clerical leadership had gained in authority and purpose under the energetic direction of Bishop Armand Charbonnel, an enthusiastic ultramontanist. Under his direction, a devotional revolution reinforced the strength of popular piety among Catholic men and women, and several new institutions drew lay people into a rich associational life that offered conviviality and spiritual renewal. A small number of middle-class Catholic men took on the leadership of various of these institutions, in the process asserting their own claims to public recognition and power. Together, the clerical and lay leaders fought hard in the political sphere to strengthen the state-funded separate schools for Catholic children – a campaign that brought them into a head-on collision with Orangemen and many other Protestants. In 1855, French-Canadian Catholics in the Legislative Assembly had been crucial in pushing through the Taché Act, which extended the rights of Catholics to the public purse for separate common schools in Canada West. Anti-Catholics were outraged. It confirmed for them the power of the Catholic Church in Canada West even though Catholics made up only a minority of the populaton. Moreover, the seriousness of the Catholic threat posed by Charbonnel appeared all the more alarming because it conicided with 'papal aggression' in Europe. When Charbonnel's seat was taken by a new bishop in April 1860, Protestants were not in the least reassured because John Joseph Lynch was an Irishman known for his Irish nationalist convictions.[5]

In 1860 no less than twenty Orange lodges dotted the Toronto map, and the city had long been home to the grand masters of the Orange Order of British North America. The grand master in 1860, John Hillyard Cameron, was a prominent member of the old Toronto establishment and a Conservative politician, whose financial reversal in the crash of 1857 had propelled him to seek a new, more popular base of political support among Orangemen.[6] About 15 per cent of the city's adult male Protestants belonged to the Order. They came from all walks of life, though the bulk of the members were men of modest means. They also hailed from diverse backgrounds. By mid-century, the Order was by no means simply an ethnic or immigrant organization of Irish Protestants, even though its roots lay in Ireland and it commemorated events in Irish history: the siege of Londonderry in 1688 and the victory of the Protestant King William III ('William of Orange') over the Catholic King James II at the battle of the Boyne River on 12 July 1690. Like their brethren in Ireland, men in Toronto were attracted to the Order by the fraternal good cheer of lodge meetings, the secret rituals, the colourful banners and marching tradition, and the political appeal of membership. In a city where politics hinged on patronage, Orangemen found it convenient to rely on lodge brethren to channel jobs and contracts their way – and away from Catholic competitors. But Orangemen were also committed to their 'principles,' and thus they were ever-vigilant both in opposing any imagined threat to freedom posed by the Catholic hierarchy and in defending Protestantism, the crown – the guarantor of the rights of freeborn men – and the imperial connection.[7]

In Toronto especially, the Orangemen had a long tradition of insistently claiming public space and recognition by marching on ceremonial and political occasions.[8] Public performers par excellence, the Orangemen had equipped themselves with bright yellow and orange robes, gorgeous silk banners with representations of 'King Billy' and slogans such as 'Never Surrender!' and fife and drum corps that added to the festive feeling and goaded opponents. Annually on 12 July – 'the Glorious Twelfth' – the Orangemen paraded through Toronto streets, as they did in so many other Upper Canadian communities, proudly proclaiming their strength in numbers and defying their enemies to challenge them. In response, some Catholics, as well as some Protestants associated with the Reform party, occasionally lashed out in anger, jeering the marchers, lobbing bricks in their direction, and engaging in hand-to-hand combat in the streets. Such violence at the time of the 1841 provincial election, which had been allowed to reach disastrous proportions by an Orange mayor and partisan police force, prompted provincial Reform politicians to sponsor a bill suppressing the Order itself, which failed to be enacted, and another bill suppressing 'party processions,' which did become law. So defiant and persistent were the Orange marchers, however, that the act became a dead letter and was revoked in 1851.[9] Under Conservative administrations in the 1850s, the Orangemen gained increasing official recognition to the point where, in 1857, the governor general, Sir Edmund Head, accepted and replied to an address from the Orange Order. This development, not incidently, contrasted sharply with the contemporary situation in Ireland, where the British state worked hard to suppress the Order's parades and demonstrations under the Party Processions Act (1850), which remained in place until 1868.[10]

Like the Orangemen, the Catholics of Toronto believed that they had a right and duty to claim public space and recognition. The Orangemen might dominate the streets annually on the Glorious Twelfth, but the Catholics would do so on 17 March, the day in the Catholic calendar devoted to celebrating the patron saint of Ireland. In the 1840s St Patrick's Day celebrations had been organized by clerics and focused on a Mass, but by 1857, with Bishop Charbonnel's blessing, the lay elite had taken charge of the festivities, which became larger, more popular, and centred on a colourful parade replete with emblems of shamrocks and harps. 'Clerically induced temperance gave way to alcoholic good cheer,' reports historian Michael Cottrell, 'and instead of expressions of loyalty and three cheers for the Queen, which had previously characterized the proceedings, mildly Anglophobic speeches were now heard.' In the words of historian Brian Clarke, the parade had become 'a demonstration for Irish freedom.'[11]

Developments far outside the boundaries of Upper Canada could provoke local Orange and Catholics, as was shown throughout the year of the prince's visit. News of Giuseppe Garibaldi's struggle on the Italian peninsula filled the international news columns of provincial newspapers. For Orangemen and many other residents of Upper Canada, Garibaldi was a hero bringing liberty at last to the hopeful masses too long oppressed by the pope and other reactionaries. The Catholic Church, on the other hand, represented Garibaldi as a cut-throat revolutionary who threatened the holy father, the papal states, and the very future of Mother Church. Bishop Ignace Bourget, the highly influential Roman Catholic bishop of Montreal, and a man of deep, ultramontane convictions, campaigned especially vigorously against Garibaldi and Italian unification.[12] Polar opposite assessments of this international scene only exacerbated the tensions between the Catholics and Protestants in Canada West.[13]

In their sectarianism, Upper Canadians were by no means unique. Witness the extreme violence between Orangemen and Catholics in New Brunswick during the 1840s and the riots that swept through

New York in 1844.[14] Yet only in Upper Canada did Orangemen cause any difficulties for the Prince of Wales and his advisers in 1860.[15] In the preceding two decades, Upper Canada's growth had outstripped that of other regions in British North America as a result of heavy immigration from the British Isles and especially from Ireland. The great majority of the newcomers were Protestants who brought with them a British nationalism that had deep anti-French and anti-Catholic roots.[16] When transplanted, it found a congenial, new home in Canada West, where a sense of political grievance festered under the political arrangements in place since the Union of the Canadas in 1841. By 1860, many Upper Canadian Protestants – not just Orangemen – bristled at what they saw as Canada West's under-representation in the legislature and the resultant political domination of the province by French-speaking Roman Catholics.[17] They also distrusted the power and militancy of the Catholic Church, especially when it was infused with the zeal of men like Bishop Lynch and Bishop Bourget. Orange militancy during the 1860 royal visit, then, emerged in the context of the deeply divided politics of the Province of Canada.

Orange Plans and Catholic Initiatives

The first indication of public controversy in connection with Orange displays and the prince's visit came in the form of letters-to-the-editor in the Toronto dailies. On 20 August the *Globe* published a letter from 'A Protestant' who asked whether it were true that the Orangemen proposed to erect an arch on King Street. It was 'not the time,' he insisted, 'to attempt any display of party feeling.' A letter in the *Leader* voiced similar concerns and urged the local program committee to 'see that nothing is done that would be likely to interfere with the harmony and good feeling that should prevail on such an occasion.'[18]

Indeed, the Orangemen had made no secret of their plans to appear before the prince. Reports on the 12 July festivities in Kingston and Toronto had casually made reference to the intentions of the Orangemen. The Kingston *Daily News* reported that celebrations for the Twelfth were expected to be more modest than usual because Orangemen, anticipating the prince's tour, planned 'to reserve their great effort for the occasion of his visit to this city.' The Toronto *Globe* had a similar report, which stated that the local Orange youth were 'reserving themselves for a grand "blow out" when the Prince arrives.'[19] A proposal that the Orangemen present addresses to the prince had been scotched at an early stage by Governor General Head,[20] but, as the visit approached, newspapers informed the public about the Orangemen's plans to build arches of welcome and noted that the reception committees in both Kingston and Toronto had assigned the Order places in the local processions. On 15 August an Orange leader in Kingston declared: 'For the last thirty years Canadian Orangemen had been boasting of their loyalty and the present was the time to prove it by being amongst the first to present themselves before the Heir apparent on his arrival in our country. No other society or body of men could turn out in such strength, or with such an amount of flags, banners, regalia, and music, as the Orangemen.'[21]

News of the Orangemen's plans enraged the Catholics of Upper Canada, and in both Kingston and Toronto they took action. The Catholics of Kingston called a 'mass meeting' at Regiopolis College on 24 August. Vicar General Angus Macdonell, who chaired the gathering of 1,000 Catholics, explained that their purpose that night was 'to protest against the Orangemen of this city, with their party banners and party emblems, being allowed a place in the procession,' the very idea of which was 'an insult to every Roman Catholic in Upper Canada.'[22] He set the tone for what followed by waxing eloquent about the profound loyalty of the Catholics of Upper Canada during his residence of more than sixty years among them. He called on the Catholics of Kingston to be 'united, temperate, yet, firm in our language,' so as to put a halt to the Orange Association, which had produced 'so much misery, wherever its obnoxious principles were introduced.' Macdonell was followed by Daniel Macarow, a Kingston barrister, who emphasized that all residents were 'equally desirous of giving to Her Noble son a right royal welcome to the city of Kingston.' He had never objected to the Orangemen's making a display on 12 July or 5 November (Guy Fawkes Day), and under Canadian law they had a right to march, 'but he did most strongly object to it on this auspicious occasion, when there was a generous rivalry amongst all classes of Her Majesty's subjects ... to see who would be foremost in extending to our Royal and illustrious visitor a hospitable welcome.' Catholics throughout the province must take 'active and energetic measures against the further aggression of Orangeism.'

After declaring the strong desire of everyone to participate in the welcome, the meeting resolved that Catholics would abstain from joining the procession if the Orangemen marched as a body, and it urged Catholics throughout the province to follow suit. Moreover, it would be impolitic, the meeting pointed out, for the prince to recognize 'any secret-politico-religious organization,' whose members sought to take 'advantage of the presence of His Royal Highness to make political capital for themselves by creating a religious feud in the community.' The meeting resolved to oppose the Orangemen's plans by 'all legitimate means' and to oppose any future candidate for public office who sanctioned the Orange demonstration on this occasion. In an attempt to remove all possible objections to the Orangemen's withdrawal from the celebrations, the meeting asked the president and members of the St. Patrick's Society to abstain from a public display, even though the meeting did 'not recognise any comparison whatever between the Orange Association and the St. Patrick's Society; the one being a secret political organization; the other purely national and benevolent.' Finally, the meeting resolved to send copies of the resolutions to the governor general, the Duke of Newcastle, the reception committee, and various newspapers of Kingston and Toronto.

The Catholics of Toronto needed no prompting.[23] Earlier on the same day as the Kingston mass meeting, a group of prominent Catholic laymen led by the community's most prominent philanthropist, Captain John Elmsley,[24] conferred with the Toronto program committee. The delegation objected to the Orangemen's arch, which was about to be erected at the intersection of King and Church streets, saying that they feared violence from both sides since the Catholics 'couldn't help feeling irritated.' In good conscience, they could not walk under an Orange arch and would therefore be 'deprived of the pleasure of walking in the procession.' Indeed, Elmsley said that, personally, 'sooner than walk under such an arch, he would rather be scalped any day!'[25] Orange arches had a long and acrimonious history in both Ireland and Canada, and Catholics knew that their self-respect and dignity were at stake.[26] After consultation, the Catholic delegates organized a committee of nine, consisting of three Orangemen, three Catholics, and three Protestants who were not members of the Orange Society, in the hope that some peaceful plan could be devised. The last three members readily agreed with the Catholics that the Orangemen should not build an arch, but when the three Orangemen took the message to their society, it promptly rejected the advice. The committee then proposed that, in place of the Orange arch, 'a national arch' be built under which 'all Irishmen should march arm in arm.' The Catholics offered to pay for it and to delegate the supervision of its construction to a Protestant clergyman, the Reverend Dr John McCaul, president of University

Strollers examining the Orangemen's arch in Toronto. The Orange mottoes 'These We Maintain' and 'Our Glorious Constitution' are shown clearly in the original etching, as is the controversial portrait of King William III. (*Illustrated London News*, 3 November 1860)

College. Few people doubted that the Orangemen would reject the idea, which they promptly did.

After the weekend, the Catholics and their supporters then visited the mayor, Adam Wilson, and asked whether he would put a stop to the construction of the Orangemen's arch. Not surprisingly, Mayor Wilson sympathized with them. His base of support had never been among the Orangemen, and he no doubt was concerned that conflict over the Orangemen's plans could derail the elaborate celebrations for which he had worked hard to win political and financial support. On the morning of 29 August, when a construction crew began breaking ground for the Orange arch at King and Church streets, the mayor, watched closely by the Catholic committeemen and their friends, ordered the workmen away.

The Orange leaders immediately took their case to the city's Board of Works, which had issued the building permit for the arch. The Orange-dominated board overrode the mayor's order and work resumed. The mayor told Catholics that his hands were tied and, in a public a letter, declared that he viewed the erection of the arch as 'unfortunate and injudicious.' The Catholic committeemen, although publicly appreciative of the mayor's efforts, took further steps to stop construction by calling a meeting of forty or fifty 'influential' Catholics at the Bishop's Palace that evening. A series of resolutions were drawn up for consideration at a 'mass meeting' to be held the following evening. Hastily prepared placards were placed in the streets to announce the event.

At least 1,000 Roman Catholics had assembled by 7:30 P.M. on 30 August in the field behind the Richmond Street Catholic School, when the Reverend Father John Walsh, rector of St Michael's Cathedral, took the chair.[27] The Catholics of Upper Canada, he said, wanted 'to take up the cheers of Lower Canada and cause them to echo along the borders of our blue Ontario.' They could not do so, however, if their feelings were 'insulted and their self-respect trampled on.' The Orangemen were that very day employed in erecting an arch 'to be decorated by their Orange flags and insulting insignia.' They intended that the Catholics of the city 'should walk beneath their yoke in token of their bondage and slavery.' From the crowd came cries of 'Never!' and 'Pull it down!' Walsh counselled peace, so that the Catholics 'might not place themselves on a level with those who flaunted yellow colours in the face of the mid-day sun.' He reckoned that the Catholics had the support of 'the vast majority of the impartial Protestants of Toronto' who 'considered this was an occasion on which all the citizens ought to act together.' Moreover, he argued that a petition to the Duke of Newcastle would bring the desired result because the British government was just then passing a law against Orange demonstrations, and 'it would be very inconsistent of the Duke of Newcastle and the prince if they gave formal recognition here to a body that was being denounced by the authorities of the Empire at home.'

Eloquence and passion marked the speeches that evening. When Father Walsh described the desire of countless Catholics to greet the royal visitor, he likened them to 'the waters of the St. Lawrence, which gathered strength and body from the tributaries that flowed into it, until they poured, a mighty flood, into the ocean.' The priest reminded his listeners that 'the soil of their native country had been repeatedly reddened by the blood of their martyred fathers in their struggle with traitors.' And he asked why Orangemen should be permitted to 'take this opportunity of raking up from the tomb of the past the ashes of our defeated fathers and flinging those ashes in our face?' Orangeism, after all, was intended to commemorate the defeat 'of our fathers' and was raised 'on the wreck of our common liberties.' Colonel Connell James Baldwin, a leading layman of the community, spoke of the Catholics' failed attempts to 'pacify the blood hounds they had to deal with.' In reply to his rhetorical question addressed to the Catholic crowd, 'Were they to bow their heads and like Roman captives march under the Orangemen's yoke?' he declared that he 'would rather die first.' Baldwin wondered whether the provincial government 'was guided by the Grand Master who had demeaned himself by wallowing through the mud at the head of the Orangemen, making himself meaner than the worm that crawled along the ground.' Each of these remarks was followed by thunderous cheers from the crowd.

The mass meeting duly endorsed the prepared motions. The first one alluded to the failed attempts to halt construction of the arch, which was 'eminently calculated to lead to a flagrant breach of the peace and perhaps to bloodshed,' and then stated that the meeting was 'reluctantly compelled as a last resource to present an earnest remonstrance to the Duke of Newcastle, soliciting protection from the premeditated and cruel insult.' The second motion put the meeting on record as 'strongly deprecat[ing] any resort to violence or physical force on the part of Catholics,' and the third announced that the Catholics would refuse to take part in the celebrations if the Orangemen persisted in their plans. It was agreed that a deputation would immediately take these resolutions for presentation to the Duke of

Newcastle. The meeting ended with three cheers for the queen and three for the pope, the *Globe* reporter wryly remarking that the latter 'were given with at least equal heartiness.'

News of these Catholic deliberations in Kingston and Toronto reached the Upper Canadian public precisely as the Toronto *Globe* launched an all-out attack on the government's mishandling of the royal visit to Lower Canada. In a series of spirited editorials,[28] the Reform organ fired the British nationalism and Protestant sentiments of many Upper Canadians. When the prince arrived in Quebec the governor general and his ministers had insulted the other members of the legislature by relegating them to the sidelines and then allowing Hector-Louis Langevin, the Quebec mayor, to address the English prince *in French*, no less! What kind of a welcome was that to a British colony?! During various ceremonies, according to the *Globe*, the Roman Catholic bishops had not only got too much attention, but they had been granted precedence above both the leaders of the non-conforming Protestant churches and the judges and members of the legislature. In an editorial pungently entitled 'Time Misspent,' the *Globe* railed against the visits the prince had been made to take of Roman Catholic institutions, such as Laval University and the Ursuline Convent. Why, in a reply to a public address at the latter institution, the prince had even been made to praise convent education, a form of indoctrination objected to by any self-respecting Protestant! Upstream at Montreal, the sins of the government were just as objectionable. When the tricolour flag of France was flown everywhere, the government had done nothing, and, in Montreal, Protestants had again been snubbed when the Presbyterians had been refused the privilege of reading their address. Far from treating the royal visit as a time-out from partisan politics, the *Globe* was doing everything possible to arouse Protestants in Upper Canada and make things difficult for the Cartier-Macdonald government.

So it was, then, that as the prince approached Canada West, Catholic and Protestant groups were both astir. Catholics and Orangemen alike were determined to assert themselves when the prince arrived, demand their due recognition, and claim their rightful places. How could both groups be satisfied? And just where did those Protestants who were not Orangemen stand, those who may have doubted the respectability and methods of the order but who also distrusted the Catholic Church of Bishop Lynch and Bishop Bourget? Much, it seemed, would depend on the Duke of Newcastle's response to the resolutions of the Roman Catholics once they reached him in Ottawa. Whom would he try to constrain: the Catholics or the Orangemen?

Newcastle's Terms

No sooner had the Catholic delegation left Toronto to visit Newcastle and Head in Ottawa than the news broke of its stunning success – or so it first appeared. Upper Canadians quickly learned that the governor general had written to the mayors of Kingston and Toronto enclosing a letter, dated 30 August, from Newcastle, which set out his policy on Orange demonstrations. The duke began by saying that he had learned that the Orangemen of Toronto were erecting an arch on the route of the procession, that they were decorating it with their insignia, and that they planned to appear in the procession wearing 'party badges.' Because an Orange display was 'likely to lead to religious feud and breach of the peace,' the duke saw it as being his 'duty to prevent ... the exposure of the Prince ... [to] a scene so much to be deprecated and so alien to the spirit in which he visits Canada.' Newcastle then made clear his 'terms': the prince would walk under no arch, nor would he visit any town where Orangemen persisted in demonstrating in their regalia. In his covering letter, dated 31 August, Head reiterated the duke's points, stating that 'any attempt to connect with His Royal Highness's reception, the public and open recognition of the Orangemen or any party association, would be viewed with extreme dissatisfaction.' In addition, Head asked the mayors of Toronto and Kingston to inform him whether there was any doubt about compliance with the duke's wishes.[29]

Protestant commentators were incensed to think that the duke had caved into Catholic threats, and newspapers spilt much ink on the matter. The duke insisted that he had adopted his terms upon learning of the Orangemen's plans and while he was still in Montreal, *before* news of the Catholic meetings or the arrival of their delegates in Ottawa. Of course, it was expedient for Newcastle to deny that the Catholics had caused him to act, but the evidence suggests that he was in fact speaking the truth – not that his denial spared him the abuse of militant Protestants who lambasted his 'Romish backsliding.'

The mayors of both Kingston and Toronto immediately swung into action in the hope of finding ways to ensure that the prince would visit their cities. The negotiations between the Toronto officials and the Orangemen were conducted behind closed doors, but news of developments in Kingston filled the pages of the province's newspapers. The Kingston reception committee formally asked that all members of the societies appear in the procession 'only as private citizens.'[30] The city council, though divided and disturbed by Newcastle's terms, nevertheless urged the Orangemen to accept them. A councillor pointed to a telegram from the grand master of the Orange Order, John Hillyard Cameron, which stated: 'I think it better to comply with the Duke's wish.' When the local Orangemen met, compliance was the last thing on their minds. In a formal resolution they declared that the prince would be honoured in Kingston by 'at least fifteen thousand Loyal Orangemen, members of the various Evangelical Churches, and of almost every grade in society, in full regalia, and with flags, banners, and music.'[31]

Mayor Strange replied to the governor general, saying that he and his councillors had taken 'every possible step' to induce the Orangemen to comply with Newcastle's terms, but to no avail. The reception committee had gone so far as to cancel the public procession; there could be no official procession with Orangemen involved.[32] It was the hope of many residents of Kingston that the duke would permit the prince to land and proceed directly and without fanfare to ceremonies at city hall, bypassing any Orange arches – a compromise that surely would enable the prince to avoid recognizing the Orange Order.

Strange was then asked to meet members of the government and the royal party at Brockville, where they stayed on the Monday night before going up to Kingston.[33] From notes[34] made by one of the delegates, it is evident that Newcastle took charge of the discussion and shot down every argument made by Strange and the other Kingstonians. John A. Macdonald, as a very interested Kingstonian, explained to the duke that Upper Canadians felt that the Catholics 'had had it all their own way in Lower Canada,' which 'made the dispute with the Orangemen peculiarly difficult to deal with as it was difficult to understand why after the course pursued in Quebec such particularity as to banners etc. was to be observed in Upper Canada.' Macdonald urged the duke to allow the visit to Kingston to take place. Newcastle rejected both the advice and the validity of the comparison made between the banners of the Catholic Church, 'which were emblematical of a faith,' and those of the Orangemen, 'which were those of a rancourous party.' Newcastle asked the delegation to meet him upon the arrival of the prince's steamer in Kingston harbour, where they could provide the latest news and he would make his final decision. There matters stood for the moment.

At Kingston and Belleville

On the afternoon of Tuesday, 4 September, as the Prince of Wales approached Kingston, the warm sunshine made it a pleasure to view the beautiful scenery of the Thousand Islands. At about 3:30, as the *Kingston* drew near town, the guns of Fort Henry boomed a royal salute. While the royal steamer plied the calm water, followed closely by two other steamers packed with sightseers, dozens of yachts circled round them, sailing lazily in the light breeze, and the blue smoke from the guns hovered in the sky above.

Marring the tranquillity of the pretty scene were thousands of Orangemen from fifty-four lodges who stood massed near the improvised wharf at the Market Battery where the prince was supposed to land and make his entry. Dressed in colourful costumes and carrying a formidable array of banners, the men were openly defiant, a fact driven home by a brass band that blasted out militant Orange tunes. When the *Kingston* drew close to the landing place, a volunteer artillery corps stationed at the wharf fired a royal salute, the steamers in the bay blew their whistles, and the bells of Kingston's churches rang out. Until this very moment, the people ashore held out hope that the prince would land immediately. Suddenly, however, the *Kingston* veered from its course, moving away from the landing place and out into the harbour, where she anchored. People worried that all their preparations might be for nought.

When Mayor Strange met with the duke, he had had to admit that evidence of the Orangemen was nearly everywhere. The mayor argued that the prince might enter the town by detouring both around where the Orangemen were standing and around their arches. Newcastle, however, refused to back down when the Orangemen at Kingston had so obviously acted in defiance of his terms.

The Orangemen had built two of the twelve arches in Kingston. The more prominent Orange arch, which stood in heart of the business district at the corner of Princess and King streets, was decorated with evergreens and a banner in orange calico bearing, in blue letters, the Orange slogan: 'Our God, Our Country, and Our Queen.' On the keystone of the arch were the talismanic dates for Orangemen, 1688 appearing on one side and 1690 on the other. Over the centre of the main arch the Orangemen had installed various devices used by the Order: the Ark of the Covenant, and above that a cherubim, and, on a silk and velvet cushion, the bible and the crown. On one side of the arch was written the names of Orange martyrs and the motto, 'In Defence of the Laws of the Land,' and on the other side appeared two transparencies, one of Garibaldi and one of the Prince of Wales, with an inscription next to it: 'The Faith of my Forefathers, and Mine.' The Orangemen made a point of including their most militant flags, a scarlet one with 'NO SURRENDER' and a blue one, with a picture of a burning bush and the motto 'Ever Burning, But Never Consumed.'[35]

About one hundred lodges – more than 15,000 men – were supposed to assemble on the morning of 4 September in Kingston's Barrie Street, with Major John Flanigan acting as grand marshal and Tom Robinson as a 'grand director of ceremonies.' Also expected were both the grand master of Central Canada, Maxwell William Strange, and the deputy grand master, Mackenzie Bowell (a future prime minister of Canada), along with the three chaplains of the Society. While the leaders appeared, the turnout was smaller than expected, which Orange spokesmen blamed on 'the Romanists,' who had spread throughout the countryside 'false and malicious reports' stating either that the demonstration had been called off or that violence was likely. It could be, however, that some of the Orange supporters did not appear because they did not want to make a demonstration and mar the royal visit. In any event, the turnout was impressive enough, the crowd stretching a half-mile back from the wharf. Many of the Orangemen had yellow, orange, or scarlet gowns with swords at their sides, some wore white sulpices and carried open bibles, and yet others had caps with tops shaped like stars. There was also a large number of boys, who simply wore orange collars or ribbons around their necks. The several marshals, including Grand Marshal Flanigan, rode horses and brandished swords, while their troops waved banners and sang their militant songs accompanied by their lodge bands and drum corps.

Adding to the splendour – or menace – was the sight of several volunteer militia companies, who assembled at the battery dressed in uniforms with the bright addition of an orange rosette or ribbon on their breasts. It was a matter of pride for the Orangemen that these volunteers and their immediate officers continued to wear the colours in defiance of the wishes, and even the orders, of commanders. Major Flanigan took off his rosette when commanded to do so, but he then put it back on in front of his men, telling them that the commander had said nothing about when to put it back on! His evasion drew cheers from Orange supporters and contempt from their critics.[36]

When Mayor Strange came ashore from the *Kingston*, he went to the

Orangemen in full regalia. The original caption identifies the figure on the left as a 'Commander,' the figure in the centre as 'Master of the Lodge,' and the one on the right as 'Director of the Lodge.' (*New-York Illustrated News*, 22 September 1860)

city council chambers and told the councillors and others present that the duke had said that if the Orange display continued past nine o'clock in the morning, then the royal party would leave Kingston harbour without landing. Some councilmen worried that Kingston was insulting the prince, or at least being a bad host by failing to comply with a guest's wishes. Others were incensed that the duke was preventing the prince from recognizing the ever-loyal Orangemen, especially after all the attention given the Roman Catholics of Lower Canada. The meeting could only agree to create a 'committee of reconciliation' to approach the Orange leaders to see what might be done about the impasse.

Meantime, outside the council chamber, it was a waiting game. At one point the *Kingston*, which had earlier moved from its anchorage, pulled close to another of the wharves, and the Orangemen rushed from the posts at the Market Battery to 'greet' the royal visitor should he try to disembark. In fact, the prince and his suite stayed aboard, but the purveyor who had prepared a dinner for the royal party to eat at their Kingston residence took the meal and other provisions aboard the steamer. As the reporter for the New York *Daily Tribune* put it, 'the unhonored visitors were fairly in condition to withstand a siege of moderate duration.' Learning of the provisioning, the Orangemen broke ranks and began drifting about the town, only to reassemble in mass meetings, where the watchword was 'No Surrender!' Speakers warned that, if the Orangemen did not turn out the next day, their society would be banned and 'the Popish host would be carried through our streets before twelve months would elapse.' Telegrams arrived from Montreal and Toronto offering encouragement and promising support.[37] Throughout the evening, members of the public gathered in knots in the streets to argue about who was at fault for the failure of the visit to come off, and to speculate about what would happen the next day. The general illumination was postponed. Orangemen fortified their resolve in taverns and shouted their defiance into the darkness.

Some people, at least, rose early the next morning. Colonel Thomas Wily, the young Canadian officer in charge of making arrangements on behalf of Public Works, was then in Kingston, and he later reminisced how that day he was 'up bright & early to reconnoitre.' On Water Street he came across the governor general doing the same, and the two 'proceeded very amicably together, "speering round."' Because things were so quiet, Sir Edmund became quite hopeful and made some final arrangements regarding the landing, which he now scheduled for ten o'clock. After leaving the governor, Wily ran into Admiral Alexander Milne, who, annoyed with the Orangemen's behaviour the day before, 'blurted out in his bluff sailor way, "I wish I had five hundred of my blue jackets here. We would soon see whether he was to land or not!"'[38]

Just before nine o'clock, the city council reconvened and learned that Orange leaders had been unwilling to meet with the committee of reconciliation. The councillors again debated the issues. They decided to reject the duke's offer to present the city's address aboard the *Kingston*, resolving instead to invite the prince once again to receive the address at the Market Battery. That the resolution referred to the desire of both Roman Catholics and Protestants to see the visit take place hardly camouflaged the council's stand: squarely in the Orangemen's camp, where public opinion in Kingston largely rested.

Meantime, Orange leaders had roused their followers from their beds and assigned them to their positions of the day previous. Sympathetic reports noted that, when the director of ceremonies, Tom Robinson, 'made his appearance on the wharf on horseback in the costume of a Knight of Malta,' he was 'eyed curiously by many gentlemen of the suite.' Indeed, the *Kingston* had drawn near and those on board sat comfortably on deck, watching the scene with opera glasses. One of them, Dr Henry Acland, sketched the scene.[39]

Journalists unsympathetic to the Orangemen penned highly derogatory reports. That of the visiting Englishman Nathaniel Woods of the *Times* presented the demonstration in the most starkly class terms. He said that it had been the work of 'a worthless' set of Irishmen, 'all belonging to the working classes.' The gentlemen connected with the Orange society in the colony had lost all control over their 'vulgar subordinates.' Leadership had been assumed by men of low standing: 'Mr. Flannigan, a butcher of Kingston,' and 'Tom Robinson, a plumber and painter in a small way of business': 'such were the men who proposed to dictate to a whole province.' Woods caricatured Robinson, saying that 'in a medley costume, like a broken-down circus rider,' he had gone 'about with others on horseback, haranguing each Lodge, exhorting them to stand by their colours and die by their colours rather than give way.' The reporter for the New York *Daily Tribune* similarly belittled this same figure, describing him as 'a vagrant painter, repulsive in feature and offensive in speech, tricked out for the occasion with cheap tinsel and dingy finery.' His followers stood throughout the day, a

'The Wood Wharf: or Orange Bitters, Kingston, Sept. 4, 1860,' by Henry W. Acland. The artist was aboard the prince's steamer *Kingston* when he sketched this scene, which gives a misleading impression of tranquillity. (National Archives of Canada, C 124448)

'senseless band of brawlers,' guarding the waterfront and relieving the monotony of their watch by 'cheering and every other expedience – smoking, drinking, insulting passersby and the like.' The same account included the words of the chorus of one of the songs that the Orangemen sang at the wharf, to the accompaniment of 'screeching fifes':

> Water, water, holy water,
> Sprinkle the Catholics every one.
> We'll cut 'em asunder and make 'em lie under,
> The Protestant Boys shall carry the day.[40]

The American reporters thought that they saw disloyalty in the Orangemen's behaviour in Kingston. It was not only that the brethren were defying the wishes of the prince and his adviser and thus challenging the monarchy, they were actively voicing support for republicanism, and more particularly for the United States. Something approaching a revolution was brewing in Kingston – or so said the more inflammatory reports in the New York press.[41] In their own account of the siege, however, the Orangemen presented themselves as staunch loyalists and manly heroes who fought on behalf of all the Protestants of Upper Canada. The Kingston Orangemen in 1860 stood firm, like the Prentice Boys of Derry in 1688, protecting their own and future generations' 'rights as British freemen.'[42]

Unlike other accounts of the siege of Kingston, the Orange one acknowledged the role played by the society's women supporters. On the afternoon of the second day, when the demonstrators were suffering from hunger and exhaustion, a couple of women, including Mrs Edward White, the sister of Major Flanigan, moved about the ranks of Orangemen in a wagon, 'dispensing bread, cheese, crackers, cakes, apples, and ice water.' What more respectable role could women possibly have played? Wives and mothers had also distinguished themselves by standing by their men and, indeed, urging them onwards in the struggle. In the Orangemen's account, one James R. Burke relates a personal experience. On the morning of the second day of the siege, when Burke was leaving to join the procession, his wife said to him 'in the presence of my only daughter, who is about 12 years of age – "if the Orangemen yield today, your child will curse you."' This admonition, he said, 'was the staff which supported me during that trying day, and recalled to my mind the time when our liberties were crushed in my native land.'[43]

At four in the afternoon of the second day, as the guns again boomed from Fort Henry, the *Kingston* weighed anchor and proceeded on her journey, without the prince having set foot in the town. The duke summed up the situation in a letter, taking the opportunity to explain himself and the imperial perspective he brought to bear on the local scene. The prince, he said, was heir to 'a sceptre that rules over millions of every form of Christianity,' and it would therefore be wrong for him to acknowledge the symbols of 'a religious and political organization' that was 'notoriously offensive to the members of another creed.' Moreover, in Ireland the Orange Order had produced 'riot and bloodshed,' and for that reason it was disapproved of by the queen and Parliament. How would it look, the duke asked rhetorically, if the duke countenanced the Orangemen's display at Kingston and then visited the north of Ireland, 'where he could not be a party to such an exhibition, without violating the laws of his country?'[44]

When Newcastle said that Orange demonstrations in Ireland were disapproved of by the queen and Parliament, he was referring not only to the long-standing position of British authorities towards the Order but also to a matter of pressing and immediate concern. In connection with that summer's July 12th celebrations in Ulster, there had been widespread disturbances triggered by the Orangemen's insistence that Protestant churches in Orange areas fly the Orange flag.[45] On the very day that the prince had landed in Newfoundland, the government at Westminster had introduced a controversial bill aimed at suppressing displays of Orange flags and emblems. Its illiberal, coercive features were much criticized, and its passage through the House of Commons did not go smoothly, though an amended measure, the Party Emblems (Ireland) Act, gained royal assent on 28 August.[46] When he corresponded with the mayor of Kingston, Newcastle knew about the July troubles and his government's difficulties with its bill, but he did not yet know of its successful passage. So it was no wonder that, as a parliamentary politician, he saw the Kingston display in an imperial context. Moreover, Newcastle privately suspected that the Orangemen of Ireland had pulled strings in Canada and encouraged their colonial brethren to use to the occasion of the prince's visit to embarrass Newcastle and the government of which he was a part.[47] No proof has surfaced of intervention by the Orange leaders in Ireland, and it is possible that Newcastle's suspicion reflects only the mindset of an imperial official who imagined that all initiatives originate in the British Isles. On the other hand, it is striking how the rhetoric of the Kingston

Orangemen in mid-August, before Newcastle announced his terms, had centred on the very theme that the Palmerston government had found so objectionable in England – the boast that no other 'body of men could turn out in such strength, or with such an amount of flags, banners, regalia, and music, as the Orangemen.'[48]

On the evening of the day that the prince sailed from Kingston, the local reception committee decided to go ahead with the ball at Kingston's Crystal Palace because there was a large quantity of fine wine and food on hand, brought in specially from Montreal. The military, who had been expected in large numbers from Fort Henry and elsewhere, did not turn out. Only two toasts were drunk, one to the queen, and one, proposed by John A. Macdonald, to the Prince of Wales; toasts to the governor general and the duke of Newcastle were conspicuous for their absence. 'A flatter or more impotent affair could not be imagined,' said one reporter. In his reminiscences, Colonel Wily recalls hearing afterwards that 'the guarantee committee for Ball expenses had to "fork out considerable" to make good the deficit.'[49]

The following morning the prince was scheduled to visit Belleville, the next place on his itinerary. Everyone wondered, of course, whether the Orangemen would make a similar stand there. The governor general ordered Wily to proceed by train to Belleville ahead of the royal party, so that he could report on the situation once the *Kingston* reached town.[50] Arriving at about 5 P.M., Wily went directly to the local authorities and learned from the mayor, Dr William Hope, that no difficulties were expected from the local Orangemen but that more would be known after a meeting at the Orange hall. The lodges that met at Belleville that evening decided that, though the men would stand as a group and dress in their regalia, they would remain at their arch. The prince could then enter the town by another route and avoid encountering them and their arch. Wily expected that the prince would indeed be able to land, and so he took pleasure in relaying the news late that evening to the *Kingston*, when she arrived in the harbour at Belleville. 'All on board,' he writes, 'seemed delighted with a prospect of relief from the three days undignified imprisonment.' Wily left the steamer and proceeded to his hotel and bed, 'completely tired out by the day's work.'

First thing the next morning, Wily, in the company of the mayor, scouted around the town. All was quiet until they approached the railway station. 'I pricked up my ears,' Wily remembers, 'at the dull booming of a distant drum. Turning a sharp corner, what should we see but a crowd of men disembarking from a train & forming into a sort of military array.' Of course, they were Orangemen from Kingston, including Tom Robinson, who immediately marched to the lodge rooms and began 'swarming about them like an angry nest of hornets.' Wily rushed off to the *Kingston*, where he found everyone 'on deck chatting cheerfully ... and enjoying the fine morning & the prospect of a pleasant day on shore.' As soon as Wily related his news, Governor Head's face 'turned as black as thunder.' Then and there, the decision was made to leave Belleville forthwith and proceed westward to Cobourg, the next town on the itinerary.

'It is pitiable to see the disappointment of the people of Belleville,' declared the telegraphed report in the Toronto *Globe*. The residents, and most especially the ladies of the town, had been toiling 'day and night' to decorate the streets and prepare a splendid welcome for the prince. Ten arches had been built, 'of a very large size, richly ornamented with garlands of flowers and banners.' There was scarcely a single house left unadorned, and along the main streets flags had been hung from roof to roof. Throughout the morning, farmers flocked into town from the surrounding district, some on horseback but most in their largest waggons, 'having brought their wives and daughters and large piles of provisions.' When they got to town, their spirits rose on seeing the pretty decorations, but then they learned the sad news and joined the rest, standing about gloomily. Though the decorations lent 'an air of gaiety to the place,' said the *Globe* reporter, 'such a quantity of sullen, discontented faces I have never before witnessed.' Colonel Wily particularly remembered seeing the young women who had expected to provide a mounted escort for the prince; there they were in the streets, 'mounted, all ready for the duty, with sad looks on their pretty faces.'[51] That evening the town illuminated – the people lighting coloured lamps and bonfires – and about 200 'Physiogs,' dressed outlandishly, performed a mock procession, which helped to lift the gloom just a little.

Meantime, along the shore at Cobourg, the prince and people were enjoying themselves at an impromptu ball held at the town's beautiful town hall. Colonel Wily had gone on ahead to reconnoitre, and he was happy to discover 'there was not going to be any trouble.' Cobourg was the home and political base of Sir Sydney Smith, a prosperous lawyer and cabinet minister in the Cartier-Macdonald government. Smith was also an Orangeman, but he had no sympathy with his rowdier brethren who threatened to ruin the tour. As Wily recalled it, in

Cobourg 'the good sense of the community, acting under the influence of the Hon. Sydney Smith, had trampled out the disaffected and turbulent element.'[52] People wondered why the Orangemen from Kingston had not come to Cobourg. Press reports said that the train carrying a group of Kingston area Orangemen had broken down en route and, as chance would have it, in a remote location along the line of the Grand Trunk Railway where the brethren could not find alternative means for reaching Cobourg. Probably government authorities had a hand in the breakdown. Writing to the queen just after arriving at Cobourg, Newcastle explained: 'A Body of 150 Orange are on their way as a Deputation from Kingston and by some curious *accident* (which will sometimes happen when the Government has the road in its own hands) the train has broken down in a wild part of the line.'[53]

In any event, the royal party's vigil on the lake had come to an end at Cobourg. For the Duke of Newcastle, who shouldered the burden of the decision making, it had been a stressful time. As he put it in his letter to the queen, he felt 'very painfully these events' and knew that the Orangemen were 'ready to tear him to pieces.' The other members of the royal entourage had not suffered in the same way, however. Writing from aboard the steamer, Dr Acland told his wife that the break in the schedule had been a godsend: 'These two days rest have been everything to us, as almost everyone is well – and I for once in thorough good spirits and enjoy myself in the quiet.' The young prince nevertheless was eager to go ashore and dance. 'It was a very pretty ball,' the prince told his mother in a letter written a few days later. And, unlike so many balls held in his honour, this one had not been crowded: 'There were not more than 200 people invited, so that there was ample room for dancing.'[54]

People wondered whether Cobourg would be the last opportunity for the prince and Upper Canadians to enjoy themselves. The next extended stay on the itinerary was Toronto, the Orange stronghold and the other flashpoint in the conflict between Catholics and the Order. Could it be that American reporters were right when they predicted that the public would be amazed to see a British prince, touring a British colony, being forced to take refuge in a friendly republic?

Toronto

Once Torontonians learned of Newcastle's terms, events transpired on two levels simultaneously: the local Orangemen proceeded with their plans for the prince's arrival in town, scheduled for Friday, 7 September; meantime, intense debates took place within the lodges and between the Orangemen, the mayor, and members of the city's reception committee. Both the preparations and the debates occurred against the unfolding developments to the east, where the intransigence of the Orangemen and the duke had become all too apparent.

The Toronto Orangemen focused their preparations on completing their impressive arch, located on the route of the planned procession, near the front of St James (Anglican) Cathedral, at the corner of – appropriately enough! – King and Church streets. The local press gave credit to a 'Mr. T. Young' for the design of the arch and to Alderman George Godson, a leading Orangeman and chairman of the city's Board of Works, for superintending its construction. The imposing structure consisted of a central arch, crowned by a watchtower that soared to a height of sixty feet, with smaller arches overhanging the sidewalks on either side. The structure was said to be 'a correct representation of the celebrated Bishop's Gate of Derry.' Its grey, stone-like colouring made the arch appear authentic, while at the same time reinforcing the charade that it was inoffensive because it was not orange in colour.[55] The design called for twenty-two transparencies, some of which were mottoes of the Order, such as the bible and the crown accompanied by 'These We Maintain' 'The Loyal Orange Institution,' and, in the watchtower at the very top, a picture of King William III on his grey charger. Torontonians showed an intense interest in these decorations, gathering at King and Church to watch the progress. As the workmen raised each of the transparencies, placing it in its appointed niche, 'it was eagerly scanned in case it might contain anything at which the Prince's adviser might take offence and thus prevent the consummation so devoutly to be wished.'[56]

Soon after Mayor Wilson learned of Newcastle's terms, the general reception committee met in an open meeting at St Lawrence Hall. District Master N.C. Gowan, the son of Ogle Gowan, the past grand master, caused a sensation in the hall by stating that 'the Orangemen were determined at all hazards to walk in the procession with party colors displayed.' On the opposite side, commentators spoke passionately about the shame that would be the city's if it were 'to go forth to the world that after inviting the Prince, he had to pass by Upper Canada – and go to the States.' One commentator declared that feeling in Toronto was stronger than at any time since the rebellion of 1837.

The following evening at 10 P.M., the general committee met again in open session at the same location, where thousands of people waited anxiously to discover how the committee would respond to decisions made by the Toronto and District Orange Lodge, which had begun meeting two hours earlier just a few blocks away. To while away the time, some musicians in the crowd played the piano and led a singsong, beginning of course with 'God Save the Queen,' followed by popular and patriotic favourites such as 'Rule Britannia,' 'I am an Englishman,' and 'A Health to the Queen.' Growing restless, at about 1:30 in the morning, the members of the general committee passed a resolution to be taken immediately to the Orange hall urging the Orangemen to join in the general welcome 'without distinction of party.'[57]

At the lodge rooms on George Street, a fierce debate was taking place among about two hundred members of the Toronto lodges and delegates from counties to the north and west of the city. At last, at nearly 3 A.M., the meeting voted on two motions. One, which called for the Orangemen to march as planned, was defeated, though a substantial minority supported it. The other resolution, which carried, declared that the Orangemen, in their regalia, would hold their own procession on the day of the visit, but that it would not interfere in any way with the citizens' procession. We cannot know for certain, but perhaps the news that the Duke of Newcastle had not backed down at Kingston helped swing the vote. In any event, Ogle Gowan announced the Orangemen's decision to the meeting of the general committee. When fears were voiced that the Orangemen's procession could not be kept separate from the general one, the Orange delegates said that their procession would occur hours before the citizens' procession. Shortly before 4 A.M., the meeting broke up 'with loud and hearty cheers for the Queen and Prince of Wales.' The *Globe* announced the next day, 'Orange Difficulty at an End.' It was a hopeful view of the matter, but one that nearly everyone in Toronto very much wanted to share. A much-relieved Mayor Wilson wrote the Duke of Newcastle assuring him that his terms would be met.

On Friday, several hours before the prince's arrival at the wharf, the colourfully clad Orangemen met in Clarence Square (near Bathurst and Front streets) and then paraded through downtown streets, cheering lustily as they passed under their own arch. Leaders did all they could to ensure a peaceful march, quickly silencing the fife when it struck 'Protestant Boys.' Upon the return to Clarence Square, Grand Master John Hillyard Cameron summoned the lodge masters and told them to instruct their members to doff their robes and regalia, disperse, and welcome the prince as private citizens. More than one Orange leader said that a day of reckoning would soon come when the governor general and his council would be called to account for handing their power over to the Duke of Newcastle.

That same day, just after six o'clock, the prince's steamer swung alongside the wharf at the foot of John Street in Toronto, and the prince stepped quickly ashore, where he and his suite were greeted by Mayor Wilson. The Prince of Wales had landed! What a relief it was to the crowd of 50,000 people, who cheered lustily. City officials formally welcomed the prince to Toronto, the voluntary societies and other groups paraded past the viewing stands, and the procession formed up and moved off towards the centre of town. 'The reception of the Prince in the amphitheatre after his landing was as grand a sight as ever met human eyes or gladdened a feeling heart,' gushed the *Globe*. Even the much-harassed Duke of Newcastle said: 'The enthusiasm of the people really knew no bounds.'[58]

It was soon evident, however, that the Toronto reception had not come off flawlessly and that Newcastle's confrontations with the Orangemen had not yet ended. In fact, two incidents marred the proceedings.

The first one centred on a contretemps between the colonial secretary and Mayor Wilson. Shortly after the procession had ended late Friday evening, Newcastle summoned the mayor to Government House. The duke was in high dudgeon. When he and the prince had passed under the infamous Orange arch on King Street, which the mayor had said was stripped of Orange mottoes, the duke had spotted a portrait of King William III illuminated near the top of the structure. The duke accused the mayor of being a liar because, in Mayor Wilson's letter informing Newcastle that his terms had been met, the mayor had explicitly stated that the Roman Catholics had objected to the portrait and so it had been removed. As a *Globe* editorial later put it, the 'Duke of Newcastle vehemently complained that he had been deceived; he protested that he had been decoyed into the city.'[59] Newcastle wanted an explanation, and if one were not forthcoming, then the prince would leave the city immediately. The mayor promised to consult his councillors and make an official statement in the morning. By midmorning, the duke had not heard from the mayor, and he wrote impatiently, once again complaining of the deception and adding that the mayor and councillors would not be welcome at the prince's levee scheduled for later in the morning.

Eventually Newcastle received the reply from Mayor Wilson, who apologized profusely and said that he had been delayed by difficulties in assembling his council.[60] Wilson explained that, after writing the duke to say that all was clear, the Orangemen had reversed themselves and retained the transparency of King William III. The mayor had consulted local Roman Catholics about the portrait, and, rather than viewing it as a representation of the Orange hero, they 'had the magnanimity to see in it ... only the representation of a good sovereign.' The mayor had thought that all was thus ready for the visit, but he admitted now that he had been mistaken in taking that decision upon himself. He ought to have transmitted news of the alteration to His Grace and His Excellency and awaited their decision. The mayor ended by expressing his hope that 'whatever omission or offence I may be chargeable with, it may not be visited in any manner upon this most loyal city.' Although the tone of the letter was conciliatory – indeed, many Torontonians thought it spineless – the duke was by no means satisfied.

The members of the prince's suite found Newcastle in a temper once he had read the mayor's apology. According to a letter penned soon afterwards by Dr Acland, the duke 'swore roundly that the Mayor was a damned blackguard and liar, and that if Canada could only be kept on such terms as dealing with fellows like him, it was not worth keeping.' It was all getting too much for poor Acland, especially since Newcastle had 'wholly lost his temper before *all* the servants!' While in this foul mood, Newcastle had drafted a sharp reply to Mayor Wilson, but, after Acland and other members of the suite intervened, the letter was 'remodelled into a gentler tone.'[61]

The duke's reply, soon published in the Toronto newspapers, amounted to a diplomatically phrased acceptance of the apology but one that nevertheless firmly took the mayor to task for his error.[62] For the moment, however, the mayor swallowed his pride and made no further reply. Acland joked to his wife that, though, as the duke had said, 'the Mayor may be a liar, and is perhaps not a gentleman,' it was fortunate that 'he was at any rate a timid man.'[63] In the wake of the reply, negotiations made it possible for the mayor and his councillors to be presented to the prince on the Tuesday morning as compensation for their forced absence from the levee on Saturday.

On Saturday evening, the prince attended the Law Society ball at Osgoode Hall, where, strange to say, he conferred the honour of the first dance on Mrs John Hillyard Cameron, the wife of the grand master of the Orange Order. It should be understood, however, that the Orange leader appeared at the ball not in the colourful robes of the grand master but in the black gown of a member of the bar. It was as the treasurer of the Law Society of Upper Canada that he played host and read the formal address of the Law Society to the prince. According to the *Times* reporter, whose representation of the events stressed the class divisions between the Orange leaders and the rank and file, the duke did not dance that night but instead 'was sufficiently occupied in receiving the congratulations of the chief members of the Orange lodges for the firm stand he had made against violent dictation.'[64]

Sunday morning brought the second of the weekend's contretemps, one that very nearly ended in a riot. Everyone knew that the prince would attend Sunday service at St James Cathedral, and it was expected that he would pass under the Orange arch to get there. Large crowds of Orangemen gathered near the arch to cheer the prince's progress. Various distinguished visitors arrived by coach along King Street, passing under the arch as they did so, but the one carrying the Prince of Wales took a detour along Queen Street, avoiding the arch entirely. Once at the cathedral, the prince and his entourage passed quickly inside.[65]

In the streets outside the cathedral, the Orangemen were furious, and word spread quickly through the city that the arch had been avoided. Some of the brethren rushed to their nearby halls, grabbed their banners and flags, and decorated the arch with them in readiness for the reappearance of the prince and duke following the service. Now the duke would see an Orange arch in all its glory! At this point the street theatre grew colourful indeed. Various Orange leaders, some of them civic politicians, intervened and tried to remove the decorations. The *Globe* reported that Alderman W.W. Fox berated the brethren and climbed a ladder so as to pull down the banners. 'The fellows on the top, seeing his purpose, commenced shaking the ladder when he was almost half way up, and finally shook not only the Alderman to the ground but the ladder into pieces, amidst the cheers of the mob below.' As the *Globe* reporter put it: 'The men in possession were determined. We doubt not that they were as valiant as if they had been on the walls of Derry withstanding a siege.' Howard, reporting for the New York *Times*, told a similar story, describing how the crowd 'hooted and yelled, calling out all manner of insulting language.'[66] In the cathedral itself, members of the congregation could hear the rising tumult outside the doors.[67]

At the conclusion of the service, the prince, the duke, and the others were met by a chaotic scene as they attempted to make their departure. Brilliant Orange banners now covered the arch, which was surrounded a howling throng. According to the *Globe*, one of the 'crazy' brethren 'cried out to the crowd to go after the carriage and draw it under the arch.' A few of the Orangemen attempted to cut the traces of the horses so that they could pull the prince and his carriage under the arch, but the prince's driver made a getaway before they could do so. The royal carriage sped off in the direction of Government House, once again detouring around the arch. The police, who had some difficulty controlling the crowd that lingered outside the cathedral, arrested two men and took them to the lock-up at city hall.[68]

The New York *Times* sensationalized the story, playing up the disorder outside the cathedral. Howard reported that, as the royal party exited the cathedral, the prince had become 'pale, and turned from the Governor to the Duke, as if asking counsel.' But the duke, 'stern and determined, strode ahead.' Once the royal party was seated in their carriage, the 'mob gathered around the horses. By order of the Duke, the coachman plied the whip; the horses reared and plunged, and, to the great danger of those in front, the *cortege* passed swiftly through, while mingled cheers, groans and hisses followed them.' The same report included a fuller account by an unnamed participant – no doubt the hero of the story, the prince's coachman. While the carriage was waiting, those in the crowd had, said 'Take the horses out, and let's drag the stubborns under the arch,' 'Down with the duke,' 'D—n the coachman,' 'To h—l with them all!' When the mob surged towards the carriage, the horses 'plunged and kicked with such violence that it was with difficulty that the coachman could restrain them.' Once the members of the royal party were seated, the coachman, 'no longer able or desirous to control the maddened steeds, gave them rein and at a furious rate they pushed through the shouting crowd to the Palace.'[69]

For the remainder of the Sabbath, the Prince of Wales did not appear publicly, but the Duke of Newcastle made a second much-reported appearance that day. Rumours reached the duke's ears that the Orangemen were saying that he was holed up, daring not to make an appearance for fear he would be personally assaulted. 'This of course could not be submitted to,' wrote the duke privately. To maintain his manly pride, Newcastle strolled over to the arch with a couple of members of the suite. As they stood examining it close up, a crowd of two or three hundred gathered and then followed the visitors back to Government House, yelling and hissing as they went. *Le Canadien* of Quebec called it a 'charivari.'[70] Three police constables quickly appeared, exercised some crowd control, and offered to accompany the duke to his residence, but, according to the New York *Times*, Newcastle called out, '"Go back; I don't need your protection. I never yet saw the crowd from which I could not protect myself."' There were reports that some in the crowd cheered the duke. Newcastle reported privately that, when confronted by the Orangemen, he had purposefully 'walked slower and slower to shew them that I knew they dare not touch me, and when I reached the gate I stopped and there were nearly as many cheers as groans.'[71]

Apparently the Orangemen had planned further demonstrations for that evening. The New York *Times* reported that the Toronto Orangemen had made effigies of Newcastle and Head, which they were going to torch Sunday night. A subsequent report explained that, before the effigies could be burned, they were 'seized by the Police, who were followed to the station by thousands of infuriated people.' Little came of these developments, and late Sunday evening the Orangemen removed their banners from the arch for fear that they might be damaged over night. The following day the masters of the Orange lodges in Toronto issued a statement expressing their regret that the Sabbath had been violated by 'a few persons who are not in connection with the Order' – a statement that does not ring true. The masters said as well that these men had been responsible for placing banners on the Orangemen's arch without the consent of either the masters or the committee in charge of the arch. At the same time, the Orange leaders voiced their regret that a society so attached to the sovereign and constitution had been 'slighted by any authority of the empire.'[72]

On the Monday, the prince, members of his suite, and various visiting and local notables made a trip through the country north of Toronto, travelling via the Northern Railway, the district's only line, through York and Simcoe counties as far as Collingwood on Georgian Bay. The idea was to let the prince view a fast-developing agricultural frontier and to give residents to the north a chance to see the Prince of Wales. The travellers sat perched atop an open flatcar, appropriately decorated for the occasion, where they could both see and be seen. The Toronto *Leader* explained gravely how the visitors would be exposed to the virtues of the city's hinterland, where 'the men who form the bone and sinew of the country' were 'by their persevering industry ... laying the foundation of Canada's future greatness.'[73]

Some of those men were also industriously preparing a special welcome for the prince and a particular nobleman travelling with him. At about ten o'clock, the train reached the town of Aurora, where two or three thousand spectators greeted the prince. Three arches spanned the tracks near the centre of town. One was a mechanics' arch, another the Masons' arch, and the third a bright orange arch adorned with a portrait of King William III, the '"glorious, pious, and immortal Monarch,"' and bearing the number of a local lodge, 'LOL–693.' The royal train stopped as a band from Buffalo played 'God Save the Queen,' the peopled cheered, and the prince bowed. And then the train rolled on, passing slowly under the Orange arch. 'The Prince himself observed the arch while the train was at the station,' noted the *Globe*, 'and with a smile directed the Duke's attention to it.' The duke's face remained expressionless, as he ignored the obvious. 'If the Duke of Newcastle had any qualms of conscience about taking his Royal charge under an erection similar to the one he so scrupulously avoided on Sunday,' observed the *Globe* reporter, 'he prudently bottled them up, as it would have been exceedingly inconvenient on this occasion to have changed the route.' The reporter for the London *Times* said that no one aboard the train 'could forbear a smile at the obstinate pertinacity displayed by the Orangemen, and the ingenious manner in which they had compelled His Royal Highness to pass under their party emblem, all bedizened as it was with the most obnoxious of their banners.'[74]

This was not yet the end of Orange demonstrations along the Northern line. At Holland Landing, standing conspicuously on the front of the platform, were the scarlet-clad officers of the local Orange Lodge, with the members grouped around their banner.[75] As they cheered the prince, the royal party scrupulously avoided recognizing them. The train eventually reached Collingwood. The Toronto newspapers reported that the official party took a short cruise on Georgian Bay; the New York papers, revealing a less certain grasp of colonial geography, had the prince enjoying a sail on the Red River! Later in the day he returned to vast and cheering crowds of Torontonians who treated his return almost like his initial landing.

The following morning, Newcastle and the prince received a delegation of about four hundred people from Belleville who apologized for the demonstration there and asked that the prince's itinerary be altered so that he could be welcomed in their town before leaving the province. In reply, the prince thanked them for their invitation but told them it was too late to change plans.[76] Privately, Newcastle patted himself on the back, dubbing the delegation's appearance 'an immense victory' and adding: 'If I have succeeded in teaching the unfortunate Majority not to be afraid of a violent & overbearing minority, I have done them a great service.'[77]

About this time, the Roman Catholics of Toronto proposed to present an address to Newcastle expressing thanks for the way in which the prince's visit to the city had been handled. One, drafted by three lay leaders of Catholic organizations and the rector of St Michael's Cathedral, said rather cryptically that the Catholics were 'anxious to make some more special manifestation, on account of recent occurrences.'[78] In fact, the address was not presented. Bishop Lynch received advice from Archbishop John Hughes of New York urging him and the community to resist the temptation to boast of triumph. Moreover, Newcastle himself had asked the bishop to suppress the address. 'The Roman Catholics have been talking of an address of thanks to me,' he explained to the prime minister, 'but I have seen the Bishop and I hope stopped it. It would do harm and I hope I am not vain enough to wish for any such recognition.'[79]

On the morning of 12 September, His Royal Highness made a splendid departure from Toronto and continued on his way, visiting the southwestern part of the province and the Niagara peninsula, where he encountered no Orange difficulties. According to Newcastle, his own tough stand at Kingston and Belleville had had a sobering effect on the Orangemen. 'The flags which were prepared in many places to plant in our faces were all furled, not an emblem nor a motto were shown elsewhere, nor a cry heard.' He took great satisfaction in his victory. 'In more than one Orange Town,' wrote the colonial secretary to his prime minister, 'I was actually cheered, but what was more agreeable I received assurances from any of the best judging men of the Colony that I had done a great good.'[80] For many Canadians, however, the departure of the royal party from the province merely freed them to speak frankly. Whether the duke had truly won the day remained much in doubt.

Reverberations

The Orange difficulty provoked intense debate. Metropolitan newspapers in England and the United States commented pointedly on the developments along the Ontario shore, and journalists from across the British North American provinces weighed in, too. In Upper Canada, the matter was a cause célèbre, one that threatened a realignment in party politics.

New York dailies were at one in representing the Orangemen as unruly Irishmen who, by showing disrespect to the young prince, had damaged the reputation of Canada. In one of its three editorials on the subject, the New York *Times* doubted whether anywhere in 'his mother's dominions' the prince could find 'a rational population before reaching the American frontier.'[81] In an editorial entitled 'The Troubles in Canada,' the New York *Evening Post* explained that the province had 'long been divided by unhappy religious feuds, which seem to be so inveterate that the parties to them cannot restrain their feelings even on occasions of the most general interest.'[82] According to the New York *Sun*, the Orangemen had caused 'an unpleasant check' on the prince's progress, and it took the opportunity to editorialize on the faults of Irishmen everywhere. 'It is singular,' declared the *Sun*, 'that Irishmen, wherever their lot happens to be cast, cannot act and behave themselves like other people.' When they emigrate in search of freedom from 'Government and party tyranny,' to Canada, or the United States, or even 'the desert of the Zahara,' they begin at once 'to revive old grievances' and organize 'not against strangers – but against each other.'[83] Irishness always meant trouble, as indeed it had on this occasion in Canada.

By contrast, the New York papers that spoke for Irish Catholics were at pains to distance their people from the turmoil and quick to blame the trouble on what the New York *Freeman's Journal* called the 'Orange bigots' and their 'vile institution.' The *Irish-American* provided a historical context for the events by recalling the tradition of Orangemen in Ireland who used to build arches over thoroughfares and decorate the structures with Orange devices so as to humiliate Catholics by compelling them to give 'involuntary homage' by passing '"under the yoke."' The Orangemen in Upper Canada had revived the practice on the occasion of the royal visit as a way to 'pay off old scores against the Catholics,' while at the same time parading in a way that would bring themselves 'eclat and official recognition from the presence of a scion of royalty.' Fortunately, however, the attempt had backfired and brought scorn on the Orangemen.[84] Not Irishness, then, but fanatical Protestant bigotry was at fault in Canada.

The London *Times*, which published two editorials on the affair, said that the Kingston Orangemen had violated the 'common decencies of hospitality' and, by 'greedily seiz[ing] the opportunity of showing off their awkward bigotry before two Continents,' had earned 'the hearty contempt of everyone of common sense in England or America.' Yet, in the second editorial, published just two days later, the *Times* showed much more sympathy for the Orangemen in the context of the political situation in the Province of Canada, where, it alleged, the Catholic Church dominated and Orangeism was 'chiefly defensive.'[85] Behind the Protestant bigotry, implied the *Times*, lay just reasons for militancy.

British North American newspapers from cities outside Upper Canada gloated at the embarrassment the Orange difficulty was causing the usually smug Upper Canadians, and they enjoyed contrasting the prince's tortured passage through the western province with his triumphal progress elsewhere in the colonies. When covering 'the disgraceful proceedings in Upper Canada,' the Saint John *Morning Freeman*, edited by Timothy Anglin, a Roman Catholic, went so far as to praise New Brunswick Orangemen, who had shown 'a degree of prudence, good sense, and good taste that did them credit, and was the very reverse of the conduct of the Toronto mob.' The Quebec *Mercury* made the same point about the Orangemen of Canada East, who had 'proved their loyalty by avoiding dissensions,' and contrasted their behaviour with 'the proceedings of the loud-throated lip-loyalists of Western Canada.' The Montreal *Gazette* thought it ironic that the discourtesy shown to the Anglo-Protestant prince had taken place not 'at the hands of the men of Roman Catholic and French Lower Canada – but of those of Anglo-Protestant Upper Canada.' *Le Courrier du Canada* boasted that 'in Lower Canada, where the population is almost entirely French and Catholic, everywhere the prince was welcomed with the most respectful loyalty.' Everything changed, however, as soon as he entered Upper Canada, where, instead of the respect owed him, 'he found only an excessive and brutal pride.' *La Minerve* of Montreal said that if French Canadians had behaved as badly as the Orangemen, English Canada would have demanded military action.[86]

In Upper Canada, the controversy was more intense and extended, as Reform and Conservative journals, each with an eye on the upcoming election, fought and refought the battles of Kingston, Belleville, and Toronto. George Brown and the *Globe* led the Reform attack, pouncing on the hypocrisy of John A. Macdonald and the other members of the Conservative ministry. Though he kowtowed to Newcastle, Macdonald was himself an Orangeman and had been a member of the government that in 1857 had overseen Governor Head's formal reply to an address from the Orange Order. Macdonald knew full well that the Orangemen were legally entitled to demonstrate their loyalty during the prince's visit, and the Canadian government ought to have insisted that the right was defended, to the point of resigning when such an important principle was at stake. Even if the Lower Canadian Catholics in the Conservative ministry would not resign, Macdonald and Sir Sydney Smith, the other Orange cabinet minister, should have done so to show their respect for Upper Canadian opinion. Instead, the ministers had clung to the spoils of office, the Catholics had gotten their way, Protestants had been humiliated for all the world to see, and the province's hard-won right to self-government had been violated by an arrogant and meddling imperial minister. Ultimately, the imbroglio showed that the Province of Canada was not fit to receive the prince: it was 'torn by dissension, because Lower Canada ha[d] been ruling Upper Canada for years in defiance of the expressed wishes of her representatives.'[87]

In response, the Toronto *Leader*, a Conservative organ, defended the Cartier-Macdonald government and attacked its opponents. The whole trouble had been stirred up by the opposition press, which for partisan purposes had appealed 'to the worst passions of the mob.' Newcastle unfortunately had not understood politics in the Province of Canada and the importance of balancing French and English, Catholic and Protestant, Canada East and Canada West. He had wrongly applied his experience in another place – 'caste-ridden' England – to a situation in 'this freer country' and thus shown 'the fatuity of Imperial statesmen who have an undue love of interference and are unable to read history properly.' (Such an argument had resonance in Upper Canada, with its long-smouldering resentment of the intervention of outsiders, whether from London, Rome, or Montreal.[88]) Macdonald had done his best to explain matters to Newcastle and get him to back down, but the duke had not yielded. Ultimately, the responsibility for advising the prince rested with the duke, who had been unable to adjust his views to local circumstances, and there was nothing Macdonald or other Canadians could do about it. Yet that was a small price for Canadians to pay for the great advantages of being part of the empire.[89]

Far from being confined to editorial columns, Upper Canadian debates abouts the events in Kingston and Belleville erupted in public meetings. Some 1,200 people packed St Lawrence Hall in Toronto on 5 October for what the newspapers dubbed a 'Protestant Demonstration.'[90] That it was. Speakers such as Henry J. Boulton, a disgruntled

Conservative, linked sympathy for the wronged Orangemen with an animus against the French Canadians. Loud cheers followed his statement that the Orangemen had 'as good a right to walk in the streets in their regalia as members of a certain religious denomination had enjoyed in the public processions in Lower Canada.' Boulton blamed the government for allowing the Duke of Newcastle and the governor to do as they pleased, and he concluded by advocating the unity of all the Protestants of the country, against whom the Roman Catholics 'would not amount to a row of pins in their way.'[91] A few weeks later at Kingston, a similar public gathering vented local anger at Newcastle and the Catholics. The Reverend A. Wilson, for instance, ridiculed the duke for having proscribed the costumes and badges of the Orangemen, and he took a swipe at the manliness of Catholic priests. If Newcastle's principle were carried to its logical conclusion, he reasoned that 'it would cause the crosses to be taken down from the Catholic churches' and the priests, those 'wearers of "black petticoats without hoops," would have to change their vestments.' The debate centred, however, on a resolution that declared that 'the course pursued by the Government renders them unworthy of the respect and support of Protestants.'[92] Meetings of Orangemen, including that of the Grand Provincial Lodge, denounced both the government for its 'popish proclivities' and the duke for his meddling – surely the work of a Roman Catholic in disguise![93] The Orangemen of Lambton County went so far as to urge all Orange lodges to withdraw their support for the imperial connection, a resolution that many other Orange bodies thought went too far and that the Toronto *Leader* dubbed 'foolish and treasonable.'[94] Yet the Grand Provincial Lodge, meeting at Hamilton in late October, resolved to withdraw the support of all Orangemen for the Cartier-Macdonald government on the ground that it had allowed 'Popish proclivities [to be] manifested at each step during the progress of the Heir Apparent to the Protestant throne of Great Britain.'[95]

Meetings such as these led Conservatives to fear for their political future in the province. Brown and the Reformers were gaining support from some Orange lodges at the same time as a breakaway Conservative faction led by Nassau Senior, the secretary of the Grand Orange Lodge of Western Canada, threatened the Conservative party from within. In preparation for an election expected in 1861, Macdonald himself took extraordinary steps to reassure Protestants that they ought to vote for Conservatives. Throughout November 1860 he travelled around the province giving public speeches defending the government's position on the Orange difficulty and other issues. According to Donald Creighton, Macdonald's biographer, John A.'s speaking tour was 'new in both his career and Canadian politics generally.'[96] At the first speaking engagement, on 9 November at the Kerby House, Brantford, Macdonald explained that he had done everything possible to alter the duke's course, but Newcastle had remained obstinate.[97] While in Canada, Newcastle's mind had remained focused on politics at home, where the government of which he was a part had a slender majority. At the very moment that the Orange issue arose in Upper Canada, the Palmerston government was seeking support for its bill suspending Orange party emblems. Newcastle believed that he could not afford to risk recognition of the Orange Order here, since doing so would have both been inconsistent with his government's position on the matter in England and put at risk the votes of Catholic MPs that were essential to his government's survival. In short, the first concern of the English parliamentarian had been Westminster politics – and not the well-being of the prince or of Canada.

Meantime, as Macdonald was making his pitch to the Ontario public, the Orangemen of Upper Canada were getting up an address to explain themselves to the queen. The provincial lodge decided on the tactic at its November 1860 meeting, and it soon had 150,000 signatures attached to a petition outlining its version of the stand-off with the Duke of Newcastle. Many commentators were sceptical that the queen would accept any such petition, but, before attempting to present it to her, Cameron undertook a speaking tour in England, where huge audiences lapped up his anti-Catholic message. Cameron was invited to present the petition directly to Queen Victoria on Valentine's Day, 1861.[98] On a bitterly cold March evening when Cameron returned home to Toronto, the Orangemen gave him a hero's welcome. After listening to their grand master gloat about how Newcastle had been made to eat humble pie, the Orangemen paraded through downtown streets as the wind howled and the snow flew. At the head of the procession the brethren carried the big transparency of 'King Billy' that had caused such controversy during the prince's visit.[99]

Where did this triumph leave the Conservatives? Macdonald's support was put to the test during the provincial election of June-July 1861. John A. ran in his Kingston seat against Oliver Mowat, a strong Reformer, who on this occasion had the backing of local Orangemen.[100] As it turned out, Macdonald won the riding because he got the support of all Catholics and of many Protestants who were not members of the

Order.[101] Overall, the provincial election results showed that the Conservatives had done well in Canada West.[102] In the longer run, the Orange difficulty did not have a big impact on politics in Canada; only among the Orangemen themselves would the crisis be commemorated. On the high holidays of Orangeism, the brethren of Upper Canada liked to burn effigies of the Duke of Newcastle along with the likes of other enemies such as Daniel O'Connell and Guy Fawkes.[103]

In conclusion, it is worth stressing that what had caused officials so much trouble was not a demonstration of *disloyalty* but rather a show of fervent loyalty to the crown, a display that superficially at least appeared to be in keeping with the spirit and purpose of the prince's visit. But the prince and his adviser found that there could be too much loyalty or, at least, embarrassing expressions of loyalty from a source with a troubling record both at home and in Canada. In Newcastle's eyes, the Orange rhetoric and militancy displayed at Kingston, Belleville, and Toronto not only resembled that of the Orangemen of the British Isles, it was part and parcel of the same movement. Immigrants had transplanted the institution, and continuing transatlantic connections maintained its nefarious activities on both sides of the Atlantic. Imperial ties similarly warranted the consistent application of a policy of repression on both sides of the Atlantic – a point made publicly at the outset of the conflict by Father John Walsh of Toronto's Catholic cathedral. Caving into Canadian Orangemen could lead only to more trouble at home, metropole and colony being inextricably linked.

From the perspective of Upper Canadians, the imperial tie had different implications in this instance, though there was no agreement about them. According to one line of reasoning, when the Prince of Wales, representing the queen, visited a self-governing colony, he ought to follow the advice of the colonial government. Yet on this occasion he had been advised by Newcastle, a member of the government of Great Britain, and a man who failed to appreciate the delicate balance in Canadian politics between French and English, Catholic and Protestant. The result of imperial meddling had been a fiasco. However, according to another interpretation, one espoused by John A. Macdonald, it was preposterous to think that when the prince moved quickly through the five colonies he would follow the advice of each colonial government in turn. The prince toured the colonies as a representative of the queen, and she had designated a member of the imperial government as the prince's adviser during the tour. It was a small price that Canadians had to pay for the prestige that came with being part of the empire. Without the imperial tie, said the Toronto *Leader* in this connection, Canada would 'at once drop to the insignificance of Illinois or that dreary State, Vermont.'[104]

The militancy of Upper Canadian Orangemen was interpreted in diverse ways by commentators at the time. Some said that their behaviour had been an expression of nationality, or what we today might call ethnicity and, in this case, Irishness: prone to intemperate displays of religious difference, Irishmen the world over always fail to control their passions, as they had done in Upper Canada. In addition to being culturally chauvinistic, such an assessment neglected the considerable self-restraint exhibited on this occasion by Irish Catholics and it ignored the diverse origins of Upper Canada's Orangemen. Equally condescending was the view that the Orange demonstration had been a vulgar, plebeian, or working-class display that the gentlemen who led the provincial order did not condone. Certainly, the street theatre had a raucous edge, and the rank and file did not always follow their leaders, as was shown by incidents like the failed attempts of Toronto's Orange leaders to pull down the banners put on the Orange arch during Sunday service. Yet analysing the class dynamics operating among Canadian Orangemen is a tricky affair, as scholarly debates have shown.[105] Although Nathaniel Woods, visiting from England, saw an insubordinate working class in Kingston, the Orange demonstrators actually included farmers from the surrounding countryside and men from nearly every rank in the local society. Class formation among workers was, at best, in a formative stage in the Kingston of 1860. Moreover, religious convictions and party feeling cut across class lines amid the contentious political scene in the Province of Canada. Passion and militancy were not the sole property of workers.

The Orange confrontation during the prince's visit to Upper Canada focused on the right of access to public space, official recognition of the Orange Order, and the forms of public ritual. Badges and banners, emblems and music became flashpoints of difference. Triumphal arches of welcome, so proudly raised and richly praised throughout the tour, in this particular context became symbols of oppression, threats to reputation, and brakes on the freedom to participate. Marching in the public processions, so widely taken up and lavishly extolled during the visit, proved to be a hotly contested matter when Orangemen did the marching. Orange arches of welcome and Orange participation in public processions provoked threats of political reprisals and clashes in the streets that bordered on rioting. Public ceremonies intended to enhance imperial relations ended up exposing long-standing social tensions. Rituals meant to demonstrate loyalty and community became triggers of confrontation between rival factions. For many Upper Canadians, the bitterness that was caused by the dispute, and the political fallout from it, called into question the value of the prince's visit to Canada. For all its appeal to authorities and the public, the royal tour came with serious risks.

6

Performing Indians

Frequently in the past, the Aboriginal peoples of Canada have played a prominent part in public spectacles of national celebration. Historians have recently noted the dramatic performance of the Kwakwaka'wakw of British Columbia at the Chicago World's Fair in 1893; the role played by Native actors in the historical pageants performed on the Plains of Abraham during Quebec's tercentenary celebrations in 1908; and the alacrity with which First Nations peoples inserted themselves into local programs of national celebration during the Diamond Jubilee of Confederation in 1927.[1] However much the Canadian state has robbed, suppressed, patronized, and denigrated First Nations peoples, governments have nevertheless found it advantageous to include Aboriginal people in celebrations that define and affirm an imagined national community. While many such performances appear at first glance to have demeaned the Aboriginal people involved, a growing body of historical scholarship calls into question this impression and suggests that the social and cultural dynamics were inevitably more complex.[2]

So it was with the 1860 royal visit to British North America. That visit not only provided an occasion for state officials and other non-Aboriginal people to appropriate and display Indians, it was also an opportunity for Native people themselves to claim public attention, affirm their own loyalism and cultural integrity, and demand redress of political grievances. For Aboriginal and non-Aboriginal people alike, Native participation in the public performances provided reassurance of the ties of First Nations with the monarchy at the same time as it raised troubling issues of representation, such as whether Native participants in public spectacles should appear in 'traditional dress' or in ways that better signified their adaptation to the colonial world around them. As we will see, state authorities in the Indian Department, notwithstanding its commitment to the assimilation of Native people, pressed for a spectacle of Indians in paint and feathers, a position that some Aboriginal people took up enthusiastically while others did not. In the end, Native involvement in the ceremonies welcoming the prince brought the First Nations peoples much public attention, but not generally of the sort they would have wanted. Press reports commented on the Native presence in ways that reinforced stereotypical racial constructions of Indians, thus underscoring the formidable obstacles to the successful assertion of Native rights.

The situation of the Aboriginal peoples who inhabited the colonies visited by the prince in 1860 varied widely because of cultural differences among First Nations, their distinct histories of contact with Europeans, the extent to which particular bands had been integrated into white-dominated economic structures or influenced by Christianity, and the different policies and practices of the various administrative regimes under which the groups fell. Yet, nearly everywhere in the regions visited by the prince, the heavy immigration from the British Isles during the previous three decades had greatly increased the pressure on indigenous peoples to change. Even where treaties guaranteed access to hunting and fishing grounds, the depletion of resources brought about by the expansion of agricultural settlements made agreements moot. Indian bands in these regions had either to move into the hunting and fishing grounds of other First Nations or to rely more on farming or jobs in the settler economy. In the Province of Canada, the state had moved furthest in developing policies aimed at schooling the children of indigenous peoples in 'the habits of industry,' promoting agricultural settlements on compact reserve lands, and exposing First Nations to the programs of missionaries who combined white, middle-class notions of respectability and moral regulation with lessons in Christianity. Results varied. If the pressure to adapt had become irresistible by 1860, nowhere were indigenous peoples choosing to accept the cultural norms of the colonizers completely. Resistance took every imaginable form, including migration to remote northern districts, passive resistance, and petitioning authorities.[3]

In the context of 1860, Euro-Canadians hardly saw the indigenous peoples as fitting seamlessly into the tour. Indians symbolized neither mid-Victorian progress nor New World prosperity. However, some of the planners of the tour came to see that Native people could be convenient foils who, in their very 'primitiveness,' sharply set off the triumphal march of civilization begun by the colonists. Moreover, Canadian promoters of the tour believed that the distinguished British visitors, as well as the reading public following their travels, would find Native people of interest, not least when they appeared as exotic and enthralling spectacles.

During the tour, the Prince of Wales, as well as imperial and provincial officials, formally and publicly recognized First Nations as collectivities, a treatment in sharp contrast to that given to African Canadians. The prince watched Aboriginal dancers perform, and he listened to addresses from First Nations and replied to them. The Duke of Newcastle accepted formal petitions from various First Nations. Yet, as we have seen, when groups identifying themselves as 'coloured people' attempted to present addresses to the prince, authorities rebuffed them, telling them that His Royal Highness was 'desirous to recognize no distinctions of race among Her Majesty's subjects residing in Canada.'[4] It appears that no one at the time pointed to what looks today to have been such a blatant inconsistency of policy. How do we account for the different treatment? Perhaps authorities were more concerned to suppress addresses from African Canadians because they criticized U.S. laws and slavery and thus raised sensitive matters that threatened imperial relations with the United States, whereas the addresses of First Nations did not. Alternatively, the policy might have resulted from the fact that, while authorities saw African Canadians as British subjects, they did not see Aboriginal peoples as being so in any straightforward sense. In 1860 First Nations were both something more, and something less. State authorities looked upon them both as sovereign nations and long-standing allies of Great Britain *and* as the crown's wards, in need of civilizing and evangelizing before they could become full subjects.

Certain members of the prince's suite paid particular attention to Aboriginal people. The Duke of Newcastle took a public interest in the First Nations on instructions from the queen, who had directed him to consult with people in Canada about the past treatment and present condition of the Indians.[5] Privately, Dr Henry Acland showed a fascination with Canada's First Nations, taking time to read about their treatment, to talk with individual Native people he encountered, and to sketch them.[6] Acland even tried to kindle in the young prince a romantic interest in Indians. As Bertie lay seasick in his bunk while crossing the Atlantic, the doctor read him verses from Longfellow's *Hiawatha* and then, half jokingly, told the prince that he was 'to play the Hiawatha among these same Northerners of the new World.'[7]

In fact, it appears that in 1860 Albert Edward personally neither had a strong interest in Canada's First Nations nor saw himself as having a special relationship with them. After seeing the carefully staged ceremony at Sarnia involving chiefs from the Ojibwa, Iroquois, and other nations, the prince briefly told his mother what had happened, adding: 'Most of the Indians were a much finer race of men tha[n] I had seen before, and they looked very picturesque in their quaint costumes.' The prince's fixing on the clothing and appearance of the Natives, as well as his perceiving them through the lens of the 'picturesque,' was perfectly in keeping, as we shall see, with the predominant British and Euro-American conventions of his day. When the Prince of Wales arrived in Brantford and took in the ceremonies involving the Six Nations Iroquois, they made little impression on him. He reported home that, at Brantford, Woodstock, and Paris, there had been 'nothing of interest, but we were obliged to stop at them as they were on our route.'[8] Yet, all around the prince, the organizers of the celebrations, the Aboriginal participants, and the journalists covering the tour repeatedly alluded to the presence of Indians and made much of the relationship between royalty and Canada's First Nations peoples.

Metaphors and Icons

During the royal tour, non-Aboriginal participants in the ceremonies and spectacles sometimes made explicit reference to Aboriginal people in their formal expressions of loyalty and welcome. The address of the citizens of Toronto used 'Indians' as a rhetorical device for highlighting the city's progress. 'The generation which saw the settler's log house succeeding to the red man's wigwam on the site of Little York,' it declared, 'has not yet wholly passed away, and yet we venture to hope that your Royal Highness will look with satisfaction on the evidence which our city presents in our streets, our railways, our private buildings, and our public institutions, of the successful results of industry and enterprise, fostered by constitutional liberty.' The achievements were those of the colonists who pushed aside the original, primitive inhabitants who had never developed the place.[9]

More often, however, non-Aboriginals erased the First Nations' presence from history by alluding to the empty lands which colonizers had come to and transformed. 'Within a century past,' declared the address of the people of Pictou, Nova Scotia, 'the primeval forest covered the soil, where, in the progress of Your Royal Highness this day, many happy homes and productive fields have presented themselves to the eye.' This advance had been made possible by 'the fostering care of the state, and from the influence of the virtues and industry which have always characterised the inhabitants of the British Islands, hence this county was originally settled.'[10] Even more bluntly, the address of the Anglican clergy in Kingston explained that the Loyalist founders of the community had been 'removed at the expense of the Imperial Government to this county, then an unbroken wilderness, inhabited solely by wild animals. Soon, however, by persevering labor, amidst hardships and privations almost insuperable, and the unwearied industry of the U.E. Loyalists and their descendants, the primeval forest was subdued and converted into cultivated farms and productive fields.'[11]

Aboriginal people were in no political position to challenge directly how colonizers used the Native imagery in their addresses, but, by participating in the public demonstrations, certain First Nations succeeded in reminding the prince and public of their history and ongoing presence. In their address to the prince, the Six Nations Iroquois (Haudenoshaunee) on the Grand River (in Canada West) alluded to this ubiquitous theme of progress but gave it a sharp twist. The address concluded by expressing the 'sincere hope' that, during the prince's travels in Canada, he would enjoy seeing 'not only the extensive improvements which are everywhere visible in this magnificent country, but also our ancient lakes and rivers and the wilds and solitudes in which Indian people delight.'[12] There was more to marvel at in the province than the transformations wrought by the colonists.

References to Native people appeared also in the visual representations that formed part of the decorations honouring the prince. Some of the transparencies that Toronto merchants commissioned artists to paint for them featured representations of Native people.[13] J. Seel's Oyster Depot, the Toronto *Globe* reported, had a transparency 'representing Britannia holding out the olive branch to an Indian.' It can be read as a boast about the Great Britain's tradition of peaceful relations with Native peoples, a cherished myth of the colonists who liked to flatter themselves by making contrasts with the bitter and violent history of Native-white relations in the United States. Alternatively, this Indian figure may be seen to represent Canada in a tableau celebrating its good relations with the mother country. The transparency on Hugh Miller's establishment showed a scene with Niagara Falls as a backdrop for an Indian warrior and three Native women. The accompanying motto read: 'Floreat Canada.' Here, Aboriginal men and women appear to stand both for Canada and for its natural beauty. Victorian spectators were familiar with the positive side of the concept of the Noble Savage – the North American Indian as an innocent child of nature – an image patriotic white Canadians happily appropriated as a symbol of their province.

Yet, in the visual representations as in the verbal ones, Indians could signify the primitive condition of the colonies before the colonizers had laid on the hand of progress. Paul, Richmond and Company, another Toronto shop described by the *Globe*, had three transparencies: 'first, the Native Indian, second the settler's log cabin, and third, laden ships.' As if it feared that readers might interpret the scenes as aspects of contemporary Canada, the *Globe* explained that the three formed a series illustrating 'the progress of Canada.' The Indian was thus juxtaposed to the dynamism of the colonizers who, by developing the region, enabled capitalism to flourish.

Aboriginal people were also depicted in the iconography decorating some of the triumphal arches raised in honour of the prince. According to the *Morning Freeman*, on the abutments of one large arch built at Saint John, New Brunswick 'were placed – on one side a squaw in full Indian dress, and a deer; on the other a bear and deer, and beneath the date of the foundation of the city, 1783.' Along with the wild animals, the Aboriginal figures signified the predominance of the wilderness at the time Saint John was founded. Another of the local arches, this one built by the firemen of Engine Company No. 3, was a Gothic structure 'surmounted by two figures of Indians holding a flag.'[14] Presumably the flag was a Union Jack and the arch's designers were referring to the support of Native peoples and the province itself for the empire.[15]

Although non-Aboriginal people erected nearly all of the arches, Native people engaged in arch building too. On the north shore of Rice Lake, in Canada West, the Mississauga raised an arch at the site where they presented an address to the prince. Similarly, the Six Nations Iroquois suggested their local prominence by erecting one of the several arches that lined the processional route through Brantford. It was decorated not with painted images but with actual men, or, as the newspapers reported, with 'four warriors who bent their bows and stood in a fixed attitude as the Prince passed.'[16] The arch projected a particular self-identity of the Six Nations as proud, autonomous allies of the crown in military conflicts of the past – a theme that remained prominent for many decades.[17] Notwithstanding the importance of women in the governance of the Six Nations, there were no women on the arch – perhaps because the Iroquois were playing to a white audience.

The illustrated press depicted Indians when covering the royal tour, although the number of such illustrations is surprisingly small given the 'imperial eyes' of the London illustrated papers, which in the nineteenth century frequently featured exotic peoples in far-flung corners of the empire.[18] A close look at one of the illustrations gives an indication of the kinds of meanings that illustrators sought to convey in their portrayal of Aboriginal peoples. One engraving, reproduced in the *Illustrated Times* (London) for 22 September 1860, was captioned: 'His Royal Highness the Prince of Wales receiving addresses at Province Building, Charlotte Town, Prince Edward Island.' The Prince of Wales appears in the distance, standing with other men on a dais in front of the provincial legislature, from which flies the royal standard. All around are the spectators, most of whom, as can be seen from the foreground, are well-dressed gentlemen and ladies. But standing in contrast to these white people is a small group of Native men set off from the rest of the crowd not only by their feather headdresses and darker skin but also by their conspicuous teepee.[19] It dominates the left half of the engraving, formally balancing the composition. Viewers are clearly meant to take note of the Native presence and appreciate the loyalty of the Indians who appeared on this occasion. Yet the humble teepee contrasts sharply with the impressive neo-classical edifice of the colonial state, which appears higher up the engraving, reinforcing its superior rank in the cultural hierarchy. Thanks to a trick of the artist, the large Union Jack flying from a flagpole behind the teepee seems to fly from atop the teepee itself, thus underscoring the loyalty of the Aboriginals but also implying subjugation by the imperial state.

The most extensive and vivid visual record of Indians from the tour is that provided by Dr Acland. During the visit he completed forty-five drawings and paintings of Aboriginal people, which form a significant part of the artwork he completed in the course of the tour. He represented the Indians he saw in a range of ways, from close-up portraits of individuals who posed for the artist to images of groups of Indians performing for the prince and other visitors. Among the latter are scenes of a group of Mi'kmaq in canoes bidding farewell to the royal party as it left Fredericton, and a depiction of an 'Indian Dance' in Montreal, with the editorial comment in an accompanying caption, 'humiliating & bad.' Acland's portraits are not of generic Indians. The

The prince receiving addresses in front of Government House, Charlottetown. Among the spectators are First Nations men wearing headdresses who stand next to their prominent teepee. (*Illustrated Times*, 22 September 1860)

portrait he identifies in pencil with the caption 'Mrs Thomas Thomas, Micmac Indian, Prince Edward Island' shows a proud and determined woman, sitting on the grass, back straight, head held high, hands clasped in her lap, with a peaked hat and a dress that demurely covers her entire body. As with Acland's other portraits of Indians, the image reflects both the conventions of European portraiture and the anthropological gaze, an interest in an individual's personality and the culture of which he or she is a part. Acland completed his original sketch of Mrs Thomas Thomas quickly on the spot in Charlottetown, as was noted in the *Examiner*, a local newspaper: 'in proof of the sympathy and interest of the Royal party towards those children of the forest, the Royal artist (Dr Ackland [sic]) made the most of the waning time before the departure of the Prince from Government House, in hastily sketching the likenesses of two or three of our native sisters, which, at some future period, may be made more public.' It would take more than a century, but eventually the sketches became part of a public collection of the National Archives at Ottawa.[20]

One of Acland's least successful portraits from an artistic point of view is perhaps the most interesting of the lot because of the story that goes with it. While in Toronto, Acland sketched a young Mohawk, Oronhyatekha, or 'Burning Cloud,' a man the artist chanced to meet in a hotel corridor. 'He was a young man, herculean, with a large ring in his nose, and painted,' explained Acland to his wife, and so he asked the youth to pose for him. As he sketched, Acland engaged Oronhyatekha in conversation and learned that the nineteen-year-old chief from the Six Nations Reserve near Brantford had succeeded in obtaining a superior education at Kenyon College in Ohio. Impressed by the young man's 'mental cultivation,' Acland offered to help him in any way he could. They met again, this time in Acland's hotel room at Niagara Falls, where Oronhyatekha had sought him out, and they again chatted at length about the troubles and traditions of Native people. Oronhyatekha expressed great pride in his people, as well as his confidence, notwithstanding the prevalent views of whites, that the First Nations and their cultures would survive. The man-to-man discussions between Acland and Oronhyatekha began a life-long transcultural friendship, renewed during Oronhyatekha's a visit to England, where the Mohawk began medical training at Oxford with Acland's help. Oronhyatekha studied only briefly at Oxford but completed his medical training in Toronto, becoming the first Aboriginal person in the province to do so. His wealth and fame came largely through his

'Mrs Thomas Thomas, Micmac Indian, Prince Edward Island,' by Henry W. Acland. The artist took the trouble to record the handsome woman's features, as well as details of her clothing. (National Archives of Canada, C 124443)

effective leadership of the Order of Foresters, a fraternal and insurance society in Canada. Even as his career advanced, Oronhyatekha continued to identify as a proud Mohawk. On occasional trips to England, he met with the Regius professor. The friendship was important to both men as they pursued their medical careers and public lives.[21]

'Indians,' then, took on various meanings when, in connection with the 1860 visit, they appeared as devices in addresses and visual displays or as artwork. While Acland's paintings suggest that he appreciated some of the complexities which lay in back of prevalent cultural stereotypes of Indians, more simplistic images prevailed on the public scene in 1860. For colonizers, Indians marked the starting point for civilization's rapid march in Canada. Both colonists and Aboriginal peoples used Indians, male and female, as icons to celebrate the distinctiveness and natural beauty of New World places and to convey political messages about the contentment of the provinces within the empire and the loyalty of First Nations to the crown. These were, of course, simplified and stylized representations of Indians, far removed both from the complex and varied cultures of actual Native people and from the many roles they played in their communities. In this respect, the iconography of Indians resembles that of women as seen in Victorian parades and public ceremonies: either relegated to being spectators or assigned a symbolic role as icons or allegorical figures representing such abstract values as truth, beauty, liberty, and national harmony, a role deemed especially appropriate given women's distance from the apparatus of the state.[22] White male organizers of nineteenth-century public festivities may well have seen 'Indians' as similarly excluded from political processes and citizenship and thus as outsiders whose images could be conveniently manipulated. Yet, in contrast to white women – as well as to Aboriginal women – actual Native men played a prominent role as performers in the public events of 1860.

On Show

Throughout the perambulations of the Prince of Wales across the British North American provinces, Native men made appearances in the celebrations of welcome, sometimes cast in their roles by the white elites that organized the events, and sometimes thrusting themselves forward into the scene.

The first public performance involving Native people during the

'Burning Cloud, Oronhyatekha, Cainsville, Brant County, Canada West, Chief Mohawk,' by Henry W. Acland. While Acland sketched Oronhyatekha in Toronto, the two men exchanged ideas and got to know one another. It was the beginning of a life-long friendship. (National Archives of Canada, C 122434)

tour was the royal entry in Halifax, where the group of Mi'kmaq men who had come to town for the occasion provided an escort. Shortly before the prince was rowed ashore by sailors of the Royal Navy, the Mi'kmaq men set off in a dozen specially decorated birch-bark canoes to greet him and accompany his barge to shore.[23] First Nations people, then, were the *first people* to welcome the prince in Halifax. The Mi'kmaq also participated in events the following day when male and female athletes paddled in races that formed part of the grand regatta, and when they took part in some of the track-and-field competitions held on the commons. No doubt, like all participants, the Mi'kmaq were encouraged to compete by the announcements of substantial cash prizes.[24]

The local press reported on preparations for the Halifax reception, including announcements about the races for 'Indians' and 'squaws,' but I have found no references to plans involving the Mi'kmaq escort during the royal entry. It may have been, then, an initiative of the Mi'kmaq themselves. Yet, clearly, the local planners knew that the Native men would be on display because there are reports in the local press about a subscription drive undertaken to raise funds for the purchase of materials from which the Mi'kmaq could fashion 'traditional' clothing appropriate for wear during the Halifax visit.[25] Blue frock coats and trousers were decorated by Mi'kmaq women using beads, colourful thread, and so on. Some athletes no doubt were induced to wear Indian costume because the subcommittee responsible for organizing the games directed all Indian participants wishing to compete for the cash prizes to dress in 'National Costume.' It is possible, however, that the Mi'kmaq men approved of the subscription drive and dressing up because they wanted to wear ceremonial clothing on a royal occasion and knew that they themselves could not afford to make the necessary purchases. At least once in the past, Mi'kmaq had chosen to dress up for a royal celebration. When Queen Victoria's marriage was celebrated in 1840, a group of Mi'kmaq had walked in procession through Halifax streets wearing clothing specially adorned, as the press reported, with 'badges, ribbons, flowers and Indian ornaments.'[26]

In Charlottetown, where the prince was greeted by a group of Mi'kmaq (possibly the group shown in the *Illustrated Times* etching), the ceremonies were simple and the political goals explicit. According to a local newspaper report, the men and women had been assembled by Theophilus Stewart, one of the colony's two commissioners of

Indian affairs. Moved by the dire poverty of the local Mi'kmaq, Stewart had been campaigning to have authorities grant the Mi'kmaq lands that they could hold with full title and farm. On the lawn of Government House, with his group assembled around him, Stewart addressed the prince on the 'depressed and unhappy condition of the resident Indians.' A Mi'kmaq woman identified as Mrs Augustine Nicolas, 'one of the Morrell section of the tribe,' presented the prince with a miniature canoe and baskets that she and her daughter had made. Dr Acland sketched some of these Mi'kmaq, and then the party broke up. A little later it was announced that the prince had donated £50 to assist the local Mi'kmaq in their farming plans, a kind gesture but one that went little distance towards solving their dilemma.[27] Appeals of this sort by the Mi'kmaq – that is, over the heads of unresponsive colonial administrators – were something of a tradition,[28] although the presence locally of such distinguished British visitors made this occasion special.

Native people featured prominently in the much-publicized spectacles in Montreal. At the 'Indian games' held on the cricket ground, athletes contested at least two lacrosse games, one between an Algonquin team and an Iroquois one, and another between Iroquois and white athletes. The Montreal reception committee chose to play up the city's reputation as a sports centre in order to entertain the royal visitor and to attract a large number of ticket-buying spectators who would help to subsidize the city's reception.[29] Immediately following the lacrosse matches, men from Caughnawaga and Oka (Kanasatake) performed 'Indian war dances.' Dressed in buckskin, paint, and feathers, the Iroquois warriors not only danced to the beat of drums but also brandished tomahawks and knives, mimicking a bloody battle complete with the scalping of enemy captives.

Commentary on the Indian games in Montreal conveyed mixed messages. On the one hand, members of the Anglo-Montreal elite presented lacrosse as an admirable example of whites' borrowing from Native peoples. In its address to the prince, the recently organized Montreal Lacrosse Club recognized the origins of the game, saying that it was a 'manly' sport 'peculiar to Canada,' one 'derived from the aboriginal Red Men of the forest, and pre-eminently adapted to test their swiftness of foot, quickness of ear and vision, and powers of endurance.' On the other hand, the participants in the Indian War Dance were variously described by white reporters either as 'demi-savages' performing feats 'too horrible to look at' or as comic entertainers who made 'the prince laugh in evident enjoyment of savage antics.'[30] In any case, sports historians have credited the games played for the amusement of the Prince of Wales both with a surge in the popularity of lacrosse, which had only recently been adopted by whites, and with the first codification of its rules.[31] And soon after the 1860 display, teams of Native players were touring widely. For the next half-century, families from Caughnawaga visited Britain and Europe, performing games and dances before royalty and public audiences, including at the Universal Exhibition in Paris. The Iroquois themselves produced the shows, which drew upon their own traditions of sports, dances, and dress.[32]

On another day during the prince's stay at Montreal, Sir George Simpson, the retired governor of the Hudson's Bay Company who had ruled his men with an iron first, arranged an outing to Île Dorval in the St Lawrence River, where one hundred Iroquois canoeists performed a water spectacle, dazzling the royal visitor and others with their colourfully decorated canoes and their rapid and meticulously synchronized paddling.[33] A canoe trip had been one of the first requests of the prince when his Canadian tour was being planned, and the queen had readily given her approval for such a trip when the Hudson's Bay Company proposed one. Dorval was the centre of the event because of its proximity to Montreal and because Simpson had a fine summer residence on the island.[34] The spectacle was a big hit with the journalists, who waxed eloquent about the fine day and splendid scene.

The prince travelled the mile or so out to the island by barge, while members of his party did so ensconced comfortably in some large canoes each paddled by ten Iroquois. Soon after the prince left the mainland, a fleet of canoes appeared from behind the island and paddled out to meet him. According to the Montreal *Gazette,* they 'darted out' in a 'line abreast,' paddling 'to the inspiriting cadences of a voyageur song.' The crews of the dozen or so large canoes were composed of one hundred Iroquois from Caughnawaga and Oka, 'being costumed *en sauvage,* gay with feathers, scarlet cloth, and paint, – the crews and craft harmonising admirably.' In his account, Gardner Engleheart, who was one of the official guests, found the sight of the canoes equally impressive: 'All dressed in scarlet, with appropriate ornamentations, and backed up as they were by the green waving woods of the island, they presented a singularly gay and striking spectacle ... The stroke of the paddle was timed by the cadence of their [the boatmen's] wild but monotonous songs.' After lunch, the guests strolled about, admiring the beauty of the place, while the band of the Royal Canadian Rifles performed on the lawn. The prince enjoyed a paddle on the river. Afterwards, the entire party boarded the large canoes and set off for the mainland, travelling first past the village of Caughnawaga, as the *Globe* reporter joked sarcastically, 'so that His Royal Highness might gain a just idea of the colossal proportion of the residences of the two thousand Indians who dwell there.'[35] The return trip was especially picturesque, the scene tinged by the light of the setting sun, and the expert paddling of the Iroquois canoeists again drew admiration from reporters. The writers all praised the Iroquois for their remarkable control of the canoes, which had moved in perfect synchrony, for their great strength and endurance, and for the way they blended so seamlessly with the natural surroundings. According to the press portrayal, then, they lived up perfectly to the image of the Noble Savage.

As a memento of this excursion, the Hudson's Bay Company presented the queen with the canoe used by her son. The *Illustrated London News* published an etching of the canoe, with an accompanying text which explained that it was forty feet by six feet, with a red hull decorated with a white streak under the gunwale, 'ending at each end with a white face, on which is painted the Prince of Wales feathers and motto.' The gunwale itself was 'ornamented alternately in black, white, yellow, and green forming a sort of chain or beadwork.' According to the report, the canoe attracted a great deal of interest among Londoners who came to see it on the River Thames.[36] In this way, then, the spectacle spanned the distance between metropole and colony not only through the words of journalists but also by means of the physical transfer of an object signifying empire.

Dr Acland produced a memento of the Dorval visit by sketching an aspect of the day that the newspapers did not cover. 'Confined Indians' is how he captioned his sketch of a group of the celebrated Iroquois paddlers who were kept away from the site of the garden-party revellers, and he adds a revealing comment: 'Sir John [*sic*: George] Simpson locks up his Indians on an Island to keep them sober.'[37] The jotting emphatically reminds us that the Dorval event was staged spectacle of colonialism. Perhaps there was justice after all: Simpson died immediately after hosting the prince, some reports saying that the excitement and work had been too much for the old fellow.

The pinnacle of the spectacles involving Native people came close to the end of the prince's tour of the provinces. Some two to four hundred

Native people, including at least eighty chiefs from various bands, congregated at Sarnia, chosen because of its large Ojibwa reserve and excellent accessibility for visitors from the north (via Lake Huron) and from the east (via the Grand Trunk Railway).[38] Most of the delegates represented Ojibwa (Anishinabe) bands, but it was reported that there were representatives of the Ottawa, Mississauga, Munsee, Potawatomi, Delaware, Wyandot, and Oneida.[39] The chiefs and warriors massed both for an intertribal grand council on the Sarnia reserve and for the prince's reception at the Sarnia railway station where they were assigned front-row seats. At the outdoor reception, the Aboriginal people presented two addresses, one of them 'a harangue' in Ojibwa, as the press reported. The prince made his replies, with the assistance of a translator. Albert Edward next presented commemorative medals (showing Queen Victoria's image) to the chiefs, each of whom came forward as the governor general called out his name. It was the only presentation of medals made by the prince during the tour, and, by all accounts, the recipients showed their pride in being honoured. The chiefs then reciprocated, presenting the prince with tomahawks, wampum, pipes, bows and arrows, and decorative work done on birchbark.[40] After these solemn and impressive ceremonies cementing the bonds between First Nations and the crown, the prince made his departure by train. Spontaneous dancing broke out among the whites on the railway platform, and some of the Aboriginal delegates were cajoled into performing their dances, too. Afterwards the Native people enjoyed a feast, the ample provisions having been donated by the prince. A similar program was planned for the prince's visit to Brantford, near the Six Nations Reserve, though the ceremonies there were rushed and shortened because of delays that reduced the time the prince had available.

The festivities at Sarnia and Brantford were carefully planned in advance from the top, under the direction of Richard Theodore Pennefather, former private secretary of Governor Head but since 1856 civil secretary and, ex officio, the chief superintendent of the Indian Department.[41] In 1860 Pennefather worked closely with Head in arranging the prince's visit to Canada, and so it must have seemed natural to him to look to the staff of his own Indian Department for assistance in making the visit a spectacular success. Pennefather instructed the district superintendents to exert themselves so that the Indians under their charge would present the sort of images that would gain approval from the press and the visiting dignitaries. The department offered to pay the travelling expenses to Sarnia and Brantford of two chiefs from each band. Not only did this make travel possible for a substantial number of performers, it gave the department leverage over the chiefs, whose deportment and dress were of concern to officials. In addition, the department encouraged the bands to send warriors at their own expense, and dozens made the trip. The outgoing correspondence of W.R. Bartlett, superintendent of the department's central district in Canada West, documents the activities of the authorities well.[42]

Bartlett was a busy man in the summer of 1860. From his Toronto headquarters he personally visited most of the bands within his sprawling district in order to rally the right sort of support for the occasion. Moral regulation was very much on his mind. In the course of his visits, Bartlett instructed his charges regarding the good behaviour the department expected of Indians who were to appear before the prince. To those bands he could not visit, he wrote letters explaining: 'None but *respectable, Sober, & well dressed* Indians will be permitted to be present.' Again and again, he reminded them of 'the absolute necessity of none but sober men going, and who can be depended upon as such.' Bartlett asked many of the delegates to assemble at Toronto and proceed to Sarnia as a group under his charge. 'By having them here,' he wrote from his Toronto office, 'we could better look after them, and prevent their being laid hold of by white people & induced to drink with them.'[43]

Bartlett, in collaboration with Pennefather, did everything possible to ensure that the Indians under his charge appeared in 'Indian costume.' Already in mid-July, Bartlett was writing to his superior at Quebec explaining that his chiefs wanted 'to attend in their Indian costumes,' but he needed instructions immediately since 'some of them may not be prepared with such and would require as much time as possible to get them ready for the occasion.' When visiting his bands, Bartlett urged them to prepare their costumes, and upon his return he worried that 'some of them w[ould] be deficient in a proper outfit.' At one point, Bartlett tried to appeal to the national pride and competitive spirit of the Mohawk councillors at Tyendinaga (near Deseronto). 'All the Bands under my charge,' wrote Bartlett, 'have cheerfully volunteered to assist their Chiefs in preparing their dresses, and I hope therefore you will not be behind the other Tribes in this respect.' Leaving no stone unturned, the district superintendent enlisted the help of missionaries, asking one of them, for instance, to ensure that only properly attired Indians left Christian Island for Sarnia and advising him: 'Let them take any war clubs and tomahawks they may possess, and what they do not possess perhaps they may borrow from those who have.'[44]

In his correspondence, Bartlett explained why he thought the Indians should look traditional. 'Our great object,' he wrote to a missionary, 'is to show the Prince of Wales how the Indians dressed in their aboriginal state, and an artist will probably be there to take sketches of everything of note during the Prince's progress. We want if possible to have a very grand affair.'[45] Nothing ought to be left to the imagination of the artist; the scene must be made to conform to artistic conventions, and, above all, it needed to be spectacular. 'I think if your Indians turn out in large numbers [too],' Bartlett wrote Froome Talfourd, his counterpart at Sarnia, 'we shall show the Prince the finest sight he has seen or will see during his tour.' Bartlett showed his own competitive spirit and keenness for recognition. 'The Mohawk are to meet at Hamilton,' he observed, 'but I hope we shall outdo them.'[46]

The insistence of the Indian Department officials that the chiefs and warriors wear traditional clothing appears to be an anomaly given the fundamental direction of the department's policy, which for thirty years had sought to 'civilize' Aboriginal people by propagating the values and habits of mainstream Euro-Canadians. If anything, by 1860 the department's campaign had intensified so that complete assimilation was the goal.[47] Yet, when it came to putting Native people on display for the edification and enjoyment of the prince and other spectators, the department took the opposite tack and encouraged the 'traditional.' I have found no evidence that Indian Department officials in 1860 had any disagreements among themselves about how the Indians ought to look, although differences surfaced on later occasions.[48] The officials accepted in 1860 that their role was to mount a spectacle for the benefit of the royal tourist and thus 'staged authenticity' was de rigueur.[49]

At Sarnia, most of the chiefs and warriors went along with the Indian Department's plan that they appear traditionally dressed. Dressing this way for such a ceremonial occasion was a means of keeping their traditions alive and honouring them. Oronhyatekha, from the Six Nations of the Grand River, was definitely a proud wearer of his special clothing. When he travelled to England in 1861, the young Mohawk took with him the ceremonial suit he had first worn on the occasion of the prince's visit, and he was photographed at Oxford wearing it. He cherished that suit for many years and kept at least one other from the visit, and to this day they continue to be carefully preserved.[50] Privately, Oronhyatekha defended wearing traditional clothing when pressed on the matter by Dr Acland in the course of private chats he and the prince's physician had at Toronto and Niagara Falls. In a letter to his wife, Acland wrote from Toronto recording his conversation with Oronhyatekha: '"Why do you wear a ring in your nose?" "I told you I take delight in all that concerns my people; this ring is part of the old Indian dress." "Well, but it is not a pleasant custom." In a sad tone, "It is the custom, that is enough."' Acland disapproved of this clinging to custom, which he thought would leave Native people behind. He told his wife that he spent a whole evening in such discussions with Oronhyatekha and 'reasoned with him against his too great confidence in the wisdom of preserving his nationality.' As it transpired, Oronhyatekha steadfastly resisted this kind of advice, and during his long life he proved adept at both maintaining the traditions of his people and succeeding brilliantly in mainstream Canada.[51]

For some of the men, the decision to dress in ceremonial garb may have been strategic – a means to gain attention and assert their claim to public space. Certainly, such a strategy had been used in the past, even by Native individuals committed to cultural adaptation. When Native missionaries from the Methodist Church toured England to raise funds for schools and church activities, they drew crowds to their lectures by promising an Indian spectacle – even though they resented being reduced to such tactics. In 1845 Kahkewaquonaby (Peter Jones) had done exactly that, and, as his biographer notes, 'at one point in his British travels he referred in a letter to his "*odious* Indian Costume."'[52] By contrast, when his niece, Nahnebahwequay (Catherine Sutton, née Sonego), gave a speech in Liverpool during a trip she made to England in early 1860 to see the queen and campaign for Ojibwa land rights, she chose to wear what she called 'simple Christian dress.' It disappointed some English people. She reported that she was 'asked by different people, why didn't I fetch my Indian dress. I tell them I had none; this was my dress; this is the way we dress.'[53]

Not all Native people agreed to dress traditionally at Sarnia: newspapers reported that some men 'appeared clothed as nearly as possible after the style of their white brethren.'[54] Bartlett named one holdout, John Sunday (Shah-wun-dais). It is not surprising to find that Sunday resisted the departmental direction; for more than thirty years this Mississauga man had been a Methodist missionary, dedicated to the evangelization of his people and to their adaption to the rapidly changing

Oronhyatekha posing in the ceremonial suit of clothing that he had worn when he addressed the prince on behalf of the Six Nations Iroquois at Brantford, Canada West. The photograph was taken in 1862 in Oxford, where Oronhyatekha studied medicine and continued his friendship with Dr Henry Acland. This suit is now in the collection of the Natural History Museum of Los Angeles County. (Trudy Nicks, 'Dr. Oronhyatekha's History Lessons: Reading Museum Collections as Texts' in Jennifer S.H. Brown and Elizabeth Vibert, eds., *Reading beyond Words: Contexts for Native History* [Peterborough, ON: Broadview Press 1996], 482)

scene around them.[55] Probably he would have sympathized with a point of view expressed in an editorial that, midway through the 1860 tour, appeared in the *Christian Guardian*, the Methodist newspaper published in Toronto. It deplored the fact that in Montreal the prince had been taken to see Indians playing 'savage games,' and it hoped that in Upper Canada the prestigious visitors could instead 'hear our Christian Indians sing, with their sweet voices, some of the songs of Zion, to hear them pray to the God of heaven.'[56]

According to the Methodist missionaries, by wearing their Sunday best rather than traditional clothing, Native people could convince the distinguished visitors that the Indians were adjusting so well that they should be treated generously when it came to negotiating access to land and resources: civilized, Christian Indians could be trusted to develop resources effectively. Later, an editorial in the *Christian Guardian*, reflecting on the failure of the First Nations during the visit to gain redress of their grievances, argued that the Indian Department's insistence on traditional dress had been part of a deliberate strategy to discredit them. The Indians had been paraded before the prince and the duke 'every where as savages.' They had been 'instructed to present themselves half-naked, with painted faces, feathers in their hair, the most grotesque forms of savage dress, and with every appearance of savage ferocity.' The point had been 'to make the Duke feel that lands could be no use to them, and they were incapable of valuing or improving that which might be conferred upon them.'[57] Of course, not all Native people had seen the Indian Department's directives in this light, as their willingness to go along with them implies, and, looking back from a distance of a few months, many Native people could well have assessed things differently from the *Christian Guardian*.

However individuals chose to dress, attending the reception of the prince appealed to Native participants. The fact that the Indian Department covered transportation and other costs of the chiefs made participation in the Sarnia ceremony feasible. At little or no expense, they could assuage their curiosity about royalty and tell stories about their encounter back home. Participants would have commemorative medals to show (now and long into the future) that they had been honoured by the queen, just as the prince and his family would have mementoes of them. Moreover, the fact that there were to be elaborate ceremonies involving opportunities for diplomacy and politics also made the opportunity appealing to the chiefs.

The Aboriginal peoples of the Great Lakes were no strangers to dip-

First Nations chiefs presenting addresses to the Prince of Wales at Sarnia, Canada West. Note the equality implied by the balance between the prince and officials on one side, and the chiefs on the other. (*New-York Illustrated News*, 29 September 1860)

lomatic rituals. From the time of first contacts with Euro-Canadian traders, the First Nations of the Great Lakes region had insisted that ceremonies become part of the diplomacy between them and the Europeans. By 1860, most Native peoples in Upper Canada were proud of their long traditions of military support for the English crown, which stretched back at least to the American Revolutionary War and through the War of 1812 and the rebellion of 1837. The royal receptions in 1860 could be seen as confirming that tradition by means of ritual.

Just as important, the ceremonies offered the chiefs an extraordinary opportunity to deal directly with a member of the royal family, an experience that had had an appeal for various Native people in the past. In 1832 Kahkewaquonaby (Peter Jones), the Mississauga and Methodist missionary, had gone to England, where he made a point of visiting Westminister Abbey, 'the place,' he recorded in his diary, 'where the Kings of England are crowned.' He took the opportunity to sit in one of the throne chairs, 'so that I can now say that I, a poor Indian from the woods of Canada, sat in the king's and queen's great crowning chairs.' Kahkewaquonaby was delighted to receive an invitation to meet King William IV and Queen Adelaide at Windsor Castle, where he talked with them and enjoyed a supper.[58] John Sunday had made a similar trip after his ordination in the Methodist Church in 1836, and he was proud to be presented to the young Victoria.[59] In 1843 a delegation of Ojibwa had travelled to England in order to see for themselves the country and the queen. A war chief Pa-tau-na-quet-a-wee-be, or Driving Cloud, it was reported, had addressed the queen through an interpreter, saying: 'Mother – myself and my friends here are your friends, your children. We have used our weapons against your enemies ... Mother – our hearts are glad at what we have this day seen – that we have been allowed to see your face. And, when we get home, our words will be listened to in the council of our nation.'[60]

On many occasions, Native people had appealed to the sovereign – either by petition or appointment in England – to gain redress of grievances by going over the heads of local officials.[61] Most recently, in the spring of 1860, Nahnebahwequay (Catherine Sutton) had left her home in Upper Canada and, with the help of Quakers in New York, gone to London to petition the queen personally about the treatment the Indian Department had given her and certain others in regard to their lands and rights. Thanks to the help of some Quakers in England, she successfully petitioned the queen for an interview. According to Nahnebahwequay's account of the meeting, the queen asked her 'many questions, and was very kind in her manners, and very friendly.' The queen promised her 'aid and protection.'[62] It was arranged that, while the Duke of Newcastle was touring Canada with the prince, he would investigate the general situation of Native people. The Canadian public was informed that the duke had been 'charged by her Majesty to enquire into the condition of her Indian subjects in this country, whose complaints have recently reached the Royal ear.'[63]

The chiefs took advantage of the chance to present petitions directly to the colonial secretary during the royal visit. While the press showed no interest in, or had no knowledge of, these petitions or the meetings the colonial secretary had with various Native groups, the petitions (twelve altogether) survive in the records of the Colonial Office and of the Indian Department, along with other papers that at least partially document the business conducted between Native groups and the duke.[64] The petitions dealt with a wide range of issues relating to the Indian Department's policies and practices, especially initiatives of the late 1850s. At risk were Native rights to land, resources, and bounties guaranteed them in treaties.[65]

The royal visit came at a time of transition, when Native rights were acutely in jeopardy. That same summer, on 1 July 1860, formal control of the Indian Department passed from the imperial government to the Province of Canada. In anticipation of the transfer, the province had been initiating various new policies and practices that Native groups strongly opposed. In 1857 the province had passed 'An Act to Encourage the Gradual Civilization of Indian Tribes in Canada, and to Amend Laws respecting Indians.' Under the act, the province gained authority to determine who was an Indian, which naturally angered Native groups because it reduced their own authority over the matter and, effectively, their self-government. The act also outlined a procedure whereby Indian men could give up their status, become enfranchised citizens, and individually claim ownership of lands shaved from reserves. This legislation posed a new threat to the integrity of bands and their lands. Moreover, by defining how Indians could become citizens, the act formalized a distinction between Indians and citizens. 'The principle was codified,' writes historian Tony Hall, 'that to be an Indian was not to be a citizen, and to be a citizen was not to be an Indian.'[66] During the late 1850s, the department also introduced a series of new measures that directly challenged long-standing resource rights guaranteed by treaties.

In response to these and other threats from the province, various

First Nations took a political initiative of their own, meeting in council at Rama in 1859 where they shared information and planned further action.[67] The grand council called by the Indian Department to coincide with the Sarnia ceremonies fit neatly into these plans, although the Indian Department hoped otherwise. Bartlett had explained to the chiefs that 'the Council was not for business.'[68] But the chiefs had a different idea and used the council for political purposes when it was convened on 11 September on the Sarnia reserve: they focussed on grievances pertaining to the Indian Department's administration of lands and resources.[69] After the council broke up, several delegates drew up a petition to present to the Duke of Newcastle, and it was signed by Chief Henry Madwayosh of Saugeen 'and 49 others.'

Although couched in the language of deference, the Sarnia petition made bold claims and demands. It began by asking Newcastle to undertake a thorough investigation of the conduct of the Indian Department. The petition then referred to specific grievances: the loss through fraud and carelessness of several hundred thousand dollars received in payment of lands; the loss of islands used as fishing stations and the government's imposition of new charges for fishing rights long guaranteed by treaties; the illegal sale of Indian lands without the permission of bands or compensation paid to them; the forcible confiscation of large tracts without adequate compensation; and government plans that would make possible the alienation of reserve lands without prior consent from bands. 'The state of things agitates the minds of our people and retards their improvement,' concluded the petition. 'We pray that something may be done speedily to set the question of Title at rest forever.'[70]

In fact, the response to the First Nations was bureaucratic and certainly not speedy. Under the constitutional monarchy of the mid-nineteenth century, the queen turned to her colonial minister to investigate the grievances, and he in turn relied on the Indian Department. Thus, the Duke of Newcastle set up an inquiry under the direction of Chief Superintendent Pennefather, who was, of course, anything but a detached investigator. In November 1860 the superintendent submitted an eighty-two-page report, along with twelve lengthy appendices, that amounted to a concerted defence of the department. Pennefather either denied the basis of the grievances or maintained that the department had now implemented the necessary controls and, within the framework of the department's new accountability to the provincial legislature, there was no possibility of further difficulties.[71] The colonial secretary took no action on Pennefather's report. Eventually, in 1862, Newcastle appended a note to the file containing Pennefather's report. 'I hope,' Newcastle wrote, 'that the Advocates of the Indians in this Country who have frequently called you and have written ... are now persuaded that there really is not much to complain of in Canada.' In fact, they were not so persuaded. The Aborigines' Protection Society regretted that the review had 'not resulted in the removal of the anomalies.' Moreover, Nahnebahwequay was outraged by the way the investigation had been conducted. 'I argue that the Duke is guilty of a great wrong towards the Indians,' she wrote, adding that he had 'made his investigation based entirely through the parties complained of to her majesty.' Nevertheless, the duke had the last word on the matter, writing dismissively on the file in 1862: 'These papers may be put by.'[72]

In the end, the Native people of Canada West benefited little from their 1860 appeal to the monarch and their professions of loyalty, a result that reflects their marginal power and importance in the mid-Victorian period, when their military support no longer figured in the calculations of the colonizing powers. Nevertheless, in future years, First Nations in Canada would sometimes pursue a similar strategy, although they would demonstrate increasing sophistication in making their appeals. As J.R. Miller has shown, in their later pilgrimages to London, Aboriginal delegates deftly combined professions of loyalty and presentations to the monarch with other tactics, such as appeals to opposition politicians, to the media, and to international organizations, so as to embarrass British and Canadian governments into taking corrective action.[73] In 1860, however, Native people had little leverage, and they operated in a context where the colonialism and race politics were daunting indeed. An examination of the press coverage of Aboriginal people during the royal tour demonstrates just how all-pervasive was the racism that the Native groups had to encounter.

Press Representations

During the prince's tour of the colonies, the local and international press took a keen interest in the Aboriginal presence, finding the spectacles featuring Native men especially intriguing. The published commentaries mix admiration and disparagement, fascination and revulsion. But, whether positive or negative, the comments reflected and reinforced predominant mid-Victorian perceptions of race and racial hierarchies. The journalists' reports on the Aboriginal presence and performances became the texts by which a wide public learned about the tour and was instructed about the meaning of racial difference.

Journalists were most admiring when Native people appeared to conform to simplified stereotypes of how Indians ought to look. The traditionally clad warriors and chiefs at Sarnia won the highest praise of all. The Associated Press account, which appeared in the largest number of newspapers, declared these Indians to be 'real red savages, majestic in mien.' According to Gardner Engleheart, the Duke of Newcastle's private secretary, many of those present were 'wild savages,' some of whom 'had never before set foot in any settlement'; he judged them to be 'the most genuine savages we have yet seen.' Nathaniel Woods told his *Times* readers that 'these were real Indians,' who had 'a wild, keen, and really savage look.'[74]

Explicit in many of the depictions of the Sarnia warriors and chiefs was praise for their muscular masculinity. The correspondent from the Toronto *Globe*, for instance, described some of the chiefs as 'tall, powerful men.' It was the 'great big fellows,' and the men who looked 'athletic' and were 'well built,' that drew particular comment, and none more so than the chief who delivered the address to the prince in Ojibwa, Chief Kanwagashi from Garden River on the north shore of Lake Huron. The correspondent for the Hamilton *Spectator* described 'The Grizzly Bear of the North' as 'a fine specimen of a savage, with a piercing eye, whose glance half ran you through.' According to the *Globe*, 'Great Bear' was 'a magnificent man.' His powerful voice added to the impression he gave. In the *Times*, Woods described the orator's voice as being 'deep, harsh, guttural' and commented on the 'quick expressive movement of his hand.' For a moment at least, according to the Hamilton *Spectator*, the Prince of Wales had stared at the orator 'and his tribe ... with something like an expression of fear.'[75]

Journalists often drew attention to the Natives' weaponry – their tomahawks, clubs, and knives – which enhanced the impression of powerful masculinity and fearsomeness. The Sarnia *Observer* commented that, given this weaponry and the 'athletic builds' of some of the chiefs at the Sarnia reception, they would 'be powerful antagonists in a hand-to-hand encounter with an opposing enemy.' Such depictions conjured up earlier times on the Ontario frontier, when the Ojibwa had been a significant military force and Britain had enjoyed support from Ojibwa warriors. Or alternatively, such images recalled the days when colonialism was more vulnerable. As Woods reminded readers of the *Times*, Iroquois men had once been dangerous enemies of the early settlers. 'Their real strength and danger,' he explained, 'had lain in their skill as huntsmen, for the craft and subtlety which enabled an Indian to surprise and kill even the most wary kind of deer, was always more than sufficient to enable him to "stalk" a colonist.'[76] In a similar vein, an account of the tour produced for schoolchildren in Canada East contrasted the peaceful Mohawk of 1860 with the ferocity of the Iroquois in times past when they had posed a threat to a fledgling French Canada. In a raid of 1689, few settlers had escaped 'the butchery,' but now the Iroquois braves formed 'a quaint escort' for the prince, singing voyageur songs in French.[77] Savage men had been tamed; the French-Canadian nation had prevailed.

The impressiveness of the Native men at Sarnia, journalists concurred, derived partly from their deportment, which conformed to admirable characteristics associated with the Noble Savage. These were Indians who exuded a natural dignity because they were so much at home in the wilderness. Even Woods complimented them on their bearing, which he found to be 'reserved and dignified.' The Indians at Sarnia, according to Woods, had 'retained all the sullen *hauteur* and studied apathy said to be peculiar to the North American Indians in the days when their voice was law to the early settlers, and they ruled the hunting-grounds from New York Island to beyond Lake Michigan.' They were self-possessed adult men, in contrast to the Native athletes at Montreal, who had simply 'made a show of schoolboy agility and strength.'[78]

The Sarnia chiefs and warriors also impressed the journalists because of their Indian costumes, their paint and feathers. Many of the reports provided precise details about the Indians' dress and adornment. The Associated Press's telegraphic report noted the painted faces, the moccasins on their feet, the silver ornaments in their noses, and the heads 'adorned with hawks' feathers and squirrels' tails.' Some of the chiefs had 'buffalo horns upon their heads; some had snake-skins tied around their waists; most of them wore feathers on their legs like so many bantam cocks. Almost all had bands around their waists, embroidered with coloured grass or porcupine quills.' The reporter for the Hamilton *Spectator* also observed the men closely:

> Some of them had head-dresses made of hawks' feathers, others of embroidered birch bark, set off with woodpecker's tails; some had buffalo horns on their crowns, others again long squirrel or fox tails hanging

> beside their ears. Some were clad in wolf or coon skins, others in well-tanned moose hide, some had tom toms, some conch shells, some hollow gourds, half filled with lumps of stone which they rattled as they walked. All had weapons of some kind, whether tomahawks, bows and arrows or war clubs. And all were horribly beautified with paint. Blue, white, red, yellow and black were all used in profusion. One man's face would be black from the eyes upwards, red from that to the nose, blue again downwards to the chin. Another athletic fellow had a bright red ochre daubed over his skin, his cheek bones relieved with white, his eyes surrounded with a halo of light blue, his nose a charcoal black.

The correspondent for the Toronto *Globe* said that some of the Indians wore 'scalps at their girdles, others were tattooed in a most extraordinary manner.' The reporter described 'one great big fellow,' who had 'blackened his face from chin up to his nostrils. Others wore patches of red, blue, or yellow paint upon their arms and cheeks.' He also noted that 'the head dresses of nearly all abounded in feathers; and upon portions of their garments, various scenes representing deeds of their own or of their forefathers were depicted.'[79]

The care that journalists took in describing the appearance of these Native men can be understood in the context of three Victorian enthusiasms. Middle-class hobbyists showed a compulsion for collecting facts and inventorying natural phenomena – God's handiwork. The detailed depictions of the appearance of the 'savages' at Sarnia paralleled the ways in which Victorians obsessively recorded and classified Indians along with rocks, butterflies, and wildflowers.[80] Commentators on the Sarnia Indians thought them to be genuine specimens, dressed and painted as they would have been before contact with whites – a judgment that was almost certainly incorrect given the many years of contact and the ongoing cross-cultural borrowing evident even in the clothing worn by Aboriginal people who were being self-consciously traditional.[81] Secondly, the descriptions of 'real savages' echoed the themes of classic colonial texts of the day: the missionary and tourist literatures which captivated readers by titillating them with stories of heathens and savages in faraway lands. To 'imperial eyes,' the Sarnia Indians who dressed with feathers and paint were exotic – intriguingly unfamiliar. Moreover, such observers at Sarnia, like many other tourists to the wilderness of frontier Ontario, thrilled at witnessing untamed forest dwellers and peoples on the verge of extinction. As Patricia Jasen has argued in her study of Ontario tourism in the nineteenth century, Victorian tourists 'looked to the Indian to satisfy their curiosity about humanity in its wild state and to confirm their confidence in civilization.'[82] Thirdly, there are signs of the search for the 'authentic,' for evidence of a simpler and better time that progress had left behind. Closely observing Indians, fresh from their homes in the northern wilderness and dressed in traditional ways, provided a poignant reminder of a vanishing way of life and fulfilled a romantic yearning rooted in nostalgia.[83]

While journalists certainly could be impressed by Indians who 'looked the part,' they just as often depicted the bodies of Aboriginal men in negative ways. When the prince reached Hamilton, a few reporters fixed on the near nudity of some of the Native men who marched in the public procession. One of them wore 'a barbarous costume,' reported the Toronto *Globe*, while the other 'had no costume at all, except a pair of moccasins and a narrow girdle round his loins. His naked body was made to look as frightful as possible by being besmeared with red paint.' The eye of the reporter for the New York *Herald* similarly fixed on a Native man 'whose only covering was a blotch of paint, like a postage stamp on each breast, a pair of moccasins, and a meager stretch of linen where something of the sort was essential.' The reporter scoffed: 'This piece of unadorned savage nature was pronounced picturesque, when seen from a distance.' In his story in the *Times*, Woods described the same man as 'a veritable Indian with a ring through his nose as big as a child's hoop, and whose costume in other respects was of the lightest possible kind, inasmuch as a few streaks of red paint and a couple of feathers constituted nearly the whole of it.'[84] For Victorians, themselves clad from chin to toe in layers of petticoats and crinolines or heavy broadcloth, stories of Native nudity bordered on the scandalous and erotic and drove home the contrast with their own modesty, respectability, and civilized demeanor. These few comments on nudity point up the silence running throughout the rest of the press coverage on native dress: nearly all the Native men, obviously, wore Euro-American clothing, or distinctively decorated items of Euro-American clothing, that concealed their bodies.

In some accounts, journalists derided Native men for lavishly adorning their bodies – a propensity that flew in the face of Victorian masculine mores. The New York *Herald* reported that in one of the processions there 'stalked a red Indian made up with a profusion of big feathers and beads and wearing a ponderous ring in his nose, after the manner of vicious bulls.' The native men's masculinity is thus disparaged because the men appear menacing and animalistic. By contrast, in an article in the Toronto *Globe*, the writer associated this same propensity for adornment with a contrasting form of masculinity: foppishness. Readers were urged not to laugh at the appearance of the Indian athletes at Montreal, whose wearing of jewellery and paint was 'merely the logical reduction to an easily realised absurdity of the white man's foppery.' The author maintained that vanity and a desire to attract the opposite sex underlay the behaviour of Indians and white people alike. 'If he [the Native man] colours his cheeks a deeper red than the pallid beauty who this night visits the ball, he uses his brush with the same intent. He desires that his squaws may the more admire him. If he puts rings round his ankles, all that can be said is that they show better there than on the little finger.'[85]

While press reports both praised and disparaged Native men, they almost universally dismissed Native women. When journalists noticed Aboriginal women at all, they generally portrayed them as part of the backdrop rather than leading players, and they almost always ridiculed the 'squaws.' 'The red men of Brantford,' observed the special correspondent of the New York *Herald*, 'were dressed in as full and gorgeous costumes as their brethren of Sarnia, but the squaws, that stood crouchingly aloof, looked wretched.'[86] No journalist went further than Woods of the *Times* in denigrating Native women. Early in his coverage of the tour, Woods drew a sketch of the dreariest streets of Halifax, where he saw 'one or two brightly dressed Indian squaws, with their flat Tartar features half hidden under a fell of long, coarse, unkempt hair; their great splay feet covered over with blanket moccasins, tramping along with their little papooses tied down hand and foot to a flat piece of board, and looking for all the world like some curious preparation of an infant being dried in the sun.' Woods denies the Aboriginal women any claim to respectable femininity and denigrates, in just a few lines, their physical features, dress, comportment, and mothering abilities.[87]

Journalists covering the royal tour also belittled people who, because of their dress, behaviour, or facial features, looked neither like Indians nor like whites but rather some mixture of the two. While the local press at Halifax, ever-ready to boost the place, presented the Mi'kmaq participants in the city's celebrations as 'gay and picturesque,' the international press saw them differently. The correspondent for the New York *Daily Tribune* complained that 'even the fantastic picturesqueness of the Indian costume was wanting'; instead, the canoeists wore 'a queer medley of round silk hats, beaded shirts, tattered trowsers, bound with gaudy ribbons and bright red moccasins.' The ceremonial blue frock coats worn by the Mi'kmaq, Woods said in his *Times* report, were a 'most un-Indian costume.' The cuffs and collars of these conventional Victorian coats had been 'ornamented with rough beadwork,' so that they made 'such a curious *melange* of the whole dress, that it was hard to say of the two whether civilisation or barbarism was most travestied.'[88] It was a strong reaction to coats that were in fact perfectly in keeping with Mi'kmaq ceremonial apparel of the period. Perhaps the hostility derived from their apparent hybridity, which profoundly threatened the journalists' sense of appropriate boundaries, of tidy racial categories. Ann Laura Stoler maintains that colonialism is premised on two fictions: that Europeans were 'an easily identifiable and discrete biological and social entity,' and that the boundaries between colonizer and colonized were 'thus self-evident and easily drawn.'[89] In Woods's eyes, these Mi'kmaq appeared to blur the lines of demarcation that were integral to Britain's imperial project.

Journalists' accounts showed both hostility towards the 'half castes,' the unappealing progeny of interracial unions, and an admiration for people of pure stock. A widely reproduced report of the Sarnia gathering praised the appearance of the Indians because their faces had not been 'whitened by the intercourse with the Anglo-Saxons.' The Hamilton *Spectator* phrased the same point a bit more saucily: 'The Indians here assembled were none of your half breeds – their faces whitened, as Governor Simcoe said, by the Christian dealings of the missionaries.' In a highly romanticized depiction of the lumberers of Ottawa, Woods lionized the men's ruggedness, bravery on the job, and their athletic appearance, which were characteristics he attributed to their 'hardy backwoods sort of life which nearly approaches that of the Indian.' But Woods had also observed among the white shantymen some 'half-caste Indians,' whom he did not admire. He wrote of their 'flat features, coarse hair, and white skins [which] betray their hybrid origin.' And he added: 'It is singular that the half-caste Indian girls are often remarkable for their beauty, while with the men the mixture of the white blood seems only to result in additional and more inveterate ugliness.'[90] If, in mid-Victorian colonial discourse, concerns about hybridity were linked to an uneasiness about interracial desire – as some scholars have suggested[91] – then Woods's comments appear more than merely gratuitous.

A related concern of some of the visiting journalists was the participation of whites in performances deemed to be Aboriginal. The correspondent for the New York *Times* ridiculed the 'Indian war dance' performed by the Mi'kmaq on the Halifax common: 'A dozen or so reddish white ruffians, led by a quack medicine doctor, who, though perfectly white, has been adopted into the Mic-mack tribe, got together and danced a sort of jig, hurrahing every now and then feebly.' Another report went so far as to insist that the white performer was not just a hoax but a con man, 'Irish by birth.'[92] The intense indignation can be understood in the context of the Victorians' deep-seated fear that 'going native' upset proper racial hierarchies.

In the *Times*, Woods drew a firm connection between the prevalence of 'half-castes' and what he called 'Indian degeneracy.' Eschewing any romantic nostalgia for a lost way of life, he delighted in the prospect of the imminent demise of Native people who were so obviously inferior. 'One feels almost a kind of wonder,' he informed readers of the *Times*, 'that the natives, as they are now seen – so sensitive to cold – so racked with rheumatism – so helpless, idle, beggarly, and drunken – could ever even in their best days, have been a people with whom treaties were made and whose courage and warlike skill made it necessary to conciliate them with offers of friendship and money.' The 'half-caste descendants' of the once-powerful tribes were 'now in Canada what the gypsies are in England – a race mostly of beggars and poachers, with the only difference that the Indians are seldom thieves.' Widening the lens, he added: 'As it is with the North American Indians, so in another century will it be with the Chinese and Japanese.'[93] More so than any of the other journalists, Woods used the participation of Native people in the program of the royal tour as a springboard for a discussion of race and imperialism, in the process participating in the ongoing construction of the English identity.[94]

In important respects, the press coverage of the Native performances during the 1860 tour resembled the visual and metaphorical references to Indians in the displays and addresses. Even as Aboriginal people were incorporated into the celebrations, they were marginalized because they appeared as stock characters rather than in all their complexity. Journalists could have complicated their accounts by reporting on the debates among the chiefs at the Sarnia grand council and the contents of the petitions, coverage that would have shown the chiefs busily engaged in political debates, honing their lobbying skills, and raising troubling issues about land claims and treaty rights. Or the press might have devoted attention to the beautiful works of art that Aboriginal women and men made for the prince, highlighting their skills and creativity.[95] However, the press preferred to sidestep thorny issues relating to politics, justice, and artistic expression, with the result that the texts about the Native presence during the visit gave white readers reassuring messages that reinforced familiar notions about racial hierarchies and progress.

Running through the press representations of Aboriginal people, as with the behind-the-scenes preparations for the performances, was a preoccupation with the appearance of Native participants. How Indians ought to look was a vexed question in 1860, but not one that divided people neatly along racial lines. Though the Indian Department was committed to a policy of assimilation, state officials knew that 'barbarism' was spectacular and would go over well with the journalists, whose pens indeed flowed freely when depicting the vivid Native presence. Only the *Christian Guardian*, speaking for Methodist missionaries, offered a counter-position when it chastised the department for staging 'savagery' and thereby giving a distorted picture of the progress that missionaries and others had made in transforming Native cultures. Aboriginal individuals themselves differed in how they chose to appear on this ceremonial occasion: as proud bearers of tradition, or as people alert to their ever-changing cultural environment.

During later royal visits, similar concerns would surface regarding the meaning of Aboriginal participation in public performances.[96] On the occasion of the 1901 visit to Canada by the Duke and Duchess of Cornwall (later King George V and Queen Mary, the son and daughter-in-law of Albert Edward), as Wade A. Henry has shown, there were sharp differences among organizers about whether the emphasis should be on mounting a colourful spectacle or showing the success of the state policy of assimilation. In the interim between the two royal visits, various developments, most notably the Riel resistance movements and their suppression, had altered the political situation, thus making officials at the turn of the century more determined to demonstrate their hegemony over First Nations. Nevertheless, in 1901, as well as during later royal visits, First Nations took the opportunity to make their presence in Canada known and to affirm their special relationship with the crown.

In 1860, the first of the royal visits to Canada, organizers and participants – not the least of them the Aboriginal peoples – engaged in 'the invention of tradition,' drawing from cultural resources to present images and performances that would become part of an established repertoire during future visits. During subsequent royal visits, although the contexts would change, debates about paint and feathers would be rehashed, the media would represent Aboriginal people in ways that continued to reflect the heritage of colonialism, and Native people would struggle to be seen, heard, and understood. Because of the vivid (if racist) representations of Indians in 1860, and thanks to the public performances of Native people before the Prince of Wales, Aboriginal people and non-Aboriginal people together fashioned a tradition: majesty in Canada would have an Aboriginal aspect.

7

Provincial Identities

During the prince's tour through British North America, spokesmen for social groups and civic and provincial governments sought to provide the public with positive impressions of their organizations and communities. For this special occasion, public postures were assumed and identities self-consciously displayed for the admiration of the prince and other distinguished visitors and for benefit of the wider world watching developments through their newspapers. It was an artificial situation and not a time for quotidian practices. Just as people donned their best outfits and decorated their towns in splendid holiday mode, in their formal addresses to the prince, they expressed themselves in studied ways. Loyalty to the crown and attachment to the empire were constant refrains. In many but not all places, the Britishness of the provincial communities was also put on display. At the same time, however, in the course of preparing for the prince and welcoming him to their communities, other identities were revealed, often inadvertently. Moreover, because there was no controlling how journalists from other places would react to the locality, the carefully crafted identities were not necessarily represented in a straightforward and flattering way by the press. Local civic promoters, in turn, often responded with outrage at what they took to be the distortions and lies propagated by scoundrels posing as honest reporters.

This chapter is based mainly on two sets of sources. It begins by examining the content of the formal addresses presented to the prince. Prepared by groups and by state and civic officials, these were mannered 'concoctions,' as a critic remarked at the time, intended to flatter the prince and queen and to celebrate ties of empire. Yet, in many cases, their authors, and those who endorsed them, succinctly conveyed meanings about who they were and how their group or community related to the monarchy and the empire. The chapter then turns to the newspapers of the period as a source for studying the ways in which several issues relating to local and regional identities were expressed in the course of planning for the royal tour and welcoming the prince. This material is approached regionally, beginning with the identities of Maritimers, then turning to French Canadians, and finally to Upper Canadians. As we will see, various identities were revealed and reasserted as part of an international conversation in the press, a discussion that sometimes grew heated and impolite. The chapter argues that, despite the best efforts of the promoters of the tour to convey an impression of seamless harmony and contentment under the crown, in fact the tour made evident the presence of social and cultural tensions. British subjects in the North American provinces, the visit showed, had not one but multiple and fractured identities. Contributions to the international historiography on public occasions draw similar conclusions about the process of identity formation.[1] Each study's significance lies in its particularities: how the various fissures actually came to light and were represented.

Addressing the Meaning of Loyalty

The addresses presented to the Prince of Wales[2] expressed a limited range of sentiments in a more-or-less formulaic way, and yet the stock phrases of 1860 do reflect cultural meanings relevant to British North Americans in the mid-Victorian period. If we were seeking frank assessments of the value of the monarchy and the British empire, the addresses would not be the place to look for them. All the addresses did what was expected: they expressed loyalty to the queen, appreciation for her decision to send the prince to the colonies, and best wishes to him on his journey. In giving them shape, however, their authors, and the community groups behind them, made choices about how best to represent such sentiments. They drew heavily from a well of cultural resources, choosing phrases that seemed appropriate for the occasion and that had meanings and resonances for their time. Concepts of Britishness abound, but not every group chose to express their attachment to crown and empire in precisely the same way.

The addresses generally have little to say about the young man to whom they were presented; it was his mother that was of interest. The queen was repeatedly referred to, not just as a beloved sovereign, but as a virtuous woman (or 'lady') and a mother admired everywhere. 'This Synod,' said the Presbyterian Church of Canada, 'hails Your Royal Highness in your visit to these parts of the American continent, recognizing in you the representative of a Sovereign, who, no less by her example of domestic virtue, than by her mild and prudent exercise of her queenly prerogative, has secured the hearty homage of her subjects, and the universal respect of the civilized world.' The Working Men and Artizans of the Grand Trunk Railway assured the prince that everywhere he went on his visit he would find 'love and attachment towards that Lady whose virtues are known and acknowledged in every land [and] in every home – Your Mother and Our Queen.' The municipal corporation of Sherbrooke, Canada East, expressed its pride in the community's relation to the sovereign, 'distinguished alike as a Queen and as a woman for those estimable qualities which have won for her the confidence and love of her people.' In making such remarks, the authors of the addresses, though speaking from the colonies, were singing from precisely the same hymnal as their counterparts in England. 'The Queen was revered in the middle-class press,' writes one historian of Victorian England, 'as the ideal sovereign and the ideal woman. ... She was the cynosure of the domestic virtues which a woman and particularly an Englishwoman was supposed to embody.'[3]

More than a little vagueness characterized references to Victoria's virtues in the addresses to the prince; listeners and readers had plenty of latitude for imagining the precise qualities that made up her queenly virtue. The city of Halifax, however, was a little more specific, referring to 'the lustre' which had been shed on the crown 'by the Christian and domestic virtues of our most gracious Sovereign.' And other addresses referred to these same virtues in ways that suggested a link between home and nation, between, on the one hand, a home made pure and good by woman's presence and Christ's love, and, on the other, a British nation whose moral strength was nurtured publicly by the royal mother and her church. An address from the temperance organizations of Upper Canada spelled out unusually clearly these kinds of connections. 'We rejoice,' it exclaimed, 'that our allegiance is due to a Sovereign whose glorious reign has never been tarnished by the exceeds of former Courts, but that the truly Christian example of your Royal mother has called forth universal commendation.' Moreover, 'many thousands' of the temperance youth of Upper Canada were 'emulating the Christian graces of our Queen,' a lady 'whose goodness and whose virtues' would form 'the choicest page of

England's history.' In echoing the veneration of Victoria so widespread in England at the time, middle-class authors of the colonial addresses, like their counterparts in the metropole, imagined that their own cherished values were exemplified fully by the queen.[4]

Many of the addresses to the prince sang the praises of the British monarchy for fostering the liberty so much enjoyed by British subjects in England and her colonies. A few of the remarks referred to the long tradition of British freedoms. The city of Toronto address, for instance, mentioned the people's cherished 'rights as freemen.' The address of Colchester County and Truro, Nova Scotia, maintained that the 'free institutions, which are the pride of Britain, have been claimed and conceded as our birthright.' The government of New Brunswick made the historical and constitutional connections more explicit, speaking of a people 'contented and happy in the enjoyment of that large measure of rational liberty which our mixed form of government secures.' The reference, well understood in 1860, was to colonial constitutions modelled on Britain's own constitutional arrangements, which were said to promote stability by balancing the powers of the monarchy, the aristocracy (or wealth), and the people.

Moreover, the New Brunswick address, like several others, drew attention as well to those newly acquired liberties associated with colonial self-government, rights granted during Victoria's reign. 'Under Your august Mother,' continued the New Brunswick document, 'the principles of self-government were fully established with ample power to regulate trade.' Nova Scotia's address similarly mentioned 'the blessings of self-government and unrestricted intercourse with all the world,' conferred upon the province during the reign of the prince's 'Illustrious Mother.' Canadian addresses were just as apt to express appreciation for colonial self-government, or, as the Legislative Council of the Province of Canada put it, for 'the institutions [that] guaranteed to us all freedom in the management of our own affairs.' The address of the Upper Canadian counties of Prescott and Russell acknowledged the 'free laws under which we have the happiness to live' and cited specifically 'a noble instance ... our own municipal institutions.' Granted by 'the most liberal and enlightened of all governments in the world,' they would 'tend to strengthen and cement more strongly and closely, if possible, than ever, our respect, regard, and attachment of the British Crown and Constitution.' In articulating such views, these colonial addresses reiterated the language of nationalism in Victorian England, which harkened back romantically to a history of expanding liberty guaranteed by the nation's flexible, unwritten constitution.[5] In addition, they gave it a Canadian twist by referring as well to recent constitutional and governmental developments, which, although in the same tradition, had taken place in the colonies.

A few of the addresses presented by certain clerical bodies made a point of expressing appreciation for the tradition of religious liberty that the colonies shared with the mother country. The address of Knox College, the Presbyterian theological school in Toronto, acknowledged 'the protection we enjoy under the shield of the British laws in the prosecution of our literary and religious labours.' Generally, however, the clerical bodies preferred to take a conservative rather than a liberal stance, emphasizing the role they played in encouraging, as the address of the Primitive Methodist Church put it, 'all necessary obedience to the Throne and Constitution of our Country.' Addresses from Anglican and from Roman Catholic clergy highlighted the order and stability that the monarchy provided and that the churches reinforced. The Anglican clergy of St John's insisted that no one else was 'more earnest in inculcating obedience to the Laws and submission to the higher powers.' The Roman Catholic bishops of Canada assembled at Quebec declared in French and English that they had always taught the people that, because God chose the rulers, 'entire submission is due to the authority that they have from high.'

A sovereign who promoted liberty was just one of many benefits derived from the imperial connection. In their address, the judges of the Court of Quarter Sessions of the United Counties of Frontenac, Lennox, and Addington (in Canada West) expressed the people's pride in 'being the free subjects of the greatest and most enlightened empire in the world' and their delight in 'the right to participate in the rich inheritance of British freedom, British triumphs, and British civilization.' The address of the municipal corporation of Sherbrooke made clear that the colonists had no wish whatever to sever the British connection, even though the people were 'situated on the borders of the neighbouring republic and intimately acquainted with the working of its institutions.' In the British empire, all were equal and shared in what the address of the city of Fredericton called, a little awkwardly, 'the universal heart-throb of our Empire of perpetual sunlight.' Usually, historians have seen this kind of assertive British imperialism as being especially characteristic of the late nineteenth century,[6] but the evidence makes it clear that the 1860 visit provided an occasion for articulating similar sentiments.

Several, but not all, of the addresses to the Prince of Wales treated the colonies and mother country as making up one corporate body that shared the same blood. 'The blood which throbs in England's heart,' boasted the magistrates of Simcoe County, Canada West, 'circulates through every member of Her mighty empire.' The address of the senate, alumni, and students of Victoria College (then located in Cobourg, Canada West) made reference to a common racial, as well as intellectual, heritage. It expressed the hope 'that the study of the unrivalled literature of our fatherland, combined with the teachings of the great masters of Greece and Rome, may render Canadian youth not unworthy of their Saxon origin and language.' It goes without saying that groups such as the Aboriginal peoples and French and African Canadians were tidily written out of this rendering of Canada.

Other communities within British North America contradicted this view of Canada as having a common Anglo-Saxon heritage. The address of the inhabitants of Gaspé referred to Canada's diverse populations, whose origins lay among the French, who first colonized the country, and among the Loyalists, who came later, but its main point was that all lived 'in peace and in friendship, respecting each other's particular views and creeds, and acting on the golden rule, "Do unto others as you would have others do unto you."' The address of the province of New Brunswick spoke of its people as deriving from three groups: the Loyalist Americans who had fled the revolution, British immigrants and their descendants, and emigrants from Europe and their offspring, this latter phrase being an oblique reference to New Brunswick's Acadian population. The address of the city of Quebec (one of the few read first in French by a French Canadian) similarly avoided any specific reference to the French origins of many citizens, but it was a forthright assertion of diversity. The address noted that the people 'derive their origin from various races, and may differ in language and religious denominations,' but it insisted that the community had 'but one voice and one heart in expressing loyalty to their sovereign, and in welcoming him who represents her on this occasion.' French-Canadian nationality could survive, alongside an English-Canadian or British nationality, within a constitutional monarchy where all bore allegiance to one crown. French Canadians could be proud Britons, not because they shared the same culture as people of British descent, but because they gloried in the freedom, prosperity, security, and stability that the British empire and monarchy provided.

The members of Laval University, a French-speaking and Catholic institution, acknowledged the university's 'special tie to Victoria,' who had granted its charter, and expressed optimism about the benefits of the empire, saying the institution would 'form a new tie between their fellow subjects of French origin and the mother country, to whose care we have been committed by Divine Providence.' The clerical nationalism of French Canada in the mid-nineteenth century presented the British Conquest of 1760 as providential: God had intervened to protect French-Canadian Catholics from the anti-clericalism that the French Revolution unleashed after 1789 in the former mother country. The church and the people were secure under British rule. 'We trust in the future destinies of the colony,' continued the Laval University address, 'which, under the protection of England, is in the enjoyment of peace and abundance, while other countries are distracted by violent convulsions.' The university went so far as to express its trust in 'the future of that glorious metropolis [London] whose influence is so weighty in controlling the destinies of the civilized world.' By drawing attention to the power of England's metropolis, the address was at once a form of flattery and a reminder to British authorities of their responsibilities – presumably the obligation to respect and protect minorities such as the French Canadians.

Several of the addresses to the Prince of Wales portrayed the colonies, and particularly Canada, as important components of the empire. The magistrates of Simcoe County in Canada West called Canada 'an integral and important portion of the empire,' while the address of the inhabitants of St John's referred to Newfoundland as being 'amongst the brightest gems of the Royal Diadem.' The address of the city of Hamilton predicted that, given local progress, 'at no distant day the British American provinces will be the most powerful support to [the] Throne.' Deference to England's hegemony was notably lacking in these assertions of colonial self-importance. At the same time, however, being part of the British empire, it was implied, gave the colonies greater significance in the world than they would otherwise have had. As things stood, they were part of 'an Empire embracing over two hundred millions of subjects,' indeed, a 'glorious globe-encircling empire.'

Sharing in the glory of the British empire did not mean slavish reproduction of metropolitan institutions or the obliteration of provincial particularities. In the British North American provinces, the local and the imperial had been smoothly combined. The address of the University of Toronto noted succinctly that 'our system is upon the model of the Institutions of our mother country, while adapted in its details to the special wants of this portion of the Empire.' And, according to the address of Upper Canada's Council for Public Instruction, there was no difficulty in fostering a local patriotism within the imperial and monarchical context. 'In the song and text books of the schools,' declared the address prepared by Egerton Ryerson, 'loyalty to the Queen and love of the mother Country are blended with the spirit of Canadian patriotism.'

Several addresses showed a quintessentially Victorian faith in colonialism and progress, and more particularly a pride in the rapid strides their own communities had made in advancing British civilization in the wilderness. The address of the town of Pictou, Nova Scotia, expressed confidence that the prince would appreciate the evidence he was seeing of the advance of settlement locally. 'Within a century past,' the address explained, 'the primeval forests covered the soil where, in the progress of Your Royal Highness this day, many happy homes and productive fields have presented themselves to the eye.' That advance had been made possible 'under the fostering care of the parent state,' because of 'the virtues and industry' which the area had acquired through its connections with 'the British islands.' Sounding a note of false modesty, the government of Nova Scotia declared its hope that the prince would observe in the province 'some faint traces of the civilization you have left at home, some indications of a desire to combine commercial activity and industrial development with the enjoyment of rational freedom.' The address of Chicoutimi, with its predominantly French-Canadian population, avoided references to any British inheritance but nevertheless made a connection to the monarchy. 'We are advancing into and clearing away the forest,' declared the address, 'and as it were, conquering a new province to add to the Crown.'

In the rhetoric of two of the addresses, racial tropes were intended to heighten the contrast between what little there had once been and how much there now was. The address of London, Canada West, reminded the prince that it had been 'only forty years since, in the locality where you now stand, none but the red Indian stood under the shade of the primeval forest.' Thanks to immigration, civilization and industry had taken their place. White mid-Victorian audiences, like the prince himself, could be expected to understand readily that the 'red Indian' was the very antithesis of the industrious settler, of the colonist who brought civilization to the wilderness.

Nothing better signified Canada's advances than the Victoria Bridge.

Several addresses dealt at length with the engineering colossus that was the occasion for the royal tour. The address of the Legislative Assembly of the Province of Canada expressed confidence that the prince would 'find in that stupendous work the most striking evidence in which the capital and skill of the mother Country have united with the energy and enterprise of this Province in overcoming the natural obstacles of the most formidable character.' Precisely the same theme was echoed in the address of the city of Montreal: 'Your Royal Highness will not fail to observe how natural obstacles, almost insurmountable in their ponderous strength and complicated variety, have been triumphantly overcome by the combined power of British enterprise and capital, and of Canadian energy and skill.' In addition to ties of sentiment and culture, the British empire had a practical worth that the Victoria Bridge both symbolized and demonstrated in a grandly substantive and useful way, a way dear to the hearts of Victorians.

The addresses prepared by cultural and religious organizations in Canada celebrated the links between their activities and similar ones in Great Britain, thus highlighting the cultural connectedness between colony and metropole. The Natural History Society of Montreal maintained that the prince would understand the importance of its work because he had attended meetings of the Royal Institution in London, while the Horticultural Society of Toronto acknowledged the encouragement that the queen and the prince consort had both given to similar societies in England. The St George's Society of Toronto explained that, 'by periodical commemorations,' it sought 'to keep alive the remembrance of the achievements of their forefathers, under the banner of their Patron Saint,' and on such occasions to give 'the time-honoured cry of "St George for Merrie England!"' Sports organizations similarly trumpeted the ties of empire that bound people together in pursuit of common goals and values. The address of the Royal Canadian Yacht Club in Toronto spoke of sailing as 'the great national sport of the British Empire – a sport so intimately connected with its naval pre-eminence.' Even the address of the Lacrosse Club (or 'Crosse Club') of Montreal, which stressed the indigenous origins of the game, acknowledged a wider, imperial context when it thanked the prince for the 'great encouragements which all manly sports and athletic games have received from the patronage and example of Your Royal Highness.'

An imperial relationship that fostered superior values and technological achievements was one worth fighting for – or so many addresses suggested. Hansport, Nova Scotia, vowed: 'Our pride is in the British institutions, laws, and flag; to uphold which, in time of need, we will ever aid with enthusiastic Volunteers.' Possibly it was at the prompting of the lieutenant governors, but the addresses of provincial governments of Nova Scotia and New Brunswick both made strong statements about military preparedness and defence. The address from the government of New Brunswick assured the prince that 'the patriotic spirit which animates the people of the parent State also pervades this portion of the Empire and that if the necessity should ever arrive, all the available resources of New Brunswick will be freely offered for the defence of Imperial interests and the maintenance of national honour.' Addresses coming from the Province of Canada preferred to dwell on a history of loyal defence rather than to make commitments for the future. The address of the city of Hamilton spoke – just a little pointedly – of the local tradition of 'loyalty which, in the earlier periods of their history, was tried by perils and sacrifices from which their fellow-subjects nearer the Throne have happily been exempt.' The militia veterans in Upper Canada recalled the glory days of 1812 and reminded the prince and others 'how large a debt the Empire owed to the lamented hero Brock, whose gallant and generous heart shrank not, in the darkest hour of the conflict, from the most discouraging odds, and whose example inspired the few with the ability and the spirit to do the work of the many.' Their Lower Canadian counterparts lovingly recalled past triumphs at Lacolle and Chateauguay but also made a nod to the present and future: 'The race of 1812 has its successors, and ... the youth of Canada know the history of their sires, and, should occasion arise, will not belie it.' The address of the St Andrew's Society of Toronto preferred to feature military traditions in Scottish history, but then it assured the prince: 'Our Scottish right hands have not forgotten their ancient cunning, but that they will be found "Ready, aye, ready," as they were of old to defend the honour and dignity of the Crown of our beloved Sovereign.'

Although the language of the addresses tended to be stilted – in an attempt to be grand – the main messages were clear enough. Under the monarchy, and especially during the reign of Victoria, the colonies had thrived and prospered, their people enjoying yet greater freedom as well as increased responsibilities. For Her Majesty's subjects living in the British American provinces, the imperial connection had fostered political, religious, and cultural well-being, for which the people of the provinces, whether of British descent or not, were truly grateful. Altogether, then, the texts of the addresses amounted to a self-satisfied celebration of the status quo. Moreover, the addresses used the rhetoric of a powerful segment of contemporary public opinion in England, one that venerated the queen and the constitution and expressed pride in nation and empire. The addresses of Canadians gave this rhetoric a local flavour by referring to provincial experience. Implicit in this imperial culture expressed in the addresses was an understanding that the destiny of the provinces was to be neither full independence nor integration with the United States – the British heritage and connection was simply too powerful and appealing. Conspicuously absent was any praise for ties to the United States – even though this was the era of the Reciprocity Treaty, when many British American localities boomed from the trade in natural products with the United States – but perhaps a royal occasion was not seen as an appropriate time for such remarks. Neither did any of the addresses broach the possibility of British North American federation, although Confederation was just around the corner. Because the addresses, when taken together, pointed to an underlying coherence and shared values among all the provinces, federation might have appeared more likely after all these outpourings of loyalty and attachment to crown and empire. At the same time, however, the royal tour also provided an occasion for revealing regional and local identities, not all of which sat comfortably together, and not all of which were flattering.

The Maritimers

Identities in the Maritime provinces were most forcefully expressed in response to criticisms voiced by outsiders, particularly members of the press covering the royal tour for newspapers outside the region. These criticisms came as a jolt. During the 1850s the Maritime provinces had been enjoying a period of economic and demographic expansion, one in which 'they came closer to being self-directing.'[7] Newspaper editors in the Maritimes expected that the visit would bring the region much-deserved attention, but they did not reckon on the negative portrayals that characterized their up-and-coming region as a backwater. In defence, the local commentators explained who they really were and lashed out at the heap of distortions surging upon their shores.

Maritime newspapermen initially saw the royal tour as an opportunity for their communities and provinces to gain the kind of recognition in Great Britain that they had long deserved but too seldom enjoyed. Yet, even as the earliest discussion of the tour began to appear in the outside press, the self-identity of the Maritimes was challenged. 'In speaking of the visit of the Prince to British America,' complained the Fredericton *Reporter* at the beginning of August, 'the London Press scarcely ever mention the British American Colonies – it is always Canada, as though our sister Colony was the only possession Her Majesty had in these parts.' But the editorial was hopeful that such neglect would soon end, and that these London newspapers would 'have a different tale to tell when they send home an account of the warm reception the Prince meets with in the Lower Provinces.'[8] The *Carleton Sentinel* expected that, thanks to royal visit to New Brunswick, 'we may soon have the powerful agency of the English press operating among the people of the British Isles and pointing their attention here.[9]

Recognition came soon enough, but not all of it was of the kind expected. As the *Morning News* put it, the foreign press had 'taken us by the hand to introduce us to the world, even though it is not always done in the most complimentary way.'[10] Neither London nor New York reporters hesitated in finding fault with people and places in the Maritimes, whether the shortcomings were real or contrived – at least, that is how it appeared to commentators in the region.

Editors in the Maritimes expressed their delight when their region and cities were praised by visiting journalists. A column in the Halifax *Constitutionalist* reproduced passages from the Toronto *Globe* that lauded the volunteers at Halifax and the displays of loyalty by the people near Windsor, but it also quoted passages that compared the streets, shops, and houses of Halifax with those at Saint John, to the detriment of the former. On another occasion, the same Halifax paper reproduced 'copious extracts' from the columns of the London *Times*, noting that there was 'much ... in these letters to approve,' especially regarding the region's abundant natural resources.[11]

One of the New York journalists anticipated a form of U.S. nationalism that would celebrate the 'melting-pot,' while also criticizing what would later be known in Canada as the 'cultural mosaic.' 'Such variety of character and countenance I had not before seen,' exclaimed the correspondent for the New York *Tribune* in reference to Fredericton. He proceeded to present a series of stereotypes: 'There were descendants of the old Welsh emigrants, from beyond the river; a profuse sprinkling of shrewd and cautious Scotchmen, ruddy in face and rough of tongue; Irishmen with mellifluous accents and everything loyal about them; original settlers, with noses of traditional tinge, full of cordiality, and laying hospitable snares for everybody; and last *and* least, a few straggling representatives of the woe-begone and degenerate Milliseet tribe of Indians, civilized to the extent of round hats and tattered jackets, but not yet rescued from the barbarism of bare legs and blankets, wandering indolently and vaguely around, the only dull and dreary objects in the busy, shifting scene.' The writer had no use for this diversity, which he blamed on an unwillingness to adapt to the North American environment and to changing times: 'It is remarkable how these diverse populations continue to preserve their individuality. It seems as if everything and everybody once planted here must become incapable thenceforward of change or advancement, and that this region, of all others in the world, has got itself detached in some inscrutable way from the universal train of progress, and is content to linger largely behind, with the brakes of sluggishness hard on, and with no earthly prospect of ever catching up, or even getting a fresh start.' The negativity and harshness of this commentary characterized much of the rest of the regional coverage by the international press. Backwardness and lethargy were featured in representations of the Maritimes penned by outsiders.

Some of the criticisms that newspapermen made were true enough, conceded certain editorials in the press of the Maritime provinces. Indeed, in response to Nathaniel Woods's columns in the *Times*, the Halifax *Acadian Recorder* freely admitted several shortcomings of its home town. 'It is useless to deny that Halifax really has not a hotel in it,' admitted one editorial, 'that its streets are not paved and are in danger, almost any day in the year, of holding the passenger fast in the mud, or suffocating him with dust; and that, architecturally speaking, Halifax is the meanest city, for its population in North America.'[12] The Saint John *Morning Freeman* actually agreed with *Times* reports which judged that the New Brunswick port had failed to match Halifax, its rival, in terms of the quality of its preparations, its volunteer rifle companies, and its illuminations.[13] As for the critical reports in the foreign press, the *Morning News* of Saint John observed philosophically that 'beneath the garb of candour there is generally a great deal of truth to be found, however distasteful it may be to have it grated into one's ears.'[14]

The Halifax *Acadian Recorder*, putting on a bright face, argued that the Maritime communities could actually benefit from the harsh criticisms. 'Instead of snarling at the stranger who speaks these truths,' the *Recorder* said, 'it would be better to admit them at once and set about remedying the evils which they set forth.' If the citizens of Halifax would only show greater enterprise, mingled with a little more taste, then Nova Scotia's capital 'would very soon be the most beautiful, most imperial looking city on the coast of North America.' And furthermore, rather than complaining about the ignorance of the English newspaper writers and their readers, the colonial governments should themselves disseminate accurate information in the metropolis so as to enlighten the people of Great Britain.[15] In effect, this magnanimity and positive approach was intended to contrast with the one-sided, negative reports that Maritime newspapers were accusing the foreign press of having published.

Yet the Maritime newspapers did not pull their punches when it came to strangers' statements that, in their view, were not only harsh but untrue or unfair. Their indignation centred on three charges made by the foreign press: Halifax's lack of enterprise, the drunkenness of people celebrating in all the cities of the Maritimes, and the feeble or shallow display of loyalty shown by the people of New Brunswick.

Halifax's lethargy was highlighted by certain journals in the United States, England, and Scotland. 'The city [of Halifax],' opined *Harper's Weekly*, 'has an old and decrepit look, as if blight had fallen upon its energies somewhere about the close of the last American war.' It described the town's public buildings as 'few and shabby' and concluded that 'altogether it seems a dreary place to dwell in.' Nathaniel Woods in the London *Times* found some good things to say but concluded that 'the whole place has an air of antiquated sleepiness about it, a kind of wood imitation of the dulness of old cathedral towns in England.' The Edinburgh *News*, taking a wider view, argued that Nova Scotia and the Maritimes had 'fallen out of notice' with the rise of Canada, Australia, and New Zealand, for which it blamed the Maritimers themselves. 'There is much need of an infusion of some of the go-ahead Yankee element in some of the districts, or of that spirit of enterprise which is so rapidly conquering Australia.'[16]

Halifax newspapers responded fiercely to these kinds of comments. The *Acadian Recorder*, which had gone out of its way to concede local shortcomings, called Woods's assertions about Halifax's lethargy 'savage' and 'the most venomous sentences he could concoct,' and it described Woods himself as 'a pompous individual' who seemed to have 'gone into a frenzy.' Fortunately, the editorial concluded: 'Any person can see with half an eye that Mr. Woods was actuated, not by any honorable motive, but solely by vulgar spite, in saying what he does.' Tit for tat!

The *Constitutionalist* answered the article in *Harper's Weekly* by first

Nathaniel Woods, special correspondent for the London *Times*. As the publication of this portrait suggests, Woods became a controversial figure in his own right. (*Frank Leslie's Illustrated News*, 20 October 1860)

feigning modesty and then making a more direct counter-attack on New York, *Harper's* home town. 'The big man, fresh from New York, of course, finds Halifax a small affair,' began the Halifax paper. It then criticized a political culture that tolerated the notoriously corrupt practices of New York aldermen, recently demonstrated yet again during a visit by a large delegation from Japan. Furthermore, said the Nova Scotia newspaper, the quality of life in Halifax was far superior to the frenzied pace of life in the sinful metropolis: 'We should rather be the slow-going, taking-the-world-easy, full-bellied contented people that we are, than be the rushing lanky excited race among whom Harper dwells.'[17]

These extended and elaborate replies make it obvious that the local press took strong exception to affronts to the city's self-image. In the mid-Victorian period, when industry and enterprise were the hallmarks of the age, these comments about lethargy cut deeply indeed. By answering the charges so forcefully, the editors were not so much engaging in a debate as *demonstrating*, by their own vigour, the inaccuracy of the criticisms. Halifax was no sleepy backwater but rather a thriving commercial centre where the spirit of enterprise thrived. So spirited was the defence that Woods himself felt compelled to answer back by taking swipes later in the tour. 'Halifax, that quaint, rickety little village,' he wrote at the end of the Canadian tour, is 'less like a town itself than the *debris* of an old one for sale, with its dusty old streets – stagnant and lethargic without being quiet – noisy without being busy.'[18]

Indignation was at least as intense, and more widespread, when strangers attacked the sobriety and respectability of Maritimers. Woods wrote disparagingly in the *Times* of the drunkenness evident in both Halifax and Saint John. In the Nova Scotian capital he had witnessed 'extensive dissipation' on the second night of the celebrations, when 'the people indulged in such a whirl of rejoicings and drinkings that the whole place seemed to have lost its senses.' The insobriety was by no means confined to the dockside: 'The stimulus given by the Prince's visit appeared to have utterly exhausted and overcome the majority of the inhabitants.' In all his life, wrote Woods, he had never seen 'so many stupefied forms as lay about the streets that night.'[19] Saint John, he reported, was no better. Vast numbers of visitors who were unable to obtain hotel accommodations fortified themselves against the night air and lay about the streets 'in attitudes indicative of the most profound oblivion to personal safety and comfort.' In a phrase that would be much quoted, he summed up by saying: 'In popular phraseology here, St. John was very "tight" that evening.'[20]

Fredericton and Charlottetown got similar treatment, but from the New York papers. The New York *Times* correspondent penned a sweeping condemnation of the situation he found at Fredericton, drawing on some racial images to enliven his account: 'The ceremony of receiving the Prince of Wales at Fredericton, N.B., over, the crowd dispersed, and, the heat parching their tongues, they took to liquor, insomuch that towards dusk the whole town was tipsy, and volunteers in uniform, Indian men and women in their outlandish dresses, bushwackers in their frieze coats, negroes in their gaudy habiliments, and plenty of other sorts of people too, might be seen in a condition anything but creditable to themselves, the province, or the nineteenth century.'[21] The New York *Tribune* found behaviour at least as shocking at Charlottetown on the night of the prince's visit. In the streets there were 'incessant, brutal bursts of drunkenness and fighting,' as 'great riotous mobs' broke through 'tavern doors' and 'deserting soldiers ... perpetually plunged into conflicts with the townspeople, and made free with their weapons.' The scene was made even more disgraceful and degraded by the presence of drunken children, no less! 'I never saw so small a place given over so utterly to bestiality,' concluded the writer.[22]

What was going on here? The accounts read either as hyperbolic exaggerations of whatever holiday celebrations may have taken place or as downright fabrications intended to enliven the dreary round of ceremonials. Newspapers in the Maritimes stated flatly that they were lies. 'The utmost sobriety prevailed throughout the visit of the Prince,' insisted the Halifax *Constitutionalist*. The 'entire absence of anything like intoxication,' which was widely remarked upon at the time, was 'fully borne out by the police reports.'[23] The newspapers of Saint John similarly leapt to the honour of their community. 'The truth is,' wrote the *Morning Freeman*, 'never was there a more sober, steady, orderly assemblage than St. John presented on that day and night.' Why, the editor himself had walked the streets of the city until midnight, and he had found 'no brawling, no drunken noise or tumult' and not 'a single person anywhere lying down.'[24] The Fredericton *Reporter* was just as extravagant in his defence of the New Brunswick capital: 'There never was in the world a more sober and well-conducted multitude than that assembled in Fredericton.' As for Charlottetown, a local paper, the *Islander*, maintained that people had been on their best behaviour: 'Noise, drunkenness and disorder were unknown.'[25]

Next, the local editorial writers counter-attacked by assaulting the integrity and respectability of the foreign correspondents. Turning the words of the New York *Times* back on the author and his American colleagues, the *Morning News* charged that their journalism was '"anything but creditable to themselves, their country, or the nineteenth century."'[26] Woods of the London *Times* was the favoured target of the editorial writers both because he had been so pointed in his comments and because he represented the single most important newspaper. Regarding Saint John, the *Morning News* said that Woods 'must have been in his cups all that day; and like the mad man thought that everybody else but himself had got astray.'[27] In a similar vein, the *Constitutionalist* likened Woods to the judge 'who having partaken rather freely during a recess in a trial, objected that the witness was unsteady, when it was the head of his lordship which was at fault.' On another occasion, the *Constitutionalist* accused Woods of talking 'like a cross child,' and the Charlottetown *Examiner* said that his charges were 'unmitigated lying, the offspring of innate blackguardism.' Obviously, the local papers enjoyed poking fun at the august correspondent, and, by doing so, they perhaps deflected his blows – to the satisfaction of readers in the Maritimes if to no one else.[28] Only the *Morning Freeman* attempted a more considered analysis, speculating that the correspondents had been misled because they had stayed at crowded hotels with bars, where 'fast young men' drank freely. Thus, the reporters 'fancy the whole cities [*sic*] "tight," when in truth they were remarkably sober and quiet.'

Attacks on Woods could get personal. In one of columns from Halifax, he had whined a good deal about the crowded and inferior hotel where he had been put in 'the smoking and drinking room.' The local paper responded by saying that 'it is not true that his room was "the smoking and drinking room,"' but if Woods 'chose to make it so, and there get into unseemly pot-house quarrels with brother reporters, it was his own affair.' In the same column in the *Times*, Woods had disparaged the Native women who were working as prostitutes in Halifax. The local paper defended the honour of the city by providing a context for such behaviour; after all, prostitution was to be expected in certain quarters of all military and naval stations. The editorial admitted that in Halifax 'a few dusky beauties perhaps do exhibit their charms at open windows to passersby,' and then turned Woods's observations back on himself: 'But this class of persons are rarely seen, and still more rarely talked about, by men of respectability and good morals, and had Mr. Woods not mentioned it, no one would have suspected him of seeking his first acquaintance here in that rank of society.'[29] The repartee gets a bit juvenile here, but the bullets fired by the *Times* correspondent had hit their mark and so the local press felt duty-bound to return fire.

The third series of charges launched by the foreign press concerned the behaviour of the people of New Brunswick during the prince's entries at Saint John and Fredericton. Nearly all the visitors had been struck by the absence of loud cheering for the prince during the public demonstrations. As Albert Edward had proceeded to his temporary residence, reported the New York *Times*, he 'drove up in solemn silence.' The crowd 'forbore to manifest the slightest feeling as he was passing up the street.'[30] Woods told the readers of the *Times* that 'in the matter of cheering, the education of New Brunswickers seemed to have been sadly neglected.'[31] The Boston *Post* thought the demonstration at Saint John 'of the weakest possible description,' and elaborated: 'The ladies would sometimes wave their handkerchiefs, and at odd moments some bold fellow would startle a big crowd around him by affecting that singularity which the utterance of a few hurrahs constituted.'[32]

As far as the local press was concerned, however, what mattered was what the foreign press said or implied about the *meaning* of this crowd behaviour. Most important, were the outsiders questioning or even impugning the loyalty of the people of New Brunswick? Clearly not, in some instances. Kinahan Cornwallis, for one, explained to the readers of the New York *Herald* that the strange behaviour amounted to 'an awe, amounting to reverence,' and it said 'nothing against their loyalty – nothing against their love of country.' He attributed the New Brunswickers' 'tame demonstration' to 'their unemotional nature.' 'What would fill a Frenchman with the bubbling gaiety of extreme ardor, and make a New Yorker boil over with the excitement of enthusiasm, would upon a native of New Brunswick produce hardly any impression deeper than would be caused by the common every-day events of life.'[33] Other writers, however, did portray the reticence of the New Brunswickers as a sign of their lack of enthusiasm for the prince and what he represented. John F. McDevitt, the correspondent of the Philadelphia *Enquirer*, said that the demonstrations at both Saint John and Fredericton 'lacked sincerity.' The people generally did not take part, he claimed. 'The government officials seemed to be the only individuals that entered into the excitement with any zeal.' The Indians who lined the route stared with 'vacant countenances,' seeming to enquire, '"What is it all about?"' Among the Celts, who, McDevitt said, made up the majority of the population, there were even 'stubborn' individuals who refused to follow the official instructions and 'uncover' as the prince passed.[34]

The Fredericton *Head Quarters* reacted with outrage, calling the charges 'the most unmitigated slander on the character of a people than whom there are none more loyal in Her Majesty's dominions.' The editor pulled apart the Philadelphia reporter's story, line by line, finding fault with many of McDevitt's facts, as well as the thrust of his report. 'Never was a Royal visitor received with more sincere loyalty and enthusiasm,' insisted the *Head Quarters*.[35] McDevitt returned the fire in a long (5,000-word) letter-to-the-editor, which the *Head Quarters* published and commented upon. The Philadelphia reporter stood by his contention that in New Brunswick 'all the "demos" that were given, were purely the work of government officials and their dependants.' He had mingled with members of the elite at the ball and was so offended by their English sycophancy and obsequiousness toward royalty that 'he was almost obliged to turn away.'[36] The *Head Quarters* had no hesitation dismissing everything McDevitt said, especially since he was an American with an anti-British bias who had come to Fredericton with such pre-conceived ideas.[37]

For all the bravado, however, there is nevertheless a defensiveness in the response of the New Brunswick press. The editors do not for a moment appear to have believed the charges of shallow loyalty, but they wished that the people had been more demonstrative during the prince's receptions. At least the local press was able to point proudly to the uproarious send-off New Brunswickers gave His Royal Highness. It was with some relief, as well as pleasure, that the New Brunswick papers could print an article by 'Mr. Spence' of the Montreal *Gazette*. 'The Prince won greater and greater enthusiasm the longer he stayed,' reported Spence. 'I have not yet seen so glorious a tribute to the Prince as that afforded at his departure from St. John.'[38]

As it turned out, then, the royal visit did bring Maritime communities to the attention of a wide public, though not generally in a way that pleased commentators in the region. To be called backward, lethargic, drunken, and disloyal in the metropolitan press called for a firm response. The result was an international conversation in the public journals of the day, one in which editors of the region's newspapers argued in defence of the Maritimers' progressiveness, respectability, and loyalty. These counter-attacks on the 'blackguardism' of the special correspondents demonstrated the forcefulness and vigour of Maritime journalists, a response that belied the representations made by commentators from away.

French Canadians

Public support for the 1860 tour of the Prince of Wales ran high in French Canada. The community's dominant elites – the Bleu politicians and the Roman Catholic bishops – strongly favoured the idea of the visit as an opportunity for the distinguished visitors and a broad reading public to appreciate fully the vigour and strength of the French-Canadian nation and the loyalty of its people. Overwhelmingly, journalists in French Canada seized the opportunity provided by the royal visit both to insist on the loyalty of French Canada and to assert the nationality of French Canadians. It was an opportunity, said one French Canadian, to display 'the national genius of the French Canadians.'[39] As events unfolded during the summer and fall of 1860, however, editorials became increasingly critical of what was happening. In parallel with the commentary of Maritime journalists, newspapers from French Canada expressed disappointment and indignation that journalists from outside the region had misunderstood or intentionally distorted local demonstrations of a proud and loyal people. Respect for *la nation* was not what it ought to be. Of course, the visit of 1860 was neither the first nor the last time that French Canadians would feel that they had been misrepresented if not betrayed.

Notwithstanding the defeat of the liberal-nationalist insurgents of 1837–8, and the Union of the Canadas in 1841, an imperial policy designed, in part, to hobble French Canada's political power, *la nation* was strong in 1860 and French-Canadian politicians were powerful in the legislature and the cabinet. The *parti bleu*, and its champion, George-Étienne Cartier, had built a political movement that garnered wide popular support both in the countryside, where most French Canadians lived, and in the cities, especially in industrializing Montreal. Moreover, the Bleu politicians worked closely with the provincial elites, notably Anglo businessmen and the Roman Catholic hierarchy.[40] Cartier and the other Bleus understood that, as British subjects with full political rights, French Canadians had the sufficient seats in the legislature of the United Province to advance the Bleu program, and, under responsible government, they enjoyed the necessary strength in cabinet both to carry out their plans and to provide the necessary patronage for party stalwarts. The opposition Rouges differed in nearly every respect from the Bleus, being anti-clerical in outlook, militantly democratic in their program for the reform of institutions, and suspicious of England's ambitions in Canada. In 1860 the *parti rouge* lacked a mass base, controlled only a few seats in the legislature, and had no representation in cabinet.[41] Its presence did little to shatter the illusion of French-Canadian unity fostered in the French-language press.

The French-language press lavished attention on the prince's visit to Canada. Newspapers followed his movements closely, mainly by cribbing from the English-language newspaper accounts that journalists translated into French. The economics of French Canadian publishing at the time made it impossible to hire special correspondents to travel with the prince. As with local papers elsewhere, those in French-speaking communities provided their own commentaries on preparations in their home towns and editors remarked upon developments of particular interest.

The French-Canadian press saw even the purpose of the royal visit as being connected to French Canada. The prince and his entourage had come on a reconnaissance mission. According to the *Courrier du Canada*, a Quebec paper that expressed the conservative views of the ultramontane clergy, the British government wanted to discover the convictions of the people of British North America but especially of French Canadians. Because war between England and France appeared imminent, imperial authorities wisely preferred to see for themselves whether there was any foundation to the accusations of disloyalty hurled at French Canadians almost daily in the English-Canadian newspapers.[42]

Whatever the motivation of the British, according to *L'Ordre*, the liberal or Rouge newspaper of Montreal, the purpose of the tour for French Canadians themselves was to show to the world their vitality, that 'we are at once a Catholic people and a happy people.' Above all, French Canadians must participate to the utmost in all the events surrounding the visit and do so as a united, Catholic, and French-speaking people.[43] Each nationality in Canada would celebrate in its own way the coming of the royal guest.[44] Loyalty to the British crown in Canada did not require being English. Loyalty was possible for *Canadiens*, though they be French in religion, manners, and civilization. The tour provided a fine opportunity for making this reality evident to outsiders who more often than not needed instruction on the point.[45]

No incident more dramatically showed the depth of French Canada's loyalty in 1860 than the tribute paid to the prince by none other than Louis-Joseph Papineau, the revolutionary leader of 1837–8, and his wife, Julie. When the prince travelled up the Ottawa River on his way to the new capital, he passed by Montebello, the estate where the province's best-known, old rebel now lived quietly. On this occasion, the chateau was gaily decked out in the flags of many nations, the people of the locality lined the river bank cheering the prince, and Papineau paid homage to the prince with a royal salute fired from his home. As the prince passed, Mme Papineau presented him with 'un magnifique bouquet,' which the prince acknowledged in a thank-you note.[46]

Initially, the French-language press was proud of how well the prince's visit to Quebec had gone. 'The Prince of Wales ... found among the French-Canadian population, so much good faith, so much faithfulness, so much loyalty,' declared *L'Ordre*. As hoped, French Canadians 'did everything to show the prince and his suite that they are still the most numerous,' claimed the Rouge newspaper. 'Many officials were astonished, after being told the contrary, to find the French in Canada alive and well.'[47] Commentators proudly pointed to impressive displays got up by French Canadians, such as the handsome arch built on Rue Saint-Laurent in Montreal by subscribers from a French-Canadian neighbourhood.[48] One newspaper pointed out that on the night of the illumination at Quebec, while the Anglican cathedral remained in the dark, the Catholic cathedral had been fully illuminated.[49] The highly active part that Mayor Charles-Séraphin Rodier played in the whole visit, and not just in his own city of Montreal, showed how demonstrably loyal French Canadians could be.[50] It was a proud moment when the prince had listened to Quebec's welcome being read *'first in French.'* Albert Edward's itinerary in the city allowed him the opportunity to see for himself the prominence of the Roman Catholic hierarchy in all the proceedings and the importance of the city's Roman Catholic institutions, which he toured.[51]

Regrettably, however, the prince and his suite had not had the same opportunity to get an accurate impression of the strength of the French Canadians in Montreal because the city's Anglo elite had taken control of the reception there. Wherever the prince went in Montreal, he was surrounded by English Canadians. 'At the Victoria Bridge, at the military review, etc., everything had an exclusively English appearance,' complained *La Minerve*. Even at the grand ball, 'the French-Canadian ladies, not convinced of the need to make themselves conspicuous at balls, were few in number,' and so 'there too those of British origin were certain to dominate by their numbers and their toilette.' Had the prince been given the opportunity to visit the city's public institutions – religious, charitable, and educational – then he would have seen for himself the 'incontestable superiority' of Montreal's French-Canadian institutions in comparison with those of all other groups.[52]

Only the coverage of the tour given in *Le Courrier de Saint-Hyacinthe*, a Rouge newspaper, contrasted markedly from the tone of other French-Canadian newspapers. Its editor, P.-J. Guitté, had the temerity to comment unflatteringly on the prince's appearance – something no other newspaper in British North America did. 'The Prince is not a handsome fellow in the ordinary sense of the word,' Guitté wrote, 'far from it. An overlong, slightly hooked nose, eyes of a pale, lack-lustre blue, a thoroughly juvenile appearance, make him a decidedly insignificant figure ... All in all, we expected *something better*.' The comment startled those in the local population, as it would have done countless others if it had been reprinted in more widely read journals. Local critics took the editor to task, and Guitté agreed to published 'a retraction' of his 'hastily written article.' Guitté conceded that the prince had personal charm, but he stated bluntly that the visit to Canada had been 'the least instructive and the most frivolous event imaginable.' These remarks further stirred the pot. It appears that the turmoil led Guitté to abandoned his newspaper, which he had edited and published for seven years. He sold *Le Courrier de Saint-Hyacinthe* in September 1860 to a publisher of quite different political leanings.[53]

Although most francophone newspapers remained fiercely proud of French Canada's showing during the royal visit, deep disillusionment set in once the francophone journalists read in the English-language press the reports and commentary on the prince's tour of Lower Canada. Instead of admiring the impressive and loyal display French Canada had made, the English-language papers, by focusing on a minor incident and distorting much else, had cast French Canada in an unflattering light, stained the honour of the French-Canadian nation, and possibly threatened its future.

The incident in question, which was not directly connected to the prince's visit, centred on remarks uttered in the heat of the moment during a meeting of the Montreal city council in early August. At the time, the council was considering a motion (not directly related to the visit) introduced by one of the anglophone councillors to honour the queen by changing the name of Montreal's 'Commissioners' Square' (Place Commissaires) to 'Victoria Square.' Two or three francophone councillors caused a ruckus, either as a tactic to delay the vote to another meeting when the francophone councillors would be more numerous, or because they lost their tempers. They saw the proposal as an attempt to do away with the French aspect of the city, and as an affront to their nationality. Rebellion had been alluded to, according to the Bleu newspaper *La Minerve*, when one of the councillors had exclaimed: 'The English would bring on another '37 if they persisted in the course they appeared to follow.'[54] Another had threatened to topple Nelson's Column in Jacques-Cartier Square if Anglo-Montreal tried to rename it, too.[55] The crowd in the council chamber had then joined in the fracas. People – possibly councillors Homier and Joseph Duhamel – had shouted remarks disrespectful of Her Majesty. Fists were raised. The anglophone councillors took flight, and the meeting ended in disarray. The English-Canadian press reacted in outrage, of course. Soon, however, two of the councillors resigned their seats, and the council unanimously supported an apology that was moved and seconded by French Canadians.

The English-language press was, in fact, divided over what the incident signified. An editorial in the Toronto *Globe*, referring to the 'insolent language and violent behaviour in the Montreal Council Chamber,' charged that 'the French inhabitants of Lower Canada' had 'seized the occasion of this happy visit to insult the Queen and pour contempt upon her loyal subjects of English origin.' The *Globe* even went so far as to claim that the incident had 'threatened the existence of British power in this country!'[56] However, the Saint John *Morning Freeman*, supportive of its Catholic brethren, criticized the way some newspapers had 'wished to make capital' of the incident, and it pointed out that the French-Canadian members of the council had repudiated the unfortunate conduct. The Montreal *Gazette*, in a show of civic solidarity with the city's French Canadians, chastised those who would judge the whole French population of Canada 'by the rubbish spoken by a few third class mob orators ... whose object at the time was to create confusion to defeat a city railway bill.'[57]

Most disturbing to the newspapers of French Canada was the London *Times*'s commentary on the fracas in a long editorial complaining about French Canadians' disrespect for the British crown and their ingratitude for all that the British had done for them.[58] Coming on the eve of the prince's visit to Lower Canada and from such a prominent newspaper, the editorial was seen by the Lower Canadian press as being not just unfortunate but deeply insulting to French Canada. *Le Canadien* of Quebec deplored both the Montreal incident itself and the fact that the *Times* represented the views of a couple of councillors as reflecting the opinion of all French Canadians. It just went to show French Canadians how vigilant they had to be in all that they said because there was always someone ready to pounce on their 'disloyalty.' *La Minerve* admitted that the Montreal incident was 'a disgrace to the honour of the French-Canadian race' but offered the reassurance that, in French Canada, no one had 'the slightest desire ... to cast a slur upon the name of our beloved Queen.' Contrary to what the *Times* maintained, French Canadians were appreciative of the benefits of British rule – representative government, the freedom of the press, and the right to manage home affairs.[59] Even more indignant, *L'Ordre* was affronted to think that the *Times* had accused French Canadians 'before all Europe of ingratitude and of infamous plots against the lives of Anglo-Saxons in connection with the ridiculous skirmish in the city council. Who would have thought that Councillor Homier would inspire in *The Times* such fear and hatred?'[60]

A second trigger for explosions over nationality and loyalty was the matter of French Canada's relationship with France and, more particularly, the French Canadians' propensity for flying the flag of that country. Certainly, it had struck British and English Canadians as strange, if not disrespectful to the prince, that during the royal visit so many Lower Canadians chose to decorate their homes, businesses, and boats with the national flag of France. Many reports noted that, in and around both Quebec and Montreal, the tricolour flew alongside the Union Jack or was waved instead of the Union Jack.[61] Predictably, some of the English-language newspapers took strong exception to the choice of flag and read into the preference a defiance bordering on treason. 'It involved,' said the Halifax *Acadian Recorder*, 'a gross insult to the Heir of the British Crown and the distinguished personages who accompanied him, as well as to all of the loyal people of these Provinces.' The Fredericton *Head Quarters* explained that with the military successes of Napoleon III in the Crimea and Italy, 'a large portion of the French in Lower Canada have regarded him as their legitimate monarch; they look upon a re-union with France as among the possibilities, and the landing of a French army on the shores of the St. Lawrence as only a question of time.'[62] Hotheads in Lower Canada hoped that France would soon strip England of her colonies. A much-reprinted article from a British newspaper, the Liverpool *Courier*, had gone so far as to claim that French agents were busy in Lower Canada fomenting revolution so as to bring Quebec back into the French empire. The flags were evidence of the agents' successes.[63]

The Montreal *Gazette* countered, saying that disloyalty was not nearly as widespread in Lower Canada as some newspapers, including the *Times*, were suggesting. To be sure, there had been some boasting about the glories of France in the wake of military victories, but things had changed recently: 'The affection for and admiration of the Emperor Napoleon, which was taking almost too strong a hue to be consistent with loyalty to our own Queen, received a rude check when he ceased to defend the power of the Holy Father in the Romagna, and the revulsion of feeling thus operated has been happily caught upon the turn by the visit of the Prince of Wales. The French Canadians [now] gave him a cordial reception.'[64] Given the new context, then, the kind of statements that the *Head Quarters* had focused on were no longer relevant.

Some French Canadians expressed shock at the idea that flying the tricolour in Lower Canada was a sign of disloyalty to the crown or disrespect for the British empire. Sometimes commentators maintained that the tricolour was flown only because it was the flag they had on hand, left over from the Crimean War years when it had been loyally flown in celebration of the alliance between England and France. The archbishop of Quebec, no less, had thought it appropriate to fly the tricolour from the cathedral, and, when questioned privately about it, he had nonchalantly replied that it was only a relic of the Crimean alliance.[65] At the other end of the social scale, the humble captain of a ferryboat that crossed the St Lawrence near Quebec told the Toronto *Globe* correspondent that he had flown it when the prince had been aboard because '"N'ai pas d'autre."'[66]

At the same time, however, some French-Canadian commentators defended flying the flag in Lower Canada as a matter of principle. *La Minerve* said that it was customary to fly both the French and English flags on solemn occasions in order to make clear both the origins of French Canadians and their particular situation.[67] In its editorials, *L'Ordre* dealt at length with the flag issue,[68] making a complicated argument that was more than a little ambiguous. At one point, for instance, it opined: 'The French flag, which is the flag of civilization, could hardly shame the royal prince of England.' In the same breath, it added: 'Neither could it wound his feelings since France is an ally of

England.' Yet *L'Ordre* insisted more vehemently still that in, Lower Canada, the tricolour was the flag of French Canadians, 'an emblem of [our] nationality.' They should carry this noble and glorious flag in all the processions to demonstrate their distinct nationality in America, and to make clear the strength of their numbers. 'A people without a flag is not a people; French Canadians insist on not being confused with other races; the French flag, therefore, will tell everyone who we are and what we aspire to become one day.' What was it that they expected to become one day: an even more powerful nation under the British crown? an independent nation? a nation in the French empire? No answer was given.[69]

There were rumours that the authorities at Quebec had tried to suppress the tricolour. *La Minerve* objected to the way outsiders called for French Canadians to hide the French flag, while the colours of all other nations could be displayed. *L'Ordre* reported that other nationalities were flying their flags – 'English, American, Turkish' – but the authorities had torn down the French flags.[70] Articles in some English-language newspapers appeared at first to confirm the rumours. The Montreal *Commercial Advertiser*, for one, claimed that no French flags had flown at Quebec because Admiral Milne had threatened that, 'if they were not struck at once, he would land men from the fleet and remove them.'[71] *L'Ordre* pointed out that in fact the French flag had been flown by many people, and it charged the *Commercial Advertiser* with having 'invented this calumny' because of 'its idiotic hatred of all that is not English.'[72] What was not reported on was that the Duke of Newcastle had asked the archbishop at Quebec to remove the tricolour from the Roman Catholic cathedral, which he had readily done. 'I found the French flag displayed every where,' wrote Newcastle to the British prime minister. 'I did not think it wise to notice it when it was displayed as an ornament on private houses.' But he had felt differently about its flying from the tower of the cathedral. He had requested its removal, believing it best 'that the people should not be taught to look upon the latter as a national flag.'[73] Had *L'Ordre* known of the duke's view, and the archbishop's ready compliance, it would have objected to both. As it was, the story never got out.

Along with defending the flying of the tricolour, the French-language newspapers objected to the attack on French Canada's ties to France. English-language newspapers had wilfully distorted developments between France and the French Canadians. 'In each of our hearts,' declared *L'Ordre*, the English newspapers see 'a traitorous aspiration toward France. Instead of instructing them, events serve only to reveal their revolting prejudice.' The *Times*, for instance, had said that French Canadians did not appreciate the freedoms the British had allowed them. But in fact, said both *La Minerve* and *L'Ordre*, it was France, through the provisions she had put into the treaties, that had enabled *Canadiens* to speak French and be Catholics a century after the conquest. French Canadians truly appreciated what had been done for them – by France, not Britain.[74]

The third way that the loyalty of French Canadians had been impugned was by George Brown's attack in the *Globe* on French Canada's handling of the prince's visit to Quebec. Unable to fault the enthusiasm that French Canadians showed for the prince, Brown turned his attention to the prominent role played during the visit by the Catholic hierarchy at Quebec. But where was the fault, asked the French-language press? The prince had come to see the province and its institutions, and so he had only naturally encountered the bishops and their work. Brown had tried to cast the hierarchy's loyalty into doubt by raising the old canard that their true allegiance was to Rome. A letter-to-the-editor in *Le Courrier du Canada* responded to the *Globe* by pointing out that, of course, the ecclesiastics swore submission to the pope in religious matters, and it asked rhetorically, 'Have they not also sworn and preached submission to the government of Her Majesty?'[75] *Le Courrier du Canada* argued that the French-Canadian clergy had contained insurrectional fires and helped to fend off invaders by always preaching 'submission and obedience to the sovereign.' 'French Canada belongs still to England,' thundered *Le Courrier*, 'thanks to the scrupulous loyalty of the French-Canadian clergy, a loyalty shown in two hard times, 1775 and 1837-38.'[76]

What was truly deplorable was George Brown's own conduct during the prince's visit. *Le Canadien* accused him of stirring up the Orangemen against the Catholics in order to gain partisan advantage from the state visit, behaviour utterly out of keeping with its purpose. Brown's blind hatred of everything Catholic and French Canadian had got the better of him. No self-respecting French Canadian could defend Brown for his conduct. He had made his political career by putting down French Canadians and by trying to eliminate their nationality.[77] He had stooped especially low when he had criticized the religious women of the Ursuline convent. Even the Quebec *Mercury* chivalrously rushed to their defence, referring to the Ursuline sisters' loyalty to the crown, the assistance they had given English soldiers, and the fine education they had provided to the mothers, sisters, and daughters of French-Canadian men, for which the latter were deeply appreciative.[78]

Once the Orange difficulty erupted in Upper Canada, the French-Canadian press suddenly found to its delight that the tables were reversed on the loyalty question. Newspapers gleefully reported the trouble that *les orangeists* were causing the prince immediately following his triumphal progress through Lower Canada. As more and more Upper Canadians rushed to defend the rights of Orangemen, the irony grew all the sweeter. 'What would they [Upper Canadian extremists] not have said,' asked *L'Ordre*, 'what would they not have done if, like the Orangemen, we had pursued the prince on the lakes and insulted him in the streets with such unparalleled boldness?' *La Minerve* answered the question: 'If French Canadians had shown their loyalty in the manner of Upper Canada, there would have been a call to arms!'[79]

As the Orange issue spiralled out of control, what had transpired in French Canada was no longer newsworthy. The fracas in the Montreal city council over renaming a square looked like small potatoes, and, for the time being at least, no one cared that the tricolour had flown in Lower Canada. French Canadians could look back on the royal visit as time when they had risen to the demands of the occasion. Their nationality had been put to a test and been proven resilient. Matters of nationality were not so clear-cut for their compatriots to the west, however.

Upper Canadians

During the early stages of public planning for the reception in Toronto, newspapers presented the occasion as an opportunity for displaying a common, non-partisan, community identity. In expressing their loyalty to the crown, Toronto public leaders spoke 'as one.' As the visit drew nearer, however, differences of opinion began to be voiced. What did it really mean to be British and Canadian? to be a colonial and a member of a new nationality?

Fervent expressions of a common identity were voiced at a public meeting which was held on 28 June 1860 in Toronto's St Lawrence Hall to consider the report of the committee of citizens charged with making preliminary plans for the prince's reception in the city.[80] The hall was packed with ratepayers, who listened to several speakers, all of them prominent public figures and, of course, men. According to the

Globe report, the crowd took part in the meeting mainly by cheering at appropriate points and showing their support for the motions.

The first speaker, the Reverend Dr John McCaul, president of University College, dealt at length with the history of Toronto, especially the deep-rooted loyalty that compelled the city to exert itself to the utmost in preparing for the royal visit. In selecting from the developments that had shaped the community, McCaul avoided those that had divided the people and focused on cherished myths that united them. Thus, there was no mention of 1837, when rebels and Tories had confronted one another on Yonge Street, exchanging musket fire. Instead, McCaul presented a version of history whose theme was the flowering in Toronto of loyalty: 'a fixed, steadfast principle, which had grown with our growth and strengthened with our strength.' According to McCaul, the community's history had begun with the coming of the United Empire Loyalists, that 'gallant band' who had been willing to abandon their properties rather than 'give up their allegiance.' They had found shelter in 'the wild woods of Canada, and carved out smiling farms and comfortable homesteads for their successors.' As they worked, they sang: 'The first musical notes which broke the silence of the remote forests of Canada were the bold tones of the National Anthem of Britons.' Moreover, it was an anthem both of nationality and of liberty, one that they could now sing fearlessly, having fled a country where true freedom was denied. That same loyalty, McCaul said, had motivated the community during the War of 1812, when once again freedom was at stake. Though the invaders had attacked Toronto and set fire to the people's homes, the enemy could not destroy the spirit of loyalty: 'That survived the conflagration. (Cheers.)' The small populace, with help from 'but a handful of regular troops,' had heroically resisted the invader and held 'this Province for the British Crown. (Cheers.)' McCaul then abruptly switched to the present, skipping over several decades, and thundered that now there never was a queen's birthday when the people did not celebrate the British connection and thank God for the blessings enjoyed under Her Majesty.

McCaul's history of his community was one that was already familiar to his audience, and, because of the efforts of people like McCaul, it would continue to be the approved interpretation of Ontario history for decades to come. He had articulated the two predominant myths concerning the origins of Upper Canada: the Loyalist Myth and the Militia Myth.[81] According to the first, Upper Canadian history had begun, not with the Aboriginal peoples, but with the United Empire

Loyalists: those brave men and women who had fled the anarchy introduced by the rebels in the American colonies. Abandoning their property and homes, the Loyalists had shown their deep devotion to the crown by fleeing north to a wilderness and beginning the hard work of colonization once again, secure only in the knowledge that they did so under the crown's protection. Their sacrifices, hard work, and fervent loyalty laid the foundations for a province that was to continue ever after as a bastion of support for the monarchy and the British connection. According to the second sustaining myth, the Militia Myth, during the War of 1812, when the republican enemy had invaded the province and threatened the freedom of His Majesty's subjects, the local population, loyal to the core, had staunchly defended themselves and their traditions. Upper Canada's gallant militia forces – the civilian population in uniform – had fought bravely and shed blood to repulse the invaders. With only a little help from the British army and His Majesty's Indian allies, the militia had triumphed and kept the Canadas British. As McCaul reminded his audience, the militia had ensured that the greatest 'blessing,' liberty, would still be enjoyed under the British crown.

Oliver Mowat, the prominent Toronto lawyer and Reform politician, was the next to speak at length that evening. He chose to elaborate on the connection between loyalty and liberty. Queen Victoria deserved the loyalty of Canadians, not so much because she was the reigning monarch, but because during her reign she had guaranteed the liberty that her subjects enjoyed. Mowat even claimed that Canadians 'acknowledged liberty as a sentiment more valuable still than loyalty.' (The *Globe*, which shared Mowat's brand of liberalism, reported that the crowd cheered at this point.) In effect, Mowat was arguing in favour of a conditional loyalty: Canadians were loyal, and should be loyal, but only if the crown stood for freedom. He continued, saying that, if there ever were to be a conflict between loyalty and liberty, 'God forbid,' then for the people of Canada, 'it was liberty which would be their choice. (Cheers.)' Conditional loyalty of this sort was no insult to the queen. Indeed, she 'rejoiced more in the loyalty of those who had such feelings, and had the manliness to acknowledge them.' Because of the freedoms enjoyed under the wise and generous queen, citizens could act like true men and express themselves honestly and openly. In other countries, such manly behaviour and liberty did not coincide. Men who fought for liberty ended up in the dungeons that foreign monarchs needed in order to cling to their thrones. But Victoria's 'safety, her confidence, lies in the hearts of the people, and long may it continue so. (Cheers.)' Mowat declared his statements to be the feeling of the meeting as a whole. Though there were political differences among the people, on such a grand occasion as the royal visit, 'they would act as one man, and speak out their feelings as with one voice.' Differences would be put aside as all joined together to cry 'God Save the Queen' and 'Long live the Prince. (Cheers.)'

Other speakers, from the arch Tory H.J. Boulton to the left-leaning reformer Malcolm Cameron, reiterated these themes, emphasizing the wonderful liberty enjoyed by Upper Canadians and contrasting it with the lack of freedom in the Kingdom of Naples and the presence of slavery in the United States. Speakers also emphasized the unanimity of sentiment in the province in support of Victoria and the population's appreciation for 'the freedom of government which they enjoyed under the benignant sway of the present Queen.' One speaker insisted that, 'throughout all Canada, they would not find among any class of the community, Clear Grits, Moderates, Roman Catholics or Protestants, a single man disaffected to the Queen and the Constitution.' As for the common people, Cameron declared: 'The mechanics and labourers of this city were second to none in loyalty, love of freedom and respect to the throne of Great Britain.'

The last to speak at length that evening was George Brown, who talked about liberty and the advantages of the British connection in a more concrete way. It was sometimes alleged, Brown said, that 'free government could not be enjoyed under the colonial system.' Under Victoria, however, Canada had been treated with 'a generosity and liberality unparalleled in the history of colonies before.' Control had shifted from Downing Street to the colonies in matters relating to public lands, the post office, commerce, and more. In fact, the people of Canada were 'left as independent and as free to control their own affairs, as were the people of Great Britain themselves, or those across the border in the United States. (Cheers.)' In foreign journals it was sometimes said, Brown continued, that 'the power of Great Britain was beginning to fail, and that she was losing her influence over her colonies.' Canadians must show otherwise by their demonstrations during the visit. The community, he said, 'ought to testify to the world on this occasion that the people of Canada felt proud to belong to the British Empire and to share in the glories of the British people. (Cheers.)'

Taking the *Globe* report on the meeting as a whole, the speeches reinforced a particular Upper Canadian identity. In both history and politics, the community – Toronto, Upper Canada, and Canada, the three being conveniently combined – was committed to the monarchy and empire. For speakers at the Toronto meeting, British imperialism in the mid-nineteenth century was not about the dominance by the metropolis over the colonies but rather signified a shared Britishness in which all could take pride, a Britishness rooted in liberty and guaranteed by the crown. The history and politics of other parts of Canada – French Canada, notably – were ignored, just as the Aboriginal peoples and women went unacknowledged. A common identity was articulated that fit the needs of the moment so that 'everyone' could unite to celebrate the prince's coming. At least at this initial stage of planning for the visit, the Toronto public appeared to have no identity crisis: the community knew exactly what it was all about. As reported, there had been complete support at a large public meeting for this particular construction of the community's history and outlook.

Differences of opinion about the province's identity appeared, however, during public discussions of a proposal that in the Toronto procession welcoming the prince there should be a large contingent of residents who would march together, each man wearing a maple leaf on his breast as a symbol of Canada.[82] The plan had originated with a 'young gentleman,' J.H. Morris, who had taken it upon himself to apply to the local program committee for a place in the procession for 'Native Canadians.'[83] In an attempt to publicize his plan and make the necessary arrangements, he called a public meeting at St Lawrence Hall for the evening of 21 August 1860. A brief editorial in the Toronto *Globe* endorsed the movement, and the paper covered the meeting closely.[84] The hall was nearly filled, mostly with young men of Upper Canadian birth, while on the platform sat various Toronto notables and the chairman, W.B. Robinson, a distinguished and senior member of the local, Canadian-born population. Morris and a few other gentlemen had prepared various resolutions, which outlined their plan.

Morris himself moved the first resolution and explained his idea. He had been struck by the fact that, though the prince was coming to Canada to meet the people of Canada, in the procession there would be large contingents from the national societies: Englishmen marching under the banner of St George, Scotsmen under the banner of St Andrew, and Irishmen under the banner of St Patrick. Yet there would be no group identifying itself as Canadian and no symbol of Canada. This was not right. 'The Prince came to see Canada,' Morris said, 'and surely it was necessary that he should be welcomed by Canadians as well as by the Englishmen, Scotchmen and Irishmen residing among them. (Hear, hear.)' He had proposed to correct the deficiency by asking for a place in the procession for those wishing to march as 'Native Canadians.' No one at the meeting objected to the plan, and indeed it was strongly supported. Yet the matter grew complicated.

In outlining his proposal, Morris repeatedly used the term 'the Canadian-born' to describe the group he called 'Native Canadians.' It was important on this august occasion, he said again and again, that 'those born on the soil be well represented.' Morris's use of the term 'the Canadian born' excluded people of British background who had been born in other colonies, a point raised at the meeting at St Lawrence Hall by Colonel William Botsworth Jarvis, the patriarch of a family at the heart of the Toronto Tory establishment. Noting that he had been born in another colony (New Brunswick), Jarvis strenuously objected to the exclusion from the movement of people such as himself – men of British colonial heritage and, in his case, with more than fifty years' residence in Upper Canada. So miffed was he that he 'took up his hat and left the Hall,' and, in a letter-to-the-editor of the *Globe*, he restated his objections.[85]

To other observers, Morris's proposal to form a Native-Canadian movement had a different weakness in that it too closely resembled the Know-Nothing movement in the United States. That movement, by means of a secret society, took exclusivity to extremes by struggling to deny public office and government patronage to anyone not born in the United States.[86] During the St Lawrence Hall meeting, Morris had felt it necessary to insist that an 'erroneous impression had gone abroad that they intended to form an exclusive society, something on the '"Know Nothing" principle.' Another speaker, the Reverend Dr Egerton Ryerson, the prominent educator, said that he supported Morris's plan, which was in no way analogous to the Know Nothingism, a movement he abhorred. Soon after the meeting, the *Globe* published a letter-to-the-editor from 'A German Resident,' who was convinced that the Native-Canadian movement was 'the beginning of a Know-Nothing movement in miniature.' If the development led to the formation of nativist societies, then the settlement of the country would be impeded because immigrants from countries such as Germany, Denmark, and Sweden would be discouraged from settling in Canada. 'Be assured,' he wrote, 'the foreign press of the United States will be glad to avail itself of the opportunity and trumpet all the world over that *Know-Nothingism*, after having been subdued there, erects its head in

Canada.' Moreover, the formation of nativist societies would have the effect of 'fostering prejudices among ourselves.' He concluded with an allusion to the Orange Order: 'God knows we have political and religious societies enough in Canada without the *Native Canadians*.'[87]

After the initial meeting and the criticisms of exclusivity, those behind the Native-Canadian movement adjusted their plan by redefining who should be publicly recognized as 'Native Canadian' at the time of the royal visit. Ryerson declared that the procession should include not just the Canadian-born but those born in 'any British Province.' Morris went further still, insisting in a letter-to-the-editor of the *Globe* written in response to Jarvis's letter that he did not mean the term 'Native Canadian' to distinguish those born here from those who were Canadian by adoption.[88] He proclaimed that, on the day of the prince's reception, his group would 'not exclude from our ranks any of our people who choose to wear our emblem the "maple leaf," and appear as one of us.' Morris had backtracked. At the public meeting he had spoken only of the Canadian-born; now he was speaking of 'all Canadians,' whether by birth or adoption. As it turned out, Morris was more a nationalist than a nativist. He did not want to divide Canadians because his priority was asserting and strengthening a Canadian nationality.

Nationalism was a theme of the St Lawrence Hall meeting. Several speakers complained that at present Canadians had no distinct national identity. In his opening speech, Morris had observed that, when a Canadian visited the United States, 'he was simply recognised as an Englishman, Scotchman or Irishman from Canada.' When he visited Great Britain, 'he was acknowledged only in the light of an American.' Morris thought that wrong and preferred that 'Canadians ... have a nationality of their own and be known to the world as Canadians.' In his letter, Jarvis agreed that Canadians needed more '*status*' in Great Britain. 'Disguise it as you may,' wrote Jarvis, 'it is nevertheless true, that a "Colonist" is not received with the same attention in England as a Yankee.' And in his rejoinder, Morris said that he was not surprised by this remark of Jarvis's, because the 'Yankee has a nationality, the Colonist none.' For that reason, Morris strongly objected to a suggestion made by Jarvis that residents form a 'Colonial Society' for all British subjects living in Canada. That name, insisted Morris, 'would be destructive to the cause of nationality and prejudicial to our importance as a race.' Apart from its immediate goal of organizing a demonstration for the prince's reception, the Native-Canadian movement aimed at fostering in Canada 'the basis of a nationality.' Morris said that he 'hoped that to-night, they might be laying the keel of a national ship which would be built up by the aspirations and deeds of the Sons of Canada.' Ryerson provided an international context by observing that 'the spirit which animated the young gentlemen in calling this meeting of Canadians was the same spirit which had laid the foundations and formed the characteristics of every country in the world.'

Because of its interest in gaining status for Canadians and recognition of a new nationality, the Native-Canadian movement promoted the maple leaf as an emblem of the country. 'If adopted,' said F.H. Heward at the St Lawrence Hall meeting, 'it would place all Canadians before the world with an emblem, which would be an evidence of their origin and nationality.' After all, 'England gloried in the Rose, Ireland in the Shamrock, and Scotland in the Thistle. Why should not Canadians as descendants of all these nationalities wreathe for themselves and wear upon their brow an emblem indicative of the land which gave them birth! (Cheers).' It was thought that the occasion of the royal visit offered a perfect opportunity to launch the emblem. For one thing, the world was watching. For another, the prince's recognition of the emblem would give it legitimacy. And so, 'wherever Canadians might go,' cried Heward, 'the maple leaf, under the sanction of His Royal Highness – and who doubted that he would sanction it? – would be an emblem of their nationality! (Cheers.)'[89]

Preparations were made to produce maple-leaf emblems for the use of the Native Canadians and others. The St Lawrence Hall meeting appointed a committee to work on the design and preparation of banners and flags. (The committee was well staffed, one of its members being the celebrated Canadian painter Paul Kane.) Jewellers set to work almost immediately manufacturing maple leaves for sale to consumers. Within a few days' time, J.G. Joseph and Company, of King Street, was advertising 'the silver maple leaf adopted by the Committee to be worn as a distinguishing badge in the procession.' The *Globe* recommended the purchase of 'maple leaves, lithographed in silver and gold by an ingenious Frenchman named Louis Cohn whose place of business is on Adelaide-street.' They were described as being 'exceedingly neat and cheap, and worthy of patronage by the Canadians who intend walking in the procession.'[90]

For all their talk of a Canadian nationality, those who discussed the idea of the Native-Canadian movement were locally oriented. At one point during the St Lawrence Hall meeting, the chairman remarked that already interest was being taken in the movement in 'all parts of the country,' and he hoped those residing outside Toronto would join in 'the great gathering.' Anticipating a future confederation of the British North American provinces, David Reesor, a Clear Grit politician from Markham, said that 'as Canadians they might feel proud to anticipate the time when the British Provinces of North America would be recognized as a great country, [and] added to the number of the great and free civilised countries of the world.' Nevertheless, the speakers' idea of 'Canada' drew only from their immediate Upper Canadian context. For them, 'Canadian history' amounted to the story of Upper Canada as sustained by the Loyalist Myth and the Militia Myths. Morris spoke of Canada's founders as being the 'brave men, known as the U.E. Loyalists,' whose homes had been destroyed and lands confiscated but whose 'love of country made them forget all.' The sons of the Loyalists, born in Upper Canada, had followed in their fathers' footsteps, fought courageously in the War of 1812, and appeared at the meeting that night. While Morris acknowledged the contribution of British immigrants to nation building in Canada, his was an exclusive nationalism, premised on notions of a white identity. It was no accident that he left out any mention of people of other backgrounds, such as Aboriginal peoples and African Canadians. Moreover, spokesmen for the Native Canadians made no attempt to take into account the people of other regions: the French Canadians and the people of the Maritime provinces. It is little wonder, then, that their movement failed to become pan-Canadian or enduring. Indeed, even in 1860, it was represented at only two receptions for the prince, at Cobourg and Toronto.

On the evening that the prince arrived in Cobourg, the first place that he had been able to land after Orange demonstrations at Kingston and Belleville, the Native Canadians provided him with a special welcome. The men, with silver maple leaves on their chests and flaming torches in hand, lined up on either side of the royal carriage. 'A long rope was attached to the carriage,' reported the New York *Times*, and the Native Canadians showed their determination 'to rope in the affection of their Prince in that novel and singular manner.' At a sprightly clip, they pulled the carriage in the procession all the way to the town hall. And what a sight it was: 'There were tall men, short men, red-faced men and whiskered men; men of delicate appearance with a little down on the upper lip; men of rough guise, whose hirsuteness would equal that of a bear; and men who had never been within a hundred feet of a carriage in all their lives.' In the eyes of the New York correspondent, then, the Native Canadians represented diversity of a sort![91]

Civic promoters of the 1860 tour had expected that the elaborate public addresses and the public spectacles mounted throughout the British North American provinces would leave the international visitors with idealized impressions that underscored loyalty, progress, and social harmony. Above all, those behind the tour hoped to enhance one identity: that of British subjects loyal to Her Majesty and proud of the British connection. And, to be sure, there can be little doubt that the tour reinforced Britishness. Yet, when the people made their preparations for the prince's coming and during the course of the visit itself, other identities had also bubbled to the surface, ones that spoke to difference rather than to a common imagined identity. Regional, racial, gender, class, religious, and political differences could not in fact be submerged, however enthusiastic the support for the young prince. While some of these identities flowed smoothly in the same current as the officially sanctioned identity of loyal British subject, cross-currents also surfaced, complicating matters. As it turned out, the royal visit proved to be a more revealing occasion than Canadians had expected – perhaps, indeed, more revealing than they wanted.

8

Royal Tourist

A royal tour implies a royal tourist. The Prince of Wales came to the British North American provinces in part to learn about them first hand by taking in the sights. His mentors believed in the adage that travel is broadening, that a vacation could help prepare the prince for his vocation. The young heir apparent did not object. Never a keen scholar, Albert Edward preferred travel to poring over books under the watchful eye of impatient tutors. And, as the prince found during his North American progress, excursions offered respite from the wearing round of state ceremonials.

It is time to consider the 1860 tour as tourism, the prince as tourist, and the writings on the visit as travellers' accounts. Of course, a tourist who is a member of the royal family is no ordinary tourist. Membership has its privileges! The prince travelled in great luxury, fussed over by servants, equerries, governors, and others. He never had to worry about making connections: trains, boats, and carriages waited for him. On the other hand, a rigid and demanding itinerary, and vigilant chaperones, left the young prince with little room for impulsive explorations – so often a source of pleasure for tourists who imagine that they have penetrated the public façade and seen the real thing. Moreover, the prince's celebrity status meant that the public's prying eyes frequently constricted his movements. As he gazed, he was gazed at, subject and object blurring in the process.

Not only did spectators peer at the royal traveller, writers did too. Public interest in the perambulations of the Prince of Wales generated a number of travellers' accounts by journalists and by members of his entourage. Most notable are the extensive writings of a few of the special correspondents who travelled alongside the prince, the published travel journal of Gardner Engleheart (Newcastle's private secretary), and the unpublished 'journal letters' that Dr Henry Acland wrote to his wife and son back home in Oxford. None of these authors was a professional or specialist in travel writing, but each felt that he could turn his hand to it. This is in itself not unusual. 'Travel writing has taken a mixed and middlebrow form throughout its history,' writes one cultural theorist of the genre. 'Anyone can have a go, and usually does.'[1] In these various accounts of the tour, the writers documented the prince's visits to various tourist locales and cast their own 'tourist gaze' on them. That is to say, they looked for the extraordinary and contrasted it with what they understood to be the everyday, the familiar.[2]

The prince's visit to St John's provided a taste of what was to come. In the Newfoundland capital, he followed the Victorian tourist agenda by visiting the public buildings, Dr Henry Stabb conducting him through the Lunatic Asylum and clergymen guiding the royal party through both the Anglican and the Roman Catholic cathedrals, which were the pride of St John's. The visit to the Anglican church caused no stir, Engleheart noting in guidebook prose only that it was 'an exceedingly pretty building, partly of native slate, partly of Galway stone, of the Early English style, but still incomplete.' The prince's brief tour of the Catholic cathedral, however, did become controversial. Militant Protestants in Upper Canada disapproved of Newcastle's allowing the Protestant prince to visit the Catholic cathedral at St John's, presenting it as evidence of the duke's 'popish leanings.' Engleheart's depiction of the Catholic cathedral shows that the duke's secretary, at least, had no such leanings. It was, he bitingly remarked, 'very pretentious in its exterior, of Irish granite, and of Italian style, but within cold and bald, and resembling a large cruciform music-hall.'[3]

In addition to touring the provincial capital, the prince saw a little of the nearby countryside. With his suite and the lieutenant governor, Sir Alexander Bannerman, the prince rode on horseback to admire the view from Signal Hill, and he went to Lake Quidi Vidi, hoping to take in the regatta that was in progress there. Many of the 10,000 people who had gathered at the lake crowded round him cheering, and the prince doffed his hat in acknowledgment. Finding the public attention tiresome, he left for the peace of pretty Portugal Cove, a fishing community about nine miles from town. At one of the fishing 'rooms,' the royal party was shown the various operations involved in preparing cod for export: cleaning, splitting, salting, drying, and packing – which the prince found, according to reports, both interesting and instructive. Although the prince tasted the cod-liver oil, he was spared 'the usual boot oiling which attends a visit to these "rooms," but some of his followers were not so fortunate, and were obliged to pay a douceur for the privilege of having a greasy hand smeared across their patent leathers.'[4]

Such was the extent of the prince's touring in St John's, but several accounts of the visit to Newfoundland included extended commentaries on the island's attractions, and, in keeping with the style of the current tourist literature on North America, they provided myriad statistics documenting the province's progress. (Accumulating and ordering 'facts' was a mid-Victorian passion.[5]) The correspondent for the Toronto *Globe,* who covered the prince's visit to Newfoundland, wrote over 5,000 words about the province, detailing its mineral resources and even providing tables showing imports, exports, and shipping activity. A lazy reporter could fill out an account easily with this kind of ready-made copy, but the *Globe* correspondent went beyond the accumulation of facts by working hard to convey the feel of St John's – or rather, the smell. 'In the town the smell of codfish prevails to a most disagreeable extent,' he wrote. It 'occasionally bursts upon the olfactory nerves with an intensity which might give rise to the suspicion that the concentrated essence of the billions of codfish murdered by man was stinking in ghostly revenge.' The widely published account by the correspondent of the New York *Tribune* provided just as many facts, most of them drawn from some published lectures by the Reverend Dr Mullock, bishop of St John's, and from the *Concise History of Newfoundland* by F.R. Page, two works he recommended to his readers. The reporter justified his extensive coverage of the population and resources of the island by referring to the widespread ignorance of people in the United States and England about the place. 'Newfoundland is indeed a *terra incognita,*' he wrote, most people believing it to be 'perpetually enveloped in the densest fogs, and inhabited by a few hundred modern Robinson Crusoes who live in a semi-barbarous style, earning a living by catching codfish.' If not every reader had an appetite for the instructive geography and history lessons that followed, they were supposedly made more palatable by being mixed in with news about the local preparations for the prince's visit.[6]

Unpublished accounts of the tour give some fleeting impressions of Newfoundland. In his own letters home, the prince admired what he saw of the island. He thought St John's 'a very picturesque sea port town,' with a 'remarkably pretty' harbour 'said to resemble Balaclava.' (Because of the Crimean War, 'everyone' in 1860 was familiar with the appearance of Balaclava.) The countryside outside St John's he found to be 'very like Scotland.' If the prince's impressions resemble ones from tourist guidebooks, where fine scenery is featured, Dr Acland's, by contrast, reflect the scholar's critical approach to travel. As a leading figure in England's public-health movement, Acland took note of the condition of the asylum and the hospital in St John's, judging them to be poorly ventilated and not well managed. Nevertheless, he added, rather patronizingly, that the health care was 'in truth ... far more than ... expected.' Acland imagined Newfoundland as an unusually simple place, 'the colony which is in all respects least developed.' It offered an ideal opportunity for observing colonial life. Always the optimist, Acland wrote that it was fortunate that the party had visited it first because, 'with fewer objects to distract the attention,' it offered 'the simplest problem for study.' The Regius professor took his touring seriously.[7]

Getting There Is Half the Fun

By 1860, the means of travelling through the well-settled parts of the British American provinces had improved enormously thanks to the convenience of coasting and river steamers and the rapidly expanding network of steam railways, which had been built only in the previous decade. Under normal circumstances, tourists, who had to be quite well off, moved from place to place in comfort on regularly scheduled trains and steamboats. But there was nothing normal about travelling during the period of the royal visit. Spectators following the prince's perambulations overtaxed the facilities, with annoying results to the travellers. The prince himself was spared such annoyances, of course, and travelled under exceptional conditions of an entirely different sort.

As a traveller from England, Nathaniel Woods praised the high quality of steamer travel in the Atlantic provinces. 'The boats that ply between Nova Scotia and New Brunswick,' he wrote, 'are admirably formed, very fast in their speed, and most ample in their means of accommodating passengers. In short they are boats of the American plan; floating hotels, of the comforts of travelling in which we English are as ignorant as of comfort in our fixed hotels.'[8] He was fortunate that he seldom had to test this impression, owing to travelling privileges extended to him as the special correspondent for the *Times*.

By contrast, the rest of the press corps travelled with the masses that followed in the prince's wake. On the trip from Shediac, New Brunswick, to the Gaspé, the reporter for the New York *Times* found the steamer so packed that people were trying to sleep 'three to a *table*!' Women sat huddled together on the planks of the deck, 'as it seemed for mutual protection,' while men caroused in the bar room, and 'every now and then a snatch of bachanalian song would be roared into your ears from one tipsy fellow's stentorian throat.' People were in a holiday mood, and fire-crackers popped at frequent intervals. Reporters said that the crowding was just as bad, if not worse, aboard the steamer *Arabian* bound for Charlottetown. 'Now commenced a twenty-four hours of discomfort,' said the correspondent for the Montreal *Gazette*, 'such as I did not remember to have suffered before.' According to the *Globe* account, so severe was the crowding that no one could move from the spot where they first got stuck. 'It was a terrible state of affairs,' he complained. 'We began to think of the black hole of Calcutta and all its horrors.' A disgusted Kinahan Cornwallis exclaimed that 'the passage was disgusting to every one of any sensibility,' but joked that he was fortunate when it came time to dash to claim a hotel room because he was unencumbered by luggage, the crew having mistakenly left it behind in New Brunswick.[9]

Not every trip was so trying. 'Howard' thoroughly enjoyed himself aboard the *Columbia*, which took him from Quebec to Montreal. As he explained to readers of the New York *Tribune*, passengers amused themselves in various ways during the trip up the St Lawrence. 'One group,' he says, 'gathered about a couple of darkies, who, with banjo and fiddle accompanying strong harmonious voices, gave out the good old-fashioned Christy's melodies.' Meantime, other travellers gathered in the ladies' cabin, 'where two pretty Canadian damsels favored us with vocal and instrumental music, aided by a fine-tone Chickering [piano]. Cards, cigars, pipes and beer filled up the chinks till late bed-time.'[10]

Train travel similarly brought pains and pleasures, even to the privileged royal travellers. The prince always travelled on special trains rather than on the regularly scheduled services. To ensure his safety, the tracks were always cleared of other trains, and the one carrying him was always preceded by another engine. Nevertheless, the train trip through parts of the back country of eastern Upper Canada, from Arnprior down to Brockville, was gruelling. By the end of the day, according to Woods, 'with the exception of the Prince, not one single member of the party was distinguishable under their hideous masks of dust.' This was despite the frequent dowsing the travellers gave themselves from the ample supply of seltzer water on hand to dilute the equally ample supply of sherry. On one occasion, members of the royal party were nearly caught without provisions to satisfy their hunger because the purveyor, Mr Sanderson, was delayed by a railway accident. His train had run over a fellow, who had both his legs cut off. The preoccupation of the journalists was not with the tragedy but with the feared lateness of the prince's meal.[11]

The prince's accommodations while travelling on British American trains were the most luxurious that could then be imagined. The railway companies wanted to treat him well, and they had the means to do it. Craftsmen in their car works performed magic on the special carriages prepared for him. The grand saloon of the car made for his use on the Great Western Railway (GWR) through western Upper Canada was said to be 'a perfect gem of a room, painted in pure white, with delicately gilded mouldings and cornices.' It had a large, handsome mirror, vases of flowers, window curtains of silk in royal blue, and four upholstered sofas and various armchairs all covered in blue silk damask. The wooden parts of the armchair intended for the prince's use were elaborately carved with Prince-of-Wales plumes and coronet and with the rose, thistle, and shamrock, intertwined with maple leaves. Beavers adorned the sofas.[12] We know from Dr Acland that the accommodations were comfortable. On the morning the prince left London, the talented physician sketched various members of the official party, including Cartier and John Rose, while they slept soundly in their GWR car as the royal party sped in the direction of Niagara Falls. Acland entitled his sketch 'After the Ball.'[13]

Sometimes the luxury went too far. For the prince's outing to the Chaudière Falls near Quebec, a sumptuous picnic was prepared by the chef, Monsieur Hardy, 'an artiste, who was once *chef de cuisine* in the establishment of the Comte de Baritenski.' The meal was intended to be served in the open air, with the guests seated on the grass, 'gipsy fashion,' but rainy weather forced the party to take shelter in the tavern of Bazil Demers in the village of Saint Nicholas. The widely reprinted bill of fare describes an extravagant feast:

GOUTER

POUR SON ALTESSE ROYALE LE PRINCE DE GALLES

Aux Chutes de la Chaudière
Lundi, le 20 d'Aôut, 1860

La Ronde de Boeuf, salée.

Le Jambon froid, decoré a la gelée.
La Mayonnaise de blanc de volaille, garnie.
Les Poulets nouveaux, rôtis.
Les Langues de Renne, décorées.
Le Pâté de foies de canards de Toulouse, trufflée
Le Pâté de Bécassines, trufflée
La Galantine de perdreux, trufflée.

Le Pâté de foies d'oles, de Strasbourg.
Les Pieds de cochon, truffés.
Les Saucissons de Lyon.
Les Sardines à l'huile.

Le Gingembre des Indes, au sucre.
Les Prunce, Reine Claude, à l'eau-de-vie.
La Marmelade d'Oranges.
Les fruits en Candis.
Les Pêches, les Poires, les Raisins, les Prunes.

Le Vin de Champagne,
Le Vin de Xérès,
Le Grand Vin de Château-Lafite, 1851.
L'Eau-de-vie de Cognac, 1834.
La Bière amère,
L'Eau de Seltz.

Reporters juxtaposed this impressive menu with the simple setting where the repast was served: a rural tavern, decorated with 'an old wooden clock, a few rush-bottomed chairs, and some of those coloured prints intended to represent scenes in scriptural history.'[14]

Dr Acland was horrified with the lavishness of this feast. It offended his evangelical sense of proper restraint; moreover, as the physician to the royal party, he was concerned for the health of the prince and his suite. He had already been worried about excess, but the picnic prompted him to act, as he explained in a letter home. After describing the menu and the fine china on which it was served (one of the sets made especially for the prince's visit to Canada), Acland wrote: 'The luncheon was so oppressively rich that I ventured for once to express my opinion of the state of affairs, and I said the Governor should report to the Council that tho' the liberality and splendour of the entertainments were most gratifying, yet that, but for state purpose, [it] would be more acceptable if in private the Prince was entertained in a more simple and less costly manner. I said the Physician ... could not but think of the contrast between this excessive luxe and the toils of those who helped to provide it.' Apparently, the advice was happily accepted and acted upon by the Canadian authorities. Even a royal tourist could have too much of a good thing.[15]

From the Sublime to the Picturesque

Everyone who travelled with the prince, whether a member of the official party or a journalist, became a travel writer and authority, slipping effortlessly into the language and conventions of the genre. It was the Victorian equivalent of snapping photographs while on a trip: we all know what ought to be captured and how a shot should be composed. So familiar is the cultural practice, it comes 'naturally.'

In 1860 much of the travel commentary in the newspapers featured the wilderness through which the royal party sometimes travelled. Vast expanses of rock and forest contrasted sharply with the urban world of most newspaper readers. Woods gave readers of the *Times* a sense of a world supposedly beyond civilization when he described the trip through Nova Scotia from Halifax to Windsor. The railway ran 'through a rugged country, where rocks seemed striving with scanty pines for the possession of the soil.' Influenced by aesthetic notions known as 'the sublime,' his account evoked the awe and unsettling fears that the wilderness signified to Victorians.[16] The 'almost primeval forests' near Windsor, he wrote, were 'more wild, more beautiful, and more impressive in their silent grandeur than can be imagined.' In writing of the scenery near Cape Gaspé, he spoke of 'the bold magnificence of this coast,' where 'the huge cliffs of steep red sandstone, lit up by the setting sun, seemed like mountains of fire, in which the dark shadows caused by rents and chasms stood out with a black distinctness that was almost terrible.' The correspondent for the New York *Times* similarly evoked the sublime, but his account was less positive. The scenery between Halifax and Windsor, he said, was 'dull, uninteresting, and monotonous – oppressive in its continuous aspect of primeval solitude – wild at times in its rough, ragged, and desolate wastes.'[17]

While staying in Quebec, the royal party made an afternoon outing to the falls at Montmorency, which struck the visitors as a very impressive natural wonder. The prince told his mother that they were 'the largest I think I ever saw,' and that, like the Chaudière Falls, they were 'well worth seeing.' The correspondent for the New York *Tribune* described the sight as 'surpassingly beautiful' and he gendered the falls as female: 'With all its impetuous velocity, the fall conveys only the sentiment of a really feminine softness.' He went on to describe the area's historical association with Wolfe and Montcalm, which, he said, added to its 'romantic and exciting interest.' Woods regarded the falls 'almost with a regretful awe' and thought it a pity that they were all but unknown outside the district, a shortcoming that reflected a lack of commercial spirit among the local French-Canadian population. 'If the Falls of Montmerenci and their Natural Steps were in the United States,' he wrote, 'there would be pictures of them everywhere, a fine hotel in their immediate neighbourhood, and thousands going to visit them annually.'[18]

In the Victorian imagination, of course, the North American wilderness was either devoid of population – unimproved by the hand of civilization – or sparsely occupied by 'savages.' To investigate the life of the Indians, Woods visited the Huron (Wendat) of Lorette (Wendake), outside Quebec. Although Lorette was recommended in all the guidebooks,[19] Woods said that 'as a tourist attraction' it was 'a delusion and a snare.' He feigned disappointment that the Indians did not live up to his expectations, which had run along the lines of 'wigwams, tomahawks, war-paint, and stalking chiefs wrapped in abnormal dignity and ragged blankets.' Instead, he found 'an Indian village about as characteristic of the Hurons as Kew.' (In fact, the guidebooks billed it as an opportunity to see what the once ferocious Iroquois had become: 'a harmless, quiet set of people.'[20]) From Woods's account it is apparent that the residents were generous and hospitable to him, but he chose to highlight other matters. An inhabitant whom the *Times* correspondent chanced to meet in the street explained to him that the marriage festivities of the chief's daughter were then going on and that he was welcomed to attend. Woods was taken to a house resembling 'a small English parsonage,' where the chief, who wore 'a plain, substantial broadcloth suit,' welcomed him. Woods hoped to find 'the people of the tribe' enjoying themselves in ways 'characteristic of the race,' but he found instead men 'in unexceptionable morning dress' and 'the "squaws" in white muslin dresses ... dancing the Lancers to the music of an excellent pianoforte!' He concludes his story with a comment intended to be amusing. 'This was enough for me,' he says. 'I had seen quite sufficient of savage life.'[21]

The picturesque vied with the sublime as a way of seeing the scenery of the provinces. Commentators warmed to pretty, pastoral scenes that conformed to notions of artistry and that signified the successful colonization of the wilderness, civilization having reshaped nature so as to make God's handiwork useful.[22] The correspondent for the New York *Times* said that the patches of cultivation amid the wilderness near Pictou, Nova Scotia, exhibited both 'the features of this continent as the white man found it and as the white man is making it.' Viewed from the comfort of a deck chair aboard the steamer, the *Forest Queen*, the cultivated fields and tidy farmhouses along the shores of the Saint John River charmed members of the royal party and the press. 'The white houses and outbuildings of the farmers,' reported the *Globe*, 'line the stream, reminding one, to some extent of the St Lawrence; though here, the residences appear on a larger scale than the shanties of the French *habitants*.' The correspondent for the New York *Tribune* described 'a region of great fertility ... the broad meadows and rich intervale lands, with unbroken chains of hills beyond, afford a series of the most delightful prospects.' The prince told his mother that 'the scenery all the way was very pretty and reminded me of the part of the Thames near Windsor rather.'[23]

The delights of the Saint John River valley were too little known, all were agreed. The writer for the New York *Times* reported that some on board the *Forest Queen* 'compared the scene to that on the Hudson – others thought it more like the English Thames – one gentleman thought it resembled the French Saone.' Indeed, they were 'all surprised to find so magnificent a river,' one 'far too little known to Summer travellers.' While the New Yorker's plug for provincial tourism was aimed at Americans, Woods had his British readers in mind when he wrote about the trip: 'Every one on board seemed much impressed by the rich luxuriance of the soil, and every one asked the question, which no one could answer, "Why were not emigrants brought there?"' He took the opportunity to describe the excellent prospects for emigrant settlers in New Brunswick and Prince Edward Island, and especially for intelligent, hard-working agricultural labourers with a capital of £100 or £150. Woods also made explicit the idea that the royal visit might have economic consequences. He explained that, if the publicity brought the colonies what they most needed – 'hardy young immigrants' – then the 'provinces will, indeed, have reason to bless the visit of the Prince.'[24]

In travelling through the countryside, the visitors encountered well-known tourist sites, which they assessed, adding their two cents to an ongoing review. Woods in particular had an acerbic pen with which he liked to destroy popular notions and well-established reputations. 'Humbolt [the travel writer] goes into extacies about the natural phenomena of the Bay of Fundy – its huge waves, its rapid currents, and the immense rise and fall of the tide,' wrote the *Times* correspondent. 'The impressions of those who cross it, as I did often, in a fog, a heavily laden boat, and during two-thirds of a southerly gale, sending in a tremendous swell, will not, however, be quite so enthusiastic.' Woods flatly panned a favourite tourist pastime below Montreal – running the rapids in the St Lawrence – and explained how it was that such a safe trip gained the reputation for being dangerous. Tourists were 'told they have accomplished a tremendous feat and as none are like to be incredulous of their own heroism, the delusion is passed on from tourist to tourist.' Woods knew exactly what he was up to. 'This language is dreadful guidebook heresy, of course, but the worst is yet come,' he wrote. 'These Thousand Islands are in their way a delusion and a snare.' To his eye, the many little islands merely choked the broad, noble river. He asked readers to imagine the scene: 'Take slips of the Isle of Dogs of all sizes, from an island as large as a footstool up to ten or twelve acres, plant the large ones with stunted firs, strew the little ones over with broken stones as if they were about to be macadamized, put them near the surface of the water in a mechanical disarray, giving confusion without picturesqueness and number without variety.' By playing the travelling curmudgeon, Woods thus kept his readers entertained between descriptions of royal ceremonials.[25]

Colonial Progress

The historical literature on Canadian tourism has highlighted the Victorian obsession with the wilderness,[26] but certainly in 1860 the towns and cities of British North America came in for their share of attention in the travel commentaries. Montreal was repeatedly reviewed and found to be attractive. Even crusty Nathaniel Woods was fulsome in his praise of Canada's leading city: 'The churches and public buildings are massive and noble looking stone structures. The houses are all lofty and handsomely built; the streets wide, clean, and most admirably paved. About the whole place too there is an air of business and wealth.' Here spoke the proud imperialist, but the correspondent for the New York *Tribune* was only a little more reserved in his praise:

'Montreal, in her nun-like dress of gray granite, is scarcely to be called a cheerful city, but she possesses much to interest the stranger.' Like others, he was struck by the attractive 'mixture of most-English English and quaintest of French peculiarities in the population.' Kinahan Cornwallis, in his *Royalty in the New World*, devoted most of the first chapter to establishing that Canada offered Americans a touch of the exotic on their doorstep. 'When you speak to a cabman he answers in a French *patois*, or with an accent which tells you that French is the mother tongue; as you pass a group of children you hear them chattering French; whenever you look up at the name of a street painted on the walls, the chances are twenty to one that it is French also; you meet Catholic priests in their vestments, with their heads covered with ordinary black silk hats; you read French names of the shops, and at the Custom-house and City Hall you find the names of the Departments painted on the doors in both languages.'[27]

Montreal's Victoria Bridge drew much attention because of the inauguration, of course. The imperialist chauvinism of Woods was blatant in his account in the *Times*: 'As an engineering triumph over natural difficulties of the most stupendous kind, it is not only without its equal in the world, but the world offers nothing which may fairly be put in comparison with it.' Hundreds of words follow, giving a multitude of relevant statistics, as well as advice that the tourist see it in winter 'when millions of tons of floating ice come crashing down.' Only then is justice done to 'its grand conception and what seems the almost super-human energy and skill necessary to carry out the idea in all its present grand perfection.' A correspondent writing in the New York *Tribune* offered a much more sober assessment. He thought that the structure impressed more 'by its figures than by its appearance. Its great length takes away from its apparent hight [*sic*] and bulk – and *length*, I have observed, is the least effective element in architecture.' No one, however, challenged the bridge's status as an engineering triumph, and for that reason alone people were encouraged to visit Montreal and see it.[28]

In the cities of British North America, Victorian tourists commonly visited public institutions and churches, and certainly the prince was no exception. It strikes us today as voyeuristic and inappropriate for casual tourists to visit functioning prisons and mental health facilities, but jails, prisons, and 'lunatic asylums' were firmly on the Victorian tourist itinerary. Toronto's 'lunatic asylum' on Queen Street, for instance, was understood to be conveniently located near the provincial exhibition grounds so that visitors could take in the two attractions on the same day: midway freaks and madmen.[29] Victorians were curious for a peak inside the still quite new institutions such as prisons, asylums, and model schools upon which social reformers had pinned high hopes for the reform of 'misfits' and of society as a whole. Still supremely confident of their ability to categorize individuals with problems, correct their moral failings, and instil 'the habits of industry,' the institution builders of the mid-Victorian period were proud to show off to the public the interiors of the massive structures, as well as their innovative methods. The civic promoters behind the prince's tour hoped that his visits to local institutions would publicize their city's up-to-date facilities and gain royal recognition and international attention for these impressive symbols of urban progress. What is more, there was a chance that the prince might show his appreciation in a tangible way by making a donation to the institution. For those, like the prince consort, General Bruce, and the Duke of Newcastle, who were concerned with the young prince's education, his visits to local and provincial institutions had an instructive purpose. Furthermore, the prince's gifts to the institutions, when they came in the form of a prestigious annual prize for student excellence, one named in honour of the Prince of Wales, would be a lasting memento of the visit and a means of strengthening the monarchical presence in the provinces.[30]

That said, the newspapers took little interest in the dull business of the prince's institution hopping, and there is little evidence that Albert Edward himself found the visits interesting. Many of these visits entailed yet more formal ceremonies involving addresses and replies. Only Dr Acland appears to have been genuinely interested in the state of colonial institutions. He went out of his way to meet institution builders and assess the results of their work. Take, for example, his 'journal letter' describing his visit to various institutions in Toronto. As with nearly every hospital he visited, Acland found the Toronto General Hospital to be deficient in its arrangements for cleanliness. But he was impressed with the Normal School, 'a very noble institution,' with its 'capital library, fine lecture Rooms, large Museum, Gallery of copies of pictures.' He attributed its success to the exertions of Dr Egerton Ryerson, who took him and other members of the royal party through the school. Acland was similarly impressed with the recently built University of Toronto: 'All was in admirable order. All well arranged. Library catalogues complete; and reading rooms most convenient for use.' Acland took special interest in the architecture of University College, a building completed less than two years before his tour and modelled, in part, on the new Oxford Museum, which Acland himself had been instrumental in getting established. 'It is our design minus the Arch – turned Norman – and gone wild,' he wrote of University College. 'But it has a certain solidity of appearance which ours lacks, is *more* ornate, less delicate, smaller in its parts – but is in many respects a very creditable building.' Acland also approved of the decision of the university authorities to enrol the prince as an undergraduate, a more appropriate honorific than a doctorate, given that the young man's actual undergraduate career was still under way.[31]

In only one instance – at Quebec – did controversy erupt over the institutions on the itinerary of the royal tourist. As we saw in chapter 5, members of the Reform opposition in Canada West attacked the authorities for having the prince visit Quebec's Roman Catholic institutions and having him accept and reply to addresses from the Catholic bishops at Laval University and the nuns of the Ursuline convent. Visiting institutions was a much more complicated and potentially controversial matter when the tourist was the Prince of Wales.

Had the prince toured Ottawa just a few years later, he would have had to devote time to visiting the Parliament Buildings and government offices, but in 1860 the city's main attraction was much more exhilarating: shooting the timber slide at the city's Chaudière Falls.[32] The lumber industry built the giant timber slide at Ottawa so that rafts of timber could be brought down the Ottawa River (and eventually to the port of Quebec) without being damaged by a tumble down the mighty Chaudière Falls. Above the falls, raftsmen broke the rafts into their component cribs, which were then diverted to the side of the falls down a series of slides, the more level passages in-between designed to slow the descent. For a fee, tourists could have a ride down the three-quarter-mile shoot. Special arrangements were made for the prince. Allan Gilmour, one of the leading lumbermen of the district, had two strong cribs made up for the occasion, one for the prince and his party and another for journalists.[33] The latter provision no doubt helps to explain the considerable coverage that the attraction received in the press.

The special correspondent of the Toronto *Globe* gave a humorous slant to his dramatic account of the ride on a timber slide in an attempt to convey a sense of the fun had by those who went down it. He pretended that the plan had been for the press to go down the slide first, to test it for the prince. 'If our crib got smashed,' he wrote, 'if we got pitched into the raging current, our heads crushed between the timbers, and our eyes and limbs, muscles and nerves generally reduced to a jelly, then the Viceroy of British North America was not to go; he was to be reserved to tell his mamma of our sad fate.' As it turned out, however, His Royal Highness would go second to none – or so the story went – and his raft had led the way. As the press crib followed, the *Globe* correspondent 'thought something dreadful was coming.' At the bottom of the first chute, 'the balks of timber strove to separate themselves from each other.' But the raft continued down, 'with the speed of lightning, splashed, plunged, [and] knocked an adventurous individual off a boom into the water.' Woods continues the story: 'Quicker and quicker the banks flew by, all thronged with people cheering and waving handkerchiefs, and faster and faster the raft plunged down, groaning and creaking, now half hidden by the boiling water.'[34]

Unpublished accounts add to the images. As the prince's crib passed along one of the more level stretches, the riders caught sight of Dr Acland standing on a bridge overhead. 'They all called out,' wrote the physician, '"drop down Acland – come, come."' He says that he 'could not resist,' and down the chain he went, landing in the midst of the group, and 'away we bounded.' More fun came at the bottom of the slide, where the wharf was crowded with spectators, most of them women eager to glimpse the prince. Preceding the crib was a wave of displaced water, as Lieutenant-Colonel. Thomas Wily says, 'on a small scale, something like a Bay of Fundy bore.' The wave surged over the wharf, immersing the people 'knee deep' in water. 'A general scattering was the result,' says Wily, 'amidst a chorus of shouts, shrieks, and screams of laughter. The women ruefully shaking "their tempestuous petticoats," alas, no longer "tempestuous." Those safe themselves enjoyed the fun immensely. None more so that the Prince & his party on the flying crib.' In Woods's view, the shoot was 'the most exhilarating adventure in all the *repertoire* of American travel.'[35]

Rest and Recreation

In addition to his busy round of sightseeing, two recreational breaks were written into the prince's British North American itinerary: a fishing trip in the Saguenay country below Quebec and a vacation at Niagara Falls. During both of them, the formalities of the state visit were put aside and the members of the royal party enjoyed some respite from public appearances. Niagara Falls was, of course, the province's top tourist attraction, but in 1860 the Saguenay was a close second, its remoteness, wild grandeur, and moody atmosphere being much celebrated by well-heeled tourists seeking the sublime.[36]

The prince's trip up the Saguenay took place when he reached the mouth of that river as he proceeded up the St Lawrence from Gaspé en route to Quebec. The plan was for a two-day fishing excursion, with a stopover at night in Baie-des-Ha! Ha!. Plans had to be revised, however, because time was lost when the *Hero* ran aground near the mouth of the Saguenay. It was decided that the prince would simply make two day trips up the river aboard the steamer *Victoria*, accompanied by the royal suite, some members of the Canadian cabinet, and Governor Mulgrave from Nova Scotia. David E. Price, the local MPP and member of the prominent lumbering family, was their guide.[37]

As luck would have it, on the first of the trips, the party encountered driving rains, heavy fog, and a stiff headwind. No attempt was made to fish. Instead, the prince and his companions aboard the *Victoria* admired the rugged scene, which was dramatically shrouded in mists, and 'consoled themselves on cigars or refreshments.'[38] On the morning of the second day, the weather greatly improved, and the royal party made an early start. 'We left the *Hero* at 6 a.m., breakfasting on aboard the *Tadoussac* steamer,' wrote Engleheart in his journal. 'Off the mouth of the river numerous seals, and large flights of gulls, were sporting and revelling in the early sunshine. The white seal is occasionally seen; one showed itself to us today.' The royal party proceeded up river fifteen miles to the Sainte-Marguerite River, where Albert Edward touched Canadian soil for the first time. 'Soon afterwards,' says Engleheart, 'eight or ten rods were whipping the water for sea-trout, which were said to abound with each flowing tide. None, however would rise to our flies.' It was disappointing, since Price had shown the prince a favourite fishing spot and members of the party were well supplied with flies from the personal fly-books of Governor Head and Alexander Tilloch Galt, the Canadian cabinet minister. The disappointing results were blamed on the lateness in the season and the heavy rains, which had discoloured the river. A local reporter, however, cast some doubt on the prince's skill at fishing, commenting wryly: 'Practice alone is needed to make His Royal Highness as expert in fishing as he already is at fowling.' The pun was undoubtedly intended![39]

On the banks of the Sainte-Marguerite, the local lessee of the river, a Mr Blackwell, had set up a camp as a base for the royal fishing party.

Special efforts had been made for the comfort of the prince and to enhance the rugged setting for the sportsmen. The tents provided for the royal party were done up in the finest of rustic furnishings. It was all very manly, and Dr Acland chose to describe the scene to his young son, Willie, rather than to his wife. 'In each tent,' he wrote, 'was a buffalo skin for us to lie on, boughs of fir trees for our carpet. Dishes of birch bark and stools and tables tied up with birch wood.' And he added that the party was accompanied by '125 canoes with Indians and Hunters.' Engleheart sketched the campsite and the manned canoes against a rugged backdrop.[40]

After a sumptuous lunch at the camp, the fishing party boarded canoes and paddled upstream to some salmon pools. The trip up took longer than expected, as the rapids in the swollen river made the paddling hard going. Time was then short for fishing, and during the session the salmon proved nearly as elusive as the trout. Price succeeded in hooking a large one, however, and passed his rod to Albert Edward. Though the neophyte fisherman played it for a while, the fish got away. By 9:00 P.M., the fishing party had returned to the mouth of the Saguenay, ready for their evening meal. The catch of the day was not on the menu.

During the prince's two-day break in the Saguenay country, he escaped the gaggle of press correspondents that normally followed in his wake. General Bruce wrote to the prince consort, telling him that 'the Prince seemed to enjoy the whole affair very much.'[41] The arrangements had been rather clever. A special excursion was laid on for members of the press, who were invited to go up the Saguenay aboard the *Flying Fish*, the most manoeuvrable vessel in the prince's squadron. The journalists were thus kept entertained and out of the way of the prince. Moreover, having made a trip similar to that of the royal party, the newspapermen had the means to produce the copy demanded of them by their editors.

Several of the correspondents, assuming here the mantle of the travel writer, filled their reports of the Saguenay excursion with lengthy descriptions of the region's scenery, ones that conformed to well-known accounts of excursions in the area.[42] The column in the Fredericton *Head Quarters*, like those in several other newspapers, made much of the impressive way the stormy weather enhanced the rugged scene. 'Such accompaniments as wind and fog,' declared the correspondent, 'are the best frames for Saguenay pictures, and the wild grandeur of this astonishing stream, so utterly unlike anything else in the world, shows to more advantage under tempestuous than with sunshiny skies.' Kinahan Cornwallis of the New York *Herald* depicted the Saguenay as 'the most sombre river in the world,' adding that it was 'the best place for enjoying a fit of the blues, or melancholy that I know of.'[43]

Nathaniel Woods, who also played up the sublime, writes of 'the terrors of the Saguenay scenery,' its 'savage wildness and gloom,' its 'huge, naked cliffs, raw, cold, and silent as tombs.' Woods goes to some lengths to evoke a sense of awe and mystery. He refers to Jacques Cartier's landing there and sending 'a boat and crew to explore its rocky chasm which were never heard of again.' It is 'Nature's sarcophagus,' where 'limestone rocks stick up white and bleached in the gloomy air like the bones of an old world.' For all its terror, though, the Saguenay was safe enough and well worth a visit.[44]

Not all the newspapermen were content to report on the scenery of the Saguenay. An amusing – or embarrassing – incident that occurred while the prince was enjoying his private time came to be repeated again and again, particularly in the U.S. press. The story originated with a report from a local correspondent in the Quebec *Chronicle.* While fly-fishing for trout, the prince and his companions had become so absorbed in his sport that they failed to notice that the rising tide had stranded them on a rock near the river's edge. By some accounts, the prince was in great danger and had to be rescued by his guide, David Price.[45] According to another version of the story, the prince was never in any danger, since the surrounding water was less than knee deep, and Price, who was already wading in the stream, simply carried the prince back to shore so that the royal visitor would not get his trousers wet.[46] The American magazine *Harper's Weekly* took up the incident in a cartoon that belittled Albert Edward by contrasting the 'imaginary prince,' who, for example, heroically slew the dragon for sport, with 'the actual prince,' who had to be carried like a child when fishing.[47] So much for the manliness of sporting life!

At Niagara Falls, near the end of his British North American tour, the prince enjoyed his second holiday in Canada. On the evening of 14 September, the royal party arrived from an exhausting tour of the southwestern part of the province. Albert Edward had three days' respite from official responsibilities: two days for touring and a day of rest on Sunday, 16 September. The press appears to have taken a rest, too, for the reports on the prince's activities are brief. 'Here for a few short days – too few by far – there was a temporary lull in the whirl-

David E. Price rescuing the prince from the rising tide on the Sainte-Marguerite River during a fishing expedition in the Saguenay country. (*Frank Leslie's Illustrated Newspaper*, 8 September 1860)

wind of addresses, reviews, processions, state balls, and noisy Orangemen,' writes Woods. 'State and pomp were scattered to the winds,' enabling the prince to go about the Falls 'without a mob at his heels' and to 'sit and watch unobserved for hours the tremendous majesty of the scenes around him.'[48]

The prince enjoyed all the usual tourist attractions at Niagara.[49] He viewed the Falls from every angle, donning waterproofs to scramble behind the wall of water, crossing to the American side for yet another angle, and climbing up Terrapin Tower on Goat Island. He drove out to the Suspension Bridge and viewed the scene from over the gorge. He boarded the *Maid of the Mist*, which pulled up close to the base of the cascade, an experience he did not much enjoy since, as he told his mother, 'we got very wet again & did not see very much.'[50] On horseback, the prince went down to the Whirlpool and then toured about the neighbouring countryside, admiring the picturesque orchards. In the evenings he took in the illumination of the Falls, the first night from Table Rock. Albert Edward even managed to relax in the park-like grounds of the handsome villa of the late Samuel Zimmerman, where he was staying, and on the nearby grounds of Clifton House, where others in the royal party were housed in comfortable cottages. Because the dining room of the Zimmerman house could accommodate only sixteen people, the dinner parties were smaller and less formal than usual. One evening, the prince went to a bowling alley, where he spent hours competing with various members of his party. Late in their game he heard dancing in a ballroom overhead and, according to reports, expressed his disappointment that he had not known about the dance and had missed the opportunity to join the fun. As the reporter for the New York *Times* observed, 'he infinitely prefers leg to arm exercise.'[51]

The tourists in the royal party thoroughly enjoyed the Falls. Engleheart describes how, upon arriving in the town after dark, members of the suite were taken down the wooded slope from the Zimmerman house to get a view of the Falls. 'We skirt the river towards Table Rock,' he writes, 'unmolested and escaping recognition by the crowds to witness the grand experiment of lighting up the Falls. Grand indeed, it was ... We lingered long on the brink of this wondrous scene.'[52] The prince wrote to his mother, telling her about the illumination of the Falls and describing the 'blue and red lights which gave them a most beautiful and fairy like effect.' He was thoroughly impressed: 'A more magnificent & grand scene I do not think I ever witnessed.' Dr Acland

Bowling ten-pins at Zimmerman House, Niagara Falls, Canada West. (*Frank Leslie's Illustrated Newspaper*, 8 September 1860)

wrote that the sight of the Falls 'far exceeds the imagination.' Engleheart criticized the usual tourist accounts of the Falls, saying that 'the affectation of being disappointed with Niagara, though fashionable, seems to me to be simply ridiculous.' One thing that surprised him was the way that the heavy vibrations shook the windows and doors where he was lodged, so that 'they rattled throughout the night.'[53]

Reporters for the North American papers gave little attention to the Falls themselves, assuming, reasonably enough, that their readers would know plenty about them, but Woods could not help but try his hand at depicting Niagara in fine guidebook fashion for his readers in the British Isles. As with so many accounts of Niagara, Woods starts his by insisting that mere words cannot convey the grandeur of the Falls, and then, missing the irony entirely, he proceeds to fill more than a dozen pages with his attempt to do so. It begins: 'Words, in fact, are powerless before the stupendous force and terror of this cataract, and all the wealth of language would be exhausted before one could tell how the great hill of waters which drops from the monstrous cliff so smooth, so green, so deep, changes ere one can mark its fall into millions of columns of spray which, darting out like white fireworks, shoot down and down till lost in the clouds of mist which always wrap the base of the Falls in dim and grand obscurity.'[54] His readers in England must have got the message: if they had never seen the Falls, then they were truly missing out. Here was travel writing that bordered on the promotional.

By all accounts, the most diverting attraction of the royal visit to Niagara Falls was the performance by the celebrated tightrope walker Blondin, who had first thrilled audiences at the Falls the previous summer. A child star of music halls in France and England, Blondin had been brought to America by P.T. Barnum, the showman, but by 1859 the Frenchman had gone solo and gained fame by his performances on a 1,300-foot-long manilla rope strung across the Niagara gorge.[55] For the 1860 season, Blondin was housed in a rustic enclosure, topped by the tricolour of France and situated near the edge of the gorge, where the prince and his party went to meet the daredevil and view the spectacle. Though the prince urged him not to assume any special risk, Blondin took the occasion to perform a daring feat: crossing the gorge on a tightrope while carrying a man on his back. For this part of the performance, Blondin removed his Indian chief's headdress and beaded coat and put on strong straps with hooks to support the legs of his passenger, a Monsieur Calcourt. The crowd was breathless as the pair inched out along the rope suspended some two hundred and thirty feet above the boiling waters of the river. Four times, Blondin stopped for a rest, lowering Calcourt to the rope and then picking him up once again. It appeared to the spectators as if the two would fall each time Calcourt clambered onto Blondin's back. After about twenty minutes, the agony of the crowd ended as the piggyback pair gained the far side. Blondin returned much more quickly – on stilts that raised him three-feet above the rope – his most dangerous act.

The members of the royal party stood awestruck and not a little terrified by the spectacle. Engleheart explains that, although the prince had begged Blondin not to cross on stilts, still he had persisted. 'The whole scene was unpleasant, yet strangely fascinating,' the secretary observed. According to others who were also there, Albert Edward had watched with rapt attention and thoroughly enjoyed himself, though he said he found the experience somewhat nerve-racking.[56] In writing to the queen, he enthusiastically described the return trip on stilts as being 'the most wonderful feat of all.' The prince added that Blondin was 'a short well made little man, and not unlike the Emperor.' (His reference was to Emperor Napoleon III, with whom he had stayed in Paris.)[57]

After the performance, the prince chatted at length with Blondin and presented him with a generous purse, and members of his suite gave something more. After this, Blondin, 'with his balance-pole and stilts across his shoulder, then walked home in his skin-fitting merino undervest and drawers, with a wreath of feathers on his head.'[58] His performance that day gained much attention in the press both because of the royal spectator and because his act had been exceptionally risky, even for him. The publicity must have done his career some good; it most certainly capped off the royal visit to the Falls.[59]

Stolen Moments

While the excursions to the Saguenay River and Niagara Falls were enjoyable, the personal accounts of members of the royal party suggest that more private and impromptu outings were the treasured highlights of the trip. Engleheart speaks warmly of quiet walks that he managed to wedge into the busy schedule, rambles taken with other members of the official group who must also have enjoyed the little escapes. On a Sunday afternoon spent outside Quebec, General Bruce and Dr Acland accompanied Engleheart on strolls through the forest at

Spencer Wood, the governor general's usual residence. They paid a visit to David Price, whom they had met on the Saguenay, and 'strolled about his charming grounds,' which adjoined those of Spencer Wood. Price pointed out to the group 'the exact spot where the first man of Wolfe's invading force climbed the steep, and surprised the picket,' the entrenchment being traceable even one hundred years later. Another Sunday afternoon, this time at Ottawa, Engleheart went for a walk along the banks of the Ottawa River with John Rose, the minister of public works, with whom he spent 'two pleasant hours.' While at Niagara he escaped two afternoons in a row with Richard Pennefather, walking on the first day 'to Mr Street's' grounds' to explore 'the wonderful islets, of which he has made so much,' and on the second to Goat Island, where he 'spent two pleasant hours with Pennefather and my sketchbook.' The prince, being an extrovert and eighteen years of age, did not cherish quiet walks in the same way, but even he liked to escape the hubbub. He told his mother that at Niagara he had taken 'a very pleasant ride in the country, wh. is very pretty.' And he added wistfully, 'I am very sorry that our time did not allow as to remain longer at Niagara, as we might have had many other pleasant rides.'[60]

On another Sunday, this time in Fredericton, the prince visited some Maliseet men who had camped near Government House. Kinahan Cornwallis, the special correspondent for the New York *Herald*, remarked how the prince had spent his Sunday evening at Fredericton in 'a stroll out to the Indian encampment at the river-side.' The next day, as the Montreal *Gazette* reported, the prince went out in 'a bark canoe with the chief, Gabriel, who is a great friend and fellow hunter of the Lieut. Governor.' A widely reproduced account from the New York *Daily Tribune* explained that the prince had been so impressed with canoeing that 'a bargain' had been 'at once struck for the primitive little craft, which is now, in consequence, the Prince's own property.'[61] For Chief Gabriel, the encounter that day was, it has been said, 'a turning-point' in his life, and subsequently in England he would renew his acquaintance with royalty.[62] For the prince, the time they spent together in Fredericton was a pleasant respite from the hoopla, if not from the eyes of reporters.

Dr Acland thrived on quiet moments away from the crowds. His inquiring scholar's mind led him to search for the unusual in his travels, and his love of sketching drew him to seek places for viewing picturesque landscapes or ones that exposed either the everyday life of the common people or Aboriginal men and women, preferably in traditional clothing. When he began writing his letter home from Fredericton, Acland said that he had 'just returned from taking a leader [a dive] into the great St John's River off a huge raft, guided by the Indian whose wigwam is on the shore.' Part way through writing the letter, he spotted 'some Indians spearing fish by torch light,' and he rushed from his desk to the riverside and joined their 'light procession as a jewelled serpent winds among the trees.' In the same letter he described an early-morning paddle that he and others in the royal party, along with a few Indians, took in canoes on the Nashwaaksis River. The trip was his opportunity to make his fine sketch of 'Southwest,' one of the Maliseet paddlers, and another of Major Christopher Teesdale, the equerry, becalmed in the 96-degree (Fahrenheit) heat. During the outing to Montmorency Falls, Acland arranged for a tour of a couple of houses in the village 'to see the manner of life in this plain but comfortable country parish.' He was charmed by what he imagined to be a simple life, well adapted to local conditions and with 'no unnecessary things.' The scene conformed to his idea of a quaint peasant life, and he made some sketches of folk life among the habitants. (Of course, he was neither the first nor the last tourist to visit rural Quebec and see the scene in this way.[63]) On another occasion, writing from Niagara, Acland described a quiet morning spent sketching in the company of one of the town's many African-Canadian guides. It was, he says, 'a lovely morning on a sullen rock, a negroe [*sic*] by my side to warn me of rocks falling, or snakes crawling.'[64]

In both his sketching and his writing, Acland shows that he savoured quiet moments. One of his sketches, which is entitled 'Delayed a Day,' depicts the royal party enjoying themselves when they were prevented by heavy rain from making their scheduled arrival at Montreal. Acland includes a caption to the misty scene: "HRH walks and geologizes with the Governor General.' That quiet escapes were precious is underscored by Dr Acland's description of a walk he took at Ottawa with the prince, Governor Bruce, and Major Teesdale. On a Sunday afternoon, the group drove out to the nearby forest so as to get a break from the crowds in the city. They 'struggled into its depths,' he writes, 'and then we strolled searching and discovering many and various things – and were ourselves undiscovered for two hours.' Acland continues: '"How strange," said His Royal Highness, kicking the stump of a fallen fir tree in the dark forest, "to feel one's feet in America. How little one would have thought it possible a time ago."' Such musings were soon interrupted, however, when the walkers were discovered by curious fans of the prince. 'We were ... tracked out,' writes Acland, 'surrounded by people and went home.' So ended what Acland presents as a delightful moment away from the crowds.[65]

Souvenirs

What tourist can resist the temptation to collect souvenirs? Items obtained along the way bring back memories of experiences in faraway places and, when shown to friends and family at home, are proof of having really 'been there.' Moreover, shopping for souvenirs and collecting specimens from nature are part of the pleasure of travelling. The royal tourist and members of his suite resembled other tourists in acquiring souvenirs, but, unlike most tourists, the prince also received many fine gifts that were meant to be mementoes of the places and people he visited. Royal tourism is extraordinary, too, in that the well-wishers who surrounded the prince everywhere he went sought souvenirs of their encounter with him. The royal tourist became not just a collector of souvenirs but also a source of them – intentionally and otherwise.

The prince's first souvenir of his visit, which was presented to him in St John's by the people of Newfoundland, was the most exceptional of the lot: a Newfoundland dog. By 1860, the breed of giant but gentle black dogs was already firmly fixed as a distinctive product of the province, which, of course, made it an appropriate gift. The presentation, which took place on the morning of his second day on North American soil, was made by some members of the provincial government, and when the prince received the dog he was said to have shown 'genuine pleasure.' (It had been said that during his Atlantic crossing he frequently had expressed the hope that he might acquire such a dog while visiting Newfoundland.) Reporters described the prince's Newfoundlander as being 'a beautiful, thorough-bred animal, of a jet but not a glossy black, and very strong.' Special attention went to the dog's collar, which had been specially made of silver by Tiffany and Company of New York, at a reported cost of $216, an extravagant and impressive amount. Three shields with the royal arms were engraved on it, the larger shield bearing an inscription noting the donors and the occasion. For the benefit of the local population, the prince removed the collar from his dog so that it could be displayed for the day in the Colonial Buildings, and, for the benefit of the wider public, the *Illustrated London News* carried an illustration showing the precise appearance of the fine collar. According to reports, when the issue of what he would call the dog came up, it was suggested that he might choose 'Avalon,' but the prince objected to naming the dog after only a part of the province and opted instead to call him 'Cabot.' For the duration of the tour, Cabot was looked after by crew members on the *Hero*, who sometimes took him ashore, where he was much admired. It is unclear whether Cabot ever lived with the prince after his return to England, but we do know that Dr Acland ended up taking care of Cabot in Oxford, where the Regius professor and the Newfoundlander were frequently seen walking together in Broad Street.[66]

The legislature of Canada presented the prince with a portfolio of photographs by the province's top photographer, William Notman of Montreal. In the mid-nineteenth century it became a practice for governments to give visiting foreign heads of state collections of photographs – which were then still a novelty – of the place or places they had visited. Notman chose 36 single views and 279 stereographs to present to the prince, the items being handsomely mounted, inserted in elegant leather folios, and put in a silver-trimmed, maple box. The views, which showed scenes from nature and of the built environment in both Canada East and Canada West, were mostly photographs that Notman had taken prior to the visit for other purposes, although some relating to the tour itself were also included. The public was invited to admire the handsome gift by the *Illustrated London News*, which published an engraving that showed the wooden case, a folio, and a photograph, and by Notman himself, who, for several years, kept a replica in his showroom in Montreal for visitors to examine.[67]

Other presentation items were also distinctively 'Canadian.' The city of Halifax presented the prince with a portrait of a local Mi'kmaq woman, Mary Christianne Paul, painted by William Gush. It is remarkable that, for all the city's mid-Victorian pride in its British military connections and commercial progress, the city chose this portrait to present as a memento of the visit. The painting shows Paul sitting on the ground, clad in a beaded, peaked hat, a jacket, a woollen skirt with ribbon, and beaded moccasins – all clothing that she, a talented artist in her own right, had made.[68] On another occasion, too, the prince acquired a painting. When he toured the Provincial Exhibition in Montreal's Crystal Palace, he was taken through the display of artwork arranged by the Art Association of Montreal, which had been founded in order to organize the show. The association offered the prince one of the paintings, and he chose a watercolour by C.J. Way entitled 'The Prince's Squadron off Gaspé Basin.' Regarded at the time as a highly appropriate choice, today the painting is in the royal collection, Windsor Castle.[69]

The prince 'shopped' for his first souvenir when he was at Sydney, Nova Scotia, visiting the Mi'kmaq camp there. He and others in his party bought moccasins from Mary Ann Gould and another woman whom they met and whose birch-bark homes they looked into. Albert Edward sent his mother a souvenir enclosed in a letter from Halifax, where he had collected a sample of sweetbriar from the grounds of the home where Victoria's father, the Duke of Kent, had lived while serving as an officer in Nova Scotia. On another occasion, while at Carleton, near Saint John, in view of reporters and a crowd of spectators, an Aboriginal woman offered him some beadwork, which he agreed to purchase. Reporters joked about the lack of pocket money among the distinguished visitors. 'The Duke of Newcastle put his hand in his pocket for money, but found none,' went one account. 'Another pocket was tried; but with no better success. The Earl of St. Germains was a richer man; he had a sovereign half hidden somewhere in the corner of his pocket, which was rapidly transferred to the squaw's palm.'[70] Attempts at purchasing Indian souvenirs did not always succeed. When Dr Acland offered to buy an ornament that a Cayuga man at Niagara Falls was wearing, the fellow refused to sell it, saying that it was his wife's.[71]

While in British North America, the prince acquired a considerable collection of artwork and handicrafts produced by various Aboriginal people, nearly all of the items having been presented to him by the artists and craftspeople or by their chiefs. Soon after his arrival at Government House in Halifax, the governor's wife, Lady Mulgrave, presented the prince with a gift that had been left at the house by a young Mi'kmaq woman. Nathaniel Woods informed readers of the *Times* that it consisted of an item for the prince, 'a cigar case beautifully worked in slips of different coloured bead ornaments,' and a similarly decorated basket intended for the queen, both made by the Mi'kmaq woman herself. When touring at Rice Lake, Canada West, the prince received baskets filled 'with Indian work' made by Mississauga women of the vicinity. Reports at the time noted that the items in the basket each had a birch-bark label attached with the name of the maker on it. During the more elaborate gift exchanges at Sarnia and Brantford, as we saw in chapter 6, the chiefs presented the prince with tomahawks, bow-and-arrow sets, peace pipes, war clubs, and wampum.[72]

Works made by Native people and connoting their way of life were standard tourist souvenirs in the mid-nineteenth century, as indeed they had been for a long period before that. In the eighteenth century, wealthy tourists visiting eastern North America from Europe had sought out handicrafts such as beadwork and decorated birch-bark, purchasing many finely made items. In the nineteenth century, as tourism began to democratize, cheaper and less carefully made 'Indian' goods came on the market and were readily available at tourist sites such as Niagara Falls. The goods acquired by the prince in 1860 were similar in type to some of these, but they were of top quality because the First Nations people who presented them were honouring a royal figure. The high quality and inventiveness of the artwork can be confirmed by viewing the actual items which have been preserved in royal collections. Ironically, although the press of 1860 showed little interest in the gifts presented by Aboriginal people, a number of the presentation items have been seen by a great many people – themselves tourists. For nearly a century, various souvenirs of the 1860 tour have been on display to tourists visiting the Swiss Cottage Museum on the grounds of Osborne House on the Isle of Wight in England. The museum was conceived by Victoria and Albert as an activity centre for the pleasure and edification of their young children, and a place to display things the children collected in their travels. Glass cases hold dried insects, stuffed birds and animals, and the like, along with the Indian souvenirs collected by Albert Edward in 1860. Moreover, interest in the prince's Aboriginal souvenirs has grown in recent years because of their discovery by the discipline of art history.

In her stimulating study *Trading Identities*, art historian Ruth Phillips analyses the items presented to the prince in 1860 as evidence of artistic expression and cross-cultural borrowing in northeastern North America. As Phillips argues, these examples of artistic expression form part of a large body of surviving material from the Indian souvenir trade of North America in the eighteenth and nineteenth centuries, artworks that have usually been ignored by art historians on the grounds that they are tourist trash and/or handicrafts made by women rather than 'true artists.' Phillips rescues the works from such condescension and creatively uses them to explore the dynamics of interaction across cultures. She argues that the mid-nineteenth century was a period of especially productive cross-cultural borrowing among Native groups and with white colonizers, even as the pressures of colonialism increased. Both because of this timing, and the fact that the visit of the

Prince of Wales called forth special artistic endeavour, the presentation works from 1860 demonstrate extreme experimentation, and thus provide exceptional opportunities for understanding the cultural change among First Nations of the northeast. Several of the items are exceptional, too, in that they are signed; that is, the birch-bark labels with the artists' names are still attached.

Although content enough to acquire some Indian souvenirs in the British provinces, the royal party left their main shopping spree for New York, expecting, no doubt, that the selection of high-class goods would be best there. At one point, the prince and members of his suite visited a big new store in Manhattan, Ball, Black and Company, which was cleared of other shoppers so that they could inspect the jewellery, silverware, and decorative objects at their leisure. They came away satisfied with many purchases.[73] Even within the royal party, imperial pride went only so far when it came to shopping; tourists with money love New York!

The royal tourist also gave gifts to some of the people he encountered, presenting his hosts with tokens of thanks, people in the service industry with tips, and charities and other institutions with donations to commemorate his visit. On the morning of his departure from St John's, for instance, among other presentations, the prince gave Lady Bannerman 'a beautiful bracelet set with emeralds and diamonds and engraved portraits of his brothers and sisters,' and he donated £50 each to the Church of England asylum for widows and orphans and to the Benevolent Irish Society.[74] The prince's generous tipping of hotel staff became a matter of public interest and record, cementing his public image as fabulously wealthy but suitably appreciative, and thus a true gentleman. Such impressions were carefully cultivated by the royal family in Victoria's time in a deliberate attempt to enhance the monarchy's popular appeal.[75]

Sometimes the prince inadvertently provided souvenirs for his admirers who overstepped the bounds of propriety and invaded his space to get a piece of him. Dr Acland was astonished by an invasion of the royal party's quarters aboard the steamer *Kingston*, after members of the suite had left them. 'One of the visitors,' he wrote, 'kissed H.R.H.'s pillow, and cut up the soap that was left into bits.' On another occasion, ladies touring the *Hero* entered the prince's stateroom and snipped the buttons from his jackets and removed hair from his combs, taking them as souvenirs. Colonel Wily reported that, before the prince had left Quebec, 'the relic hunters had commenced work': people had approached the chambermaids where the prince was staying for 'the hair scrapings from the Prince's brushes & combs.' 'Howard' of the New York *Times* described the Quebec intrusion more colourfully still. 'Actually I blush to record what transpired in these rooms,' he wrote of the palace after the prince's departure. 'Men, women and children seemed possessed by some insane desire of making asses and flunkies of themselves. They tried the bed and all the chairs, they drummed on the piano and smashed tumblers, they cut off the tassels from the curtains and stole a sheet of music from the stand, they carried off some water left in a basin and cut up a copy of Tuesday's *Times* into a thousand pieces, each being anxious to preserve something that His Royal Highness had owned, used, or had about him.'[76]

Writers had found much that was remarkable about both the prince's experience of tourism and British North American tourist sites. His Royal Highness travelled in luxury and comfort, pampered in his elegant railway carriages and by meals that went to excess, but he had to contend with large, persistent, and curious crowds that made him the most gazed at of the gazers. When fly-fishing, he could not simply wade through the rising tide but had to be carried and then suffer the ridicule of the American press for failing to present the image of the virile sportsman.

In their commentaries, journalists and members of the royal party alike looked for the extraordinary when they cast their eyes on the landscape and populace of British North America. Wilderness scenes triggered notions of the sublime, the raw and terrifying beauty of nature at its most rugged and untouched, as well as of the Noble Savage – a world and its inhabitants that contrasted utterly with the civilization of home, whether home was London, New York, or some other metropolis. And yet this same land also displayed the marks of progress, achievements made possible by Europeans and their descendants who colonized the place. It was so fitting that the Victoria Bridge was the centrepiece of the royal tour: the engineering marvel, whose vast span epitomized what civilization could accomplish in the mid-nineteenth century, was itself a new and awe-inspiring tourist attraction, especially when viewed with massive ice floes heaving against the unshakable, man-made foundations. The British North American provinces had much to offer tourists, whether royal or common: wilderness wonders and tangible evidence of colonial triumphs.

The end of the prince's Canadian tour did not bring an end to his tourist experience. Quite the opposite. As the prince turned towards the United States, no longer was he expected to squeeze tourist attractions into a schedule dominated by occasions of state. Albert Edward could make tourism his full-time activity – or that, at least, had been the plan.

9

Renfrew in the Republic

On the evening of 20 September, the Prince of Wales arrived in the United States, entering at Detroit, Michigan. Albert Edward crossed the Detroit River from the Canadian side aboard the steamer *Windsor.* 'The view from the hurricane deck of that steamer,' declared a widely reprinted report from the Detroit *Daily Advertiser,* 'was one of the most striking that the imagination can conceive.' All the homes and warehouses lining both shores of the river for a distance of more than three miles were illuminated. The spars and lines of the hundreds of steamers and sailing vessels, those at anchor and those circling the *Windsor,* held lanterns that shone in blue, red, green, yellow, and white. The prince's steamer gleamed brighter than the rest, with red lanterns forming triumphal arches. From the shore and river, rockets shot into the night sky so that 'darkness was almost turned into day.'[1]

Mid-way across the river, Albert Edward himself underwent a change, casting off his royal identity as Prince of Wales and assuming that of Lord Renfrew, one of his lesser titles. In bidding farewell to his Canadian hosts – and most notably the governor general, Sir Edmund Head – the official, state visit to the five British colonies came to an end and a 'private' tour of the republic began. The formalities, which were now deliberately downplayed, took place aboard the *Windsor,* where Mayor Christian H. Buhl of Detroit greeted Baron Renfrew, welcoming him both to 'the commercial metropolis of the state of Michigan' and to the United States. The baron acknowledged the remarks with merely 'a courteous bow and a simple expression of thanks.'[2]

By all accounts, however, the immense and irrepressible crowd at Detroit made a mockery of the idea that the visit was in any way 'private.' Thirty thousand cheering and curious people gathered in the broad streets of the Michigan metropolis, pushing as close as they could get to the landing place at the foot of Woodward Avenue. 'Humanity lost its individuality,' declared the *Daily Advertiser*, 'and mankind and womankind was but a conglomerate mass from the dock's edge to Jefferson Avenue.' At the landing place, 'a scene of the wildest confusion ensued,' reported the New York *Times*. 'Such struggling, pushing, fighting and yelling was never heard.' Risking their bonnets and crinolines, women jostled to get a better spot, uttering 'soprano exclamations' and defying the rule that it was 'the masculine species who are supposed to be exclusively entitled to go in crowds.'[3]

The plan had been for Renfrew and his party to disembark, walk to carriages waiting a few steps away, and then join a procession to their hotel, the Russell House. However, the people were packed in so tightly at the dockside that the guests could not even disembark let alone reach the carriages. 'If the Detroiters had been drawn up to resist British invasion, they could not have done it more completely,' observed the reporter for the Chicago *Press and Tribune*. Six hundred firemen, torches in hand, were supposed to keep the way clear, but they found themselves overwhelmed by the throng. Several men in the crowd climbed into the waiting carriages to get a better view, but the firemen jumped up and knocked them down. At the same time, people at the front of the crowd began to clamber aboard the prince's steamer – either to avoid being pushed into the river or 'for the gratification of their curiosity.' Some of them succeeded in reaching the deck, where they added to the jam on board, while others found themselves 'unceremoniously pitched back from whence they came.' In the confusion, Richard Pennefather, Governor General Head's secretary and superintendent-general of Indian affairs in the Canadas, fell into the water and nearly drowned, as a paddlewheel swept him under and 'tore skin off his shoulder.'[4]

If Albert Edward were to escape, a ruse was needed. When at last the firemen cleared a narrow passageway by thrusting their torches against anyone who encroached, General Bruce and other gentlemen from the prince's party went ashore as decoys, distracting the crowd by standing ostentatiously in the open carriage that Albert Edward was supposed to have taken. The people cheered the impressively dressed men, assuming one of them to be the prince. Meantime, Albert Edward was hustled off the steamer and into another carriage, which squeezed through the crowd and 'by dint of strong horses and skilful driving' reached the Russell House unnoticed and in safety.[5]

The visit to Detroit called forth both denunciations and apprecia-

Canadians bid the prince goodbye and Americans welcome him. The illustration top left, entitled 'Out rolled,' refers to an incident in Washington where Harriet Lane, the niece of President James Buchanan, beat the prince at bowling. The one top right, entitled 'Rolled out,' shows a spill caused by the prince's spurs at dance in Canada. (*Harper's Weekly,* 20 October 1860)

tions of American crowd behaviour. Canadian and English commentators maintained that the display had been excessive and out of control. 'Disorder reigned supreme,' declared the Toronto *Globe*; 'chaos had come again.' The police presence had been inadequate, and the prince had been placed in genuine danger from an American mob – however well-meaning the cheering people had been. Above all, the event had shown that Americans 'neglected to cultivate the love of order as ardently as they have cherished the love of liberty.' The report in the London *Times* similarly grumbled about Detroit's poor arrangements, at one point referring to the 'mob of dirty boys and rowdies.' By contrast, the Detroit *Daily Advertiser* was not at all sure that the crowd's exuberance was to be regretted. Should the future constitutional ruler of Great Britain have 'the sagacity to penetrate the surface,' he would realize that he had witnessed 'a great popular demonstration, unrestrained by the resources of a more artificial state of society.'[6]

The Detroit entry, as represented by the press, introduces several themes that stand out in the newspaper coverage of Renfrew's romp through the republic. Now that Albert Edward was no longer on a state visit, formal ceremonies were far fewer and downplayed. Instead, attention shifted to the American crowds that greeted the baron everywhere he went – their size, their composition, their appearance, their conduct. It fell to journalists to tease out cultural meanings from what was seen and said and done. America's reputation and American values went on display for the world to view and it remained to be seen how they would be assessed.

Albert Edward's trip through the United States would be exhausting, involving over 2,600 miles of travel in a thirty-day period from 20 September to 20 October. From Detroit, he visited Chicago and then proceeded to Dwight, Illinois, where Renfrew and his party enjoyed a respite from the crowds during a shooting holiday. Even though the holiday in 'the West' was short, journalists said that the frontier had had its legendary effect, giving the young aristocrat a new 'robustness' and stimulating 'the flow of animal spirits before unknown to him.'[7] After Dwight, the pace was gruelling as the party raced from place to place between St Louis, Missouri, and the eastern seaboard.[8] No visit to the south had been included in the original itinerary, the excuse being that the climate was too unhealthy,[9] but, after public pressure for such a visit from various quarters, a brief stay in Richmond, Virginia, was added to the itinerary.[10] The royal party then moved up the coast, going as far north as Portland, Maine.

The Crowds

In American cities, the crowds that congregated to see the Prince of Wales – for it was he and not Baron Renfrew whom they came to see – gained a great deal of attention in the press. The ceremonies and pageantry took centre stage in the coverage of Albert Edward's appearances in British North American centres, and the crowds were represented as a chorus or backdrop, but in the United States the crowds themselves became the leading players. Because British officials discouraged civic processions in U.S. cities (with the exception of New York), the American public during the tour was not represented in its familiar component parts, with, for example, the fraternal orders following a well-rehearsed script.[11] Public gatherings were generally much more spontaneous. Press reports therefore focused on the makeup of these crowds. How large were they? Who turned out? How did they behave? These were the burning questions in the republic where democracy reigned.

According to press reports, enormous crowds met Albert Edward almost everywhere he went. In Chicago the throng inside the railway station numbered 15,000, 'while outside the rush was fairly awful.' The New York *Times* correspondent estimated the assemblage at the Pittsburgh railway depot to number 'at least ten thousand people.' When he arrived at Boston, according to the New York *Daily Tribune*, 'the multitude that filled the streets surpassed in numbers any that had ever before been gathered in New England.' New York topped all the other cities, where 200,000 to 500,000 people lined Broadway to greet the prince. In the New York *Herald*, Cornwallis – possibly with the aid of a thesaurus – described that crowd as being 'huge, immense, enormous, exaggerated, stupendous, infinite and indefinite.'[12]

For fear that daily reports would get monotonous, writers turned to metaphors and similes in an effort to vary their accounts of the throngs. Images drawn from nature were the preferred embellishment. In Detroit the 30,000 people presented 'a sea of upturned faces.' The crowd outside the Chicago terminus pressed past the barrier and 'rushed down the platform like a torrent.' In New York the people 'met the eye in exceeding ocean stretches, swaying together as if with the irresistible tidal throb.'[13] In another account, Gotham's masses 'were revealed in one volcanic throe of enthusiasm,' or alternatively, there appeared 'a multitude countless as the leaves of the forest.' 'All the streets were jammed,' reported the New York *Evening Post*, 'and people clustered in windows and on all the housetops on every side, like huge swarms of bees.' Another reporter wrote that along Broadway 'clusters of crinoline hung out upon the balconies like grapes on trellised vines.' And a reporter for the New York *Times* wrote self-consciously about the overworked water metaphor, but then let his pen flow like Niagara:

> The comparison of a multitude of people to an ocean has become trite and wearisome from repetition, but by no other simile can you express the character of the tidal mass which yesterday billowed through Broadway. The current of omnibuses and carriages was tapped very early in the day, and turned off into by-streets; but their separate channels were supplied by two longitudinally [sic] currents of humanity, flowing in opposite directions. It was as two rivers, running counter to each other in the same bed, their waters touching yet not mingling. That on the right steadily flowed downward to the Battery; that on the left surged ceaselessly uptown. At the Bowling Green the counter currents met, and an eddying, maelstromic whirl was the result, engulfing staid but curious matrons in its pool and spinning elderly gentlemen around in unaccustomed evolutions.[14]

Journalists delighted in describing the diversity of the people who made up the crowds. At the White House levee for the prince, there were 'ladies, gentlemen, officers, workmen, children, nurses, rowdies and drivers.' The Richmond *Whig*, using the racist language of the old south, characterized those at the local railway depot on the occasion of the prince's departure as being 'a crowd of ladies, gentlemen, boys, and niggers following in a run.' Outside New York's Academy of Music on the evening of the ball, 'the street was densely packed with male and female, aged, middle-aged, youthful, juvenile and even infantile specimens of the curiosity-loving public.' Down Broadway, at the time of the prince's entry, 'rich and poor were mingled together,' declared one account. 'The merchant prince, the hard-worked mechanic, the silk-attired lady, and the cotton-dressed drudge; all degrees and conditions of men of that great republic stood side by side in this unparalleled congregation of humanity.'[15]

If anything, the mixing went almost too far, it was suggested. 'The quantity of well-dressed ladies and children, mixed in with the not over fragrant crowd of unscoured publicans and sinners,' wrote Cornwallis, 'was painfully amazing to behold.' The correspondent for the

New York *Times* made the same point about the diversity of the crowds in Pittsburgh:

> There were all sorts and conditions of men, all kinds of women, and all sizes of children. Miners with dirty faces, skull caps, rolled-up shirt sleeves, tucked-up trousers and open mouths; tradesmen with bundles under their arms and amazement in their eyes; lazy men quietly puffing a weed and leaning heavily against convenient posts; gentlemen who were manifestly out of place; fat women in black; thin women in striped calico; short women in muslin; flashy women in flounces; brazen women in flats; modest women in veils; and cautious women with umbrellas; tall, lank, thin boys, whose parents supposed them to be at school; little fat boys, with caps on wrong side before, whose mothers probably did *not* know they were out, and diverse other creatures whose peculiarities I have no time or strength to describe.

In Cincinnati, the shouts of the diverse voices were enough to drive people mad. 'A great portion of the people were German, French, or Irish,' read one report, 'and the jargon of these folk, mixed up with all the known dialects of the American language – produced a state of things by no means favourable to the continuation of perfect sanity.'[16]

Of greater interest still was the behaviour of the crowds and what it signified. Commentators heaped praise on cities where conduct was becoming. 'The police kept admirable order,' wrote one correspondent from Chicago, 'and the party were enabled to walk slowly through a large open space, giving all present a fine view of the Prince.' Woods told readers of the *Times* that, though the crowds were immense in Philadelphia, they were 'decorous, cordial, and ... almost affectionate.' Upon Albert Edward's return to his hotel, 'there was no mobbing, no intrusive forwardness, nothing in word, look or gesture which was not of such kind respect as would have gladdened any Englishman to witness.' The policing was much admired at Albany, where 100 men did duty, along with two militia regiments that served as the prince's escort. 'There was,' observed the correspondent of the New York *Times*, 'a vast crowd present whose good order was enforced by the hickory clubs of the policemen.'[17] In Boston, the enthusiasm and decorum had been wonderfully impressive. 'A Fourth of July could hardly be more universally celebrated,' declared the New York *Daily Tribune*, 'and would never be celebrated with such order and perfect good feeling.' The prince was escorted through Boston by the Governor's Body

Guard and a mounted police, but the reporter for the New York *Evening Post* insisted that 'really, with a rational people, self-respecting and loving order for its own sake, there seems to be no occasion for a police on such an occasion as yesterday.'[18]

Enthusiasm had to be kept within bounds, and, when it was not, the reporters detailed the shortcomings of the local population. At Cincinnati, outside the prince's hotel, the Burnet House, 'in point of struggling, crushing disorder,' wrote Woods, 'there was almost an unpleasant repetition of what had occurred at the Detroit landing.' In several places, rude people were reported to have intruded on the privacy of the prince and his suite. As the royal party travelled by train west from Detroit, at the stations en route persons 'climbed up to and looked in the window, and called out, "Bring him up," "Let's see him," and so forth.' Similarly, when the party rode through the streets of St Louis, 'the curiosity of some of the "roughs" led them to commit the indiscretion of running close alongside of the carriage and staring at the occupants through closed windows.' One of the prince's travelling companions, the young Lord Hinchingbrooke, wrote home to his father in England and described in astonishment how the Americans would jump up and look in the windows of the railway carriages, asking which was the prince. 'They take me for him very often,' he wrote, 'and put out very dirty hands, asking me to shake hands with them.' The young aristocrat did not, however, characterize the behaviour as rude, preferring to call it 'wonderfully free and easy.'[19]

The levee that President James Buchanan hosted for the prince at the White House brought the American crowd under particularly close scrutiny. When the doors to the East Room were thrown open, 'the rush was terrible,' reported *Harper's*, what with people clambering in and jumping out of windows. The special dispatch to the New York *Times* described the throng's 'pell-mell' entry as 'mobbish.' Some ladies climbed onto the chairs placed around the walls, craning their necks in an effort to see the prince, and those who could not get chairs climbed onto the shoulders of the gentlemen who accompanied them. 'No telegraphic statement can do justice to the inexcusable lack of prearrangement of the preservation of decency, not to speak of order,' sniffed the New York *Times* reporter. 'The royal party have certainly seen Democracy unshackled for once.'[20] In contrast to the levees in Canada, where well-dressed men were presented, in Washington men and women alike were welcomed and no matter their attire. Ladies appeared in bonnets and shawls, observed Woods, while their tobacco-chewing male companions 'sauntered into the room with their hands in their pockets.' Some of the men, said the reporter for the New York *Daily Tribune*, appeared 'slightly unclean and possibly worse, and a few ... spat on the carpets.' In the capital of the United States, democracy 'doth insist upon free participation in all social festivities and solemnities such as this.'[21] While the reporters enjoyed joking about the 'gaucheries,' pride, too, was expressed regarding the inclusiveness of the affair. Even the reporter for the London *Times*, a dreadful snob, thought that the reception 'showed well for the American people.' He conceded that, if the queen were receiving the president at Buckingham Palace and *anyone* could attend 'without distinction of rank, dress, or calling,' he doubted that 'the assemblage on such an occasion would even bear comparison with that at the White House to meet the Prince.'[22]

Most controversial of all was the behaviour of the crowds in Richmond, Virginia, because the coverage of the prince's flying visit there reflected the bitter political divisions between north and south. Local newspapers proudly described the enthusiastic welcome given by the people of the city. The Richmond *Whig* reported that the streets near the royal party's hotel 'were thronged with thousands of men, women, and boys – white and black – eagerly awaiting the arrival of the "live Prince."' Only with the aid of the reception committee did the distinguished guests 'get into the Hotel without being overrun by the excited multitude.' The New York *Times*, however, described how 'the mob' swarmed the prince, leaving him 'mussed and spoiled.' When he at last gained his room, 'flushed and panting, he reclined upon a lounge, refusing peremptorily to exhibit himself at the window.' During the evening, dozens of people occupied the rooms of the building opposite where the prince was dining, and they peered through second-storey windows at the royal party throughout the meal. As the bemused correspondent for the New York *Times* succinctly put it: 'The night was warm, the windows open, and the crowd curious.'[23]

That the next day was Sunday brought the visitors no relief from the insistent spectators of Richmond. Outside St Paul's Church, where Albert Edward and his suite attended morning service, a crowd numbering several thousand persons gathered, 'representing all classes of society, and all complexions.' As he moved off in his carriage, they followed 'in hot pursuit, determined to see His Royal Highness if perseverance would enable them to do so.' Word got out that in the afternoon the prince would visit the First African Church, which became 'a great point of attraction for whites as well as blacks.' Had

Working out in Washington. The original caption reads: 'The Prince of Wales accompanied by Miss Harriet Lane, Mrs. Secretary Thompson, the Duke of Newcastle, etc., exercising in the gymnasium of Mrs Smith's Young Ladies' Institute.' (*Frank Leslie's Illustrated Newspaper*, 20 October 1860)

the prince actually gone to worship there, commented the Richmond *Whig*, 'he might have been led to suppose that no inequality of race was observed here, as both colors occupied the pews of the church promiscuously.' Actually, the prince did not visit the First African Church, although members of his suite did so. Thinking that one of the visitors was the prince, reported the New York *Times*, 'the excited congregation rose, saying, all over the house "He's come," he's come."'[24]

The northern press drew particular attention to the rude behaviour of the white crowds in Richmond. When, in the company of the mayor and the governor, Albert Edward and others had examined the city's famous statue of Washington, 'the rude, ill-bred crowd pushed in' and annoyed the party 'beyond endurance, while they insulted them with such remarks as he (Washington) "socked it into you at the Revolution"; "He gave you English squirts the colic."'[25] When news of the incident reached London, an indignant editorial appeared in the *Times*. Nowhere in the northern free states could there be found 'a class so ruffianly and depraved as are the lower class of whites at the South,' declared the *Times*. 'Fancy a mob of four or five hundred slave-dealers, horse-dealers, small planters, liquor-store keepers and loungers, together with probably a large sprinkling of blackguardism from Ireland, and you will probably have the crowd that rushed after the Prince of Wales and the Duke of Newcastle.'[26]

Other people leapt to the defence of Richmond. In his book on the tour, Woods took a different position than the *Times* editorial and sympathized with the way 'poor Richmond' had woken up 'one morning and found itself notorious throughout the United States for blackguardism, and ruffianly inhospitality of every kind.' Woods maintained that the Republican press had wildly exaggerated the impertinence of 'a few boys' whose insults had been 'uttered *sotto voce*.'(!) The local press in Richmond similarly insisted that the press attack had been made 'for political effect, to prejudice the North against the South.' The reception committee at Richmond issued several statements denying the report of the New York *Times*, and fortunately it was able to refer to a public letter from Lord Lyons, the British ambassador, to the municipal council, thanking the city for its 'cordial welcome.'[27]

What behaviour was truly characteristic of the American people – the rambunctious enthusiasm or the orderliness? Reflecting on the issue, the New York *Times* reprinted an item from the London *News* – a letter from 'an English gentleman travelling in America' who was in

Chicago during the prince's reception there. 'Every man,' wrote the Englishman, '– some of them workpeople – is anxious that the Prince, who will some day be King of England, should form a just judgment of the American people.' Most of all, the people of Chicago were 'bent upon convincing him that they are not the barbarians they are often supposed to be.' The people delighted in congratulating themselves on their own fine behaviour. 'Again and again,' reported the visitor, 'I have heard them rejoice that ... the masses have behaved in the streets of Chicago with perfect decorum.' He concluded by reassuring readers that 'property and life are as secure here as in the old country.'[28]

In planning the tour of the United States, British authorities had worried about crowd behaviour. When the idea of the U.S. tour was first broached, Lord Lyons, the British ambassador, had written from Washington, saying that while the proposal had merit, he was concerned because American crowds were 'curious and violent' and there would be no way 'to secure for the Prince rest and freedom from intrusion.'[29] Newcastle, by contrast, remained confident that the American public would present no serious problem. 'I have not the smallest apprehension of insult,' he noted privately, 'though the greeting may probably be somewhat rough and vulgar.'[30] As it turned out, officials and commentators in the daily press agreed that nearly everywhere the American crowds had been exuberant but sufficiently self-disciplined – true to the American character.

Republicans and Royalty

In the midst of reporting on the latest developments in Lord Renfrew's progress through the United States, commentators occasionally wondered why Americans were showing such interest in Albert Edward. After all, he was a representative of royalty, and Americans were republicans, and as Americans liked to point out, the prince's mother was no more sovereign than each and every American. Moreover, the Prince of Wales was a representative of Great Britain, the nation against which the Americans had revolted in 1776 and fought again in the War of 1812. Clearly, some explaining needed to be done to account for America's love affair with the Prince of Wales.

'So long as the Prince of Wales was in Canada,' observed the Philadelphia *Public Ledger and Daily Transcript*, 'a sort of loyalty, it was said, made the crowds rush to see him; but no sooner did he pass over into the United States than the rush became ten times greater.' This had a little to do with the fact that 'the young ladies ... all want to see him, to know how he dances, and the young men to imitate the cut of his coat and the style of his dress.' It had more to do with the fact that, once king, he might do more 'to shape the future than anyone else on the globe,' and so it was only natural for people to be curious and hope 'to form some conception from the play of his countenance.' Questions of peace and war might one day be decided by him, and, as king of all the British North American colonies, the neighbours of the United States, he could make decisions of profound importance to the security of Americans. Similar explanations appeared in other newspapers, too. And an editorial in the the London *Times* reminded its British readers: 'It is not for those who see princes every day to estimate the curiosity of those who hear of them only across a hemisphere, or know them only through newspapers and books.'[31]

The Irish nationalist and Catholic press of New York, not surprisingly, was troubled by the immense interest in the prince and it had a quite different explanations for his apparent popularity. 'He came to America to parade himself as a show,' said the *Irish-American*, and 'everybody in America rushes to see shows.' The *Freeman's Journal and Catholic Register* made the same point: Americans like to view anything '*bizarre*,' and the prince had been 'a kind of "What is it," like Barnum's little idiot negro.'[32] It was also the case that New Yorkers liked holidays, and they were 'well enough pleased to have a holiday to look at him.' Alternatively, offered the *Freeman's Journal*, Americans 'do not like the grim constraint of Puritanism,' and so, 'just from the exuberance of spirits,' they were apt 'to overdo a demonstration.' The editor of the *Irish-American*, thinking along the same lines, explained that Americans are 'before all things, good humored' and like to make a visitor '"feel good" while he stays.'[33] Moreover, the American public had been readied by 'the system of *advertising*,' perpetrated by a part of the press 'bent (and *bennett*) on it' – the allusion being to James Gordon Bennett, the editor and publisher of the New York *Herald*, the city's largest daily.[34] Whereas, for many Americans, time had lessened their hostility towards the British, it was not so for Irish Americans. They could neither forget nor forgive, said the author of a letter to the editor of the *Irish-American*, because for the Irish people 'the sufferings have continued, even under the reign of the Prince's mother, who allowed *two million* of the people to die of famine.'[35] The voices of the Irish-American press were thus stridently hostile and so stood out starkly against the chorus of supporters for the prince and his visit.

In the mainstream press, Albert Edward's visit provided an occasion for reflecting upon the ties between England and the United States. It was widely agreed that the mutual respect and goodwill between the two nations that existed in 1860 derived from a common history, various shared cultural values, and common blood.

Editorial writers found themselves on the weakest ground when they turned to history as a source of mutuality linking England and the United States, given the two wars fought between them. The New York *Times* reached back to the colonial era, saying that the prince's visit was a 'vivid reminiscence of that elder union,' and it reminded its readers that America owed her greatness at least in part to the institutions that Great Britain had provided for the Thirteen Colonies. The editorial could not ignore the fact that the union had been sundered, but it maintained that the British had now conceded that the American position had been just. Indeed, by making this visit, the prince was paying homage to the American people for 'the justice of the cause in which our fathers contended against the crown which he inherits.' The London *Times* put the matter less starkly, maintaining that the British had become used to recognizing 'revolutions and new dynasties by dozens.' It added, alluding to Italy, that 'at this moment we are actively sympathizing with a people struggling to exchange a despotic for a constitutional master.' In drawing a parallel between the American War of Independence and Garibaldi's liberal revolution, which was then immensely popular in England, the *Times* was in effect going some distance towards conceding the justice of American revolutionaries' cause. In the current atmosphere of goodwill, then, both the British and the Americans could put aside their history of bitter conflict.[36]

Recent history, it was argued, had helped make possible this changed perspective. Before Victoria's reign, argued the London *Spectator*, the Americans had been in the habit of antagonizing the English crown in matters political, territorial, and commercial, but during her reign 'every one of these trans-Atlantic prejudices ha[d] been softened to such an extent that each one is now ready for removal.' The New York *Times* similarly argued that the passage of time had altered circumstances. The United States was now so wealthy, influential, and powerful that she was 'strong enough to be unaffectedly cordial and ... generously forgetful.' Meantime, 'sober second thought' was 'obliterating from the English mind the angry memories of long ago together with the jealousies of more recent years.' And if there were any doubt about how much had changed, declared the *Times*, then 'one look at

'Lord Punch: "Now, my boy! There's your pretty cousin Columbia – you don't get such a partner as that every day!"' (*Punch*, 20 October 1860)

the Prince of Wales ought to convince the citizens of the United States that the England of 1860 and England of 1770 are very different things.' In contrast to the foppery of George III, the prince appeared simply as a well-dressed gentleman.[37]

When it came to cultural matters, the ground appeared firmer for supporting the Anglo-American entente. Naturally, newspapers pointed to a common language and shared literary tradition. A poem, written for the occasion of the prince's appearance on the Boston Common and entitled 'The Prince's Welcome,' includes the lines: 'Our welcome breathes his native tongue./ A kindred sense of Shakespeare's art,/ Of Milton's verse, so grand, sublime.' An accompanying text declared that England's 'literature is ours also; the great poets, historians, orators, and judges have lived and written for us, and not alone for the island that gave them birth.'[38]

Moreover, England and the United States shared a love of liberty and attachment to free institutions. Nothing could 'totally sunder nations,' declared the New York *Times*, which have 'a common origin and language' and 'develop themselves by the practice of the same free institutions.' The *Times* promised that the Americans' warm welcome for the prince would be 'an evidence of the strong attachment and admiration for Old England and her free institutions that is felt by our people.' *Frank Leslie's Illustrated Newspaper* of New York boasted that England and the United States were 'the two greatest and the only free nations on earth.' A more cordial understanding between the two – which the visit was encouraging – would enable them 'to make other peoples as free as ourselves.' Thus, the editor hailed 'the tour of the British Prince in this Republic' as 'a promise of better times for the enslaved nations of the world.'[39]

In the rhetoric of the visit, shared cultural values also provided the pretext for the Americans' willingness, indeed enthusiasm, for embracing, not just Great Britain and its liberal institutions but also England's royal family. Editorial writers and other American journalists who supported the visit were confronted with the awkward fact that the prince was descended from the George III, who had oppressed the American people and forced upon them the War of Independence. In gender and family, the writers found a way out of the dilemma.

Rather than presenting Albert Edward as the descendant of that oppressor George III, the leading New York newspapers instead portrayed Albert Edward as the son of an ideal mother. Queen Victoria represented a purity in domestic life that all Americans could admire.

'Distracted and disjointed as this country seems at this moment,' observed the New York *Times* upon the prince's arrival in North America, one bond united American families: 'respect for the purity of domestic life, and for the innate nobleness of woman's nature.' Victoria, who embodied these ideals, had exerted 'a powerful influence in the increase of domestic purity in English life.' And so it was, then, that her son carried 'a higher claim to the friendly reception of our best people.' The New York *Daily Tribune* made a similar point at the time of the prince's entry into the metropolis. The cheering crowds of New Yorkers had made it clear that, notwithstanding the revolution, the American people were 'still so loyal to the domestic virtues that have made the name of Victoria illustrious; and this sentiment of respect and admiration for purity and charity was the key-note of the whole affair.' According to the special correspondent of the New York *Herald* who observed the same scene, New Yorkers had 'hailed the coming and showered hearty blessings upon the head of the son of that peerless Queen, whose virtues shed a halo round the throne of England, and constitute the pride and joy of all where England's tongue is spoken and England's honor loved.' The poet of the Boston Common, referring to 'The wife and mother, – England's Queen/ Who finds no equal, knows no peer,' urged fellow Americans: 'In veneration bow us down/ At gentle Virtue's holy shrine.'[40] Such veneration of Victoria's domestic virtues would become increasingly widespread in the years ahead, as her long reign continued and her widowhood added poignancy to the story.[41]

According to the rhetoric of newspapers supporting the visit, what ultimately tied England and the United States together was blood. The word signified both that the two countries were branches of the same family and that they were parts of a greater body: the Anglo-Saxon race. According to the New York *Times*, Americans were welcoming the Prince of Wales so enthusiastically because, as in Britain, he was 'the head of their race,' or 'a bit of the true stock, and shows them what they have all come from.' A Boston pundit, referring to the commonalities of the English and the Americans, insisted that the visit had helped to highlight the fact that 'the spirit and temper of the race is the same on either side of the Atlantic.' Furthermore, so keenly did England want to cultivate cordial relations with the United States that 'within the limits of reason there is not a point that England would not gladly concede to secure her from a quarrel with her own flesh and blood.'[42] An editorial in the Chicago *Daily Evening Journal* observed that 'we Yankees forget sometimes that we are full brothers to the subject of the British Queen.' And it then joked that Americans were 'full brothers on the father's side by the Land; on the mother's by the Language: "father land" and "mother tongue."' Cornwallis, the correspondent for the New York *Herald,* maintained that the 'graver import of the visit' of the prince to the United States had been the 'securing more firmly of the general interest of the two great sections of the Anglo-Saxon race.' Throughout his coverage of the tour, Cornwallis referred to 'the ties of consanguinity' between the two 'branches of the Anglo-Saxon race,' ties that led Americans to 'hail Victoria's son as they would a brother.'[43]

Affection often leads to romance. A cartoon entitled 'The Next Dance!' that appeared in the London publication *Punch* shows the Prince of Wales and fair Columbia being introduced by 'Lord Punch.' He says in the caption below: '"Now, my boy! There's your pretty cousin Columbia – You don't get such a partner as that every day!"' Several of these themes are succinctly expressed in a jaunty poem by 'Sigma' entitled 'The Coming of the Prince,' which was published in *Frank Leslie's Illustrated Newspaper.* Part of the poem reads as follows:

> What thinks the royal youth?
> Will his guess be near the truth?
> Of this more than cordial greeting of the 'rebels to the Throne?'
> Does he deem it compensation
> Of a penitent young nation,
> A return to that allegiance we so long have ceased to own?
>
> No No! young heir to Britain ...
> We greet thee for thy mother –
> We hail thee as a brother,
> We hold thee as a symbol of the race from whence we sprung.[44]

The Ladies

In the press coverage of Albert Edward's tour through cities of the United States, women figured prominently, taking their places in the crowds and at the balls. As in British North America, the journalists portrayed 'the ladies' as an embellishment to the scene, but in the United States, even more than in the colonies, the press cast women, or at least young, white women, as potential fiancées for the prince. Journalists spun a fairy tale and invited America's damsels to imagine themselves in a leading role. In the weeks leading up to the tour, the New York press portrayed Albert Edward as a handsome prince charming who might well be smitten by an American girl and make her his princess. The New York *Herald* urged every young American girl to 'put on her most bewitching smile' for 'to catch a prince is no common achievement.' After it had been established in Newfoundland and Nova Scotia that the prince loved to dance, American ladies were urged to 'be prepared, armed at all points, [to] show the Prince of Wales that they can dance better than the damsels of the British Provinces.' The real-life Albert Edward looked a little young for the role cast for him – but not to worry. Though it was admitted that Albert Edward's charms were 'boyish,' American women were reminded that he was near the age of 'Don Juan, who, in his travels, made such havoc among hearts.' And, like Don Juan, the Prince of Wales was '"handsome, slender, but well knit."'[45]

Reporters pointed out that it was unlikely that the Prince of Wales would marry a subject, and so, while the young ladies of British North America might fantasize about marrying Albert Edward, America's daughters were actually better positioned to do so. Indeed, other princes had married American women. Who knew whose hand might be taken by the heir apparent to the throne of England? As the English satirical journal *Punch* put it:

A spark's a spark, and tinder tinder,
And certain things in Heaven are written;
And is there any cause to hinder
The Prince of Wales from being smitten?

Transcendent charms drive even monarchs frantic,
A German Princess must he marry?
And who can say he may not carry
One of Columbia's fascinating daughters
O'er the Atlantic?[46]

There is no better illustration of this romantic theme than a full page of cartoons, headed 'The Prince and the Ladies,' which *Harper's Weekly* ran at the height of America's love affair with the prince.[47] In the first cartoon, where two well-dressed young ladies are pictured reading together, the caption is as follows: 'Emily reads: "The number of British

Princes who have married commoners is very large indeed, and any virtuous and amiable girl may become the wife of a member of the Royal Family. The Duke of Clarence married Mrs. Jordan, George the Fourth married Mrs. Fitzherbert, James married Ann Hyde –" Now Mary, I ask you, why should not – ?' In the remaining cartoons, American ladies, in all their variety, are shown readying themselves for the eligible prince. The ladies are all represented as white, which is underscored by the presence of a stock character, the mature and plump African-American mammy.

While the press depicted white American women as 'cunning girls,' to use a phrase of *Harper's*, it often portrayed Albert Edward as the world's most eligible bachelor. 'The Prince was decidedly a "heart smasher,"' the young ladies of Washington supposedly said as the prince left the nation's capital. Even amidst an immense crowd, Albert Edward could set hearts a-flutter or provoke a jealous competitiveness among the fair sex. On Broadway 'the feminine display was indeed remarkable' when, as the prince passed, the young ladies' 'bright glances' shot 'athwart each other to reach the Royal carriage.' The New York *Times* correspondent described the following scene at Pittsburgh: 'When the ladies waved their handkerchiefs, the Prince took off his hat – when they "did so some more," the Prince bowed his head – when they smiled he smiled, and when he smiled they blushed.' Prince charming, indeed![48] When visiting Philadelphia, where Albert Edward enjoyed performances of *Martha* and the first act of *La Traviata*, he spent the intervals between scenes 'examining closely the beauties,' moving his seat at one point in order to 'ogle the ladies to their heart's content.' The situation became downright comical, it was reported, when the leading ladies on stage could not keep their eyes off the royal youth. 'Both Martha and Nancy, when in the height of their distress at being entrapped into service, found time to eye, from under their handkerchiefs, Albert Edward.' He in turn, 'seemed bent on mischief' and brought 'his lorgnette ... fully to bear on the pretty faces of the actresses.'[49]

Not all the writers could keep up the pretence that Albert Edward was likely to sweep an American damsel off her feet in a story-book tale of princely romance. Cornwallis of the New York *Herald* bluntly asserted that the ladies of Harrisburg 'appeared to have fallen desperately in love, notwithstanding the improbability of that love being ever returned.'[50] Other accounts frankly reported on the mixed reactions of American women to the prince. According to the Philadelphia *Public*

Ledger, among the women in the crowd present for the prince's departure from the City of Brotherly Love, 'there were pretty free criticisms upon his appearance.' While some thought him 'a "nice little fellow," others could see no beauty whatever in him. One young woman exclaimed disappointedly, "why he's just like one of our fellows!"' Similarly, the ladies at the ball held in Boston had exclaimed variously: '"How pretty," "What a dear," "Looks like any other young man," "Bless me, how plain," "How I *should* like to dance with him."' The New York *Times* reported that, truth be told, the general opinion of Baltimore ladies was: '"He's a nice little fellow, but not overly handsome."' Another correspondent did an even more thorough rewrite of the prince-charming tale, telling readers that at New York the women regarded the prince as only 'a boy,' but the mature Duke of Newcastle truly excited their admiration: 'The Herculean shoulders of His Grace, his full chest, his height, and his noble bearing, met the feminine idea of a complete man.'[51]

Throughout most of the reporting, however, journalists stuck to the story that the women of the United States were smitten with the prince, so much so that they pushed at the very bounds of appropriate feminine decorum. At the Boston ball, the ladies who pursued the prince 'jostled him and impeded his movements.' In order to get a satisfactory view of his dancing, they would hurry 'in flocks' up the stairs to the balcony, in the process not worrying much 'upon the order of their rushing up, so that the object could be gained.' So crowded was it at the prince's end of the dance floor, reported another observer at Boston, that the prince 'was very uncomfortably pressed, jostled and pushed.' New York ladies were no better, however – or so said the Boston press. 'I am told,' exclaimed a reporter for the Boston *Courier* who was covering the New York ball, 'that the poor youth is literally *covered with black and blue spots* – painful remembrances of the ball; that women who had given up all hope of being introduced to him pushed him, punched him, pinched him, jostled him, squeezed his arm when they thought they could do so unobserved, touched his coat and stared at him with a wonderment incredible.'[52]

Not only was American femininity damaged by such unbecoming behaviour, but so too was the very reputation of the nation. When the prince toured the Capitol at Washington, reported the New York *Times*, 'several ladies tested the nap of his coat; others crowded before him, and nothing was omitted which could add to any opinion he might previously have formed concerning the most radical ideas of Democratic freedom which prevail in the capital of the United States.' Especially since their brazen behaviour took place in Washington, these daughters of the republic were seen as tarnishing the image of their country and values at its heart.[53]

In conclusion, then, the visit of Baron Renfrew to the United States prompted various assessments of Anglo-American relations. From the point of view of Irish Americans who drew on the fundamentals of Irish nationalism, those relations could not be separated from the fact of English oppression – perpetuated down to the present under the reign of Albert Edward's mother. By contrast, the metropolitan dailies imagined a history of shared traditions, culture, and blood, and looked fondly at Victoria, under whose motherly virtues the bonds between the English and the Americans had grown all the stronger.

Above all, however, the press had turned Renfrew's visit to the United States into an opportunity for examining the meaning of American nationality. Attention had focused on the appearance and behaviour of the crowds of Americans who greeted Albert Edward. Because the visit was unofficial, civic processions – the staged and much rehearsed representations of the public – had generally been avoided and the people had simply come out en masse, in all their racial and class diversity, to see the prince. Even in Washington, informality and spontaneity had prevailed. The unruliness of American crowds was read by some as democracy gone wild, a lack of self-restraint, a fawning after royalty that was unbecoming to republicans. Alternatively, the unrestrained enthusiasm of American crowds was represented as the generous hospitality of a free and easy people, untrammelled by the fear of police and soldiers. Women who pursued the prince were variously depicted as rude, unladylike representatives of American womanhood, or as damsels doing what was expected of young ladies who had the chance to meet a real-live prince. What could not be denied was the fascination Americans had with the royal visitor – and with themselves.

The comments on African Americans in the press coverage of the prince's visit to Richmond – fleeting as they were – point up the resounding silence that runs throughout the press's treatment of the tour of the rest of the United States. Journalists took almost no notice at all of African Americans; it was nearly as if they did not exist. Given the history of race relations in the United States to 1860, it is not surprising to see that African Americans were excluded from municipal welcome ceremonies, concerts, and elegant balls, and that the press simply took their absence as being 'natural.' Yet, when vast crowds came out to see the prince, surely there were some blacks among them. Notwithstanding the press's propensity for depicting American crowds as diverse, journalists seldom represented racial difference as being an aspect of the diversity. American Indians, both as symbols and as a living presence, were also entirely missing from coverage of the U.S. part of the tour – in sharp contrast to the prominence of First Nations during the preceding Canadian tour. Such erasures form part of a wider American cultural practice, as Mary Ryan reminds us in her study of civic festivities in nineteenth-century United States. 'The disorganized and least powerful citizens,' she writes in reference to racialized minorities, 'were virtually barred from the parade of civic differences.'[54]

The visit to New York City – the highpoint of the prince's American sojourn – would bring into even sharper relief these same features of the press coverage: the sentimentalization of Anglo-American commonalities, the oppositional voice of Irish Americans, the contested representation of American crowds and American womanhood, and the erasure of racial minorities.

10

New York, New York

The prince's visit to New York was the pinnacle of his tour of the United States and a significant moment in the social life of the city. From the earliest days of planning the American tour, the idea had been that a visit to *the* great American commercial and financial capital would be a crowning triumph in the royal progress, where the extravagance of the reception would be grander and the welcome more public than anywhere else in the United States. With alacrity, the social elite of Gotham took on the role of welcoming His Royal Highness, determined to outdo the welcome given by their counterparts in cities with smaller claims to metropolitan status. And the 'Upper Ten Thousand' or 'Upper Tendom,'[1] as the city's social elite was called, succeeded brilliantly, helped in no small measure by the strength and talent of the great metropolitan daily newspapers. In a way that far surpassed the efforts of newspapers elsewhere in the United States, the New York press fostered interest in the prince's visit. The coverage was more thorough and livelier than in other newspapers – which accounts both for the tremendous public interest of New Yorkers in the prince's coming and for the unusually rich body of sources available to the historian.[2] We are fortunate to have, as well, the delightful accounts of the visit penned by George Templeton Strong, the prolific diarist and man-about-town whose anglophilia and lofty social position put him at the heart of the preparations for the prince.[3]

Coming as the visit did near the end of the lengthy North American tour, the people of New York were more than primed to participate in a grand public reception, one that frankly welcomed the Prince of Wales and not just Baron Renfrew. In 1860 New York had a population of more than 1,000,000, and at least 200,000 people – many reports said

500,000 – lined Broadway to greet the prince as he entered the city. Just as interesting, nearly one-quarter of New Yorkers were Irish immigrants whose spokesmen saw themselves and their community as exiled from a homeland that was oppressed by the government that the Prince of Wales represented. Their reactions, as reported in the Irish press centred in the city, forms a vital part of the story and the single most important instance of republican hostility to royalty visiting America.

The Hospitalities of New York

New York was the first city in the United States to extend an invitation to the prince. The mayor, Fernando Wood, wrote on 8 May 1860 to G.M. Dallas, the American ambassador to Great Britain, asking him to call the attention of Her Majesty's government to the invitation extended to the prince 'by the Corporation and citizens of New York.'[4] Before the invitation came, and immediately after receiving it, British officials fussed about whether such an invitation should be accepted. Given that the U.S. tour was supposed to enhance Anglo-American relations, there was an obvious appeal to having a grand reception in the leading city of the United States – a city renowned for its splendid public receptions for prominent visitors to America.[5] That the metropolis was not a capital made it an especially appropriate place for festivities welcoming Baron Renfrew on his unofficial visit. Yet there was a risk in putting the heir to the British throne in the hands of New Yorkers and their civic leaders, whose respectability and support for England were doubted.

Initially, top British officials had grave doubts about the wisdom of the prince's accepting an invitation from New York. Lord Lyons, the British ambassador at Washington, had told the foreign secretary, Lord John Russell, that if such an invitation came, it should be declined mainly because the 'respectability of the Municipal authorities is generally in inverse ratio to the populousness of the Towns which they govern. New York is, I suppose, the lowest of all. The object of these municipal entertainments is to show off the guest to the Mob, to extract speeches from him, & to have him shaken by the hand, & pulled about, by as many people as possible.' E.M. Archibald, the British consul at New York, canvassed opinion among pro-British members of the New York elite, including diarist George Templeton Strong, who noted that when asked for his opinion he had 'advised against the royal imp accepting public hospitalities, for the tender mercies of the Common Council are cruel.'[6]

At the time, respectable New York was scandalized by the behaviour of New York councillors when, that summer, they had welcomed the first official delegation of Japanese to visit the United States. City politicians had hosted a ball, where vast amounts of champagne had been consumed (at public expense) and hundreds of cases more had been passed out the backdoor of the ballroom to appreciative friends of the officials. The city's tab for the visit had topped $100,000, a colossal sum. Mayor Wood, who had both hosted the Japanese and invited the prince, was himself looked down upon by the Upper Tendom, notwithstanding the wealth he had accumulated. After all, Wood's power base lay among the common people to whom he had once sold groceries. Wood's modern biographer refers to him as 'the model for corrupt political bosses, with close ties to Tammany Hall.'[7]

A second and related concern of British officials was New York's Irish population, whose political leaders stridently denounced British misrule in Ireland. At the outset of deliberations regarding a possible invitation, Archibald had advised against the visit on the ground that the New York Irish 'might attempt to show rudeness or disrespect to the prince or even to get up a disturbance.' However, the consul revised his assessment after prominent New Yorkers assured him that fears of Irish hostility were 'entirely groundless, while with all the rest of the community ... the *enthusiasm* of the reception would be boundless.' Lyons was less certain, but he was somewhat reassured when the invitation was publicly endorsed by New York's Roman Catholic archbishop. 'Dr. [John] Hughes, who is an Irish man himself & has great influence with his countrymen,' Lyons said, 'would exert himself to keep his flock from misbehaving themselves.'[8]

British officials ultimately came round to the idea of accepting the invitation from New York. When the invitation arrived in England, it was accompanied by a memorial signed by a great many prominent New Yorkers, a signal not only that they endorsed the visit but that they planned to intervene in it so as to counterbalance the doubtful respectability of the civic officials.[9] On 21 June, Foreign Secretary Lord John Russell replied to Mayor Wood, accepting, on the prince's behalf, the offer of the hospitalities of New York and predicting that the visit would be 'a means of strengthening ... the relations of friendship and regard which bind this country to the United States of America.'[10]

By mid-July, newspapers in North America were trumpeting the news that the prince would visit New York. The Toronto *Globe*, however, could scarcely believe it and questioned the wisdom of the British decision given that so many members of the municipal council were from 'the least respectable class.' Moreover, the *Globe* added, there were rumours that the visit was already leading to trouble at New York's city hall between the Irish and other councillors. Newspapers in the metropolis itself had worries, too. The New York *Daily Tribune* thought that the news must be 'a mistake.' It was not, the editorial joked, that 'we grudge the $50,000 or so that our Municipal legislators will steal under the pretense of entertaining him – we are so used to being skinned that we do not mind a flea-bite like that.' No, the problem was that the young prince would gain such a bad impression of Americans and their institutions by coming into close contact with the councilmen. 'Let the Booles and Bagleys get hold of him,' said the *Tribune*, 'and he will ever after labor under an invincible loathing of American ideas and institutions.'[11]

Almost as worrisome for New York's reputation was the flunkeyism of wealthy New Yorkers who were rifling off invitations to the prince in the hope that he would stay with one of them. The New York *Daily Tribune* found this scramble undignified and hoped that there would be some limit to it, otherwise manufacturers would soon be seeking publicity for themselves and their companies by offering to provide their wares to the distinguished guests. The New York *Times* also thought that the men with mansions were in danger of exposing New York 'to ridicule.' It joked about the diplomatic difficulties that the offers of private residences posed for the prince and his advisers, who could easily cause resentment by accepting one offer over another. 'If the brown stone-front of Jenkins is taken, while the marble of Smithson is left, infinite undemocratic heart-burnings must inevitably ensue. Why should Union Square be snubbed that Fifth Avenue may forever cherish the fine aroma of a princely presence? Why should Washington Heights be contemned, that Broadway and the Bloomingdale Road may be exalted?' George Templeton Strong, who witnessed the manoeuvres of the millionaires at close hand, confided in his diary: 'I hope the community won't utterly disgrace itself before [the prince] goes away. The amount of tuft-hunting and Prince-worshipping threatens to be fearful.'[12]

Prominent New Yorkers took the initiative in organizing the reception for the prince. Nine 'millionaires,' including William B. Astor, Robert B. Minturn, and Maunsell B. Field, called a meeting at the Merchants' Bank on 14 August. The meeting resolved to invite the prince and his suite to a public dinner 'to be presented by the citizens of New York.' A general committee of arrangements was appointed, which included 160 names of wealthy and prominent gentlemen, from bankers to clergymen. Peter Cooper served as chairman, General Winfield Scott as vice-chairman, and Maunsell B. Field as secretary. Several subcommittees were struck, including one that was delegated to proceed immediately to Canada, where the prince was visiting and Lord Lyons was on hand. It was correctly surmised that the prince and his suite would accept no invitations from Americans until Lyons had been consulted.[13] John Jacob Astor, ex-governor Hamilton Fish, and ex-governor John A. King – 'men of character,' said the New York *Times* – pursued the prince and his suite to Montreal. After learning from the prince's advisers that a ball would do better than a dinner, the delegates discarded their elegantly engraved invitation to a public dinner in New York and had a new one embossed that referred to a dance. It came as no surprise when the prince happily accepted this invitation.[14]

The shift from a dinner to a ball proved to be awkward for those committeemen who regarded dancing as sinful. The press delighted in the hypocrisy of evangelical plutocrats wrestling with their consciences. Some of the committee decided that, if the ball were to be called 'a reception,' then they could take part, although they would personally avoid the dance floor. For others, such a name change did not resolve the moral issue at all, and they withdrew. In an editorial entitled 'Promiscuous Dancing,' the New York *Daily Tribune* poked fun at the apparent hypocrisy of the committeemen whose names appeared on the list organizing the ball but who were better known to the public 'from their connection with Foreign Missions, the Tract Enterprise, the Fulton Street Businessmen's Prayer Meeting.' Hitherto, such men were agreed about the sinfulness of dancing – though they could not agree about the propriety of other matters, 'such as making black men work for white without wages.' How could it be, then, that 'a crime' such as dancing became 'harmless or even praiseworthy' simply because a prince got into the act?! It was going to be a treat to attend the ball and witness 'the Directors of the Sabbath School Union twirling in the giddy gyrations of the polka.'[15]

During this same period, newspapers also generated excitement concerning where the prince would lodge in New York. Which of the city's splendid hotels would be favoured? Or would the distinction go to Mayor Wood, who owned a palatial villa at Broadway and 77th

Street. The New York *Times* denigrated this latter option. An editorial mocked the taste of the owners of hideous villas that were a mishmash of architectural styles. It also drew on racial and other stereotypes to make fun of the kind of eclectic guest list that the mayor would draw up for entertainments he hosted at his residence: 'a social circle uniting fragments of the aboriginal Indian with others of the primeval Paddy-whack, blending the frivolity of the antediluvian patriarch with the solemnity of the Saratoga belle, and commingling the more popular exuberance of the domestic Boole with the tastes of the exotic Yahoo.'[16] In the end, the prince and his suite chose to stay at the newly built Fifth Avenue Hotel, a grand marble structure at Twenty-Third Street. It was fitted up specially for the occasion with carved rosewood furnishings and a valuable collection of fine art.

The Royal Entry

The entry of the Prince of Wales into New York dazzled the distinguished guests, the hosts, the hundreds of thousands of people who participated, and, presumably, the countless newspaper readers who experienced the spectacle vicariously. Certainly, there was plenty to read about. Descriptions of the royal entry ran to many columns of cramped print in the metropolitan dailies. Reading through the material must have taken nearly as long as the entrance ceremonies themselves, which began about noon on 11 October and finished soon after six o'clock in the evening, when the public procession up Broadway began. As the New York *Daily Tribune* anticipated, however, the prince's arrival in town had at last brought 'a deep sigh of satisfaction' and an end to 'the agony of expectation which ha[d] bound the millions and the fashionable world of New York so long.'[17]

In order that the entrance could be made by water, the prince and his suite left their train carriage at South Amboy, where they were met by the *Harriet Lane*, the government cutter that President Buchanan had dispatched. Welcoming the prince aboard was General Winfield Scott, a distinguished military figure and the vice-chairman of the ball committee, and Peter Cooper, chairman of the ball committee. There followed introductions to dozens of other millionaires, who got the jump on the municipal officials who were waiting at New York and feeling more than a little sidelined.

The reception by the mayor was to take place at Castle Garden, conveniently close to the Battery, where the prince was to review the troops. Since 1855, Castle Garden had been the reception centre for countless others entering New York under quite different circumstances: it was the city's immigrant inspection station, the forerunner to Ellis Island. The visiting journalist from the London *Times* remarked that it looked like neither a castle nor a garden, but it served well enough as a landing place for the royal party. Local journalists were impressed by the transformation of the place effected by the commissioners of emigration. For the occasion, the immigrants 'with their boxes and dirty bedding' had been banished to a shed and stables beyond the walls so that they would not 'disfigure the stately scene.'[18]

The presence of members of the Common Council on this occasion was a matter of uncommon interest. The councillors were miffed that Mayor Wood had cut them out of any significant role in preparing for the visit, and they had made their annoyance plain in council meetings.[19] Five aldermen and eight councilmen turned up at Castle Garden, but several stayed away, most notably the 'Celtic members.' A report in the *Daily Tribune* said that the group at the castle was 'bravely led by Boole,' though even he had struggled hard with whatever conscience he had before deciding to attend.[20]

At 2:15 in the afternoon, the prince made his landing at Castle Garden. It was an altogether impressive sight: 'the gaily decked-out shipping on both the North and East rivers, the saluting from the merchant shipping and from the forts; the crowds which throng the pier-heads and darkened the roofs of every house-top; and the dazzling uniforms and brisling bayonets of the military which occupied every foot of space upon the Battery.' As the prince stepped up to the mayor, the band of the Twelfth Regiment played 'God Save the Queen.' Mayor Wood greeted the prince with a short, prepared text, to which the prince briefly replied, while the Duke of Newcastle and Alderman Frances Boole stood nearby. The prince then withdrew to exchange his civilian clothing for his military uniform in preparation for his review of the troops, which was shortly to follow on the Battery. According to the reporter for the *Daily Tribune*, it was at this point that Boole 'summoned his faithful and bore down after royalty.' The military guard firmly held them back until the prince was out of reach of the city fathers, though they 'stormed for their rights, threatened, coaxed, and called for help.'[21]

At the Battery, all was ready for the military review. Spectators by the thousands, who had begun to arrive five hours earlier, jammed in wherever they could find a place, lining the rooftops of surrounding buildings and peering from every window. A force of 300 police kept the public from the parade ground, which in any event was crammed with some 7,000 militiamen from local regiments. General Sandford, as commander of the First Division of the New York State Militia, invited the prince, now dressed as a British colonel, to review the troops, and he did so, riding up and down the neat ranks. The prince was impressed by their appearance and privately compared them to 'our Guards.' The correspondent for the London *Times* sang their praises, too, presenting the New York militia as an inspiration for the people of Great Britain, where the volunteer movement was the coming thing. A correspondent for a Canadian newspaper remarked that 'nothing could better illustrate the self-dependent character of the American people – one of the main characteristics to which they owe their rapid growth and present greatness.'[22]

When the review was complete, the prince took a short ride in a specially built carriage to the city hall. Outside the city hall the prince mounted a platform for a second review of the troops, who had followed behind his carriage. As company after company passed him by, the officers saluted and the prince 'touched his chapeau.' Seven military bands appeared in succession, each trying to play 'Hail Columbia' louder and better than the one before. Drums rolled constantly. And the crowds, kept behind a strong iron chain by a vigilant police, cheered on and on. Woods of the *Times* articulated the essential message of the whole event, saying 'there was no pomp or pageantry attempted of any kind, no grand liveries or gilded coaches. It was such a welcome as only a whole people and a free people could ever give.'[23]

From ten in the morning, people had been seeking good locations from which to view the military reviews at the Battery and city hall or the procession up Broadway to the Fifth Avenue Hotel. People grabbed every vantage point until the multitude filled the streets from curb to tree branch to chimney top. 'To the boys,' reported Cornwallis of the New York *Herald*, 'the lamp-posts and iron railings were a godsend.' Parlours in the best hotels facing onto the streets of the procession fetched 'fabulous prices' from hundreds of gentlemen who had booked them days in advance for their families and friends. Prices for seats in the viewing stands and for standing room in shop and office windows ranged from fifty cents to five dollars. 'Ladies,' it was reported, had run 'severe gauntlets to get them without a murmur.' Meanwhile, members of the 'aristocracy' who owned 'palaces' with balconies facing onto Fifth Avenue invited friends and made a party of the afternoon. Higher up on the rooftops, observed a report in the New York *Times,* stood the 'dense masses of chambermaids, waiting-maids, cooks, housekeepers and nurses, with their appropriate following of cousins, uncles, brothers-in-law, and husbands to dead sisters.' According to the special correspondent writing for the Toronto *Leader,* Barnum's Museum was crammed with people who had paid the usual twenty-five cents a head, 'but the curiosities were all neglected.' The freaks were allowed to sleep, 'the people having taken possession of the top of the building and every window.'[24]

The crowds waited and waited, growing ever more restless as afternoon turned to evening. George Templeton Strong, who along with some other gents viewed the scene from a window of the exclusive New York Club, noted in his diary that 'all Broadway was one long dense mass of impatient humanity.' Even from his commodious perch, the waiting seemed endless. 'We watched and waited,' he wrote that evening, 'and united in denunciation of F. Wood, Mayor, whom we assumed to have got the Prince in his grasp and to be detaining him with a speech.'[25] The second military review at city hall was taking far too long.

At ten past five, the authorities, sensing at last the impatience of the crowd, cried 'Halt!' and Albert Edward at last got into his carriage for the procession up Broadway. Thousands of people had already given up and headed home, the growing darkness having dashed all hope of seeing the prince. People were hugely disappointed, said the daily press. The ladies on Fifth Avenue had waited in hope of 'smothering the prince in bouquets thrown by the whitest of hands,' but they had seen nothing of the prince. 'Fifth Avenue was disappointed,' it was reported in a Canadian paper. 'Fifth Avenue was in a state of intense grief.' And the disappointment extended to the multitude. 'Many of the female portion,' wrote Cornwallis of the New York *Herald,* 'burst into tears when they found he had gone by without their having seen him.' The *Daily Tribune* saw the women's behaviour differently, saying that, 'with squelched bonnets, skirts, and babies,' they had 'led on desperate charges upon the police.' Militiamen to the rear of the cortège left their ranks to deal with the angry members of the crowd, threatening some 'with true martial discipline.' The delay fell upon the whole town, the New York *Times* quipped, 'like a crushing and withering blight. What energies were not wasted! What hopes were not decayed!'[26]

Only the flickering gaslight of the street lamps lit the scene at

Twenty-Third Street by the time the prince and the other dignitaries at last reached the Fifth Avenue Hotel. They hurried into the marble palace, seeking refuge from the throng. The Caledonia Club Band, by serenading the party from the street, coaxed the prince onto the balcony for an appearance. But it was brief, because, as the prince explained in a letter to this father, 'after arriving at our Hotel we were very glad to get our dinner and go to bed, as we had had a very tiring day.'[27]

Assessments of New York's welcome came quickly, and they were overwhelmingly favourable. The reporter for the London *Times* hyperbolized, saying that it had been 'an ovation as has seldom been offered to any monarch in ancient or modern times.' The New York papers were just as fulsome. According to the New York *Herald*: 'No grander ovation to the representative of the elder branch of the Anglo-Saxon race was possible. Here the entente cordiale with England was proclaimed to the skies by hundreds of thousands of freemen.' But the New York *Times* slammed the masters of ceremonies, whose 'stupid blunder' had prevented two-thirds of the people of New York from seeing the prince before nightfall had come. 'We hardly know to whom it did more injustice – to our visitor, whom it robbed of the gentlest half of his welcome, or to our citizens, for whom it wasted their precious hours of liberal good-will.'[28]

Private comments from several individuals echo these public assessments of the day's events. The banker Baron Solomon de Rothschild, who was living in New York at the time, observed incredulously that a population of a million New Yorkers had 'greeted the royal scion with more enthusiasm than they would have shown for a liberator of their own country.' Strong noted succinctly on the evening of the prince's arrival: 'What a spectacle-loving people we are!' The amazement extended to the royal party itself. Dr Henry Acland wrote home to his wife from the Fifth Avenue Hotel ('a *white marble* hotel, much larger than the whole of Queen's College!'), saying: '*Not less* than half a million people received us last night on entering. It was an altogether overwhelming spectacle.' The Duke of Newcastle told the queen how impressed he was by 'the enthusiasm of more than half a million of People worked up almost to madness and yet self-restrained within the bounds of the most perfect courtesy by the passage through their streets of a Foreign Prince.' He observed that, while he had not shared the fears of those who expected that New Yorkers would insult the prince, he had 'never ventured to hope for anything approaching the scene which occurred here.' Even the young prince, who in his letters to his parents seldom let himself appear strongly impressed by what he saw in North America, ventured that it had been 'by far the finest reception we have had & shows that the feeling between the countries could not be better ... I believe that there were 300,000 people in the streets, which was wonderful!' There was no mention in any of these accounts of Boole or any of the other municipal politicians.[29]

Irish New York

During the lead-up to the prince's visit to New York, and throughout his stay there, the mainstream press kept the Irish Catholics in the background, as it did African Americans. Differences of religion, ethnicity, and race were generally submerged in the coverage, which insisted that all New York was welcoming the prince. Of course, the Irish-American press of the city bellowed a dissonant counterpoint to the cheery tune of community harmony sung by the rest of the press. In 1860 some 200,000 Irish-born were living in New York,[30] a number that provided a critical mass which could have generated serious problems for the royal party. In fact, during the visit itself, it appeared as if no challenge from the Irish marred the celebrations, although there was an acknowledgment of some trouble coming from the officers and men of the city's 69th (Irish) Regiment. Only after the prince had departed did their response to the celebrations become truly controversial. Ultimately, the visit by the Prince of Wales laid bare some serious ethnic and class tensions in New York.

On just a few occasions did the mainstream journalists covering the tour allude to the presence of Irish people in the city and then it was to underscore their keen participation in the celebrations. A reporter for the New York *Times* described an incident on Broadway, where he had allegedly overheard an Irish woman in the crowd admonish a policeman who obstructed her view. 'I want to see my Prince,' she had said. A man standing nearby had inquired, 'Is he your Prince, my good woman?' She replied, 'Indeed he is!' a sentiment immediately echoed by 'a colored individual in the crowd.' While the reporter acknowledged the Irish woman's right to claim the prince as her own, he denied the African American the same right: 'Nay, thought our reporter, thou at least can not claim him, – he is not the Prince of Darkness.'[31]

A pair of cartoons in the number of *Harper's Weekly* that appeared just before the prince's arrival in New York also relied on racist stereotypes to insist that the Irish were full participants in the welcome. The cartoon, entitled 'Before the Prince's Arrival,' has two disreputable-looking men complaining in the street about the reception to be given 'the son of that oppressor of Oul' Ireland' and swearing, 'It'll be a long day before thi' iver see an Irishman bend his knee or take his hat ov to the bloody Saxin!' The second image shows a crowd of Simeon-faced figures bowing before the young prince. As they fawn over him, they cheer 'Hooroo for the Prince of Wales!' One of them offers his cab service, 'an divil a Cint will I charge.' These are men – well, scarcely men at all, given their ape-like features – who lack the convictions to go with their politics. Hypocrites all, they nevertheless contribute to the general warmth of the welcome – according to *Harper's*.[32]

These were scarcely the images that Irish Americans had of themselves; their own newspapers insisted that the Irish of New York were proud republicans, true to American political ideals, who stood alone in defying elitism, hypocrisy, and oppression. In contemplating the arrival of the prince, the New York *Freeman's Journal and Catholic Register* predicted that 'the chief trouble' would be 'in the conduct of the American flunkeys of what affects to be fashionable society in New York.' Such people would 'run after the young man, toady him, and seek to fete and fool him.' When a reader learned that 'the flunkeys of New York' were offering their mansions for the use of the prince, 'J.M.C.' pondered the selfish motives of these alleged Christians, asking, 'How many of the poor have they sheltered or solaced during the year?' The Irishmen of New York would not grovel like this; they would ignore him. 'So let him come,' said the *Freeman's Journal*, 'and dance, and dine, and drive, and enjoy himself or be bored, as the case may be. It is nothing to us – nothing at all to the real American people.' True Americans were '*republicans*' and 'believe, in the *new* world, that the honors, dignities and emoluments of the government are not fit things to be transmitted and inherited.'[33]

Similar points were made by the *Irish-American*, the secular voice of New York's Irish, which declared that 'the spirit of flunkeyism ... was at the root of the whole affair.' New Yorkers had fawned over 'unearned rank and title,' when they should have put on 'an exhibition of the might and majesty of a free people.' A letter-to-the-editor took the New York *Herald* to task for declaring that '"the New York Committee of Reception represents all classes of citizens,"' a statement the letter writer called 'a most deliberate falsehood.' 'Who in that committee,' he rhetorically asked its members, 'represents the carpenters?

Who the bricklayers? Who the masons? Who the plasterers? Who the blacksmiths? Who the poor men blasting your rocks from one end of the year to the other? Who represents the hod carriers? Is there one amongst you who will carry the hod for the three or four months of summer to the top of a five or six storey house? Where would all your splendid mansions and your princely palaces be but for these men?' Working-class consciousness, then, as well as national consciousness, welled up when the Irish of New York observed the social establishment claiming to speak for all.[34]

The Irish press maintained that, while the mainstream dailies were not discussing it, the government of Lord Palmerston had a hidden agenda. 'Let us expose to the world,' declared a letter in the *Irish-American*, 'this subtle scheme of Palmerston and his ministry, to gain the moral support of the United States, preparatory to making war upon France and its ruler, that chivalrous ally of downtrodden nations, struggling for Freedom.' The writer called for a mass meeting to expose the matter, though nothing came of the proposal. Another writer, commenting on the attempts of British officials 'to extract from these gala scenes' an assurance of '"American sympathy" with Britain in the approaching European troubles,' estimated that in the case of a war with France, 'for every *one* American citizen who will cross the sea to aid her, *ten*, will come to deal her, if possible, her mortal blow.'[35]

Although the Irish-American newspapers were seriously concerned about the visit of the Prince of Wales, they could also find humour in all the fuss. A long poem, entitled 'The Prince of W(h)ales: The Fete of the Fishes,' appeared in the *Irish-American*. Parodying the response of New Yorkers and mocking the prince himself, it begins:

In the beautiful harbor of Gotham one day
'Twas rumored a fish had come into the Bay
From afar, where still rank among fishes prevails –
As it should among ours – called the Prince of W(h)ales.

And n'er since the days of the old prophet Jonas,
Who swallowed a whale, such commotion was known, as
Thereon straightway followed 'mong creatures with scales,
All mad to pay court to the Prince of W(h)ales.

Yet the fish was not large, and the fish was not fat,
Scarce 'A No. 1:' but no matter for that,

A certain descent certain greatness entails
And a very great fish was the Prince of W(h)ales ...[36]

Given all the enthusiasm for the prince in New York, the local Irish nationalists were fortunate to be able to point to the heroic behaviour of the Irishmen of the 69th Regiment, proud republicans whose principles forbade them to participate in the 'universal spectacle.' With the news that General Sandford had ordered the First Division of the state militia to parade for the reception of the Prince of Wales, the *Irish-American* responded with an editorial questioning the authority of the general 'to order, officially, citizens who are his equals, if not his superiors in everything, to quit their legitimate employments and sacrifice time and trouble and money to do honor to a youth, whom many regard only as the representative of a tyranny which they cordially detest.' The editorial urged members of the Irish companies in the various regiments to hold to their decision to parade but 'neither shoulder a musket, draw a sabre, nor fire a gun to honor the entry into New York of the representative of their relentless persecutor – England.' The editor mistakenly reported that the 69th Regiment, which was known as the Irish regiment, had been excused from duty – presumably by the top brass, who feared the embarrassment of a whole regiment's defying orders. As it transpired, the 69th was ordered out, but its commander, Colonel Michael Corcoran, refused to comply with the order. The metropolitan daily newspapers predicted that Colonel Corcoran would likely face a court-martial as a result.[37]

In 1860 the 69th Regiment was the strongest of the Irish militia units of New York and one of three that had been formed in 1853 to further the Irish nationalist struggle. (The plan had been that, while Britain was preoccupied with fighting in the Crimea, Irish-American militia units could play a crucial role in the liberation of Ireland from English rule.) The regiment's elected commander, Michael Corcoran, was a twenty-seven-year-old postal clerk. He had been born in Donegal and emigrated to New York in 1849, where he became a leader of the Fenian movement for Irish freedom.[38] For a man with such convictions, parading in honour of British royalty was utterly detestable, and for him to comply with orders might would have been a disgrace and personal setback. By refusing to order his men out, the colonel stood by his convictions, thus becoming a hero among his compatriots and a martyr for the cause.

The *Irish-American* reported the news of Irish defiance with pride and glee. It commended the 69th Regiment, listed the names of the various Irish captains in other regiments who had not been in the ranks for the celebrations, and mentioned a lieutenant who had demanded his discharge from service before the prince's parade had begun. Nearly all New York had 'flocked in crowds to do homage to a meritless youth,' a display that was 'humiliating to the student of our history, humiliating to the admirers of our institutions, humiliating to the advocate of democracy and the growth of liberty.' But Colonel Corcoran and the 69th, 'at the very zenith of this excitement,' had shown that 'we are not hirelings to be marched and countermarched in illustration of the abandonment of our principles and the degradation of our country.'[39] Meantime, the mainstream press lambasted the 69th for insulting the distinguished guest and blasted its commander for defying orders. As an Irish-American commentator put it, 'the FitzFanners and Van Sycophants are outraged.'[40]

The defiance of the 69th Regiment gained increasing attention in the weeks after the prince's departure from New York. The *Irish-American* and other newspapers published several resolutions passed by groups expressing their solidarity with the men of the 69th Regiment. For instance, a resolution of a mass meeting of the Irish-born residents of Boston declared that the 69th should have the support of every Irishman, and commended its commander for his 'patriotic and manly refusal to obey an unjust order, or to bow the knee in the temple of liberty, to a representative of monarchy.'[41] And the stakes were raised on 15 November, when the senior military authorities ordered the court-martial of Corcoran for disobeying orders. 'We shall be glad to see the issue joined,' declared an editorial in the *Irish-American*, 'for it is evident that General Sandford forgets that the men whose misfortune it is to be commanded by him are not hireling soldiers, but his equals and fellow-citizens, who freely give their services to the State.' They were not bound to follow the command of someone whose 'flunkeyism may prompt him to act in a manner derogatory to the dignity of Republican manhood.'[42] The court-martial, which began on 8 January 1861, lasted for many weeks. It was Corcoran's defence that 'military processions and displays were not the legitimate objects of the militia' and that the major-general had acted beyond his power by ordering out the division on this occasion. The detailed coverage of the trial made for dull reading because of the complex and technical issues, which centred on the amount of discretion the major-general had in calling out the division for 'purposes not expressly for exercise.'[43]

More interesting was the news of the support work done by Corcoran's admirers. Mass meetings moved their confidence in him and in the justice of his case. A convention of Irish societies, which met at the Hibernian Hall to plan New York's parade for St Patrick's Day, declared its approval of his action against 'a manifestation of sycophancy and toadyism' that was 'unworthy of the American name and contrary to the spirit of true Republicanism.' An elaborate presentation ceremony drew attention to the 'handsome flag' given to the 69th and a sword given to Corcoran by the 'citizens of New York.' The 'Irishmen of San Francisco' presented the 69th with a large gold medal, with an inscription expressing their approval of 'the manly course' pursued by the regiment.[44] Topping off the rituals of support was a ball held in January at the Academy of Music, the very hall where the grand ball for the prince had taken place three months earlier. The intention had been to fill the hall not with 'a vast display of borrowed jewellery and milliner's work' but rather 'with an assembly of rational Republican citizens, with their wives daughters, sisters and sweethearts – the "fair daughters of Erin" and of Columbia – whose charms are not purchased in Broadway repositories, but come from the hand of the great Creator.' The *Irish-American* declared the ball to have been a great success, with the Academy crowded to utmost capacity with swirling dancers – a contrast to the 'complete fizzle' that had been organized for the prince, an affair that had been 'as flat as a bad keg of diluted lager.'[45] Public spectacles, then, were by no means the monopoly of authorities!

In the end, Colonel Corcoran was never convicted by the court-martial. As the trial dragged on, events growing out of the conflict between north and south overtook those in the courtroom. Authorities in the north needed Irish immigrants to enlist in the military. When the Confederates attacked Fort Sumter, Corcoran publicly called all men to defend the Union. His trial was quashed. Irish-American volunteers rushed into the army, and especially into the 69th Regiment. On 23 April, New York gave the 69th an enthusiastic send-off. This time, the militia did march in procession through the streets of New York – and the cheering came from all quarters. Before long, Michael Corcoran would be a war hero.[46]

The refusal of the 69th Regiment to parade in honour of the Prince of Wales galvanized Irish New York's opposition to the celebrations. In the aftermath of the visit, working-class pride, republican manhood, and the nationalisms of two countries came together in the rhetorical attacks on a local elite that toadied to monarchy. It was the only sustained and militant assault on the idea of royalty during the whole of the prince's North American tour. Yet the incident had limited impact on the tour itself and on the tone of the coverage in the mainstream press. The press gave far more attention to the contributions and behaviour of those who endorsed the goodwill tour. No subject drew more interest than the grand ball, designed to be the cream on the cake of the New York visit.

New York's Ball

'The event of the age transpired last night,' – so began the *Commercial Advertiser*'s coverage of New York's brilliant ball honouring the Prince of Wales.[47] The ball, held at New York's Academy of Music on Friday, 12 October, was as extravagant as the press coverage of it. With energy and panache, the New York newspapers did their bit to make the ball the pinnacle of social events, as though the city's pre-eminence in America and the nation's claim to greatness depended upon it. American womanhood went on display for all the world to admire. And if the event failed to come off exactly as expected, even that might reveal aspects of the American character.

The ball was an exclusive affair. Members of the ball's general committee, which was composed of 400 wealthy and influential men, had to subscribe $70 each, which gave them seven invitations each. But members had to nominate individuals whom they hoped would be invited, and these names were evaluated by the Invitation Committee. The secretary would then issue non-transferable invitations to the approved nominees. In addition, the Invitation Committee issued two hundred complimentary invitations to special guests.[48] The New York *Tribune* put a highly favourable and nationalist gloss on the arrangements, saying that it would result in an event that would show off 'a republican aristocracy, sprung of the same energy and talent which give such a prodigious total to the great sum of American life.'[49] Cornwallis of the rival New York *Herald* thought the arrangements were a mistake. 'In a democratic country like this,' Cornwallis opined, 'an exclusive gathering of the kind ought not to have been tolerated.' Furthermore, the guest list was bound to be 'composed of old fogies.'[50]

Who would be at the ball became the most talked about topic in high society during the weeks leading up to it. In the words of the *Commercial Advertiser,* it was 'that for which thousands of fair ladies have sighed, and which has excited more envy than any other event that has happened in New York for years.' The New York *Daily Tribune* said that 'the struggle for tickets exceed[ed] in desperation any military campaign.' Pressure from the Upper Tendom was so great, says the historian of New York's 'aristocracy,' because of 'the fact that the guest list for the ball indicated who was "in society" and who was not.'[51]

As the committeemen delighted in – or agonized over – choosing their guests, they were also busy with their assigned tasks in preparing for the ball. Among the tasks at hand was the job of overseeing preparations for the site of the extravaganza. 'The greatest difficulty we at present encounter,' wrote Charles Augustus Davis, the chairman of the committee on the hall and supper, 'is the want of a House *big eno'*.' He was concerned to accommodate both '*Wide Crinolines* and comfort.'[52] The Academy of Music was the best locale, and, under the supervision of Isaac Brown, the sexton of Grace Church and social adviser to New York's great hostesses, a dance floor was constructed above the sloping concert-hall floor and theatre seating, and the mezzanine was converted into dressing rooms.[53] The school of medicine that was located next door offered its kitchens for the use of the staff preparing the supper, and one of its floors for use as supper rooms. The space between the two buildings had to be enclosed and passageways constructed to link the two. Painting, carpeting, lighting, and furnishing were required on a grand scale, as well as flags, bunting, and flowers galore. At one point it was reported that $12,000 had been allocated for the temporary decorations alone.[54] 'Some splendid sofas were offered *gratis*,' reported Davis to a friend, 'if I would only give a certificate that the Prince had seated himself on them!' Davis pondered the meaning of such offers: 'Is this *Loyalty*, or has it a little of the *Everlasting Dollar* in it? Perhaps a little of both.'[55]

Though the committee had exclusive control over the decorating, it became a kind of public event. The newspapers published endless details, such as the precise dimensions of the various rooms. Letters-to-the-editor commented on the choices made by committeemen. Thus, 'An Artist' wrote the New York *Times* expressing his horror that green was to be a predominant colour, on the grounds that 'its effects upon the countenance are most trying, and indeed injurious. To those of full sanguineous tint it produces the complexion of the squaw, upon the sallow it gives the complexion of a person in the last stages of yellow jaundice.'[56]

In the choice of decorations, patriotism combined with luxury. The entrance had a canopy formed of Union Jacks and Star-Spangled Banners, and the entry hall was draped with silks of red, white, and blue, while English and American flags were 'looped in the semblance of waving cornices round the ceiling.' Deep damask carpeting ran from the curb, up the steps, and down the hallway. The ballroom itself was 'a vista of gilding, yellow satin, wreathed pillars, crimson velvet, and flowers.' To dazzle the crowd, much extra lighting had been installed, including enormous gas-lit chandeliers of Florentine gold from which fresh flowers hung gracefully. Three lavishly appointed private rooms were prepared exclusively for the prince's personal use.[57]

The ball supper was said to be a triumph, too, one that demonstrated the superb talent available on the local scene in New York. With pink and white drapery, the rooms of the medical college had been transformed into exotic tents. On the buffet tables, the magnificently presented dishes, with their elegant-sounding French names, were provided by Lorenzo Delmonico, the owner of Manhattan's best restaurant. In mid-nineteenth century New York, the renowned Delmonico's served conspicuously expensive and extravagant fare to a well-heeled clientele appreciative of both the excess and the deferential service.[58] The journalists covering the royal ball showered praise on Delmonico, pointing both to the way he 'marshalled' his 'regiment of most faithful and active waiters' and to the many 'delicacies' that he had created 'with the true artistic power.'[59] New York had truly arrived when it could boast a banquet on such a 'tastefully luxurious scale.' The menu said it all – and in French, too:

Consommé de Volaille
Huîtres à la Poulette
Saumon Truites
au beurre de Montpellier
Filets de Boêuf à la Bellevue Galantines de Dindes à la Royale
Pâtés de Gibiers à la Monderne Cochons de Lait à la Parisienne
Pains de Lièvres Anglais Historiés Terrines de Nérac aux Truffés
Jambons de Westphalie à la Gendarme
Langues de Boêuf à l'Écarlate
Mayonnaises de Volailles Salades de Homards à la Russe
Grouses
Bécassines Bécasses
Faisans
Gelées au Madère Macédoines de Fruits
Crèmes Françaises Glaces à la Vanille et Citron
Petits Fours Charlotte Russe

Pêches, Poires, Raisins de Serre, etc.
PIÈCES MONTÉES
La Reine Victoria et le Prince Albert
Le Great Eastern   Le Vase de Flora
Silver Fountain, etc. etc.[60]

Preparations had also been under way in the homes and workshops of New York, since everyone going to the ball had to have the finest jewellery and formal wear for the occasion. Mrs August Belmont, married to one of the richest men of the city, was said to be the envy of all the ladies when she purchased a splendid diamond rivière, which had been admired for weeks in a display case at Tiffany's. According to the *Commercial Advertiser*, the women had 'exhausted all the ingenuity and the patience of their milliners in providing the most elegant and chaste costumes for the ball.' Mauve, magenta, and solferino were the fashionable colours. The New York *Times* correspondent, noting that many dowagers would dress in black velvet, surmised that 'the busy fingers of modistes throughout the metropolis must have been marvellously blackened during the past fortnight by working in velvet.' It was said that one particularly popular modiste had been responsible for no less than forty-six of the dresses worn at the ball. A history of fashion reports that it was well known that the prince's ball would set the trends of the era. The celebrated Mme (Ellen Curtis) Demorest not only designed several gowns for the evening but, as a journalist and publisher of the *Mirror of Fashion*, she declared that because 'all the ingenuity and resources of the most celebrated modistes were brought into play on this occasion, the toilets may therefore be considered as fairly indicative of the standard for full dress during the winter.'[61]

Even the men, for whom formal wear meant black suits and white cravats, purchased new attire for this special occasion and fussed about just what was most fashionable. In his diary, George Templeton Strong mocked the discussions at a meeting of the reception committee: 'Shall it be white vests and black cravats or vice versa? Are silk vests considered provincial in Paris? What manner of gloves prevailed at the Tuileries when Governor Fish was last there?' Nevertheless, Strong himself went out and bought a brand new pair of patent-leather shoes for the ball.[62]

On the evening of 12 October, all was ready for the grand event. Strong arrived early, at eight o'clock, along with other committeemen. 'The doors were not yet opened to the common herd,' he joked in his diary, 'but my exalted official position on the committee admitted me by the royal entrance on Fourteenth Street.' He was delighted with what he saw: 'The house looked brilliant, blazing with light and decorated with great masses of flowers.'[63]

In addition to the crowd assembling inside the Academy of Music, onlookers crowded the street to watch the arriving beauties. 'The unfashionable masses,' wrote the reporter for the *Daily Tribune*, 'stood thickly – and their wives with them – on the side-walks of Fourteenth-street and Irving place, opposite the Academy, and looked at the disgorging of divinity from the carriages.' Some hundreds of policemen exercised effective crowd control and kept the masses behind a barrier. 'A broad river of cobble-stone,' reported the New York *Times*, 'ran between the invited and the *out*vited, so that no unpleasant mingling might occur.' 'The ladies sprang in quick succession like fairies in a pantomimic scene, glittering with diamonds and floating in lace.' Those watching in the street, however, were 'not quite as well dressed as the others.' Indeed, the 'monotony of their rags [was] unrelieved by a single gleam of Solferino or the most remote hint of Magenta.' These onlookers stood in amazement, if not anger: 'The lean-eyed, hungry-mouthed crowd on the opposite pavement looked over and wondered how so much wealth could be in the world and they so poor.' But the air outside was fresh, and there was pleasure to be had in gazing, as well as in being gazed at. When a particularly beautiful woman stepped down from a carriage, the crowd would express their approval by cheering and sharing in her joy if only momentarily and vicariously. They 'clapped their hands and shouted their delight that some were happy, though they were miserable.'[64]

As more and more guests entered the Academy, the crush grew terrific. One of the two bands played music for promenading, but most people congregated at the front of the hall, near where the prince was to make his entrance. According to the *Evening Post*, the men talked about how they planned to enlighten the prince in regard 'to the expense of the entertainment,' while the women talked of dancing with him or at least getting 'near enough to ascertain whether he ever shaved.' Strong recorded in his diary that he found himself waiting next to Mayor Wood, and he had 'a very intimate talk with that limb of Satan.'[65]

At half past ten, the waiting ended with the prince's arrival. All eyes were on him as one of the bands played 'God Save the Queen' and 'Hail Columbia.' Cornwallis of the New York *Herald* reported that only a few of the ladies climbed up on chairs to get a better view, and they did so 'gracefully.' The reporter for the *Daily Tribune* said that the ladies nearest the prince, the ones who had fought to get close at an early hour, were well-behaved, although everyone had 'expected hysterics.'[66] Introductions and a promenade were supposed to occur in the short interval before the prince would have the first dance, a Strauss quadrille, with 'Mrs. Governor Morgan.' The crush was so great, however, that it proved impossible to clear the way and begin a promenade, and the selected guests could not get close enough to be introduced to the prince. Everyone stood awkwardly, during several minutes of silence, when there was no band music and no one knew quite what to do. Their predicament ended suddenly and in a completely unexpected way.

With a loud crash, the catastrophe of the evening began. A giant Sèvres vase fell to the floor, breaking into pieces and spraying those nearby with water and roses. As people gasped in surprise, another vase smashed down. And then suddenly a large section of the dance floor collapsed, sending dozens of guests downwards. No one was sure what was happening. Some people assumed that it was a Guy Fawkes plot. Everyone feared the worst: that panic would break out in the jammed hall. But Hamilton Fish leapt to reassure the throng. The floor had sunk only a few feet. No one had been hurt, though many were rattled. Strong noted that his wife, Ellie, 'went down into one of the pits and was frightened.' Fortunately for her, she 'did not lose her footing'; fortunately for him, neither did she lose 'her self-possession.'[67]

An extended interlude then took place. The prince and his suite were hustled away to their withdrawing rooms to seek champagne and stronger drink. Many of the other guests headed to the supper rooms, where they scrambled for the libations. Meantime, a score of carpenters were found, who wedged timber supports into place and hammered away, while Sexton Brown of the house committee supervised. It was nearly another two hours before the program could resume. In his diary Strong poked fun at the sight of 'Brown peering down into the oblong hole [who] looked as if engaged in his ordinary sextonical duties at an internment.' In a more sober vein, he wrote that 'there was a general sense of failure and calamity. Everything looked bilious. Everyone said the whole floor was unsafe. There could be no dancing; the ball was a disgraceful fiasco.' People pointed their fingers at the committeemen, blaming them for the disaster. Strong felt compelled to defend his honour, explaining to anyone who would listen that 'the Reception Committee had nothing to do with the arrangements of the house.'[68]

It was not until midnight that the prince accompanied Mrs Governor Morgan onto the floor for the opening dance. At last, at about two o'clock, the prince, it was reported, 'seemed to be getting into the merits of the occasion.' In contrast, Strong spent the rest of the night 'dawdling about and wishing it were over.' He got home at daylight, 'weary and worn' after nearly nine hours spent in his 'new patent leathers.'[69]

The Saturday newspapers, which brimmed with assessments of the ball, focused on the collapse of the floor and the overcrowding – and their implications. The cave-in succeeded in typifying, wrote one of the correspondents for the New York *Times*, 'the salient trait of our wild, reckless, and brilliant civilization': Americans could take catastrophes in their stride and rise to greater triumphs. Although the ballroom floor had been 'tossed about for some time like a ship in a blusterous sea,' there had been 'little ... dismay or alarm.' Accustomed to weathering 'the storms of panics in Wall-street and Tammany Hall,' the committeemen were 'little concerned about an incident which threatened neither to break the banks nor to render asunder the Union.' And not only had 'the solid men of New York' worn their 'usual air of prosy and business-like placidity,' the ladies, too, had shown a poise that did the nation proud. Only one woman had fainted. Most had 'seemed to enjoy the thorough Americanism of the thing.' Joking among themselves, one lady had quipped 'that even the timber of America revolts against royalty.' For these daughters of Columbia, 'all was wit, fun, and good nature.'[70]

A hard-headed editorial in the same newspaper gave a different spin to the event. In 'Lessons of Adversity,' the New York *Times* admitted that, before the eyes of the world, New York had blundered badly, and to make matters worse, America's reputation for practicality had been damaged. 'Is it absolutely impossible for us to do anything *well*?' asked the editorial. 'We pride ourselves greatly on our practical qualities, – and yet it is precisely there that our failures occur.'[71]

An editorial in the *Evening Post* similarly worried about the reputation of the United States. More than any event during the prince's tour, the ball had focused the attention of the world, and most especially of the British, on the claims to status of the United States. 'In the character of the assembly, its claims to distinction, its deportment under circumstances calculated to put the best breeding to a severe trial,' said the

Dancing and gazing at the Academy of Music, New York. At least some guests are depicted as enjoying themselves notwithstanding the embarrassment caused by the floor's collapse. (*Frank Leslie's Illustrated Newspaper*, 27 October 1860)

Post, 'there was everything for an American to feel proud of, and for a foreigner to respect.' The ball was nearly a triumph, except for the fiasco of the collapsing floor, which appeared to confirm 'what John Bull terms, not without reason, our national vice, our recklessness of life, as exhibited in our hasty, imperfect, hand-to-mouth methods.' Altogether, it had been 'inconceivably humiliating.'[72]

Where should the blame be placed – apart from on the American character? The *Post* attributed the 'miserable fiasco' to the contracting carpenter whose attempt to save five or ten dollars imperiled the lives of hundreds of people and the reputation of the nation. The New York *Times* thought otherwise, placing blame for 'the stupid blundering' on the 'sheer incompetency ... of the persons in charge.' The committeemen had failed both to assess the capacity of the Academy and to supervise the construction of the false floor. People had been selected to arrange for the ball, even though they had no competence let alone expertise in such matters. 'A man may be respectable,' fumed the editorial, 'and rich and benevolent, and yet know no more about supervising a public ball than he does about construing Sanscrit.' The editorial concluded: 'Our failures would not be wholly lost, if they taught us to be more thorough, and to guard against the same mishaps in future.'

In back of the floor's collapse lay the bigger problem of overcrowding. The crush was so bad in the ballroom, reported the *Daily Tribune*, that the guests pressed 'hard against each other's fineries, crushing fresh flowers brandished by dainty fingers' and making 'a jelly of the costliest silks and laces, the whitest shoulders, and the most stunning heads of hair.' A rumour – one characteristic of New York – had it that the excessive crowding was the result of a fraud perpetrated by the ticket-takers operating in collusion with the police at the doorways: together they had accepted bribes and admitted far more people than had actually been invited. But the organizers denied the truth of such statements. The chairman of the committee on police and carriages explained publicly that, in order to answer the charges being made, an official count was made during the ball of the locked ticket boxes. No counterfeit tickets were found. Of the 3,195 tickets issued for the event, 3,025 had been taken in at the door. The committeemen had simply miscalculated the amount of room needed for crinoline and hoops.[73]

Offsetting the dismal reflections on the blunders of carpenters and committeemen were some happy thoughts about the sumptuousness of the event – most especially the feminine beauty that had been displayed. As the New York *Times* clumsily put it, there had been 'an overflow of ripe loveliness.'[74] Such beauty and opulence did credit to America. Cornwallis of the New York *Herald* asked rhetorically: 'For beauty and the display of diamonds, where could their like be met?' After grumbling about there being too many dowagers, a reporter for the New York *Times* added: 'Velvet and dowagers have this merit, that they imply diamonds, and the implication on this occasion was verified in fact.' Worth singling out in this regard was 'Mrs. Kirkland, of this City,' whose dress was 'adorned with black lace flounces, trimmings of gold, and a blaze of diamonds which recalled to many the splendid *soirees* at the Hotel Thorn in Paris.' So glittering was the display that one 'might almost have fancied himself in St. Petersburg.' The republican aristocracy sparkled every bit as brilliantly as the courts of Europe.[75]

In response to these kinds of discussions of female splendour, there came a reaction in the New York *Times* from 'One of the Visitors at the Ball.'[76] The writer insisted that, 'far more than the display of jewellery and finery,' what gave 'the glow of beauty' to the ball was 'the cheerfulness and graciousness of the ladies.' The 'independence and free and easy manners of American ladies presented a remarkable contrast to the stateliness of those of England.' The author surmised that the Prince of Wales had appreciated this very contrast and would have attributed it to 'its true source, the great sense of liberty of the American woman on account of the greater reverence paid to her and of the more unsophisticated and unconventional views of life which here prevail.' The men at the ball, by contrast, appeared to be a sombre lot, nearly all of them dressed in black, and yet the vitality of America's manhood had burst forth in every one of them, even if the polish were lacking. 'What some of the male New York leaders of fashion lack in intellectual refinement and culture,' wrote one observer, 'they make up in boisterous energy and audacious enterprise.' True, some of the calls during the quadrilles resembled 'gongs and railway whistles' rather than 'dignified utterance of polished men of the world.' But 'there was on the other hand a refreshing absence of the stiffnesses and etiquettes which chill many of the gatherings at the courts of Europe.' Writing privately in his diary, Strong saw things differently. He sneered at Peter Cooper, the philanthropist who had made a fortune in glue and paint, saying that in his formal attire fellow 'looked like one of Gulliver's Yahoos caught and cleaned and dressed up.' From a completely different perspective, the *Irish-American* also denigrated the men who attended the ball, saying that, because the committee of four hundred was 'mostly composed of "old fogies" of fifty or sixty,' their guests had been 'other fossils of the same calibre.'[77]

The behaviour of a few of the guests at the ball caused eyebrows to be raised. It was widely reported that many unusually rude guests – most of them so-called ladies – had swarmed the prince, plucking at his jacket and pinching and bruising him. In his diary, Strong expressed disgust at the way 'Walker, the Presbyterian bookbinder,' had aggressively thrust his daughter into the prince's arms for a dance, and admiration for His Royal Highness, who 'evaded this ambitious plebeian rather gracefully for so young a person.' The Duke of Newcastle noticed this kind of behaviour and in a private communication wrote witheringly that the poor prince had been 'somewhat persecuted by attentions not in strict accordance with good breeding.'[78]

The behaviour and reactions of the prince's dance partners also varied. Strong was bemused by 'Miss Helen Russell,' who was so overcome when presented to the prince that 'her voice failed her for fear, and she astonished H.R.H. with a series of contortions and muscular twitchings before she succeeded in articulating an audible word.' On the other hand, Fanny Kemble, an actress from London whose memoirs of life in New York delighted the late Victorians, was astonished by the attitude of her daughter, Fan, who was one of the few young ladies who danced with the prince at the Academy ball. When Fanny asked her daughter whether she had 'laid up in lavender the satin shoes in which she danced with such a partner,' Fan had shrugged and chuckled, saying only that he was a 'nice little fellow, and danced very well.' Fanny commented to a friend: 'Think ... of the shock to my rather superstitious respectful loyalty at hearing my future sovereign, the future sovereign of England, Scotland, Ireland, Wales, and India, clapped on the shoulder by this monkey of a democratic damsel of mine.'[79]

The prince himself was characteristically nonchalant when reporting back to his mother about the New York ball. Bertie told her about the crowding, saying that '3,000 were invited and 5,000 came, which of course was not an improvement.' He said that it had been 'very difficult to move,' and he mentioned the late start on account of the floor's giving way. Nevertheless, the prince concluded generously: 'In spite of these disasters I must say it was a very pretty sight.'[80] Had the ball's organizers seen the prince's letter, they would probably have been more than satisfied with the royal judgment.

In the long run, leading New Yorkers remembered the ball not for its problems but as a highlight in the social life of the metropolis. Even today, New Yorkers and visitors to the city can see in the Museum of the City of New York a gown worn at the 1860 ball, carefully preserved in all its magnificence. Our prolific diarist, George Templeton Strong, joked that, having shaken the hand of the prince at the ball, he was thinking of having his 'right-hand glove framed and glazed, with an appropriate inscription.' Had he only done so, it, too, might yet be on display![81]

Conclusion

On the morning of 20 October, the prince and his suite left Boston, the last site of grand festivities, and proceeded by train to Portland, Maine, the port of departure for home. Earlier there had been talk of leaving the United States from New York, but rumour had it that the naval officers feared that too many tars would jump ship in Gotham's busy harbour. (As it was, reports put the number of desertions from the royal squadron during the tour at 140.[1]) Portland's comparative quiet, as well as its fine harbour and good rail connections, made it the officers' choice, a favour that the city of Portland reciprocated by hosting a ball in their honour on 18 October.[2] Upon reaching Portland, the prince was greeted by the usual throngs of curious and enthusiastic well-wishers, as well as by many dignitaries from New England and Canada. A luncheon at the Prebble House provided an opportunity for the prince and members of his suite to renew friendships with men such as John Rose, the minister responsible for the visit to Canada, and Montreal's irrepressible mayor, Charles-Séraphin Rodier. As farewells were said, it was reported that 'the eyes of more than one or two of the illustrious visitors glistened with moisture from the well of feeling.'[3]

A little before three o'clock in the afternoon, the prince left the hotel for the waterfront. For the last time, an American crowd shouted and waved handkerchiefs as Albert Edward stepped aboard the barge that carried him swiftly to the *Hero*, whose yards, like those of other British vessels in the harbour, were manned by cheering tars. As the prince boarded her, a salute thundered and the royal standard went up. Before five o'clock, all was ready for the Atlantic crossing. The royal squadron weighed anchor, and one last salute was given as the *Hero* and her escort steamed past the forts near the mouth of the harbour.

Not far out to sea, heavy swells forced the little *Flying Fish* to fall behind the *Hero,* whose only escort for the homeward trip was the frigate *Ariadne,* as had been the case on the outbound crossing. She carried the lesser members of the prince's entourage, including the prince's chums – Charles Eliott and the Honourable Mr C. Ellis, a naturalist – as well as Nathaniel Woods of the *Times.* Aboard the *Hero,* Captain Seymour reassigned the members of the prince's suite their familiar berths. Eager to be home, passengers and crew looked forward to an arrival at Plymouth in as little as two weeks' time, so long as the weather held.

It did not. Storms, which had dogged the prince throughout his travels in North America, marred the voyage home as well. Cold, rain, hail, and heavy fog can be expected on the North Atlantic in late October, and, as it turned out, the presence of royalty was no protection. Heavy seas and persistent headwinds slowed the passage, and nasty squalls drove the vessels off course. On many occasions the two ships were blown far apart, and on a few they came so close together that serious damage was only just averted. Even so, squalls knocked both vessels onto their sides, ripped mainsails and foresails, and washed howitzers into the sea, where they sank without a trace. 'The *Ariadne* creaked and groaned in every timber,' wrote Woods: 'The wind moaned and howled through the shrouds in every tone of hoarse and dangerous anger, while the clouds of hail drove over everything, and kept ringing and spinning from the deck like small shot.'[4] Between the gales, the ships were becalmed, rolling uncomfortably in the heavy swells for days on end. Both vessels were sailing ships with auxiliary steam engines. The *Ariadne* carried enough coal for her to have steamed clear across the Atlantic, but the *Hero* could carry only sufficient for emergencies. During periods of calm, the *Ariadne* tried towing the mighty *Hero,* but the equipment was not up to the task. By 1 November, the *Hero* and her escort were within 600 miles of Great Britain; five days later they still had 430 left to go. By 11 November, they were farther away than they had been a week earlier.

As the journey dragged on, everyone aboard grew increasingly impatient. 'Towards the end of this voyage,' wrote Hinchingbrooke, who travelled aboard the *Hero*, 'the Duke of Newcastle became so irate at the wind coming always ahead that he vowed he would not go on deck again until the wind changed.'[5] Even Dr Acland's bright spirits dampened for once. In lengthy letters (which could not be mailed), the physician grumbled to his wife. He blamed the bad weather on the

Departing for home. For the long, arduous return voyage, the *Hero*, shown in the lead, would be accompanied only by the *Ariadne*. (*Illustrated London News*, 24 November 1860)

timing of the voyage, which was just one result of Newcastle's 'cramming everything into too short space, nearly killing us.' The earnest doctor groused about the slipping standards among members of the suite, commenting: 'To what lengths of looseness and badinage Bruce would allow conversation to go I had no idea!' For all his worldliness and superiority, General Bruce was not above 'mixing with apparent satisfaction in light talk with young men – and very loose innuendo.'[6] Tut-tut!

Sailors and travellers made the best of things. 'We often danced in the evening with the midshipmen for partners,' Hinchingbrooke recalled.[7] Special celebrations were arranged on 9 November, the day the prince turned nineteen. The sailors got a double ration of grog that day, and the midshipmen arranged for an afternoon meal in the gunroom, opening the stern port to clear the air and setting up tables for the birthday party. The ship's officers, the 'middies,' and members of the suite enjoyed a convivial dinner, sharing jokes and laughter, and enjoying a rendition by the ship's band of 'The Roast Beef of Old England.' In the memory of one of the midshipmen, the meal ended abruptly when suddenly a great wave poured through the stern port, swamping everyone – the birthday boy included – in icy sea water.[8]

England's roast beef looked increasingly appealing at this point, since the ship's supplies of fresh food had begun to run out by 7 November. Mr Ellis, the naturalist travelling with his menagerie on board the *Ariadne*, half-jokingly offered the royal party 'a racoon and a greyhound' to roast for supper! By 11 November, all the meat and vegetables aboard the *Hero* had been consumed and, as Acland noted, there was 'no beer, no bitter, no wine.' Understandably, 'even the sailors [were] disheartened.' The entire crew and all the passengers, including the prince, were reduced to rations drawn from the ship's salt store. 'We have many speculations ... of what you all think of our tardy movements,' wrote Acland, who added darkly: 'I dare not think neither of what may be, nor has been, nor what will be.'[9]

In England, concern for the late arriving royal squadron grew by the hour.[10] The queen and prince consort, who were deeply worried about the fate of their son, contacted the Admiralty, which sent out search crews to look for the royal squadron. On 13 November, dispiriting news arrived at Windsor that the *Gorno* had returned to Plymouth, 'not having any intelligence of the squadron.'[11] At last, on the night of 14 November, amid heavy fog in the Channel, the red signal rockets that the *Hero* sent into the sky were spotted by the *Himalay*, one of the search vessels sent by the Admiralty. The wayward ships were directed towards the Cornish coast, which they soon reached.

At breakfast the next day, the queen learned that the squadron had been sighted, and shortly afterwards, as she noted in her journal, 'telegrams showered in from Plymouth,' informing her of the squadron's arrival in port. 'We felt much pleased to think of Bertie's safe arrival at last,' the queen wrote.[12] Before 10 A.M. on 15 November, the *Hero* and the *Ariadne* had both cast their anchors inside the breakwater at Plymouth. Salutes were fired as the royal standard came down from the *Hero* and the prince stepped with relief onto the terra firma of the Royal William Victualling Yard.

By noon, Albert Edward and his suite were aboard the royal train, bound for Windsor. At every station along the way, crowds cheered the prince's safe return. By 6:30 that evening, the train had arrived at Windsor station, where the prince was greeted by his father and a guard of honour. The town's inhabitants cheered and church bells rang out as the prince proceeded to the castle. Queen Victoria noted in her journal that her husband returned from the station 'with dear Bertie, looking extremely well.' After hearing briefly from Newcastle, St Germans, and Bruce about the trials of the voyage home, the royal family spent some private time together. That evening the queen hosted a dinner for the prince's travelling companions and others such as the Duke and Duchess of Somerset. 'Bertie, who sat next to me,' wrote the queen, 'talked a great deal of his voyage & travels, the fatigues & exertions of which must have been very great.' When the queen praised the Duke of Newcastle for 'all he had done,' he was 'touched to tears' and 'spoke in great praise of Bertie.' She summed up by writing: 'It was a happy & satisfactory return, for which we must be truly thankful.'[13]

Assessments of the tour began to be made well before the royal party arrived home in England, and the judgments continued to be recorded in the months and years that followed. The congratulatory tone of the conversations at the queen's dinner party pervaded both private and public assessments made of the tour by those closely involved, as well as by commentators in the mainstream press.

'Everyone' agreed that the prince had truly shone during the tour. 'The prepossessing appearance and social qualities of the Prince were of immense assistance in fanning the fire of his popularity,' wrote Kinahan Cornwallis of the New York *Herald*. 'His fondness for dancing

LATEST FROM AMERICA.

H. R. H. JUNIOR (TO H. R. H. SENIOR). "NOW, SIR-REE, IF YOU'LL LIQUOR UP AND SETTLE DOWN, I'LL TELL YOU ALL ABOUT MY TRAVELS."

An Americanized Prince of Wales recounts his exploits abroad to his disapproving father. (*Punch*, 10 November 1860) aroused the interest of the ladies to a very high pitch indeed.'[14] From Canada, the tour organizer, John Rose, wrote to Bruce saying that the prince's 'kind and gentle demeanour' had taught 'the mass of the people' no longer to regard royalty as 'the stern and unapproachable thing they were accustomed to consider it.'[15] From Boston, Lord Lyons informed the foreign secretary, Lord John Russell, in England: 'The excellent impression made upon the Americans is chiefly due to the kind and gracious manner in which the Prince received the attentions which were paid to him – to the patience and good humour with which His Royal Highness bore what was fatiguing and irksome; and to the judgment and (if I may use the expression) tact with which he maintained his dignity.'[16] Away from his school books, amid a whirl of festivities, the young prince had found his *métier*. In the process, his character had developed. Bruce assured the prince consort that, as a result of Albert Edward's assuming public duties in North America, he had 'grown and strengthened both in mind and body and become more fitted on the whole to meet the work and responsibilities of his ripening years.' Lord John Russell wrote the queen from the Foreign Office, saying that he had heard on good authority that 'the accounts in the newspapers of the reception of the Prince of Wales are by no means exaggerated.' Since the Prince of Wales's arrival coincided with Prince Alfred's from Cape Town, Lord Palmerston formally congratulated the queen on the safe return of both her sons, 'who in such different parts of the Globe have by their admirable Bearing spread wide over the world the high and deserved Reputation of the Royal Family of England.'[17]

The royal parents read the newspaper coverage of the tour and received many flattering comments on its success, which puzzled them a little when the praise focused on their son. The prince consort wrote to a confidant in amazement: 'Bertie is generally pronounced "the most perfect production of nature."'[18] For once the queen was persuaded that her eldest son had accomplishments. She explained to her daughter in Germany that Bertie had been 'immensely popular everywhere,' adding perceptively and frankly: '[He] really deserves the highest praise, which should be given him all the more as he was never spared any reproof.'[19]

At the end of their duties, officials at all levels felt relief and a sense of satisfaction with a job well done. Newcastle's tears at the Windsor dinner were both a sign of his happiness that his work met with royal approval and an indication of his fragile emotional state at the moment when he was at last relieved of a great responsibility. Similarly, at the close of the Canadian tour, Colonel Thomas Wily had 'felt [his] shoulders equally relieved of a burden that had weighed heavily on them for a month or more.'[20] At a celebration enjoyed by the organizers on the night of the prince's departure from Canada, the men behaved, recalled Wily, 'like a lot of schoolboys, our tasks ended, the school doors shut behind us with unlimited holidays looming ahead.'[21] Several weeks later, after the prince had left the United States, Lord Lyons reflected with pleasure on the visit and the role he himself had played. 'The Prince of Wales' tour in the United States went off completely to the satisfaction of all parties from beginning to end,' he wrote. 'It was rather hard work for me, as he never went out without me, nor I without him, and I had quantities of letters to write and people to see and keep in good humour. Nevertheless H.R.H. himself and all the people with him were so agreeable that on the whole I enjoyed the tour very much while it was going on. I look back to it with unmixed satisfaction.'[22]

Those people who assisted the prince received commemorative gifts in recognition of services rendered. A couple of months after the prince's departure from Canada, for instance, five officers of the Grand Trunk Railway's western division were given 'handsome medals' struck at Her Majesty's Mint in recognition of their work in transporting the prince throughout Canada West.[23] In Hamilton, at the end of the Canadian tour, General Bruce had presented Colonel Wily with a jewellery box from the prince. To the young officer's evident delight, the box contained 'five massive gold vest buttons with three shirt studs bearing the [Prince-of-Wales] "Plumes" in gold, on a ground of deep blue enamel.'[24] Wily also received an honorarium of $600 from the government and Commissioner John Rose's 'warm thanks for ... constant and valuable co-operation.'[25]

The members of the journalistic fraternity, Woods of the *Times* and the artist G.H. Andrews of the *Illustrated London News*, who had been privileged from the start, were also suitably recognized by the royal family for their services. Andrews gained both financially and in prestige when the Prince of Wales bought a series of illustrations completed by the artist from sketches made during the tour.[26] In the case of Woods, sweet reward came in the form of continued access to the royal family. For instance, in 1863 Woods was one of just a handful of reporters given the privilege of attending and reporting on the Prince of Wales's wedding ceremony in St George's Chapel, Windsor – an event that won great public interest and approbation to the benefit of journalists, publishers, and the monarchy alike.[27]

In recognition of services rendered during the tour, the queen wished to confer high honours on certain members of the suite. The Duke of Newcastle, Lord Lyons, and Sir Edmund Head were all given the distinction of the Order of the Bath, or KCB.'[28] The queen also wanted to confer the latter honour on General Bruce because, as she explained to Palmerston, nothing could 'exceed the tact & judgment & the zeal with which General Bruce discharges his important duties.' The prime minister would not agree, arguing that Bruce's services had been of a private rather than a public nature, to which Victoria replied: 'The watching over and training the youth of a future sovereign is, in the Queen's opinion, one of the greatest public services which can be rendered in a monarchy.' Still, Palmerston would not budge, and Bruce never got his KCB.[29]

Meantime, as those nearest the prince indulged themselves in the warm glow of mutual admiration, the prince's recent hosts were confronting the cold reality of totalling up expenses and paying the bills. The New York *Times* lauded Mayor Fernando Wood for keeping a tight lid on expenditures in connection with the prince's visit to New York – such a sharp contrast to the scandalous extravagance of the earlier visit by the Japanese embassy. Nevertheless, the editorial acknowledged that Wood had a problem on his hands because the members of the common council would balk at approving any amount for fear of 'the backlash at the polls from Irish voters.'[30] In Toronto the organizers of the visit squabbled among themselves over petty matters, in the process dredging up the earlier charges of corruption within the decorations committee and arguing about whether that committee or the general one should be credited with revenue from the sale of leftover materials.[31] In Montreal the decade-long dispute over the tangled finances of the Crystal Palace was only just beginning.[32]

Widespread interest swirled around the auctions held in Canadian cities to liquidate the stock of special items commissioned by the province for use during the visit. Attention focused both on the premium prices paid and on the individuals who had the cash and an interest in acquiring them. At the auction in Toronto, Colonel George Taylor Denison, the scion of an old Toronto family and a keen monarchist, paid $47 for a handsome plate-glass mirror, which had been valued at $40. The *Globe* reporter observed that, 'as the prince had surveyed his features in it,' that surely made it 'worth $7 extra.' The item that drew the most interest among the spectators at the auction was the bed slept in by the prince, a finely carved piece in black walnut produced in the

Toronto shops of Jacques and Hay. When it was put on the block, there was a 'commotion in the crowd,' and the gentlemen gallantly allowed the ladies 'to occupy the best places.' Bidding for the bed started at $100. '"It cost that sum to pay the wage of the man who did the carving," exclaimed Mr [Robert] Hay. "Put him out," shouted several gentlemen.' In the end the bed sold 'to Mr A. Manning for $170,' a price the manufacturer thought too little by at least $60.[33] Overall, however, bidding was strong and the prices high.

These auctions brought the provincial government some income to offset expenditures, but on the whole the Department of Public Works settled a great many accounts, some of them hefty indeed by the standards of the period. The department paid $26,293 to Jacques and Hay for the several suites of furniture and some carpentry work; one wine merchant was paid $3,729, and four hotel owners received a total of $12,885.[34]

Colonel Wily, who assisted the work of the departmental accountant and clerks, had to do some careful auditing since some of the accounts were misdirected or heavily padded. Several government departments, for instance, attempted to bill the commissioner of public works for the cost of illuminating buildings in Quebec, and the sums were far from paltry: the Civil Secretary's Office, $1,751; the Receiver General, $1,261; the Quebec court house, $1,000. Commissioner Rose refused to pay.[35] One of the worst offenders for overcharging came from within Rose's own department: the chief engineer in charge of construction of the Parliament Buildings in Ottawa. He sent in such 'very large Bills' in connection with the laying of the foundation stone that the commissioner insisted on 'a full enquiry ... into the necessity or propriety of the outlay.'[36] When I.M. Sanderson complained about the amount he received for his culinary magic, Rose stood firm, saying that $2,000 was adequate remuneration, given that all expenses had been covered and Sanderson had gained public recognition that would benefit his career. Rose deducted $757 from an account totalling $4,101 sent by the proprietors of the Royal Hotel in Hamilton, noting an 'overcharge' for accommodating extra gentlemen and servants, a 'gratuitous and unauthorized expenditure' for fitting up the hotel for the royal levee, an 'exorbitant charge' in connection with a luncheon, and 'an unheard of charge' for breakage and damage to carpets and furniture. Notwithstanding such disputes, however, Wily recollected that, overall, things went smoothly because people were held to the contracts that they had signed in advance. When all the accounts were sorted out, it was found that the department had paid out about a half-million dollars on the prince's visit.[37]

The amount of money spent by governments, municipalities, and private individuals in hosting the prince appeared staggering, a fact that raised the question of how worthwhile the expenditures had been. The New York *Herald* devoted a long editorial to the subject, which the London *Times* picked up for the benefit of British readers. The gist of its argument was that, if nothing else, the visit had provided an economic boost by putting into circulation in North America between $4,000,000 and $5,000,000. The prince himself had contributed by spending heavily while in the United States. 'Special trains cost rather dear,' noted the editorial, 'and so do extensive suites of apartments in fashionable hotels.' Moreover, his personal generosity was to be admired, and not only by hotel staff and other persons who had benefited from his largesse. 'Checks for various sums, from $500 to $1,000 for distribution among servants, testified to his liberality and his credit at the bankers.' Altogether, during his stay in the United States, 'he could not have managed to expend in that time less than $100,000 – a mere bagatelle, to be sure, to one who has the British Treasury at his back.' By such an argument, then, the *Herald* hoped to subdue fears about civic overspending and answer criticisms coming from 'some narrow-minded philosophers of the utilitarian school.'[38]

More generally, commentators in England and the United States hailed the visit as a triumph in promoting goodwill between the two countries. In a speech given just after the prince's return to England, Lord Palmerston observed that the visit had 'awakened the deepest interest in the mind of every Englishman.' The Americans' 'cordiality, the heartfelt kindness, the generous hospitality' had been extraordinary, and the display boded well for yet stronger ties in the future between Britain and the United States – 'those two great branches of the same noble and ... illustrious stock.' In a speech three weeks later, Newcastle declared that the visit 'had done more to cement the good feeling between the two countries than could possibly have been effected by a quarter of a century of diplomacy.' The *Times* ran an editorial that similarly praised the good effects the visit would have on Anglo-American relations: 'The Prince of Wales, while showing the feelings of a true-born Englishman, elicited the feelings of all true-born Americans, and so brought the two face to face and made them feel they were brothers.'[39]

On the other side of the Atlantic, similar sentiments prevailed in public assessments of the tour's effects. 'The queen and people of Great Britain,' said the New York *Times*, must be highly gratified at the way in which their Prince has been received in the United States, for the enthusiasm and cordiality of the popular greeting have exceeded all the expectations of Americans themselves.' According to Cornwallis of the New York *Herald*, the visit had secured 'more firmly the general interests of the two great sections of the Anglo Saxon race.' Mixing metaphors, a Boston journalist declared that the tour had made the two nations 'truer, deeper, better friends' and predicted that in the future '"God save the Queen" and "Hail Columbia" will be twin-sisters in the world of harmony and of patriotism.'[40]

Predictably, Queen Victoria and President Buchanan expressed the same sentiment when they publicly exchanged messages in December 1860. The queen referred to the 'affection' that she expected 'to prevail between the two countries, to their mutual advantage, and to the general interests of civilization and humanity'; the president alluded to 'that consciousness of common interest and mutual regard which have in the past, and will in the future bind together more strongly than treaties, the feeling and the fortunes of the two nations which represent the enterprise, the civilisation, the constitutional liberty of the same great race.'[41]

In the months immediately following, the goodwill allegedly built up by the prince's visit was put to an onerous test and found to be less robust than the queen and the president had imagined. By April, the Civil War had broken out in the United States, and the hostilities strained Anglo-American relations to the breaking point. British public opinion tended to favour the south, which naturally angered the people living in the northern states that the prince had so recently traversed in apparent triumph. The general sense was that, as an exercise in goodwill diplomacy, the impact of the visit had been utterly ephemeral. When the *Trent* affair of November 1861 brought Britain and the Union government to the brink of war, the happy days of the visit were a distant memory if they were not forgotten completely by the people of the northern United States and of England alike. Sir Sidney Lee, Albert Edward's official biographer, maintains, however, that the visit *did* have a salutary impact on diplomacy during the Civil War years. At the time of the *Trent* affair, when the British public clamoured to go to war against the north, Palmerston was tempted to yield. 'The queen and Prince Consort,' writes Lee, 'confessing that the Prince of Wales's American tour was still an efficient motive-force on their minds, urged with success on the Prime Minister a moderation which in the result insured a peaceful settlement.'[42] More recent histories by diplomatic historians have not credited the visit with having had the same influence, however.[43]

Yet the visit's importance need not be viewed narrowly as a factor in diplomatic relations because, as commentators in 1860 were so well aware, the tour was an occasion for showcasing and celebrating civic and national values. According to an editorial in the New York *Times* appearing on the day of the prince's departure from the United States, the true significance of the visit to the nation's leading city had been the prince's encounter with 'Democratic Crowds.'[44] The royal visitor and the members of his suite had come to the United States 'to move in Democratic crowds; they were as curious to see us as we were curious to see them.' And what a show the New York crowds had made! They were 'the glory of her Democratic institutions.' In great European cities the state would never allow such crowds to assemble, and even in London, there would have been 'an endless array of policemen to keep order.' Nothing of the kind had been needed in New York. In spite of 'many sores and excrescences on the body politic, the heart must be sound while so vast an assemblage of people are under perfect self-control and so fully capable of self-government.' Even though there were some people in the crowds who disapproved of the ovation, seeing it as 'an indorsement of Royalty – the Prince was as safe from insult as he would be in his mother's boudoir.' Furthermore, the New Yorkers could teach the Canadians a thing or two about courtesy – an allusion to the Orange difficulty. And in comparison with the English, New Yorkers were much more demonstrative. Nevertheless, 'that sound common sense which they inherit from their Anglo-Saxon ancestry preserves them from frivolity and extravagance in their amusement.'

This editorial nicely encapsulates the ways in which, when all was said and done, the leading American journals went about representing their communities in 1860: triumphal in tone, they stressed the positive, downplayed the negative, and generalized sweepingly about national and racial characteristics. America's vitality, self-discipline, and democratic values had been splendidly displayed for all the world to admire. Dissonances such as Major Corcoran's insubordination and the defiant show of Irish-American opposition to royalty were sidelined or ignored. Embarrassments such as late start to the New York procession, which left everyone in the dark, or the dance floor's collapse at the Academy of Music, were conveniently forgotten. Constraints on the freedom of women and racialized minorities to exercise democratic citizenship went unmentioned in a discourse that hid differences in the language of 'crowds,' 'people,' and 'community.' Class and racial hiearchies, which had left the masses outside the Academy of Music to watch the Upper Tendom flaunt their jewels and wealth, were submerged in crowds portrayed as uniformly democratic and Anglo-Saxon. There were no 'Others' within New York, but only 'Others' beyond the nation – in this instance, the Europeans suffering under misrule, the heavily policed English, the discourteous Canadians.

As for British North America, commentators in the provinces and Great Britain preferred to stress the good effects that visit had had in strengthening imperial bonds. The prime minister, Lord Palmerston, told a London audience that the visit would 'cement more closely those ties which ... are long destined to bind together that portion of the queen's dominions and the mother country.' Just back from the tour, Newcastle was much more effusive when he explained to a gathering in Nottingham, England, that no one who had not personally witnessed the enthusiasm of the people could imagine the intensity of the colonists' commitment to the crown and empire. 'The enthusiasm which he saw came from the inmost hearts of all those who displayed it,' he insisted, and 'it was not a mere demonstration of the towns and populous places, but an enthusiasm exhibited in every back street and thinly populated locality.'[45]

In Canada, public commentators looked hopefully to the visit's benefits. One observer pointed to the advantage Canada would have over other 'dependencies of the crown' now that the future monarch had 'seen the country and its people, [become] acquainted with its vast resources and growing prosperity, [and] knows our wishes ... and requirements.' The Toronto *Globe* observed that, now that the prince and the English public had had a chance to get to know Canada better, 'those things which concern us will henceforth be looked upon as of greater importance, more interest will be taken in our welfare, more attention will be paid to our desires.' John A. Macdonald made the same point when speaking in Brantford, Canada West, on 12 November 1860. In addition to being an honour to Canada, he said, the 'visit would be a great and permanent advantage. It had called the attention of the world to the position and prospects of Canada. Our great resources, our magnificent country, would be considered, thought of, called to the attention of the whole civilized world in a manner we had never before known.'[46]

Macdonald, however, balanced this optimism with some sobering remarks about what the world had seen of Canadians. 'It was quite true,' he said, 'that in this world there was no perfect happiness, and we had an instance of it in this case. Although the visit of the Prince of Wales had been a source of great pleasure to the people, it had been accompanied in some respects with disappointment, in some degree with heart burnings, in some degree with mistakes.' Macdonald then discussed the Orange difficulty, explaining the awkward position his government had found itself in when the Duke of Newcastle, as adviser to the prince, had let his priorities as a party politician at Westminister affect his decision making in Canada. By preventing the prince from recognizing and thus lending legitimacy to the Orangemen of Canada, the imperial minister had meddled in local affairs and ignored the essential compromise at the heart of Canadian politics, and thus clumsily upset the delicate balance between French and English, Catholics and Protestants.

Whether or not they agreed with Macdonald's analysis of the causes of the 'heart burnings,' Canadians accepted that the visit's success had been seriously tempered by the Orange troubles and by the various derogatory ways in which journalists had portrayed and explained them. Partisan and religious differences had destroyed the illusion of a contented, united community so carefully crafted by the civic and provincial promoters of the tour. In the pages of the great metropolitan dailies, Canada had appeared as a place riven by class, ethnic, and religious feuds that threatened public peace, as well as provincial progress and prosperity.

In reflecting on these troubles, some commentators, most notably from New York, looked to the confederation of British North America as a way for Canadians to move beyond narrow differences. 'There is so much petty party bickering now in the North American colonies,' declared Cornwallis of the New York *Herald*, 'that the system must be enlarged to avert the catastrophe of its breaking in pieces.' He had found 'a strong popular feeling in the Provinces favorable to ... consolidation.' 'The pride,' he said, 'of having a national name and national character on a wider scale than the present may have much to do with the popular sentiment in favor of such an organization.' An editorial in the New York *Evening Post* pointed out that the combined population of the colonies was 'over four million souls, a million more than the number of American colonists when they declared their independence from Britain.' But it noted, too, that unlike their southern neighbours, the colonists of 1860 were 'proud of their model Queen and, since they have been allowed to govern themselves, of their model government.' What they wished for now was 'to have a national name and a national character.' The New York *Times*, though more sceptical about the likelihood of confederation coming about, nevertheless acknowledged that there might 'be something grand in the idea of a union of the British Provinces under a Vice-Regal chief, whose sway will extend from Labrador to Vancouver's Island, and from the United States boundary to the North Pole.' Of course, these thoughts were in the air in Canada, too, and before long confederation would become a goal of British policy makers (including Newcastle) and then, in 1867, a reality. However inadvertently, the royal visit, and the Orange difficulty that it triggered, played at least a small part in making confederation appear to be more necessary and attractive.[47]

The negative assessments by the international press of British North America are revealing in other ways, too. Local journalists had objected strenuously to depictions of their communities as lacking adequate loyalty, morality, or order. When New Brunswickers, Nova Scotians, and Prince Edward Islanders felt that they had been treated as mere provincials, the local newspapers insisted otherwise, in the process demonstrating an alacrity that belied the critics. When French Canadians saw outsiders exaggerate the significance of a minor skirmish in the Montreal council chamber, or misinterpret the meaning of flying the tricolour flag of 'la civilization,' then they defended themselves vigorously. And when Protestant Upper Canadians read depictions of the Orange imbroglio that showed a misunderstanding of Canadian politics, they leapt to explain themselves. Identities were articulated and sharpened in the process. By contrast, little or no defence was made by these same people when First Nations were depicted and attacked in racist terms by journalists; indeed, the reports of local and international dailies were of a piece when it came to representing indigenous peoples. And when groups of African Canadians sought to present addresses of loyalty and welcome to the prince, they were not only fobbed off by state authorities but almost completely ignored by the press. The visit showed clearly, for anyone who cared to notice, who was in and who was out. It was one thing to be snubbed by the Duke of Newcastle and create an uproar heard in London and New York. It was quite another to be snubbed and face indifference and silence.

Yet the public festivities and the exuberant press reports of them generally underscored the delight and pride that the British North Americans took in living within Britain's glorious empire and being ruled by Queen Victoria. Above all, the visit of her son had been a time for jubilant celebrations that put the provinces' loyalty and progress on show. Even in French Canada, where the conquest of 1759–60 could never be forgotten, the 1860 royal tour was an occasion for expressions of pride and satisfaction: pride in the resilience of the French-Canadian nation and satisfaction with the religious and civil liberties possible within the imperial framework and with the self-government that had been achieved during Victoria's reign. In other communities heavily settled by Loyalists and British immigrants, and with strong, ongoing transatlantic connections, the 1860 royal visit was a time when the Britishness of the North American provinces was powerfully asserted and reinforced. French-Canadian allegiance and British cultural chauvinism were hardly the same thing. The two could collide disastrously, but, as frequently occurred during the Prince of Wales's progress through Canada, they could also run in tandem.

When large crowds in British North American cities cheered as the prince passed through their streets, the press reports took it – as the media did in England during the same period – as evidence of popular support for the monarchy. An heir apparent who honoured British subjects with his presence deserved the support of the people, certainly no less so in colonies that had recently, under Victoria's sceptre, come to enjoy additional constitutional rights with the introduction of responsible government. The press played a vital role in creating a sense of participation in the royal tour. The blanket coverage seemingly of every detail of the prince's progress involved the mass readership of British North American newspapers in the tour. This saturation of the news, along with the persistently positive gloss put on the prince (though not on every aspect of the tour) by all newspapers except the Irish-American ones, made the monarchy more familiar, more easily understood, and more a part of the local scene. In 1860 the royal tour, a tradition hitherto confined to the British Isles, had been extended for the first time to the North American colonies and it largely reproduced the cultural practices of England: effusions of loyalty, civic displays of local pride, media constructions of national belonging. Royal populism gained new ground in 1860. At the same time, the state visit to the British provinces brought 'Canada' and its excited displays of loyalty to the attention of a broad public beyond the colonies. Similarly, Albert Edward's unofficial but triumphal tour of the United States put American national characteristics on public display. The New World encounter with royal spectacle, though not without 'heart burnings,' had been a proud experience for nearly all concerned.

Notes

Introduction

1 New York *Times*, 29 Aug. 1860.
2 Frederick H. Armstrong, 'Rodier, Charles-Séraphin,' *Dictionary of Canadian Biography* vol. 10 (Toronto: University of Toronto Press 1972), 624–6.
3 New York *Times*, 29 Aug. 1860; the Montreal civic address and the prince's reply are reproduced in A British Canadian [Henry James Morgan], *The Tour of H.R.H. the Prince of Wales through British America and the United States* (Montreal: John Lovell 1860), 90–3.
4 Nathaniel Augustus Woods, *The Prince of Wales in Canada and the United States* (London: Bradbury and Evans 1861), 115–16.
5 E.A. Heaman, *The Inglorious Arts of Peace: Exhibitions in Canadian Society during the Nineteenth Century* (Toronto: University of Toronto Press 1999), 91–2.
6 In 1860 many commentators referred to all of British North America as 'Canada.'
7 The standard work on Canada in the period, W.L. Morton's *The Critical Years: The Union of British North America, 1857–1873* (Toronto: McClelland and Stewart 1964) gives the tour less than two pages. Studies focusing on the visit deal with local matters. See Bonnie Huskins, '"A Tale of Two Cities": Boosterism and the Imagination of Community during the Visit of the Prince of Wales to Saint John and Halifax in 1860,' *Urban History Review* 28 (1999): 31–46; Anne MacDermaid, 'The Visit of the Prince of Wales to Kingston in 1860,' *Historic Kingston* 21 (1972): 50–61. For a recent, unpublished study that deals in part and at length with the visit, see Wade Andrew Henry, 'Royal Representation, Ceremony, and Cultural Identity in the Building of the Canadian Nation, 1860–1912' (PhD thesis, University of British Columbia 2001).

8 On Canadian royal visits, see Robert M. Stamp, *Kings, Queens, and Canadians: A Celebration of Canada's Infatuation with the British Royal Family* (Markham, Ont.: Fitzhenry and Whiteside 1987); Tom MacDonnell, *Daylight upon Magic: The Royal Tour of Canada, 1939* (Toronto: Macmillan 1989); Phillip A. Buckner, 'Daylight upon Magic: Deconstructing the Royal Tour of 1901,' paper given at the Boundaries Conference, University of Edinburgh, 1996. Studies of royal tours to other colonies include Jane Connors, 'The 1954 Royal Tour of Australia,' *Australian Historical Studies* 25 (1993): 371–82; Jane Connors, 'Betty Windsor and the Egg of Dukemburg: Men, Women, and the Monarchy in 1954,' *Journal of Australian Studies* 47 (1996) 67–80; Kevin Fewster, 'Politics, Pageantry and Purpose: The 1920 Tour of Australia by the Prince of Wales,' *Labour History* 38 (1980): 59–66; Phillip A. Buckner, 'The Royal Tour of 1901 and the Construction of an Imperial Identity in South Africa,' *South African Historical Journal* 41 (1999): 127–46; Judith Bassett, '"A Thousand Miles of Loyalty": The Royal Tour of 1901,' *New Zealand Journal of History* 21 (1987): 125–38.

9 Alan J. Lee, *The Origins of the Popular Press, 1855–1914* (London: Croom Helm 1976); Paul Rutherford, *A Victorian Authority: The Daily Press in Late Nineteenth-Century Canada* (Toronto: University of Toronto Press 1982); Michael Schudson, *Discovering the News: A Social History of American Newspapers* (New York: Basic 1978); Peter W. Sinnema, *The Dynamics of the Pictured Page: Representing the Nation in the Illustrated London News* (Aldershot, U.K.: Ashgate 1998); James L. Crouthamel, *Bennett's New York Herald and the Rise of the Popular Press* (Syracuse, N.Y.: Syracuse University Press 1989).

10 Much of the detailed coverage of the tour in the French-language newspapers of Lower Canada was cribbed from the English-language press and translated into French. As a result, in this book I have not quoted extensively from these newspapers in the belief that readers of a book in English would prefer to read the quotations in the original English.

11 See *Illustrated London News*; London *Illustrated Times*; *Frank Leslie's Illustrated Newspaper* [New York]; *New-York Illustrated News*.

12 The six books are: Morgan, *Tour of H.R.H.*; Robert Cellem, *Visit of His Royal Highness the Prince of Wales to the British North American Provinces and United States in the Year 1860* (Toronto: Henry Rowsell 1861); Pierre-J.-Olivier Chauveau, J. Lenoir-Rolland, J. Phelan, *The Visit of His Royal Highness, the Prince of Wales to America* (Montreal: Journal of Public Instruction for Lower Canada 1860); Kinahan Cornwallis, *Royalty in the New World: or, the Prince of Wales in America* (New York: Doolady 1860); George D. Engleheart, *Journal of the Progress of H.R.H. the Prince of Wales through British North America and his Visit to the United States, 10th July to 15th November, 1860* (London: privately

printed 1860); Woods, *Prince of Wales*. A more specialized 'instant book' is Duke of Newcastle, ed., *Addresses Presented to H.R.H. the Prince of Wales during His State Visit to British North America, with the Replies Thereto, July, August and September 1860* (London: privately printed 1860). With the exception of the volumes by Engleheart and Newcastle, all the others rely extensively on newspaper materials. Cornwallis's book is a lightly edited compilation of his newspaper columns from the New York *Herald*; Woods's book presents his 'letters' from the *Times*, only slightly expanded and altered.

13 Allan Nevins and Milton Halsey Thomas, ed., *The Diary of George Templeton Strong: The Civil War, 1860–1865*, 4 vols. (New York: Macmillan 1952), vol. 2.
14 Royal Archives (RA), VIC/T 3/51–8 and VIC/Add A3/17–22.
15 RA, VIC/Z 466 and 467.
16 National Archives of Canada (NA), MG 24 A 34, Henry, Duke of Newcastle Papers, reel A-307.
17 Oxford University, Bodleian Library, Acland Family Papers, MS Acland, d.12–13.
18 NA, MG 40–Q40, Sir Henry Wentworth Acland Fonds, 2000809739–200081287.
19 Victor E. Graham and W. McAllister Johnson, *The Royal Tour of France by Charles IX and Catherine de Medici: Festival and Entries, 1564–66* (Toronto: University of Toronto Press 1979); Alexandra F. Johnston and Wim Husken, eds., *Civic Ritual and Drama* (Amsterdam: Rodopi 1997); Edward Muir, *Ritual in Early Modern Europe* (New York: Cambridge University Press 1997); Barbara Wisch and Susan Scott Munshower, eds., *All the World's a Stage: Art and Pageantry in the Renaissance and Baroque* (University Park: University of Pennsylvania Press 1990).
20 Brooks McNamara, *Day of Jubilee: The Great Age of Public Celebrations in New York, 1788–1909* (New Brunswick, N.J.: Rutgers University Press 1997); Susan G. Davis, *Parades and Power: Street Theatre in Nineteenth Century Philadelphia* (Philadelphia: Temple University Press 1985); Mary P. Ryan, *Civic Wars: Democracy and Public Life in the American City during the Nineteenth Century* (Berkeley: University of California Press 1997). On Canada, see especially P.G. Goheen, 'The Ritual of the Streets in Mid-19th-Century Toronto,' *Environment and Planning D: Society and Space* 11 (1993): 127–45; Bonnie Huskins, 'The Ceremonial Space of Women: Public Processions in Victorian Saint John and Halifax,' in Janet Guildford and Suzanne Morton, eds., *Separate Spheres: Women's Worlds in the Nineteenth-Century Maritimes* (Fredericton: Acadiensis Press 1994), 145–59; Craig Heron and Steve Penfold, "The Craftsmen's Spectacle: Labour Day Parades in Canada, the Early Years," *Histoire sociale/Social History* 29 (1996): 357–89.

21 Eric Hobsbawm, 'Introduction: Inventing Traditions,' and David Cannadine, 'The Context, Performance and Meaning of Ritual: The British Monarchy and the "Invention of Tradition," *c.* 1820–1977,' in Eric Hobsbawm and Terence Ranger, eds., *The Invention of Tradition* (Cambridge: Cambridge University Press 1983), 1–14, 101–64.

22 See, for example, Walter L. Arnstein, 'Queen Victoria Opens Parliament: The Disinvention of Tradition,' *Historical Research* 63 (1990): 178–94; Paul S. Fritz, 'The Trade in Death: The Royal Funerals in England, 1685–1830,' *Eighteenth-Century Studies* 15 (1982): 291–316. Cannadine himself has gone on to situate the rituals of modern Britain within wider contexts by studying the 'rituals of royalty' in far-flung traditional societies and by exploring how the English viewed British (and other) royal rituals within their own empire. (See David Cannadine, 'Introduction: Divine Rites of Kings,' in David Cannadine and Simon Price, eds., *Rituals of Royalty: Power and Ceremonial in Traditional Societies* (Cambridge: Cambridge University Press 1987), 1–19; David Cannadine, *Ornamentalism: How the British Saw Their Empire* (London: Allen Lane/Penguin Press 2001).

23 William M. Kuhn, *Democratic Royalism: The Transformation of the British Monarchy, 1861–1914* (London: Macmillan 1996); see also Jeffrey L. Lant, *Insubstantial Pageant: Ceremony and Confusion at Queen Victoria's Court* (London: Hamish Hamilton 1979).

24 Changing understandings of monarchy in Britain are usefully explored in two works by Frank Prochaska, *Royal Bounty: The Making of a Welfare Monarchy* (New Haven, Conn.: Yale University Press 1995); *The Republic of Britain, 1760–2000* (Hammondsworth: Allen Lane/Penguin Press 2000). Canadian studies of the crown include David E. Smith, *The Invisible Crown: The First Principle of Canadian Government* (Toronto: University of Toronto Press 1995); W.L. Morton, *The Canadian Identity,* 2nd ed. (Toronto: University of Toronto Press 1972); Jacques Monet, *The Canadian Crown* (Toronto: Clarke Irwin 1979); Henry, 'Royal Representation, Ceremony, and Cultural Identity'; Victoria R. Smith, 'Constructing Victoria: The Representation of Queen Victoria in England, India, and Canada, 1897–1914' (PhD thesis, Rutgers University 1998).

25 Richard Williams, *The Contentious Crown: Public Discussion of the British Monarchy in the Reign of Queen Victoria* (Aldershot, U.K.: Ashgate 1997).

26 John Plunkett, *Queen Victoria: First Media Monarch* (Oxford: Oxford University Press 2003) 15.

27 On popular constitutionalism more generally, see James Vernon, *Politics and the People: A Study in English Political Culture, c 1815–1867* (Cambridge: Cambridge University Press 1993). Two recent Canadian studies that touch

on this theme for one region are Carol Wilton, *Popular Politics and Political Culture in Upper Canada, 1800–1850* (Montreal and Kingston: McGill-Queen's University Press 2000); and Jeffrey L. McNairn, *The Capacity to Judge: Public Opinion and Deliberative Democracy in Upper Canada, 1791–1854* (Toronto: University of Toronto Press 2000).

28 Linda Colley, *Britons: Forging the Nation, 1707–1837* (New Haven, Conn.: Yale University Press 1992).

29 David Waldstreicher, *In the Midst of Perpetual Fetes: The Making of American Nationalism, 1776–1820* (Chapel Hill: University of North Carolina Press and the Omohundro Institute 1997). See also John Bodnar, *Remaking America: Public Memory, Commemoration and Patriotism in Twentieth Century America* (Princeton, N.J.: Princeton University Press 1992); John R. Gillis, ed., *Commemorations: The Politics of National Identity* (Princeton, N.J.: Princeton University Press 1994).

30 H.V. Nelles, *The Art of Nation-Building: Pageantry and Spectacle at Quebec's Tercentenary* (Toronto: University of Toronto Press 1999).

31 See, for example, Ronald Rudin, *Founding Fathers: The Celebration of Champlain and Laval in the Streets of Quebec, 1878–1908* (Toronto: University of Toronto Press 2003); Colin M. Coates and Cecilia Morgan, *Heroines and History: Representations of Madeleine de Verchères and Laura Secord* (Toronto: University of Toronto Press 2002); Alan Gordon, *Making Public Pasts: The Contested Terrain of Montreal's Public Memories, 1891–1930* (Montreal and Kingston: McGill-Queen's University Press 2001); C.J. Taylor, *Negotiating the Past: The Making of Canada's National Historic Parks and Sites* (Montreal and Kingston: McGill-Queen's University Press 1990); Peter E. Pope, *The Many Landfalls of John Cabot* (Toronto: University of Toronto Press 1997); Jacques Mathieu and Jacques Lacoursière, *Les Mémoires Québecoises* (Quebec: Les Presses de l'Université Laval 1991); Norman Knowles, *Inventing the Loyalists: The Ontario Loyalist Tradition and the Creation of Usable Pasts* (Toronto: University of Toronto Press 1997).

32 Benedict Anderson, *Imagined Communities: Reflections on the Origin and Spread of Nationalism*, rev. ed. (London: Verso 1991).

33 An important overview of the literature is Phillip A. Buckner, 'Whatever Happened to the British Empire?' *Journal of the Canadian Historical Association* 4 (1993): 3–32.

34 Catherine Hall, *Civilizing Subjects: Metropole and Colony in the English Imagination, 1820–1867* (Chicago: University of Chicago Press 2002). For another impressive example of the new imperial history, see Linda Colley, *Captives: Britain, Empire and the World, 1600–1850* (London: Jonathan Cape 2002).

Chapter 1: Proposal, Planning, and Players

1 The idea that Great Britain enjoyed an 'age of equipoise' during the mid-Victorian years has been both reasserted and complicated by recent historiography; see especially Martin Hewitt, ed., *An Age of Equipoise? Reassessing Mid-Victorian Britain* (Aldershot: Ashgate 2000); K. Theodore Hoppen, *The Mid-Victorian Generation, 1846–1886* (Oxford: Clarendon Press 1998). See also Neville Kirk, *Change, Continuity, and Class: Labour in British Society, 1850–1920* (Manchester and New York: Manchester University Press 1998). In Canadian history, the mid-Victorian years lie between the rebellion era of 1837–8 and the troubled years of industrialization and western expansion in the immediate post-Confederation decades.

2 Sir Sidney Lee, *King Edward VII: A Biography*, 2 vols. (London: Macmillan 1925), 1:85. During the Crimean War, offers of assistance had come to the British government from various of the British North American colonies, where militia units or newly recruited volunteers were prepared to take the place of garrisoned regulars sent for duty elsewhere. (J. Mackay Hitsman, *Safeguarding Canada, 1763–1871* [Toronto: University of Toronto Press 1968], 156–9.) Raising troops in Canada for the British army was considered at the same time, but it was not until the Indian Mutiny in 1857 that a regiment (the Royal Canadians) was actually raised; even it was organized, equipped, and paid at English expense. See C.P. Stacey, *Canada and the British Army, 1846–1871: A Study in the Practice of Responsible Government*, rev. ed. (Toronto: University of Toronto Press 1963), 96–106.

3 On mid-Victorian imperialism and 'Little Englandism,' see A.G.L. Shaw, ed., *Great Britain and the Colonies, 1815–1865* (London: Methuen 1970); Ronald Hyam and Ged Martin, *Reappraisals in British Imperial History* (Toronto: Macmillan 1975), 91–106; P.J. Cain and A.G. Hopkins, *British Imperialism: Innovation and Expansion, 1688–1914* (London: Longman 1993); William P. Morrell, *British Colonial Policy in the Mid-Victorian Age* (Oxford: Oxford University Press 1969); Ronald Hyam, *Britain's Imperial Century, 1815–1914: A Study of Empire and Expansion*, 3rd ed. (New York: Palgrave Macmillan 2002).

4 On the relative political stability of mid-century Canada, see Jacques Monet, *The Last Cannon Shot: A Study of French-Canadian Nationalism, 1837–1850* (Toronto: University of Toronto Press 1969); J.M.S. Careless, *The Union of the Canadas: The Growth of Canadian Institutions, 1841–1857* (Toronto: McClelland and Stewart 1967); W.L. Morton, *The Critical Years: The Union of British North America, 1857–1873* (Toronto: McClelland and Stewart 1964); Allan Greer and Ian Radforth, eds., *Colonial Leviathan: State Formation in*

Mid-Nineteenth Century Canada (Toronto: University of Toronto Press 1992).

5 Hostile remarks are cited by Cecilia Morgan, *Public Men and Virtuous Women: The Gendered Languages of Religion and Politics in Upper Canada, 1791–1850* (Toronto: University of Toronto Press 1996), 89–90; Allan Greer, *The Patriots and the People: The Rebellion of 1837 in Rural Lower Canada* (Toronto: University of Toronto Press 1993), 190–7. On republicanism in the period after the visit, see Henry A. Wade, 'Severing the Imperial Tie? Republicanism and British Identity in English Canada, 1864–1917,' in Colin M. Coates, ed., *Imperial Canada, 1867–1917: A Selection of Papers Given at the University of Edinburgh's Centre of Canadian Studies Conference - May 1995* (Edinburgh: University of Edinburgh, Centre of Canadians Studies 1997), 177–86.

6 John Gustavus Norris, *Mr J.G. Norris and the Visit to Canada of H.R.H. the Prince of Wales* (Ottawa: privately printed 1876). Published on the occasion of the Prince of Wales's visit to India, Norris's pamphlet gives an outline and relevant documents regarding his role in the 1858 invitation.

7 The views of the Toronto *Leader* and Toronto *Colonist* are reflected in the critical account in A British Canadian [Henry James Morgan], *The Tour of H.R.H. the Prince of Wales through British America and the United States* (Montreal: John Lovell 1860). Morgan later apologized for his 'share in the general crusade against [Norris],' believing after learning more of the incident that Norris had been 'somewhat unfairly judged by the public.' See Henry James Morgan, *The Visit of the Prince of Wales to Canada in 1860: Mr. Morgan's Reply to 'Observer' in Full* (Toronto: Privately printed 1888).

8 'Resolution of the Common Council of the City of Toronto,' 6 Dec. 1858, in Morgan, *Visit of the Prince of Wales*, 22.

9 Ibid., 9–12, 14.

10 Cartier's fondness for the culture and society of England's upper class is best documented in Brian Young, *George-Étienne Cartier: Montreal Bourgeois* (Kingston and Montreal: McGill-Queen's University Press 1981), 45–8.

11 J.-C. Bonenfant, 'Cartier, Sir George-Étienne,' *Dictionary of Canadian Biography*, vol. 10 (Toronto: University of Toronto Press 1972), 142–52, quotation at 145.

12 Alastair Sweeny, *George-Étienne Cartier* (Toronto: McClelland and Stewart 1976), 122.

13 For context, see Bruce W. Hodgins, 'The Attitudes of the Canadian Founders toward Britain and the British Connection: A Personal Re-examination,' in Coates, ed., *Imperial Canada*.

14 Morgan, *Tour of H.R.H.* 14.

15 Michael Bliss, *Right Honourable Men: The Descent of Canadian Politics from Macdonald to Mulroney* (Toronto: Harper Collins 1994), 8–9. See also Donald Creighton, *John A. Macdonald: The Young Politician* (Toronto: Macmillan 1952).

16 J.M.S. Careless, *Brown of the Globe*, 2 vols. (Toronto: Macmillan 1959); J.M.S. Careless, *The Pre-Confederation Premiers: Ontario Government Leaders, 1841–1867* (Toronto: Ontario Historical Studies Series and the University of Toronto Press 1980); W.L. Morton, *The Critical Years: The Union of British North America, 1857–1873* (Toronto: McClelland and Stewart 1964); Christopher Moore, *1867: How the Fathers Made a Deal* (Toronto: McClelland and Stewart 1997).

17 'Address to the Queen's Most Excellent Majesty,' in Morgan, *Tour of H.R.H.* 14.

18 The complications in handling Smith are documented in National Archives of Canada (NA), MG 24 A 34, Henry, Duke of Newcastle Papers, reel A-1610, Correspondence with Governors, June 1859–Dec. 1860, Newcastle to Sir Edmund Head, 29 July 1859 (private); Toronto *Globe*, 15 March 1860; Donald Swainson, 'Smith, Sir Henry,' *Dictionary of Canadian Biography* vol. 9 (Toronto: University of Toronto Press 1976), 725–6; Newcastle's words are cited by Lee, *King Edward VII*, vol. 1, 83.

19 NA, Newcastle Papers, reel A-307, Newcastle Letterbooks, Newcastle to the Duke of Cambridge, 21 Oct. 1859.

20 NA, Newcastle Papers, reel A-1610, Newcastle to Head, 9 Aug. 1859 (private). At the time Rose was deeply involved with the teetering finances of the Grand Trunk Railway (GTR). Had it gone bankrupt, it would have been embarrassing for the Conservative ministry in Canada, and all the more so if the bankruptcy had occurred at the time of a royal visit that featured the GTR's Victoria Bridge. As it turned out, just as the prince was leaving North America, the GTR's latest financial embarrassment was publicly announced. The New York *Times* noted the irony of the timing and mocked Canadian extravagance in an editorial entitled, 'A Royal Funeral' (16 Oct. 1860).

21 Morgan, *Tour of H.R.H.*, 15–16.

22 Stanley Triggs et al., *Victoria Bridge: The Vital Link* (Montreal: McCord Museum 1992).

23 Richard Williams, *The Contentious Crown: Public Discussion of the British Monarchy in the Reign of Queen Victoria* (Aldershot, U.K.: Ashgate 1997), 196–7.

24 John Plunkett, *Queen Victoria: First Media Monarch* (Oxford: Oxford University Press 2003), 45.

25 *Journals of the Legislative Assembly of the Province of Canada*, 28 Feb. 1860, citing the speech of the governor.
26 London *Times*, 20 and 26 March 1860.
27 NA, Newcastle Papers, reel A-1610, Newcastle to Dundas, Mulgrave, and Manners-Sutton, 9 March 1860, and to Bannerman, 10 March 1860.
28 W.S. MacNutt, *New Brunswick: A History, 1784–1867* (Toronto: Macmillan 1963), 376–7.
29 Fredericton, *Reporter*, 30 March 1860.
30 NA, Newcastle Papers, reel A-1610, Newcastle to Head, 17 Feb. 1860.
31 Royal Archives (RA), VIC/Z 466/11, Sir Edmund Head to the Duke of Newcastle, 10 March 1860.
32 Kinley E. Roby, *The King, the Press and the People: A Study of Edward VII* (London: Barrie and Jenkins 1975), 58.
33 NA, Newcastle Papers, reel A-1610, Newcastle to Head, 13 June 1860 (private); see also copies of Head's letters and memoranda to Newcastle (February and March 1860) in RA, VIC/Z 466/10, 11, 12.
34 RA, VIC/Z 466/4, Duke of Somerset to Prince Albert, 8 March 1860; VIC/Z 466/6 Prince Albert to the Duke of Somerset, 10 March 1860.
35 NA, Newcastle Papers, reel A-1610, Newcastle to Head, 28 April 1860 and 13 June 1860.
36 Andrée Desilets, 'Taché, Sir Étienne-Paschal,' and Peter Baskerville, 'MacNab, Sir Allan Napier,' *Dictionary of Canadian Biography* vol. 9 (Toronto: University of Toronto Press 1976), 519–27, 774–8.
37 NA, Newcastle Papers, reel A-1610, Newcastle to Head, 13 June 1860.
38 NA, Colonial Office Records, CO 42/624 contains considerable correspondence about this matter, including denials from the French government that it was behind Boilleau's manoeuvres.
39 In 1855 the Commandant de Belvèze, the captain of *La Capricieuse*, had made his own 'princely progress' through Canada, delivering over fifty speeches and being greeted by throngs of French Canadians. The visit ended the century of isolation between France and Canada. Even though it occurred at the height of the French-British alliance during the Crimean War, the excitement caused by Belvèze led London to protest to Paris. See Mason Wade, *The French Canadians, 1760–1967*, 2 vols. (Toronto: Macmillan 1968), 1:297–302; Jacques Portes, '*La Capricieuse* au Canada en 1855,' *Revue d'Histoire de l'Amérique Française* 31 (December 1977): 351–70; Eveline Bossé, *La Capricieuse à Québec en 1855* (Montreal: La Presse 1984).
40 NA, France, Ministère des Affaires Étrangères, correspondance consulaire politique, Angleterre, vol. 35; a series of despatches from G. Boilleau, French consul at Quebec, to M. Thouvenel in Paris (microfilm).

41 CO 42/625, George Arbuthnot to Newcastle, 20 January 1860.

42 CO 42/625, George Arbuthnot to G.A. Hamilton, 24 March 1860.

43 On criticisms of the 1875 tour amid the anti-monarchism of the 1870s, see Antony Taylor, 'Republicanism Reappraised: Anti-monarchism and the English Radical Tradition, 1850–1872,' in James Vernon, ed., *Re-reading the Constitution: New Narratives in the Political History of England's Long Nineteenth Century* (Cambridge: Cambridge University Press 1996), 177.

44 CO 42/625, T.F.E. to George Arbuthnot, 11 April 1860; George Arbuthnot to Newcastle, 20 April 1860; copy of treasury minute, 30 June 1860; NA, Newcastle Papers, reel A-1927, copy of W.E. Gladstone to Lord Palmerston, 22 Dec. 1859.

45 John A. Macdonald emphasized these points, and cited references, in a speech he gave on 12 Nov. 1860. See Toronto *Globe*, 13 Nov. 1860.

46 David M.L. Farr, 'Rose, Sir John,' *Dictionary of Canadian Biography*, vol. 9 (Toronto: University of Toronto Press 1982), 766–72.

47 NA, MG 29 E 1 (F46), Thomas Wily Papers, Thomas Wily, 'A Reminiscence of the Visit of the Prince of Wales to Canada in 1860.' Details of his work can also be found in NA, RG 11, Public Works, vol. 771, the outgoing correspondence of the Department of Public Works for 1860.

48 Railway companies were paid at the rate of $3 per mile for royal trains. (See NA, RG 11, vol. 771, T. Trudeau to Covert and Fowler, Cobourg, 31 Oct. 1860.) Kirwin charged at the rate of $8 per horse per day and was eventually paid a total of $1,618.25 for his services. (NA, RG 11, vol. 771, T. Trudeau to W. Kirwin, 5 Dec. 1860.)

49 Letter from Dr Henry Acland, cited in J.B. Atlay, *Sir Henry Wentworth Acland, Bart.* (London: Smith, Elder 1903), 277.

50 In 1857 the five-storey Rossin House had been opened by Marcus and Samuel Rossin, members of the city's fledgling Jewish community. (See William Denby and William Kilbourn, *Toronto Observed: Its Architecture, Patrons, and History* [Toronto: Oxford University Press 1986], 157.) Until his death in a railway accident in 1857, Samuel Zimmerman was a prominent businessman with extensive interests in land, transportation projects, and banking. (See, J.K. Johnson, 'Zimmerman, Samuel,' *Dictionary of Canadian Biography*, vol. 8 [Toronto: University of Toronto Press 1985], 963–7.) Richard Juson, a hardware merchant and nail manufacturer, owned one of Hamilton's best estates, located at the bottom of the escarpment not far from the centre of town. (See John C. Weaver, *Hamilton: An Illustrated History* [Toronto: Lorimer 1982], 60.)

51 NA, RG 1, Canada State Books (Minutes of the Executive Council), vol. 5, reel C-119, 22 May 1860, 166–7.

52 Toronto *Globe*, 6 Aug. 1860, reproduces Rose's letter to Buchanan, dated 31 July 1860.
53 Toronto *Globe*, 15 Aug. 1860.
54 Letter of Dr Henry Acland, cited in Atlay, *Sir Henry Wentworth Acland*, 275.
55 Toronto *Globe*, 26 July and 16 Aug. 1860.
56 NA, RG 11, vol. 771, T. Trudeau to Sharpee and Company. Pall Mall, London, England, 22 June 1860.
57 Wily, 'Reminiscence,' 271. The Shiners were Irish shantymen who for class, ethnic, and political reasons and in the context of weak institutions of authority, had earlier disturbed the peace of Ottawa; see Michael S. Cross, 'The Shiners' War: Social Violence in the Ottawa Valley in the 1830s,' *Canadian Historical Review* 54 (1973): 1–26. Various letters and records relating to security in the John A. Macdonald Papers and in the records of the Dominion Police in the National Archives are silent on security for the 1860 visit. At the end of the tour, an official at the Department of Public Works sent E.J. Causesoll of Montreal $100 for distribution among 'Sergeant McLauglin and the four men of the Government Police Force, who accompanied H.R.H. throughout Canada.' The letter acknowledged Commissioner John Rose's 'very high appreciation ... of the manner in which their arduous duties were performed,' and he thanked them for the 'readiness which they evinced in aiding to keep order.' (NA, RG 11, Public Works Records, outgoing correspondence, 1860, vol. 771, T. Trudeau to E.J.Causesoll, 8 Oct. 1860.)
58 Plunkett, *Queen Victoria*, 44.
59 Roby, *The King, the Press and the People*, 18–55.
60 Plunkett, *Queen Victoria* 13–67.
61 Williams, *Contentious Crown*, 10–30; Frank Prochaska, *The Republic of Britain 1760–2000* (London: Allen Lane 2000), 65–97; Margaret Homans, *Royal Representations: Queen Victoria and British Culture, 1837–1867* (Chicago: University of Chicago Press 1998).
62 Williams, *Contentious Crown*, 200.
63 Biographical information is drawn especially from Lee, *King Edward VII*, vol. 2; Philip Magnus, *King Edward the Seventh* (London: John Murray 1964); Giles St Aubyn, *Edward VII: Prince and King* (New York: Atheneum 1979). The prince's first public engagement was the laying of the foundation stone for a school of art at Lambeth, England, in June 1860, shortly before his departure for Canada.
64 Magnus, *King Edward*, 27.
65 The prince consort to the Princess Royal, 17 Nov. 1858 cited by Magnus, *King Edward*, 27.
66 Biographical details are drawn from F. Darrell Munsell, *The Unfortunate*

Duke: Henry Pelham, Fifth Duke of Newcastle, 1811–1864 (Columbia: University of Missouri Press 1985); assessments of the fifth duke's abilities are noted at 2–3 and 284–8.

67 James A. Gibson, 'The Duke of Newcastle and British North American Affairs, 1855–64,' *Canadian Historical Review* 44 (1963): 142–56.

68 Kinahan Cornwallis, *Royalty in the New World; or the Prince of Wales in America* (New York: M. Doolady 1860), 276; Oxford University, Bodleian Library, MS ADD d.12, Acland Family Papers, Henry Acland to Sarah Acland, 5 Aug. 1860.

69 Cornwallis, *Royalty in the New World*, 278.

70 Ibid., 277–8.

71 The original letters, carefully preserved by the family, survive in tact in the Acland Family Papers (MS Acland, d.12, d.13, d.91, especially) at the Bodleian Library, Oxford University. Much of the correspondence is also available on microfilm in NA, Sir Henry Acland Fonds, MG 40 Q40; the original drawings and paintings are in this collection.

72 Cornwallis, *Royalty in the New World*, 279; Lee, *King Edward VII*, 1:58, 154–6.

73 Lee, *King Edward VII*, 1:87.

74 Mrs Steuart Erskine, ed., *Memoirs of Edward, Earl of Sandwich, 1839–1916* (London: J. Murray 1919).

75 Woods, who has been described as 'the best of descriptive reporters,' had recently covered the Crimean War, the opening of Covent Garden Opera House and the Westminster Clock Tower, and the maiden voyage of the *Great Eastern*. (See *The History of the Times, vol. 2, The Tradition Established, 1841–1884* [London: *The Times* 1939].) The *Times*'s famous editor, John Delane, called Woods 'a very pleasant fellow' who had done 'whole reams' of 'good work.' (See John Delane to John Rose, 12 June 1860, in Arthur Irwin Dasent, *John Thadeus Delane, Editor of The Times*, vol. 2 [New York: Scribners 1908], 9.)

76 Another applicant for the same privileges was denied them. See NA, RG7 G23 vol. 1, Arthur Harvey (of the New York *Times*) to Governor Head, 18 July 1860, and accompanying draft reply.

77 Plunkett, *Queen Victoria*, 218–19.

78 On the illustrated press, see Plunkett, *Queen Victoria*; Peter W. Sinnema, *Dynamics of the Pictured Page: Representing the Nation in the Illustrated London Ne* (Aldershot: Ashgate 1998); Mason Jackson, *The Pictorial Press: Its Origins and Progress* (London: Hurst and Blackett 1885); Paul Hogarth, *Artist as Reporter* (London: Gordon Fraser Gallery 1986). Art was more important than photography in the visual record of the 1860 tour, but only two years

later, when the Prince of Wales toured the Near East, a photographer was officially attached to the royal party.

79 Oxford University, Bodleian Library, Acland Family Papers, MS Acland d.12, Henry Acland to Sarah Acland, 8 July 1860.

80 Ibid., 9 July 1860.

81 Robert Cellem, *Visit of His Royal Highness, the Prince of Wales to the British North American Provinces and United States, in the Year 1860* (Toronto: Henry Rowsell 1861), 9–10, reproduces a newspaper account, and the story is retold in Morgan, *Tour of H.R.H.*

82 As cited in the Halifax *Constitutionalist*, 2 Aug 1860.

83 Toronto *Globe*, 26 July 1860.

84 Acland Family Papers, Henry Acland to Sarah Acland, 10 July 1860.

85 Cornwallis, *Royalty in the New World*, 51. Note, however, that in the later-life recollection of a midshipman aboard the *Hero*, the cabins for the prince's use were 'lined with a pretty pattern of chintz picked out by the Queen.' (Lieut. Thomas Bunbury Gough, *Boyish Reminiscences of His Majesty the King's Visit to Canada in 1860* [London: John Murray 1910], 6.)

86 Inserted in Lee, *King Edward VII* I, at 89.

87 RA, VIC/T 3/52, 'Bertie' [the Prince of Wales] to 'Mama' [Queen Victoria], 24 July 1860; RA, VIC/Z 466/44, General Bruce to Prince Albert, 22 July 1860; Acland Family Papers, Henry Acland to Sarah Acland, 15 July 1860.

88 RA, Vic/Z 466/44, General Bruce to Prince Albert, 22 July 1860; Gough, *Boyish Reminiscences*, 101–4.

89 Acland Family Papers, Henry Acland to Sarah Acland, 15 July 1860; RA, Vic/Z 467/16, extract of letter from Miss Catherine Sinclair, 19 Aug. 1860; Gough, *Boyish Reminiscences*, tells of the prince's boyish fun, though, as the former midshipman tells it, the prince got his dowsing at his birthday dinner on the homeward journey (209–15).

90 Cornwallis, *Royalty in the New World*, 47.

91 Public Archives of New Brunswick, MG 6/34, Diary of George F. Hill, 2 Aug. 1860. George Hill, a visitor from Maine, talked with the sailors when he went to see the celebrations welcoming the prince to Saint John.

92 London *Times*, 24 July 1860.

93 Prince Albert to Baron Stockmar, 27 April 1860, cited by Theodore Martin, *The Life of His Royal Highness the Prince Consort*, 5 vols. (London: Smith Elder 1880), 5:15–16.

94 London *Herald*, 29 June 1860, and London *Chronicle*, 29 June 1860, both reprinted in Toronto *Globe*, 16 July 1860.

95 Williams, *Contentious Crown*, 93–117. As Williams notes, however, Queen

Victoria actually continued behind-the-scenes to intervene frequently in political affairs and to hold pronounced partisan views.

96 Liverpool *Post*, 11 July 1860, reprinted in Toronto *Globe*, 28 July 1860.

97 London *Saturday Review*, reprinted in Toronto *Globe*, 26 July 1860.

Chapter 2: Fit for a Prince

1 Ottawa *Citizen*, 24 July and 1 Sept. 1860.

2 Bonnie Huskins, '"A Tale of Two Cities": Boosterism and the Imagination of Community during the Visit of the Prince of Wales to Saint John and Halifax in 1860,' *Urban History Review* 28 (October 1999): 31–46.

3 Toronto *Globe*, 2 June 1860; names included: George Brown, William Allan, Henry Draper, William H. Boulton, John Hillyard Cameron, F.W. Cumberland, William B. Jarvis, William McMaster, and Sandford Fleming.

4 Toronto *Leader* and Toronto *Globe*, 7 June 1860.

5 Ibid., 21 June 1860.

6 Ibid., 29 June 1860.

7 *Minutes of the Council of the Corporation of the City of Toronto for 1860* (Toronto: 1861), app. no. 178, 'Final Report of the Standing Committee of Public Walks and Gardens for the year 1860,' 372–3; and app. no. 179, 'Final Report of the Standing Committee on Wharves, Harbors, etc.,' 373–4; City of Toronto Archives, 'Minutes of the Toronto Board of Works,' 2 Aug. 1860, 'Report of A. Brunet, City Engineer,' 7 Sept. 1860.

8 City of Toronto Archives, 'Minutes of the Toronto Board of Works,' 7 Sept. 1860; *Minutes of the Council of the Corporation of the City of Toronto for 1860*, app. no. 140.

9 London *Times*, reprinted in *Globe*, 11 Sept. 1860.

10 Montreal *Pilot*, 21 Aug. 1860.

11 Toronto *Globe*, 10 Aug. 1860 regarding Halifax.

12 Robert Cellem, *Visit of His Royal Highness the Prince of Wales to the British North American Provinces and United States in the Year 1860* (Toronto: H. Rowsell 1861), 154–5.

13 Nathaniel Augustus Woods, *The Prince of Wales in Canada and the United States* (London: Bradbury and Evans 1816), 94.

14 Saint John *Morning News*, 23 July and 1 Aug. 1860; Fredericton *New Brunswick Reporter*, 10 Aug. 1860; Halifax *Acadian Recorder*, 4 Aug. 1860.

15 Barrie *Northern Advance*, 5 Sept. 1860.

16 Toronto *Globe*, 4 Aug. 1860.

17 Ottawa *Citizen*, 25 Aug. 1860.

18 Woods, *Prince of Wales*, 17.

19 Port Hope *Guide*, reprinted in *Globe*, 13 Sept. 1860.
20 Woods, *Prince of Wales*, 112. See Colleen Skidmore, '*Concordia Salus*: Triumphal Arches at Montreal, 1860,' *Journal of Canadian Art History* 19 (1998): 85–109.
21 Fredericton *New Brunswick Reporter*, 17 Aug. 1860; New York *Tribune*, 23 Aug. 1860.
22 Woods, *Prince of Wales*, 67.
23 Cellem, *Visit of HRH*, 155–6.
24 Halifax *Constitutionalist*, 2 Aug. 1860; Cellem *Visit of HRH*, 257.
25 Cellem, *Visit of HRH*,109; Halifax *Constitutionalist*, 2 Aug. 1860.
26 Cellem, *Visit of HRH*, 304; no further details given or comment made.
27 Ottawa *Citizen*, 18 Aug. 1860.
28 Woods, *Prince of Wales*, 162; Toronto *Globe*, 4 Sept. 1860; Ottawa *Citizen*, 1 Sept. 1860; Ottawa *Union*, 29 Aug. 1860.
29 *New Brunswick Reporter*, 17 Aug. 1860; Barrie *Northern Advance*, 26 Sept. 1860.
30 Mark Francis, *Governors and Settlers: Images of Authority in the British Colonies, 1820–60* (London: Macmillan 1992), 34. For some examples of arches built later in Canada, see Chuen-yan David Lai, *Arches in British Columbia* (Victoria, B.C.: Sono Nis Press 1982). Arches were also built as part of the Corpus Christi processions in Montreal; see Christine Sheito, 'Une fête contestée: la procession de la Fête-Dieu à Montréal au XIXe siècle' (MA thesis, Université de Montréal 1983).
31 Karen Stanworth, 'Rhetoric, Ritual, and the Fashioning of Public Memory in Washington's America,' *Histoire sociale/Social History* 29 (1996): 311–31; David Waldstreicher, *In the Midst of Perpetual Fetes: The Making of American Nationalism, 1776–1820* (Chapel Hill: University of North Carolina Press and the Omohundro Institute 1997), 120.
32 M. James, 'Ritual, Drama and the Social Body in the Late Medieval English Town,' *Past and Present* 98 (1983): 3–29; John Prebble, *The King's Jaunt: George IV in Scotland, August 1822* (London: Collins 1988).
33 Roy Strong, *Art and Power: Renaissance Festivals, 1450–1650* (Berkeley: University of California Press 1984).
34 Lawrence Bryant, *The King and the City in the Parisian Royal Entry Ceremony: Politics, Ritual, and Art in the Renaissance* (Geneva: Librairie Droz 1986).
35 Michael McCormick, *Eternal Victory: Triumphal Rulership in Late Antiquity, Byzantium, and the Early Medieval West* (Cambridge: Cambridge University Press 1986).
36 Toronto *Leader*, 16 June 1860.
37 Francis, *Governors and Settlers*.

38 Royal Archives (RA), VIC/Z 466/37, Newcastle to Prince Albert, 4 July 1860.
39 Archives of Ontario, MS 4, John Beverley Robinson Papers, reel 6, minutes of meeting, 7 July 1860, Rossin House, Toronto.
40 Montreal *L'Ordre*, 18 July 1860.
41 Halifax, *Acadian Recorder*, 7 July 1860; see also 26 July and 4 Aug. 1860.
42 National Archives of Canada (NA), RG 7 G23, vol. 1. Trade unionism in Canada was in its infancy, which may account for the weak response. It is also possible that unions did not take up the opportunity because they did not see it as part of their purview, just as almost no businessmen drafted addresses on behalf of their firms.
43 Toronto *Globe*, reprinted in *Head Quarters*, 6 June 1860; Toronto *Leader*, 16 June 1860; Fredericton *Headquarters*, 4 July 1860; Saint John *Morning News*, 15 June 1860; *New Brunswicker*, reprinted in *Acadian Recorder*, 25 Aug. 1860.
44 Toronto *Globe*, 3 Aug. 1860.
45 Michael Wayne, 'The Black Population of Canada West on the Eve of the American Civil War: A Reassessment Based on the Manuscript Census of 1861,' in Franca Iacovetta with Paula Draper and Robert Ventresca, eds., *A Nation of Immigrants: Women, Workers, and Communities in Canadian History, 1840s-1960s* (Toronto: University of Toronto Press 1998), 58–81.
46 'Resolutions of a Convention of Colored People Assembled in Toronto, 3 Aug. 1860,' in Toronto *Globe*, 11 Aug. 1860; NA, RG 7 G23, vol. 1, 'Petition of Queen's Subjects Residing on the Elgin Settlement at Buxton,' signed 20 Aug. 1860 by the Rev. William King, Samuel Burrill, Rev Thomas W. Stronger, Thomas Scott, H.K. Thomas, James J. Rapier [sp?]. On Buxton, see Howard Law, '"Self-Reliance Is the True Road to Independence": Ideology and the Ex-Slaves in Buxton and Chatham,' in Iacovetta, *Nation of Immigrants*, 82–100.
47 NA, RG 7 G23, vol. 1.
48 Ibid., draft of reply from the governor general to A.R. Green, 8 Sept. 1860, and undated draft in reply to Sam Gale's letter of 25 Aug. 1860.
49 Toronto *Leader*, 13 Oct. 1860.
50 On black newspapers, see Jane Rhodes, *Mary Ann Shadd Cary: The Black Press and Protest in the Nineteenth Century* (Bloomington: University of Indiana Press 1998).
51 Woods, *Prince of Wales* 13.
52 Toronto *Globe*, 5 Sept. 1860; Saint John *Morning Freeman*, 2 Aug. 1860; St Lawrence Hall advertisement, clipping in the collection of Mr Norman Shelman, Toronto.
53 Toronto *Globe*, 3 and 5 Aug. 1860.

54 Saint John *Morning Freeman*, 31 July and 2 Aug. 1860.

55 Tori Smith, '"Almost Pathetic ... But Also Very Glorious": The Consumer Spectacle of the Diamond Jubilee,' *Histoire sociale/Social History* 29 (1996): 333–56.

56 Toronto *Globe*, 10 Aug. 1860.

57 Alfred Sandham, *Medals Commemorative of the Visit of H.R.H. the Prince of Wales to Montreal in 1860* (Montreal: privately printed 1871). The Hoffnung medal had on one side a view of Victoria Bridge, with an inscription reading 'the Greatest work of engineering skill in the world, publicly inaugurated and opened in 1860'; on the other side appeared 'the arms of the city, surmounted by a beaver, with an Indian on each side, the whole supported by a lion.'

58 Smith, '"Almost Pathetic,"' 335–6; Woods, *Prince of Wales*, 13.

59 David Cressy, *Bonfires and Bells: National Memory and the Protestant Calendar in Elizabethan and Stuart England* (London: Weidenfeld and Nicolson 1989), 18–24.

60 For a cultural historian's treatment of illuminations in the electrical age, see Keith Walden, *Becoming Modern in Toronto: The Industrial Exhibition and the Shaping of a Late Victorian Culture* (Toronto: University of Toronto Press 1997), 304–11.

61 Toronto *Globe*, 7 Aug. 1860.

62 Quebec *Mercury*, 7 July 1860.

63 The Canadian government issued instructions to keepers of government buildings for the night of illuminations. At least one 'steady and reliable person' was continually to check for hazards and flames and to ensure that a hose, axes, and water buckets were on hand. See 'Instructions to House Keepers and Guardians of Government and Public Buildings,' printed flyer in NA, RG 11, Public Works, vol. 711, T. Trudeau to Sippell, 22 Aug. 1860.

64 Toronto *Globe*, 7 Aug. and 8 Sept. 1860.

65 Ottawa *Citizen*, 25 Aug. 1860.

66 Toronto *Globe*, 29 Aug. 1860; Law Society of Upper Canada Archives, 19–3–1, General Journal, 1858–78, entries for 4 and 13 Sept. 1860.

67 NA, RG 7 G14, vol. 25, J. Rose to Sir Fenwick Williams, 10 Nov. 1860.

68 Ottawa *Citizen*, 22 Sept. 1860.

69 Ibid.

70 Ottawa *Citizen*, 8 Sept. 1860; Ottawa *Union*, 5 Sept. 1860.

71 Detailed descriptions of illuminations appear in Toronto *Globe*, 8 and 11 Sept. 1860.

72 Mary Ryan, *Women in Public: Between Banners and Ballots, 1835–1880* (Baltimore, Md.: Johns Hopkins University Press 1991).

73 Edwin C. Guillet, *Cobourg – 1798–1948* (Cobourg: privately printed 1948), 44.
74 Port Hope *Guide*, reprinted in *Globe*, 13 Sept. 1860.
75 Toronto *Globe*, 28 July 1860.
76 Cellem, *Visit of HRH*, 28.
77 Ibid. 29.
78 Oxford University, Bodleian Library, Acland Family Papers, MS Add. d.12, Henry Acland to Sarah Acland, 21 July 1860.

Chapter 3: Right Royal Welcome

1 Toronto *Globe*, 9 Aug. 1860, reprinted in Robert Cellem, *Visit of His Royal Highness the Prince of Wales to the British North American Provinces and United States in the Year 1860* (Toronto: Henry Rowsell 1861), 30–9.
2 New York *Herald* account, reprinted in Kinahan Cornwallis, *Royalty in the New World; or, the Prince of Wales in America* (New York: M. Doolady 1860), 18–25.
3 Toronto *Globe*, 9 Aug. 1860; New York *Herald* report in Cornwallis, *Royalty in the New World*, 19, 21.
4 St John's *Newfoundland Express*, 7 Aug. 1860.
5 Royal Archives (RA), VIC/Z 467/15a, Extract of letter enclosed in RA, VIC/Z 467/15 Lady Hardwicke to the queen, 27 Aug. 1860. Lady Hardwicke describes the author only as 'the wife of the Archdeacon' at St John's and 'the daughter of Dr Fulford, Bishop of Montreal.'
6 St John's *Newfoundland Express*, 7 Aug. 1860, letter to the editor from Edward Newfoundland, 30 July 1860.
7 RA, VIC/Z 466/44, General Bruce to Prince Albert, 22 July 1860 (with later additions); RA, VIC/T 3/53, General Bruce to Sir Charles Phipps, 24 July 1860.
8 The prince consort to the Dowager Duchess of Coburg, 5 Aug. 1860, excerpted in Sir Theodore Martin, *The Life of His Royal Highness The Prince Consort*, vol. 5, 3rd ed. (London: Smith, Elder 1880), 149.
9 H.H. Scullard, *Festivals and Ceremonies of the Roman Republic* (Ithaca, N.Y.: Cornell University Press 1981); Barbara Wisch and Susan Scott Munshower, eds., *All the World's a Stage: Art and Pageantry in the Renaissance and Baroque* (University Park: University of Pennsylvania Press 1990); Lawrence M. Bryant, *The King and the City in the Parisian Royal Entry Ceremony: Politics, Ritual, and Art in the Renaissance* (Geneva: Librairie Droz 1986); Edward Muir, *Ritual in Early Modern Europe* (New York: Cambridge University Press 1997); Bonner Mitchell, *1598: A Year of Pageantry in Late Renaissance Ferrara* (Bing-

hamton N.Y.: Medieval and Renaissance Texts 1990); Bonner Mitchell, *The Majesty of the State: Triumphal Progresses of Foreign Sovereigns in Renaissance Italy, 1494–1600* (Florence: L.S. Olschki editore 1986).

10 See especially Robert Darnton, 'A Bourgeois Puts His World in Order: The City as a Text,' in his *The Great Cat Massacre and Other Episodes in French Cultural History* (New York: Vintage Books 1985), 107–43.

11 Mary P. Ryan, *Civic Wars: Democracy and Public Life in the American City during the Nineteenth Century* (Berkeley: University of California Press 1997), 59.

12 Nathaniel Woods, *The Prince of Wales in Canada and the United States* (London: Bradbury and Evans 1861), 18; see also Cellem, *Visit of HRH*, 51–5; the account by the correspondent for the New York *Daily Tribune*, which appeared in the Toronto *Globe*, 2 Aug. 1860; the *Globe*'s own correspondent's report, published on 9 Aug. 1860; the Halifax *Constitutionalist*, 2 Aug. 1860; Cornwallis, *Royalty in the New World*, 34–41.

13 Toronto *Globe*, 9 Aug. 1860.

14 Oxford University, Bodleian Library, Acland Family Papers, MS Add d.12, Henry Acland to Sarah Acland, 2 Aug. 1860.

15 Peter Burroughs, 'Phipps, George Augustus Constantine, 3rd Earl of Mulgrave,' *Dictionary of Canadian Biography*, vol. 9 (Toronto: University of Toronto Press 1982), 686–7. Burroughs notes that Mulgrave had been treasurer of the royal household at the time of his appointment to Nova Scotia in 1858; on the death of his father in 1863, when he became 2nd Marquess of Normanby, he returned to England and became lord-in-waiting to Queen Victoria.

16 Toronto *Globe*, report of its correspondent, 9 Aug. 1860.

17 'The Prince's Tour in British North America,' *Journal of Education for Upper Canada* 13 (September 1860): 131.

18 Saint John *Morning Freeman*, 4 Aug. 1860; Saint John *Morning News*, 4 Aug. 1860. Charles Fisher had gone to Halifax and Windsor for the celebrations, and he reported back on them to Samuel Tilly, a fellow member of the New Brunswick government, urging action and making suggestions. See National Archives of Canada (NA), MG 27 I D1, Samuel L. Tilley Papers, vol. 58, Fisher to Tilley 1 and 2 Aug. 1860.

19 *Morning Freeman*, 4 Aug. 1860; Cornwallis, *Royalty in the New World*, 53.

20 Woods, *Prince of Wales*, 46.

21 New York *Times*, 8 Aug. 1860.

22 New York *Evening Post*, 7 Aug. 1860.

23 Public Archives of New Brunswick, MS 36, George Hill Papers, vol. 34, Diary of George F. Hill, 2 Aug. 1860. My thanks to Gail Campbell and Phillip Buckner for bringing this document to my attention.

24 *Globe*, 18 Aug. 1860.
25 Cornwallis, *Royalty in the New World* 68–9; Woods, *Prince of Wales* 70.
26 *Globe*, 17 Aug. 1860.
27 A British Canadian [Henry James Morgan], *The Tour of H.R.H. the Prince of Wales through British America and the United States* (Montreal: John Lovell 1860), 53. Philip M. Vankoughnet, the cabinet minister responsible for crown lands, had been unable to leave Quebec.
28 RA, VIC/Z 466/74, General Bruce to Prince Albert, 14 Aug. 1860.
29 Woods, *Prince of Wales*, 75.
30 Toronto *Globe*, 21 Aug. 1860.
31 New York *Herald*, 19 Aug. 1860; New York *Times*, 20 Aug. 1860.
32 New York *Times*, 23 Aug. 1860.
33 New York *Herald*, 19 Aug. 1860; Lieutenant Thomas Bunbury Gough, *Boyish Reminiscences of His Majesty the King's Visit to Canada in 1860* (London: John Murray 1910), 139; Cornwallis, *Royalty in the New World*, 79; Woods, *Prince of Wales*, 79.
34 New York *Times*, 23 Aug. 1860.
35 Ibid.
36 Toronto *Globe*, 22 Aug. 1860.
37 Cellem, *Visit of HRH*, 126.
38 NA, MG 24 A 34, Henry, Duke of Newcastle Papers, reel A-307, Newcastle to Queen Victoria, 30 Aug. 1860; RA, VIC/Z 467/1, General Bruce to Prince Albert, 20 Aug. 1860.
39 Toronto *Globe*, 22 Aug. 1860.
40 Acland Family Papers, Henry Acland to Sarah Acland, 3 Sept. 1860.
41 Ottawa *Citizen*, 1 Sept. 1860; Toronto *Globe*, 3 Sept. 1860; Woods, *Prince of Wales*, 151.
42 RA, VIC/Add A 3/18 'Bertie' [the Prince of Wales] to 'Mama' [Queen Victoria], 2 Sept. 1860.
43 William Davies to James Davies, 15 Aug. 1860, in William Sherwood Fox, ed., *Letters of William Davies, Toronto, 1854–1861* (Toronto: University of Toronto Press 1945), 118.
44 RA, VIC Z/ 467/33, General Bruce to the prince consort, 11 Sept. 1860; Newcastle Papers reel A-307, Newcastle to Queen Victoria, 12 Sept. 1860; RA, Vic/Add A 3/19, 'Bertie' [the Prince of Wales] to Mama [Queen Victoria], 11 Sept. 1860.
45 NA, France, Ministère des Affaires Étrangères, correspondance consulaire politique, Angleterre, vol. 35/111, G. Boilleau (Quebec) to M. Thouvenel (Paris), 17 April 1860.
46 Ryan, *Civic Wars*, 15.

47 On distinctions between processions and parades, see Roberto Da Matta, 'Carnival in Multiple Planes,' in John J. MacAloon, ed., *Rite, Drama, Festival, Spectacle: Rehearsals Towards a Theory of Cultural Performance* (Philadelphia: Institute for the Study of Human Issues 1984), 218–19; and Ronald Rudin, 'Marching and Memory in Early Twentieth-Century Quebec: La Fête-Dieu, la Saint-Jean-Baptiste, and le Monument Laval,' *Journal of the Canadian Historical Association* 9 (1999): 211–13. The parading tradition in Canada has been studied in: John R. Porter, 'Processions et défilés,' in *Le grand héritage: l'Église catholique et des arts au Québec* (Quebec: Musée du Québec 1984); H.J.J.B. Chouinard, *Fête nationale des Canadiens-français célébrée à Québec, 1881–1889* (Quebec: Belleau et Cie 1890); Rémi Tourangeau, *Fêtes et spectâcles du Québec: région du Saguenay-Lac-Saint-Jean* (Quebec: Nuit Blanche Éditeur 1993); Allan Gordon, *Making Public Pasts: The Contested Terrain of Montreal's Public Memories, 1890–1930* (Montreal and Kingston: McGill-Queen's University Press 2001), 145–215; Bonnie Huskins, 'The Ceremonial Space of Women: Public Processions in Victorian Saint John and Halifax,' in Janet Guildford and Suzanne Morton, eds., *Separate Spheres: Women's Worlds in the 19th-Century Maritimes* (Fredericton: Acadiensis Press 1994), 145–60; Craig Heron and Steve Penfold, 'The Craftsmen's Spectacle: Labour Day Parades in Canada, The Early Years,' *Histoire sociale/Social History* 29 (1996): 357–89; Michael Cottrell, 'St. Patrick's Day Parades in Nineteenth-Century Toronto: A Study of Immigrant Adjustment and Elite Control,' *Histoire sociale/Social History* 25 (1992): 57–73; P.G. Goheen, 'The Ritual of the Streets in Mid-19th-Century Toronto,' *Environment and Planning D: Society and Space* 11 (1993): 127–45; Peter G. Goheen, 'Negotiating Access to Public Space in Mid-Nineteenth Century Toronto,' *Journal of Historical Geography* 20 (1994): 430–49; Peter G. Goheen, 'Symbols in the Streets: Parades in Victorian Urban Canada,' *Urban History Review* 8 (1990): 237–43; Peter G. Goheen, 'Parading: A Lively Tradition in Early Victorian Toronto,' in Alan R.H. Baker and Gideon Biger, eds., *Ideology and Landscape in Historical Perspective* (New York: Cambridge University Press 1992), 330–51.

48 On processional routes, see Peter G. Goheen, 'Parades and Processions,' plate 58 in R. Louis Gentilcore, ed., *The Historical Atlas of Canada*, 3 vols. (Toronto: University of Toronto Press 1993), vol. 2.

49 Bonnie Huskins, '"A Tale of Two Cities": Boosterism and the Imagination of Community during the Visit of the Prince of Wales to Saint John and Halifax in 1860,' *Urban History Review* 28 (1999): 31–46.

50 Toronto *Globe*, 21 June 1860.

51 Woods, *Prince of Wales*, 114.

52 Founded in Montreal in 1834 to promote French Canada's 'fête nationale,'

the Société Saint-Jean-Baptiste spread to Quebec soon afterwards. From the 1840s, the lay society organized annual parades that were essentially secular, although the Roman Catholic clergy, eager to assert themselves, cooperated with the Société and gave the parades their blessing. See Rudin, 'Marching and Memory,' 227.

53 Quebec, *Le Courrier du Canada*, 1 Aug. 1860; Cellem, *Visit of HRH*, 128; Ottawa *Citizen*, 1 Sept. 1860; New York *Times*, 7 Aug. 1860.

54 Saint John *Freeman*, cited in Halifax *Constitutionalist*, 2 Aug. 1860; Toronto *Globe*, 8 Aug. 1860.

55 Jan Noel, *Canada Dry: Temperance Crusades before Confederation* (Toronto: University of Toronto Press 1995).

56 Saint John *Freeman*, cited in Halifax *Constitutionalist*, 2 Aug. 1860.

57 'Proceedings of the Central Canada Temperance Convention, held at Kingston, 17 Aug. 1860,' in Toronto *Globe*, 20 Aug. 1860.

58 See Bradley Rudachyk, '"At the Mercy of the Devouring Element": The Equipment and Organization of the Halifax Fire Establishment, 1830–1850,' *Collections of the Royal Nova Scotia Historical Society* 61 (1982): 165–84.

59 Fredericton, *New Brunswick Reporter*, 3 Aug. 1860.

60 Cornwallis, *Royalty in the New World*, 43; Toronto *Globe*, 10 Aug. 1860. Horace Greeley was a prominent New York publisher and politician and an outspoken abolitionist.

61 New York *Times*, 7 Aug. 1860.

62 Huskins, 'Ceremonial Space of Women.'

63 Toronto *Leader*, 30 Aug. 1860; Belleville *Hastings Chronicle*, reprinted in Toronto *Globe*, 2 Sept. 1860. Lucy Stone (1818–93) was a prominent American campaigner for the rights of women and for the abolition of slavery. In Canada, the campaign for women's rights had only just begun by 1860, the 1859 Married Women's Property Act being its first (partial) victory. See Lori Chambers, *Married Women and Property Law in Victorian Ontario* (Toronto: University of Toronto Press and the Osgoode Society for Canadian Legal History, 1997), 70–91.

64 Morgan, *Tour of H.R.H.*, 187.

65 Toronto *Globe*, 22 and 27 Aug. 1860.

66 Ibid., 22 Aug. 1860.

67 NA, Newcastle Papers, reel A-307, Newcastle to Queen Victoria, 7 Aug. and 12 Sept. 1860.

68 Toronto *Globe*, 2 Sept. 1860.

69 Saint John *Morning Freeman*, cited in Halifax *Constitutionalist*, 2 Aug. 1860; Toronto *Globe*, 8 Aug. 1860; New York *Times*, 8 Aug. 1860. On the anti-labour bias of the *Globe*, see Christina Burr, *Spreading the Light: Work and*

Labour Reform in Late-Nineteenth-Century Toronto (Toronto: University of Toronto Press 1999), 15–19.

70 New York *Times*, 23 and 29 Aug. 1860. On the American parade as a highly evolved display of national pride, see Susan G. Davis, *Parades and Power: Street Theater in Nineteenth Century Philadelphia* (Philadelphia: Temple University Press 1985); Ryan *Civic Wars*.

71 Hellmut Kallmann, Gilles Potvin, Kenneth Winters, eds., *Encyclopaedia of Music in Canada* (Toronto: University of Toronto Press 1981), 54–7.

72 New York *Herald*, 19 Aug. 1860. The reporter added that Canadians considered it to be 'the equal of Dodsworth's Band,' a celebrated band that would perform during the prince's visit to New York.

73 Toronto *Globe*, 25 Aug. 1860.

74 New York *Times*, 29 Aug. 1860.

75 Woods, *Prince of Wales*, 103–5.

76 *Frank Leslie's Illustrated Newspaper* [New York], 18 Aug. 1860.

77 Fredericton *New Brunswick Reporter*, 3 Aug. 1860; Saint John *Morning Freeman*, 4 Aug. 1860.

78 Ottawa *Union*,11 Aug. 1860; Ottawa *Citizen*, 7 Aug. and 1 Sept. 1860; Morgan, *Tour of H.R.H.*, 138; Acland Family Papers, MS Add d. 12, Henry Acland to Sarah Acland, 2 Sept. 1860.

79 Kingston *British Whig*, 8 Sept. 1860; Toronto *Globe*, 7 Sept. 1860.

80 Ryan, *Civic Wars*.

Chapter 4: Princely Duties, Princely Pleasure

1 *Punch*, a journal of middle-class radicalism, made gentle pokes at the royal family in the 1850s, and it also attacked the intrusions of journalists into the lives of members of the royal family. See Richard Williams, *The Contentious Crown: Public Discussion of the British Monarchy in the Reign of Queen Victoria* (Aldershot, U.K.: Ashgate 1997), 13–15; John Plunkett, *Queen Victoria: First Media Monarch* (Oxford: Oxford University Press 2003), 213; M.H. Spielmann, *The History of Punch* (London: Cassell 1995).

2 New York *Times*, 25 Aug. 1860; Fredericton *Head-Quarters*, 4 July 1860.

3 National Archives of Canada (NA), MG 21 A34, Henry, Duke of Newcastle Papers, reel A-1610, Correspondence with Governors, 1859–60, Newcastle to Head, 27 April 1860; NA, RG 7 G 23, Office of the Governor General, Royal Visits, vol. 1, draft reply to letter of P. Kempson, reeve of Fort Erie, to R. Pennefather, 7 Sept. 1860.

4 NA, Newcastle Papers, reel A-1610, Newcastle to Mulgrave, 30 June 1860.

5 London *Times* article reprinted in *New-Brunswick Reporter*, 21 Sept. 1860.

6 Toronto *Globe*, 31 Aug. 1860.
7 Toronto *Globe*, 9 Aug. 1860.
8 Nathaniel Augustus Woods, *The Prince of Wales in Canada and the United States* (London: Bradbury and Evans 1861), 92.
9 NA, Newcastle Papers, Newcastle to Queen Victoria, 24 July and 18 Aug. 1860; RA, Vic/Add A 3/18, 'Bertie' [the Prince of Wales] to 'Mama' [Queen Victoria], 2 Sept. 1860.
10 New York *Daily Tribune*, 22 Sept. 1860.
11 Toronto *Globe*, 20 and 25 Aug. 1860; Montreal *L'Ordre*, 18 July 1860.
12 NA, RG 7, sheriff of York and Peel to R. Pennefather, 20 Aug. 1860.
13 NA, RG 7, G 23/1, Dunbar Ross to R. Pennefather, 20 Aug. 1860, and Hector L. Langevin, mayor of Quebec, to R. Pennefather, 16 Aug. 1860.
14 NA, Newcastle Papers, Newcastle to Lord Palmerston, 1 Sept. 1860.
15 Newcastle had been definite about the order of precedence; see his instructions: NA, RG 7 G1, vol. 7, Circular from the Duke of Newcastle, 3 May 1860.
16 Toronto *Globe*, 25 Aug. 1860; Fredericton *New Brunswick Reporter*, 14 Sept. 1860.
17 Memorial printed in Toronto *Globe*, 8 Sept. 1860.
18 Toronto *Globe*, 30 Aug. 1860. The slight was in fact an oversight that authorities rectified in Kingston harbour, where the Presbyterian moderator read his address to the prince aboard his steamer.
19 NA, Newcastle Papers, reel A-1610, Newcastle to Head, 29 July 1860 [*sic*: 1859?]; Newcastle to Head, 9 May 1860.
20 Robert Cellem, *Visit of His Royal Highness the Prince of Wales to the British North American Provinces and United States in the Year 1860* (Toronto: Henry Rowsell 1861), 136.
21 Michèle Brassard and Jean Hamelin, 'Belleau, Sir Narcisse-Fortunat, 1808–94,' *Dictionary of Canadian Biography* vol. 12 (Toronto: University of Toronto Press 1990), 86–7; Donald Swainson, 'Smith, Sir Henry,' *Dictionary of Canadian Biography* vol. 9 (Toronto: University of Toronto Press 1976), 725–6.
22 Toronto *Globe*, 24 Aug. 1860; New York *Times*, 25 Aug. 1860.
23 See, for example, Toronto *Globe*, 22 and 25 Aug. 1860.
24 New York *Times*, 27 Aug. 1860.
25 Fredericton *Head Quarters*, 4 July 1860; Woods, *Prince of Wales*, 159.
26 Cornwallis, *Royalty in the New World*, 57.
27 Woods, *Prince of Wales*, 126–7.
28 Saint John *Morning Freeman*, 1 Sept. 1860; Saint John *Morning News*, 3 Sept. 1860.

29 On Freemasonry in Canada, see J. Ross Robertson, *The History of Freemasonry in Canada from its Introduction in 1749 ...* (Toronto: Hunter Rose 1899); Jeffrey McNairn, *The Capacity to Judge: Public Opinion and Deliberative Democracy in Upper Canada, 1791–1854* (Toronto: University of Toronto Press 2000) 69–83.
30 Toronto *Globe*, 24 Aug. 1860; Ottawa *Union*,12 Sept. 1860.
31 Ottawa *Citizen*, 21 Aug. 1860; Montreal *Pilot*, 4 Sept. 1860; Toronto *Globe*, 4 Sept. 1860.
32 RA, Vic Add A./3/18, 'Bertie' [Prince of Wales] to 'Mama' [Queen Victoria], 2 Sept. 1860.
33 I.F.W. Beckett, *Riflemen Form: A Study of the Rifle Volunteer Movement, 1859–1908* (Aldershot, U.K.: Ogilby Trusts 1982).
34 J. Mackay Hitsman, *Safeguarding Canada, 1763–1871* (Toronto: University of Toronto Press 1968), 155–64.
35 Under the 1855 act, there still was provision for the old (or 'sedentary') militia: the compulsory service required of male residents who were untrained and obliged to muster only once a year. Hitsman, *Safeguarding Canada*, 158.
36 C.P. Stacey, *Canada and the British Army, 1846–1871: A Study in the Practice of Responsible Government* (Toronto: Royal Commonwealth Society and the University of Toronto Press 1963), 89–116. For the wider context, see J.L. Granatstein, *Canada's Army: Waging War and Keeping the Peace* (Toronto: University of Toronto Press 2002).
37 NA, Newcastle Papers, Newcastle to Mulgrave, 30 June 1860. Newcastle to Head, 27 June 1860.
38 Royal Archives (RA), Vic/T 3/54, 'Bertie' [Prince of Wales] to 'Mama' [Queen Victoria], 5 Aug. 1860; Sydney, N.S., *Cape Breton News* clipping in the Charlottetown *Examiner*, 14 Aug. 1860.
39 Halifax *Constitutionalist*, 9 Aug. 1860. See Desmond Morton, *A Military History of Canada*, 3rd ed. (Toronto: McClelland Stewart 1992), 86–7.
40 'The Prince and the Volunteer Force: Official Order, 18 August 1860,' *Globe*, 29 Aug. 1860.
41 'Militia Generals Orders, 28 August 1860,' in *Globe*, 6 Sept. 1860.
42 Halifax *Constitutionalist*, 11 Aug. 1860.
43 Ottawa *Citizen*, 1 Sept. 1860.
44 Cellem, *Visit of HRH*, 205.
45 Ottawa *Union*, 12 Sept. 1860.
46 Toronto *Globe*, 10 Aug. 1860; Woods, *Prince of Wales*, 29.
47 Toronto *Globe*, 10 Aug. 1860; Cornwallis, *Royalty in the New World* 43; Woods, *Prince of Wales*, 29.

48 RA, Vic T3/54, 'Bertie' [Prince of Wales] to 'Mama' [Queen Victoria], 5 Aug. 1860.
49 Toronto *Globe*, 27 Aug. 1860.
50 Woods, *Prince of Wales*, 221–2.
51 Halifax *Constitutionalist*, 7 and 9 Aug. 1860.
52 A. Fortesque Duguid, *History of the Canadian Grenadier Guards*, 1760–1964 (Montreal: privately printed 1965), 31; New York *Times*, 22 Sept. 1860.
53 Cited in John Ross Robertson, *Robertson's Landmarks of Toronto*, series 2 (Toronto: J. Ross Robertson 1896), 783–4.
54 Toronto *Globe*, 14 Aug. and 8 Sept. 1860.
55 St Catharines *Post*, reprinted in Toronto *Globe*, 4 Aug. 1860.
56 Toronto *Globe*, 19 Sept. 1860.
57 Archives of Ontario (AO), MU 4, John Beverley Robinson Papers, minutes of meeting at Toronto, 7 July 1860. The address was prepared by Sir John Beverley Robinson, Sir Allan MacNab, and Archibald McLean.
58 Toronto *Globe*, 19 Sept. 1860.
59 Niagara *Mail*, as cited in Ruth Mackenzie, *Laura Secord: The Legend and the Lady* (Toronto: McClelland and Steweart 1971), 101.
60 NA, RG 7, G23, vol 1, 'Petition of Mrs Secord,' 10 Sept. 1860.
61 Niagara *Mail*, 17 March and 3 April 1861.
62 Colin M. Coates and Cecilia Morgan, *Heroines and History: Representations of Madeleine de Verchères and Laura Secord* (Toronto: University of Toronto Press 2002), 123–94.
63 Woods, *Prince of Wales*, 258; Toronto *Globe*, 20 Sept. 1860.
64 Cellem, *Visit of HRH*, 41.
65 Cornwallis, *Royalty in the New World*, 29.
66 Toronto *Globe*, 10 Aug. 1860.
67 New York *Times*, 8 Aug. 1860.
68 Account from the *Sun*, reprinted in Halifax *Constitutionalist*, 4 Aug. 1860.
69 New York *Times*, 8 Aug. 1860.
70 Woods, *Prince of Wales*, 165; Ottawa *Citizen*, 25 Aug. 1860.
71 Toronto *Globe*, 5 Sept. 1860.
72 Halifax *Constitutionalist*, 9 June 1860.
73 Cellem, *Visit of HRH*, 42–5.
74 Woods, *Prince of Wales*, 130; Toronto *Globe*, 29 Aug. 1860.
75 Woods, *Prince of Wales*, 130–3; Cellem, *Visit of HRH*, 172.
76 Woods, *Prince of Wales*, 133.
77 Saint John *Morning Freeman*, 1 Sept. 1860.
78 Woods, *Prince of Wales*, 130; Cellem, *Visit of HRH*, 172.

79 Cellem, *Visit of HRH*, 223.
80 Ibid., 99.
81 Woods, *Prince of Wales*, 55.
82 Cellem, *Visit of HRH*, 233.
83 Montreal *Pilot*, 18 Sept. 1860.
84 Cellem, *Visit of HRH*, 100.
85 Ibid., 235.
86 Ibid., 62.
87 Ibid., 223.
88 Montreal *Gazette*, 11 Aug. 1860.
89 'The International Dance,' reprinted from the New York *Methodist* in the *Christian Guardian*, 14 Nov. 1860.
90 Cornwallis, *Royalty in the New World*, 30.
91 New York *Herald*, reprinted in Toronto *Globe*, 4 Aug. 1860.
92 *Harper's Weekly*, 22 Oct. 1860.
93 Ibid.
94 RA, VIC/T 3/54, 'Bertie' [Prince of Wales] to 'Mama' [Queen Victoria], 5 Aug. 1860; RA VIC/Add A 3/19, 'Bertie' [Prince of Wales] to 'Mama' [Queen Victoria], 11 Sept. 1860; New York *Times*, 12 Sept. 1860.
95 For the tour, the *Hero*'s band was expanded to about fifty men, to make it 'equal to the occasion.' A retired officer later described it as 'by far the best naval band' that he had ever heard. See Lieutenant Thomas Bunbury Gough, *Boyish Reminiscences of His Majesty the King's Visit to Canada in 1860* (London: John Murray 1910), 9.
96 Cellem, *Visit of HRH*, 173–4.
97 The diary entries (for 12–14 Sept. 1860) were given to me by Adam Crerar, whose father is transcribing the diary of his ancestor Jessie Anne Hope for a forthcoming volume to be published by the Champlain Society. I thank most sincerely both Adam and his father.
98 New York *Times*, 30 Aug. 1860.
99 Woods, *Prince of Wales*, 102.
100 Cornwallis, *Royalty in the New World*, 135, 160.
101 Toronto, *Christian Guardian*, editorial, 12 Sept. 1860.
102 Ibid., 8 Aug. 1860.
103 Ibid., 12 Sept. 1860.
104 Montreal *Witness*, 4 Aug. 1860.
105 *Christian Guardian*, 24 Oct. 1860.
106 Halifax *Acadian Recorder*, 14 July 1860.
107 Ibid., 4 Aug. 1860.
108 Cornwallis, *Royalty in the New World*, 44, 58. Ticket prices and sales were

also much discussed at Charlottetown; see Charlottetown *Examiner,* 24 July 1860; Charlottetown *Islander,* 10 Aug. 1860.

109 Barrie *Northern Advance,* 26 Sept. 1860.

110 New York *Daily Tribune,* 5 Sept. 1860.

111 Toronto *Globe,* 15 Aug. 1860.

112 Toronto *Globe* editorials, 22, 23, 24, 25, 29 Aug. 1860.

113 Cellem, *Visit of HRH,* 233, 279.

114 New York *Times,* 10 Sept. 1860; Ian Malcolm, 'Robert Sutherland: The First Black Lawyer in Canada?' *Law Society Gazette* 26 (1992): 183–5.

115 New York *Daily Tribune,* 19 Sept. 1860.

Chapter 5: Arch Rivals

1 See, however, Anne MacDermaid, 'The Visit of the Prince of Wales to Kingston in 1860,' *Historic Kingston* 21 (1972): 50–61; J.D. Livermore, 'The Orange Order and the Election of 1861 in Kingston,' in Gerald Tulchinsky, ed., *To Preserve and Defend: Essays on Kingston in the Nineteenth Century* (Montreal and Kingston: McGill-Queen's University Press), 245–60.

2 On Orangeism in Upper Canada, see especially: Cecil J. Houston and William J. Smyth, *The Sash Canada Wore: A Historical Geography of the Orange Order in Canada* (Toronto: University of Toronto Press 1980); Hereward Senior, *Orangeism: the Canadian Phase* (Toronto: McGraw-Hill 1972), and 'The Genesis of Canadian Orangeism,' *Ontario History* 60 (1968): 13–39; Ogle R. Gowan, *Orangeism: Its Origin and History* (Toronto, 1859); Gregory S. Kealey, 'The Orange Order in Toronto: Religious Riot and the Working Class,' in G.S. Kealey and Peter Warrian, eds., *Essays in Canadian Working Class History* (Toronto: McClelland and Stewart 1976), 13–35; W.B. Kerr, 'When Orange and Green United, 1832–9: The Alliance of Macdonnell and Gowan,' Ontario Historical Society *Papers and Proceedings* 34 (1942): 13–42. On Orangeism elsewhere, see Dominic Bryan, *Orange Parades: The Politics of Ritual, Tradition and Control* (London: Pluto 2000); Frank Wright, *Two Lands on One Soil: Ulster Politics before Home Rule* (Dublin: Gill and Macmillan 1996); T.G. Fraser, ed., *The Irish Parading Tradition: Following the Drum* (New York: St Martin's Press 2000); E.W. McFarland, *Protestants First: Orangeism in Nineteenth Century Scotland* (Edinburgh: University of Edinburgh Press 1990); Hereward Senior, *Orangeism in Ireland and Britain, 1795–1836* (London: Routledge and Kegan Paul 1966); Scott W. See, *Riots in New Brunswick: Orange Nativism and Social Violence in the 1840s* (Toronto: University of Toronto Press 1980); Michael Gordon, *The Orange Riots: Irish Political Violence in New York City, 1870 and 1871* (Ithaca, N.Y.: Cornell University Press 1993).

3 J.R. Miller, 'Anti-Catholic Thought in Victorian Canada,' *Canadian Historical Review* 66 (1985): 474–94.

4 Brian S. Osborne and Donald Swainson, *Kingston: Building on the Past* (Westport, Ont.: Butternut Press 1988); Louis J. Flynn, 'Bishop Edward John Horan,' *Historic Kingston* 24 (1976): 43–54; J.E. Rea, *Bishop Alexander Macdonnell and the Politics of Upper Canada* (Toronto: Ontario Historical Society 1974).

5 Brian P. Clarke, *Piety and Nationalism: Lay Voluntary Associations and the Creation of an Irish Catholic Community in Toronto, 1850–1895* (Montreal and Kingston: McGill-Queen's University Press 1993); Michael Cottrell, 'St. Patrick's Day Parades in Nineteenth-Century Toronto: A Study of Immigrant Adjustment and Elite Control,' in Franca Iacovetta, Paula Draper and Robert Ventresca, ed., *A Nation of Immigrants: Women, Workers, and Communities in Canadian history, 1840s–1960s* (Toronto: University of Toronto Press 1998), 35–54; Gerald J. Stortz, 'John Joseph Lynch, Archbishop of Toronto: A Biographical Study of Religious, Political and Social Commitment' (PhD thesis, University of Guelph 1980); Charles W. Humphries, 'Lynch, John,' *Dictionary of Canadian Biography* vol. II (Toronto: University of Toronto Press 1982), 535–8.

6 Donald Swainson, 'Cameron, John Hillyard,' *Dictionary of Canadian Biography* vol. 10 (Toronto: University of Toronto Press 1972), 118–24; Ogle R. Gowan was also a resident of Toronto. On Gowan, see Hereward Senior, 'Gowan, Ogle Robert,' *Dictionary of Canadian Biography*, vol. 10, 309–14; In *The Orangeman: The Life and Times of Ogle Gowan* (Toronto: James Lorimer 1986), a historical novel, Don Akenson depicts the rape charge and scandal.

7 Houston and Smyth, *The Sash Canada Wore*, 142–59; Gregory S. Kealey, 'The Orangemen and the Corporation,' and Barrie Dyster, 'Captain Bob and the Noble Ward: Neighbourhood and Provincial Politics in Nineteenth-century Toronto,' both in Victor L. Russell, ed., *Forging a Consensus: Historical Essays on Toronto* (Toronto: University of Toronto Press and the City of Toronto Sesquicentennial Board 1984), 41–86, 87–115.

8 Peter G. Goheen, 'Negotiating Access to Public Space in Mid-Nineteenth Century Toronto,' *Journal of Historical Geography* 20 (1994): 430–49; Peter G. Goheen, 'Parading: A Lively Tradition in Early Victorian Toronto,' in Alan R.H. Baker and Gideon Biger, eds., *Ideology and Landscape in Historical Perspective* (Cambridge, U.K.: Cambridge University Press 1992); P.G. Goheen, 'The Ritual of the Streets in Mid-Nineteenth Century Toronto,' *Environment and Planning D: Society and Space 11 (1993): 127–45*; Kealey, 'Orangemen and the Corporation,' 41–86.

9 Kealey, 'Orangemen and the Corporation,' 51–9.

10 On state suppression of the Orangemen of Ireland, see James Loughlin, 'Parades and Politics: Liberal Governments and the Orange Order,' in Fraser, *Irish Parading Tradition*, 27–9; Bryan, *Orange Parades*, 29–43. In England in the 1860s, the Conservative Party was meantime making headway within the working class by appealing to Orange values. See Neville Kirk, *Change, Continuity and Class: Labour in British Society, 1850–1920* (Manchester and New York: Manchester University Press 1998), 95–107.

11 Cottrell, 'St Patrick's Day Parades'; Clarke, *Piety and Nationalism*.

12 Philippe Sylvain, 'Bourget, Ignace,' *Dictionary of Canadian Biography*, vol. 11 (Toronto: University of Toronto Press 1982), 101.

13 René Hardy, *Les zouaves: une stratégie du clergé québécois au XIXe siècle* (Montréal: Boréal 1980); A.I. Silver, *The French-Canadian Idea of Confederation, 1864–1900* (Toronto: University of Toronto Press 1982), 227–37.

14 See, *Riots in New Brunswick*; Gordon, *The Orange Riots*.

15 In 1860 New Brunswick was nearly completely free of any Orange demonstrations. The local press noted after the problem had occurred in Upper Canada that a few people at Portland had begun to decorate an arch with Orange colours but their attempt had been swiftly 'nipped in the bud.' Saint John *Morning Freeman*, 8 Sept. 1860.

16 Linda Colley, *Britons: Forging the Nation, 1707–1837* (New Haven, Conn.: Yale University Press 1992).

17 For those unfamiliar with the troubled politics within the Union of the Canadas, let me explain. Under the Act of Union, 1840, an act of British Parliament, the two colonies of Upper Canada and Lower Canada were united, effective 1841. Each half of the new province had an equal number of seats in the legislature, even though the population of English-speaking Canada West was much smaller than that of Canada East. During the next two decades, most French-Canadian politicians shrewdly formed a bloc and made strategic alliances that gave them much clout. Meantime, because of British immigration, the population of Canada West grew much more-rapidly than that of Canada East. By 1860 the Reform opposition in the legislature, which had the backing of the majority in Canada West, was demanding 'representation by population' and railing at 'French and Catholic domination.' Confederation in 1867 was intended to resolve the conflict by creating a federal structure that both divided the province into its original halves and united the two with the Maritime provinces of Nova Scotia and New Brunswick.

18 Toronto *Globe*, 20 Aug. 1860; Toronto *Leader*, 25 Aug. 1860.

19 Kingston *Daily News*, 1 July 1860; Toronto *Globe*, 13 July 1860.

20 It was not until after the prince's visit to Canada that the Orange grand

master, J.H. Cameron, revealed to the public that he had consulted the governor general well before the visit about the appropriateness of the Order presenting addresses to the prince. Upon consulting with the prince's advisers, Governor Head had had his views confirmed that such addresses would be '"very embarrassing"' (Toronto *Leader*, 6 Oct. 1860; Cameron cites, with permission, Head's letter of mid-August). Both Head and Cameron insisted that they had never discussed the matter of Orange arches or Orangemen's marching in processions.

21 William Shannon, *Narrative of the Proceedings of the Loyal Orangemen of Kingston and Belleville, on the 4th, 5th, and 6th of September, 1860, in connection with the Visit of H.R.H. the Prince of Wales, to Central Canada* (Belleville, Ont.: M. Bowell 1861), 6.

22 Kingston *British Whig*, 26 Aug. 1860.

23 I have found no evidence to suggest that the hierarchy coordinated Kingston and Toronto meetings as part of a province-wide campaign. On the contrary, it is clear they were being reactive. A letter from Bishop Edward Horan of Kingston to Bishop Lynch of Toronto on the eve of the Kingston visit indicates that this was the first discussion between the bishops on the Orange matter. See Archives of the Roman Catholic Archdiocese of Toronto, Bishop Lynch Papers, L.AG 04.01, Bishop Horan to Bishop Lynch, 2 Sept. 1860.

24 Elmsley had been a member of York's Anglican elite but had converted to Catholicism in the 1830s after his marriage to a Catholic. Substantial landholdings at Toronto provided the basis for his philanthropy. He was locally known as 'Captain' because he owned and sailed a steamship on Lake Ontario. [See Henri Pilon, 'Elmsley, John,' *Dictionary of Canadian Biography*, vol. 9 (Toronto: University of Toronto Press 1966), 239–42.

25 Toronto *Globe*, 31 Aug. 1860.

26 On the symbolism of Orange arches, banners, and so on, see Neil Jarman, *Material Conflicts: Parades and Visual Displays in Northern Ireland* (Oxford and New York: Berg 1997). In 1790 the first recorded Orange arch appeared in Ulster. (Jarmen, *Material Conflicts*, 48).

27 Ibid.

28 Ibid., 20, 23, 28, 30, and 31 Aug. 1860.

29 Toronto *Globe*, 5 Sept. 1860.

30 National Archives of Canada (NA), RG 7, G23, Office of the Governor General, Royal Visits, David Shaw, secretary of Kingston Reception Committee, to Sir Edmund Head, 31 Aug. 1860.

31 Toronto *Globe*, 4 Sept. 1860.

32 Kingston *British Whig*, 3 Sept. 1860.

33 Ibid.

34 Ibid.

35 Shannon, *Narrative*, 24–5.

36 Nathaniel Augustus Woods, *The Prince of Wales in Canada and the United States* (London: Bradbury and Evans 1861), 187–8; Shannon, *Narrative*, 30.

37 New York *Daily Tribune*, 7 Sept. 1860; Shannon, *Narrative*, 23. The carrying of the holy host by Catholics through the streets of Canadian cities was sometimes contested by Protestants. See Christine Sheito, 'Une fête contestée: la procession de la Fête-Dieu à Montréal au XIXe siècle,' MA thesis, Université de Montréal, 1983; Martin A. Galvin, 'The Jubilee Riots in Toronto, 1875,' Canadian Catholic Historical Association *Report* 1959, 93–107.

38 NA, MG 29 E 1 (F 46), Thomas Wily Papers, Colonel Thomas Wily, 'A Reminiscence,' 221–2.

39 Shannon, *Narrative*, 35; NA, MG 40-Q40, Sir Henry Acland Fonds, Album no. 5, drawing 176.

40 Woods, *The Prince of Wales in Canada*, 183, 187; New York *Daily Tribune*, 7 Sept. 1860.

41 New York *Evening Post*, 6 Sept. 1860. It is possible that, wishing to find drama and trouble, the reporters mistook the band music and cries of American visitors who included a militia corps and their band from nearby Oswego, N.Y.

42 Shannon, *Narrative*, 32–3.

43 Shannon, *Narrative*, 35; James R. Burke to William Shannon, 9 March 1861, printed in Shannon, *Narrative*, 41–2.

44 A British Canadian [Henry James Morgan], *The Tour of H.R.H. the Prince of Wales through British America and the United States* (Montreal: John Lovell 1860), 149. (Morgan reproduces the full correspondence.)

45 *Hansard's Parliamentary Debates*, vol. 160 (London: Cornelius Buck 1860), 1155–7.

46 Ibid. 1510–11, 1618; *Journals of the House of Lords for 1860* (London: Queen's Printer 1860), 317.

47 NA, MG 24 A 34, Henry, Duke of Newcastle Papers, reel A-307, Newcastle to Lord Palmerston, 12 Sept. 1860. He wrote, in part: 'I have heard on good authority that the movement was ordered from home and much was to be founded upon it if it had succeeded.'

48 Shannon, *Narrative*, 6.

49 *British Whig*, 7 Sept. 1860; New York *Daily Tribune*, 8 Sept. 1860; Wily, 'A Reminiscence,' 227.

50 Wily, 'Reminiscence' 223–7.

51 Toronto *Globe*, 7 Sept. 1860; Wily, 'Reminiscence,' 226.

52 Wily, 'Reminiscence,' 227.

53 NA, Newcastle Papers, reel A-307, Newcastle to Queen Victoria, 6 Sept. 1860.

54 Ibid.; Oxford University, Bodelian Library, Acland Family Papers, MS, Add d.12, Henry Acland to Sarah Acland, 3 Sept. 1860; RA, Vic Add, A/3/19, 'Bertie' [Prince of Wales] to 'Mama' [Queen Victoria], 11 Sept. 1860.

55 Toronto *Globe*, 8 Sept. 1860.

56 Ibid.

57 Toronto *Globe*, 6 Sept. 1860.

58 Toronto *Globe*, 10 Sept. 1860; NA, Newcastle Papers, Newcastle to Queen Victoria, 12 Sept. 1860.

59 Toronto *Globe*, 10 Sept. 1860.

60 Mayor Wilson's statement, Toronto *Leader*, 18 Sept. 1860. All correspondence relating to the mayor and the decorations, along with some additional remarks by the mayor, appear in the *Minutes of the [Toronto] City Council for 1860*, no. 141, 241–51.

61 Acland Family Papers, Henry Acland to Sarah Acland, 11 Sept. 1860.

62 Toronto *Globe*, 12 Sept. 1860.

63 Acland Family Papers, Henry Acland to Sarah Acland, 11 Sept. 1860.

64 Ibid. 213.

65 Robert Cellem, *Visit of His Royal Highness, the Prince of Wales to the British North American Provinces and United States, in the Year 1860* (Toronto: Henry Rowsell 1861), 236.

66 New York *Times*, 10 Sept. 1860.

67 Toronto Central Reference Library, Baldwin Room, Larrett Smith Diaries, 9 Sept. 1860.

68 Toronto *Globe*, 10 Sept. 1860. Reports from the City of Toronto police court highlighted the drunkenness of the two men arrested outside the cathedral. One was fined $4, the other $3. See Toronto *Globe*, 14 Sept. 1860.

69 New York *Times*, 10 Sept. 1860.

70 *Le Canadien* [Quebec], 21 Sept. 1860.

71 NA, Newcastle Papers, reel A-307, Newcastle to Palmerston, 12 Sept. 1860.

72 'Resolution of a Meeting of the Masters of the Various Orange Lodges in the District of Toronto Held Yesterday,' Toronto *Daily Leader*, 13 Sept. 1860.

73 Toronto *Leader*, 11 Sept. 1860.

74 Toronto *Globe*, 11 Sept. 1860; Woods, *The Prince of Wales in Canada and the United States*, 219.

75 Toronto *Globe*, 11 Sept. 1860.

76 Kingston *British Whig*, 15 Sept. 1860; Woods, *The Prince of Wales in Canada and the United States*, 222–3.

77 NA, Newcastle Papers, reel A-307, Newcastle to Palmerston, 12 Sept. 1860.
78 Archives of the Roman Catholic Archdiocese of Toronto, Bishop Lynch Papers, L.AE 11.01, 'Address to Your Royal Highness, Signed on Behalf of all the Societies,' by James Stock, John Walsh, W.J. MacDonell, and J. Elmsley.
79 Newcastle Papers, reel A-307, Newcastle to Lord Palmerston, 12 Sept. 1860.
80 Ibid., Newcastle to Lord Palmerston, 30 Sept. 1860.
81 New York *Times*, 6, 7, and 11 Sept. 1860.
82 New York *Evening Post*, 6 Sept. 1860.
83 New York *Sun* editorial reprinted in the Kingston *British Whig*, 11 Sept. 1860.
84 New York *Freeman's Journal and Catholic Register*, 15 Sept and 27 Oct. 1860; New York *Irish-American*, 15 Sept. 1860.
85 London *Times* 21, 23 Sept. 1860.
86 Saint John, *Morning Freeman*, 15 Sept. 1860; Quebec *Mercury*, 6 Sept. 1860; Montreal *Pilot*, 6 Sept. 1860; Montreal *Gazette*, editorial reprinted in Kingston *British Whig*, 10 Sept. 1860; *Le Courrier du Canada*, [Quebec], 7 Sept. 1860.
87 Toronto *Globe*, 17 Sept. 1860; see also 19 and 20 Sept. 1860. George Brown spoke publicly along the same lines at a rally in Kingston; see *Globe*, 27 Nov. 1860.
88 Paul Romney, *Getting It Wrong: How Canadians Forgot Their Past and Imperilled Confederation* (Toronto: University of Toronto Press 1999).
89 Toronto *Leader*, 8, 11, and 13 Sept. 1860.
90 Letters written by Thomas D'Arcy McGee, the Reformer and Catholic, show that the Roman Catholics were eager to take part in a public meeting, but there is no indication in the press that they actually did so. Although the mayor had called a public meeting, the newspapers consistently referred to it as a 'Protestant' meeting or demonstration. See NA, MG 29 D 15, James George Moylan Papers, letters of T.D. McGee to J.G. Moylan, n.d.
91 Toronto *Leader*, 6 Oct. 1860.
92 Ibid., 6 Nov. 1860.
93 Ibid., 29 Oct. 1860. Historians have sometimes taken the allegation seriously and reported that Newcastle was sympathetic to the Catholics of Upper Canada because he was a Roman Catholic; see, for instance, Kealey, 'Orangemen and the Corporation,' 74. The duke was, in fact, an Anglican. Indeed, his father was an ultra-Protestant, but the fifth duke was known as a High Church Anglican from the time he was an undergraduate at Oxford. See F. Darrell Munsell, *The Unfortunate Duke: Henry Pelham, Fifth Duke of*

Newcastle, 1811–1864 (Columbia: University of Missouri Press 1985), 14, 126–7, 140.

94 Toronto *Leader,* 13 Oct. 1860.

95 Ibid., 29 Oct. 1860.

96 Donald Creighton, *John A. Macdonald: The Young Politician* (Toronto: Macmillan 1952), 304.

97 Toronto *Globe,* 12 Nov. 1860.

98 Shannon, *Narrative,* 53.

99 Toronto *Globe,* 21 March 1861.

100 Livermore, 'Election of 1861 in Kingston,' 245–59.

101 Ibid., 253; Stortz, 'John Joseph Lynch,' 121–2.

102 Creighton, *John A. Macdona* 259, 314–17; Cottrell, 'Irish Catholic Political Leadership,' 104–113.

103 Cottrell, 'Irish Catholic Political Leadership,' 218.

104 Toronto *Leader,* 8 Sept. 1860.

105 Kealey, 'The Orange Order in Toronto'; Houston and Smythe, *The Sash Canada Wore.*

Chapter 6: Performing Indians

1 Paige Raibmon, 'Theatres of Contact: The Kwakwa̱ka̱'wakw Meet Colonialism in British Columbia and at the Chicago World's Fair,' *Canadian Historical Review* 81 (June 2000): 157–90; H.V. Nelles, *The Art of Nation-Building: Pageantry and Spectacle at Quebec's Tercentenary* (Toronto: University of Toronto Press 1999), 164–97; Robert Cupido, 'Appropriating the Past: Pageants, Politics, and the Diamond Jubilee of Confederation,' *Journal of the Canadian Historical Association* 8 (1998): 156–86.

2 In addition to the above studies, see Cecilia Morgan, '"A Wigwam to Westminster": Performing Mohawk Identity in Imperial Britain, 1890s–1990s,' *Gender and History* 5 (2003): 319–41; Wade A. Henry, 'Imagining the Great White Mother and the Great King: Aboriginal Tradition and Royal Representation in the "Great Pow-wow" of 1901,' *Journal of the Canadian Historical Association* 11 (2000): 87–108; Trudy Nicks, 'Indian Villages and Entertainments: Setting the Stage for Tourist Souvenir Sales,' in Ruth B. Phillips and Christopher B. Steiner, ed., *Unpacking Culture: Art and Commodity in Colonial and Postcolonial Worlds* (Berkeley and Los Angeles: University of California Press 1999), 301–15; E.A. Heaman, 'Making a Spectacle: Exhibition of the First Nations,' chapter 10 of her *The Inglorious Arts of Peace: Exhibitions in Canadian Society during the Nineteenth Century* (Toronto: University of Toronto Press 1999); Karen Dubinsky, 'Local Colour in the "Contact Zone": The

Spectacle of Race,' chapter 3 of her *The Second Greatest Disappointment: Honeymooning and Tourism at Niagara Falls* (Toronto: Between the Lines 1999); Daniel Francis, *The Imaginary Indian: The Image of the Indian in Canadian Culture* (Vancouver: Arsenal Pulp Press 1992), 97–143; Peter Geller, '"Hudson's Bay Company Indians": Images of Native People and the Red River Pageant, 1920,' in S. Elizabeth Bird, ed., *Dressing in Feathers: The Construction of the Indian in American Popular Culture* (Boulder, Colo.: Westview Press 1996), 65–78; Keith Regular, 'On Public Display,' *Alberta History* 34 (1986): 1–12; Glen Mikkelsen, 'Indians and Rodeo,' *Alberta History* 34 (1986): 13–19; Donald B. Smith, *From the Land of Shadows: The Making of Grey Owl* (Saskatoon: Western Producer Prairie Books 1990); Veronica Strong-Boag, '"A Red Girl's Reasoning": E. Pauline Johnson Constructs the New Nation," in Veronica Strong-Boag et al., eds., *Painting the Maple: Essays on Race, Gender, and the Construction of Canada* (Vancouver: UBC Press 1998), 130–54.

3 See Olive Patricia Dickason, *Canada's First Nations: A History of Founding Peoples from Earliest Times* (Toronto: McClelland and Stewart 1992), 216–73; J.R. Miller, *Skyscrapers Hide the Heavens: A History of Indian-White Relations in Canada*, rev. ed. (Toronto: University of Toronto Press 1991), 41–115; William Wicken, *Mi'kmaq Treaties on Trial: History, Land and Donald Marshall Junior* (Toronto: University of Toronto Press 2002); Bill Parenteau and James Kenny, 'Survival, Resistance, and the Canadian State: The Transformation of New Brunswick's Native Economy, 1867–1930,' *Journal of the Canadian Historical Association* 13 (2002): 49–71.

4 National Archives of Canada (NA), RG 7 G23, Office of the Governor General, Royal Visits, vol. 1, draft of the provincial secretary's reply to A.R. Green, 8 Sept. 1860.

5 Newcastle's biographers cover the North American tour but neglect the Aboriginal theme; see John Martineau, *The Life of Henry Pelham, Fifth Duke of Newcastle, 1811–1864* (London, 1908), 290–301; F. Darrell Munsell, *The Unfortunate Duke: Henry Pelham, Fifth Duke of Newcastle, 1811–1864* (Columbia: University of Missouri Press, 239–43.

6 Oxford University, Bodleian Library, Acland Family Papers, Sarah Acland's Letters from Her Husband 1860 (MS Add. d.12 and 13) and 'Burning Cloud' (MS Add, d.91); Trudy Nicks, 'Dr Oronhyatekha's History Lessons: Reading Museum Collections as Texts,' in Jennifer S.H. Brown and Elizabeth Vibert, eds., *Reading Beyond Words: Contexts for Native History* (Peterborough, Ont.: Broadview Press 1996), 483–508; J.B. Atlay, *Sir Henry Wentworth Acland, Bart.* (London: Smith, Elder 1903), chapter 10; Gayle M. Comeau-Vasilopoulos, 'Oronhyatekha,' *Dictionary of Canadian Biography*, vol. 13 (Toronto: University of Toronto Press 1994), 792; Jim Burant et al.,

'Sir Henry Wentworth Acland,' in their *A Place in History: Twenty Years of Acquiring Paintings, Drawings and Prints at the National Archives of Canada* (Ottawa: National Archives of Canada 1991), 55–8.

7 Oxford University, Acland Family Papers, Henry Wentworth Acland (MS Acland d.91), Henry Acland to Sarah Acland, 15 July 1860.

8 Royal Archives (RA), VIC/Add A 3/20, 'Bertie' [the Prince of Wales] to 'Mama' [Queen Victoria], 16 Sept. 1860.

9 'Address of the Citizens of Toronto,' in Robert Cellem, *Visit of His Royal Highness the Prince of Wales to the British North American Provinces and United States in the Year 1860* (Toronto: H. Rowsell 1861), 215–16.

10 'Address of the Inhabitants of the County of Pictou,' in Cellem, *Visit of HRH*, 74–5.

11 'Address of the Archdeacon of Kingston and Clergy of the Archdeaconry within the Diocese of Toronto,' Kingston *British Whig*, 3 Sept. 1860.

12 NA, RG 7 G 23, vol. 1, 'Address of the Chiefs, Sachems, and Warriors of the Six Nations Indians Residing on the Grand River, Done in General Council, August 20, 1860.'

13 All descriptions of Toronto transparencies are from Toronto *Globe*, 7 Sept. 1860.

14 Saint John *Morning Freeman*, 4 Aug. 1860.

15 Bonnie Huskins suggests that, during the prince's visit to Nova Scotia, it was made clear that 'the Amerindians ... played an important role in Nova Scotia's "official" historical memory and sense of colonial identity.' See her '"A Tale of Two Cities": Boosterism and the Imagination of Community during the Visit of the Prince of Wales to Saint John and Halifax in 1860,' *Urban History Review* 28 (Oct. 1999): 38.

16 Toronto *Leader*, 15 Sept. 1860.

17 Carl Benn, *The Iroquois in the War of 1812* (Toronto: University of Toronto Press 1998), 190; Veronica Strong-Boag and Carole Gerson, *Paddling Her Own Canoe: The Times and Texts of E. Pauline Johnson (Tekahionwake)* (Toronto: University of Toronto Press 2000), 30.

18 Peter W. Sinnema, *Dynamics of the Pictured Page: Representing the Nation in the Illustrated London News* (Aldershot, U.K.: Ashgate 1998). In contrast to the theme I emphasize here (the partial incorporation into the colonies of loyal Natives), Gillian Poulter examines the ways in which British and French-Canadian artists used Native figures to signify the 'Other' in paintings and engravings of Lower Canada. See her 'Representation as Colonial Rhetoric: The Image of "the Native" and "*the habitant*" in the Formation of Colonial Identities in Early Nineteenth-Century Lower Canada,' *Journal of Canadian Art History* 16 (1994): 10–25.

19 The teepee was not only imagined by the artist. The Toronto *Globe* correspondent reported from Charlottetown that 'in the square was the tent of an Indian chief, who ... with his warriors and squaws paddled out to meet the Prince, and joined his voice with that of the applauding throng' (17 Aug. 1860).

20 Charlottetown *Examiner*, 12 Aug. 1860; Burant et al., *A Place in History*, 54–8.

21 Acland Family Papers, d.12, Henry Acland to Sarah Acland, 2 and 21 Sept. 1860, and d.91, 'Burning Cloud'; Nicks, 'Dr Oronhyatekha's History Lessons,' 483–508; Atlay, *Sir Henry Wentworth Acland*, passim; Comeau-Vasilopoulos, 'Oronhyatekha,' 792; Burant et al., *A Place in History* 55–8.

22 Mary Ryan, 'The American Parade: Representations of the Nineteenth-Century Social Order,' in Lynn Hunt, ed., *The New Cultural History* (Berkeley: University of California Press 1987), 131–53; Mary P. Ryan, *Civic Wars: Democracy and Public Life in the American City during the Nineteenth Century* (Berkeley: University of California Press 1997), 65–8; Bonnie Huskins, 'The Ceremonial Space of Women: Public Processions in Victorian Saint John and Halifax,' in Janet Guildford and Suzanne Morton, eds., *Separate Spheres: Women's Worlds in the 19th-Century Maritimes* (Fredericton: Acadiensis Press 1994), 145–60. See also Ruth Roach Pierson, 'Nations: Gendered, Racialized, Crossed with Empire,' in Ida Blom, Karen Hagemann, and Catherine Hall, eds., *Gendered Nations: Nationalisms and Gender Order in the Long Nineteenth Century* (Oxford and New York: Berg 2000), 43–4.

23 In the memory of a storyteller who was a midshipman aboard the *Hero* that day, the Mi'kmaq had come alongside in their canoes, bearing an address that they had hoped to present, but they had arrived too late since the prince had gone ashore; he met with them later. This account does not square with the newspaper ones, which have the canoes providing an escort for the prince and his barge. See Lieutenant Thomas Bunbury Gough, *Boyish Reminiscences of His Majesty the King's Visit to Canada in 1860* (London: John Murray 1910), 124–5.

24 The Halifax *British Colonist*, 26 July 1860, announced prizes of $10 and $5 respectively for the first and second prizes in the Indian 'flat race' and mentioned that the winner could run in the champion race.

25 Huskins, 'Tale of Two Cities,' 37–8.

26 Halifax *Nova Scotian*, 7 May 1840, cited by L.F.S. Upton, *Micmacs and Colonists: Indian-White Relations in the Maritimes, 1713–1867* (Vancouver: University of British Columbia Press 1979), 136.

27 Charlottetown *Examiner*, 21 Aug. and 10 Dec. 1860; L.F.S. Upton, *Micmacs and Colonists*, 119; Acland's sketches may be found in NA, MG 40-Q40, Sir Henry Acland Fonds, album 2/74–6.

28 Reid, *Myth, Symbol, and Colonial Encounter*, 83.
29 NA, RG 7, G 23, vol. 1, Memorandum from the Montreal Reception Committee to R. Pennefather, 18 Aug. 1860.
30 'Address of the Crosse Club of Montreal,' in Morgan, *Tour of H.R.H.*, 222; Toronto *Globe*, 22 Aug. 1860; Toronto *Leader*, 28 Aug. 1860; Cornwallis, *Royalty in the New World*, 97.
31 Don Morrow, 'Lacrosse as the National Game,' in Don Morrow et al. *A Concise History of Sport in Canada* (Don Mills, Ont.: Oxford University Press 1989), 46–8.
32 David Blanchard, 'For Your Entertainment Pleasure – Princess White Deer and Chief Running Deer – Last "Hereditary" Chief of the Mohawk: Northern Mohawk Rodeos and Showmanship,' *Journal of Canadian Culture* 1 (1984): 99–116; Nicks, 'Indian Villages and Entertainments,' 304–5.
33 Toronto *Leader*, 28 Aug. 1860; Cornwallis, *Royalty in the New World*, 97.
34 NA, MG21 A34, Henry, Duke of Newcastle Papers, A-1610, Newcastle to Sir Edmund Head, 13 June 1860.
35 Morgan, *Tour of H.R.H.*, 125, reproduces an article from the Montreal *Gazette*; Gardner D. Engleheart, *Journal of the Progress of H.R.H. the Prince of Wales through British North America and His Visit to the United States* (London: privately printed 1860), 45; Toronto *Globe*, 31 Aug. 1860.
36 *Illustrated London News*, 1861.
37 NA, MG40-Q40, album 3/137.
38 The reserves in the Sarnia area are described in Peter S. Schmalz, *The Ojibwa of Southern Ontario* (Toronto: University of Toronto Press 1991), 176–8.
39 Toronto *Globe*, 17 Sept. 1860; *Sarnia Observer*, 21 Sept. 1860.
40 Presentation items from the tour, many of which are still in the Royal Collection, are discussed and shown in illustrations in Ruth B. Phillips, *Trading Identities: The Souvenir in Native North American Art from the Northeast, 1700–1900* (Seattle: University of Washington Press/Montreal and Kingston: McGill-Queen's University Press 1998).
41 Douglas Leighton, 'Pennefather, Richard Theodore,' *Dictionary of Canadian Biography* vol. 9 (Toronto: University of Toronto Press 1976), 627–8. Note that Pennefather continued to act as superintendent for several months after the transfer from imperial to Canadian authority.
42 NA, RG 10, Records of the Department of Indian Affairs, vol. 545 is the relevant letterbook of outgoing correspondence sent by Bartlett, mainly from his Toronto office, in July, August, and September 1860. Henceforth: Bartlett Letterbook.
43 Bartlett Letterbook, W.R. Bartlett to Chief Henry Madwayosh and John Kadahgegwow, 27 July 1860; W.R. Bartlett to the Rev. Allen Salt, 27 July

1860; W.R. Bartlett to R.T. Pennefather, 11 July 1860; W.R. Bartlett to Froome Talfourd, 11 Aug. 1860.

44 Bartlett Letterbook, W.R. Bartlett to R.T. Pennefather, 11 July 1860; W.R. Bartlett to the Mohawk Councillors, Tyendinaga, 3 Aug. 1860; W.R. Bartlett to the Rev. A. Salt, 17 July 1860. In contrast to the tercentenary celebrations in 1908, when Indians, no matter their nation, were clothed as Plains Indians, 'traditional dress' in 1860 had not yet firmly acquired the Plains connotation, which developed in tune with the popular Wild West Shows of the 1880s. (See Nelles, *The Art of Nation-Building*, 174–6.) That is not to say that cross-cultural borrowing, possibly including from Plains Indians, was absent from the 'traditional' clothing worn for the 1860 celebrations – quite the contrary. See Ruth B. Phillips, 'First Nations Gifts for a Royal Prince: Unsettled Arts in an Era of Settlement,' McCready Memorial Lecture, Art Gallery of Ontario, 21 Jan. 2002.

45 Bartlett Letterbook, Bartlett to the Rev. Allen Salt, 27 July 1860.

46 Bartlett Letterbook, Bartlett to Froome Talfourd, 11 Aug. 1860. The Mohawk display in fact took place in Brantford.

47 Dickason, *Canada's First Nations* 247–56; John L. Tobias, 'Protection, Civilization, Assimilation: An Outline History of Canada's Indian Policy,' and John S. Milloy, 'The Early Indian Acts: Developmental Strategy and Constitutional Change,' in J.R. Miller, ed., *Sweet Promises: A Reader on Indian-White Relations in Canada* (Toronto: University of Toronto Press 1991), 212–58.

48 Heaman notes that as early as 1865 such disputes arose in connection with Canadian exhibits abroad (*Inglorious Arts of Peace*, 300). Similar concerns about appropriate representation surfaced in connection with later public events involving Indian participation in the Calgary Stampede (see Regular, 'On Public Display') and in the royal visit of 1901 (see Henry, 'Imagining the Great White Mother') and the 1939 visit (see Tom MacDonnell, *Daylight upon Magic: The Royal Tour of Canada – 1939* [Toronto: Macmillan 1989], 131–2).

49 The phrase comes from the important theoretical study first published in 1976: Dean MacCannell, *The Tourist: A New Theory of the Leisure Class*, 2nd ed. (New York: Shocken 1989). See also Jane C. Desmond, *Staging Tourism: Bodies on Display from Waikiki to Sea World* (Chicago: University of Chicago Press 1999).

50 Oronhyatekha's clothing, which is in the collection of the Museum of the County of Los Angles; another suit of clothing, worn by Ojibwa Chief John Tecumseh Henry in 1860, is in the collection of the Royal Ontario Museum (ROM). See Nicks, 'Dr Oronhyatekha's History Lessons,' 500. These and

other articles worn in honour of the 1860 royal visit were part of a special exhibit on Oronhyatekha at the ROM in the spring of 2002.

51 Acland Family Papers, MS Acland d.12, Henry Acland to Sarah Acland, 2 Sept. and 21 Sept. 1860. See also Atlay, *Sir Henry Wentworth Acland*, chapter 10; Comeau-Vasilopoulos, 'Oronhyatekha'; and Jim Burant et al., *A Place in History*, 55–8.

52 Donald Smith, *Sacred Feathers: The Reverend Peter Jones (Kahkewaquonaby) and the Mississauga Indians* (Toronto: University of Toronto Press 1987), 204, citing Victoria University Archives (Toronto), Peter Jones Collection, Peter Jones to his wife, Eliza Jones, 8 Nov. 1845.

53 Liverpool *Courier*, 15 Sept. 1860, as cited in Celia Haig-Brown, 'Seeking Honest Justice in a Land of Strangers: Nahnebahwequa's Struggle for Land,' *Journal of Canadian Studies* 36 (2001–2): 155. For further discussions of Native women's dress and performance, see Morgan, 'Performing Mohawk Identity in Imperial Britain,' 331; Mary Elizabeth Leighton, 'Performing Pauline Johnson: Representations of the "Indian Poetess" in the Periodical Press, 1892–95,' *Essays on Canadian Writing* 665 (1998): 141–62; Strong-Boag, '"A Red Girl's Reasoning,"' 130–54.

54 Sarnia *Observer*, 21 Sept. 1860.

55 Bartlett Letterbook, W.R. Bartlett to R.T. Pennefather, 7 Aug. 1860; G.S. French, 'Shah-wun-dais' (or John Sunday), *Dictionary of Canadian Biography*, vol. 10 (Toronto: University of Toronto Press 1972), 647–8.

56 *Christian Guardian* (Toronto), 5 Sept. 1860. Opposition to Indian dances was much more intense during the royal visit to Canada in 1901; in the interim, state officials had focused on stamping out traditional dancing as forms of resistance to departmental authority and Christianity. See Henry, 'Imagining the Great White Mother,' 96, 106; Katherine Pettipas, *Severing the Ties That Bind: Government Repression of Indigenous Religious Ceremonies on the Prairies* (Winnipeg: University of Manitoba Press 1994).

57 *Christian Guardian*, 30 Jan. 1861.

58 Smith, *Sacred Feathers*, 136–8; the quotation that Smith cites is from Peter Jones, *Life and Journals of Kah-ke-wa-quon-na-by by (Rev. Peter Jones), Wesleyan Missionary* (Toronto: Anson Green 1860), entry for 23 Feb. 1832.

59 French, 'Shah-wun-dais,' 647–8.

60 Charles Stuart, *A Short History and Description of the Ojjibeway Now on a Visit to England* (London: n.p. 1844), 11–12.

61 J.R. Miller, 'Petitioning the Great White Mother: First Nations Organizations and Lobbying in London' (paper presented to the Canada and the End of Empire Conference, Institute of Commonwealth Studies, University of London, April 2001, 4–10).

62 Nahnebahwequa's account is in Robert Alsop and Thomas Hodgkin, M.D., 'Nah-ne-hab-wee-quay,' *Aborigines' Friend, and the Colonial Intelligencer* (January–December 1860), 155, and cited in Haig-Brown, 'Seeking Honest Justice,' 153. Queen Victoria described Nahnebahwequa as being 'of the yellow colour of the American Indians, with black hair' and as being 'dressed in a strange European dress with a coloured shawl and straw hat with feathers. She speaks English quite well, and is come on behalf of her Tribe to petition against some grievance as regards their land.' RA, Queen Victoria's Journal, 19 June 1860, as cited in Haig-Brown, 'Seeking Honest Justice,' 154.

63 Toronto *Globe*, 1 Sept. 1860.

64 NA, Colonial Office Records, CO/42, vol. 624; NA , RG 10, vol. 266.

65 Rhonda Telford, 'The Anishinabe Presentation of Their Fishing Rights to the Duke of Newcastle and the Prince of Wales,' *Papers of the Alqonquian Conference* 30 (1999): 374–96.

66 Tony Hall, 'Native Limited Identities and Newcomer Metropolitanism in Upper Canada, 1814–1867,' in David Keane and Colin Read, eds. *Old Ontario: Essays in Honour of J.M.S. Careless* (Toronto: Dundurn 1990), 161. See also Miller, *Skyscrapers Hide the Heavens*, 110–13; Milloy, 'Early Indian Acts,' 147–50.

67 Janet Chute, *The Legacy of Shingwaukonse: A Century of Native Leadership*, (Toronto: University of Toronto Press 1998), 175–8.

68 Bartlett Letterbook, W.R. Bartlett to R.T. Pennefather, 7 Aug. 1860.

69 Chute, *Legacy of Shingwaukonse*, 176; Bartlett and his colleague Froome Talfourd refused to attend the council because they did not want to 'be parties to or recognize in any way this grievance meeting,' but they learned about what occurred from Francis Assikinack, the interpreter, who attended the council and provided a memorandum on what he heard. (See W.R. Bartlett Letterbook, Bartlett to R.T. Pennefather, 25 Sept. 1860.

70 NA, RG 10, vol. 266, 163, 326–9, 'Petition Signed by Henry H. Madwayosh and 49 Others.'

71 NA, Colonial Office Records, CO/42, vol. 624, f. 266–949, 'Report of R.T. Pennefather to His Grace, the Duke of Newcastle.'

72 Ibid., Newcastle to the Superintendent of Indians in Canada, 1862; 'Twenty-fourth Annual Report of the Aborigines' Protection Society,' 1862, in *The Colonial Intelligencer and Aborigines' Friend, 1859–1866*, 2:17; Nahneebahwee-quay to the Friends of New York, 30 March 1861, in J.C., 'Nah-nee--bah-wee-quay,' *Friends' Intelligencer* 5 April 1861, 119, cited by Haig-Brown, 'Seeking Honest Justice,' 157.

73 J.R. Miller, 'Petitioning the Great White Mother,' 16–28.

74 The Associated Press account appeared, for instance, in the Toronto *Globe*, 14 Sept. 1860, and the Toronto *Leader*, 16 Sept. 1860; Gardner D. Engleheart, *Journal*, 61; Woods, *Prince of Wales*, 231.

75 Toronto *Globe* , 17 Sept. 1860; Hamilton *Spectator*, 20 Sept. 1860; Woods, *Prince of Wales*, 23. On representations of Native masculinity, see Elizabeth Vibert, 'Real Men Hunt Buffalo: Masculinity, Race, and Class in British Fur Traders' Narratives,' *Gender & History* 8 (1996): 4–21; Morgan, 'Performing Mohawk Identity,' 324–6.

76 Sarnia *Observer*, 21 Sept. 1860; Woods, *Prince of Wales*, 35.

77 Pierre-J.-Olivier Chauveau, J. Lenoir-Rolland, J. Phelan, *The Visit of His Royal Highness, the Prince of Wales to America* (Montreal: Journal of Public Instruction for Lower Canada 1860), 53. (The pamphlet was simultaneously published in French.)

78 Woods, *Prince of Wales*, 231.

79 Toronto *Globe*, 14 Sept. 1860; Hamilton *Spectator*, 20 Sept. 1860; *Globe*, 17 Sept. 1860.

80 Carl Berger, *Science, God, and Nature in Victorian Canada* (Toronto: University of Toronto Press 1982); Suzanne Zeller, *Inventing Canada: Early Victorian Science and the Idea of a Transcontinental Nation* (Toronto: University of Toronto Press 1987).

81 Ruth Phillips makes this point in reference to the suit of clothes worn by Oronhyateka in her 'First Nations Gifts for a Royal Prince.' On hybridity in the art forms of First Nations of the region more generally, see Phillips's *Trading Identities*.

82 Patricia Jasen, *Wild Things: Nature, Culture, and Tourism in Ontario, 1790–1914* (Toronto: University of Toronto Press 1995), 17; see also, R.G. Moyles and Doug Owram, *Imperial Dreams and Colonial Realities: British Views of Canada, 1880–1914* (Toronto: University of Toronto Press 1988), 184; Bill Parenteau, '"Care, Control and Supervision": Native People in the Canadian Atlantic Salmon Fishery, 1867–1900,' *Canadian Historical Review* 79 (1998): 1–35.

83 Cultural anthropologists have looked closely at the concept of 'authenticity' as it relates to folklore; see Regina Bendix, *In Search of Authenticity: The Formation of Folklore Studies* (Madison: University of Wisconsin Press 1997). In the twentieth century, such notions were reformulated as 'antimodernism'; see Ian McKay, *The Quest of the Folk: Antimodernism and Cultural Selection in Twentieth-Century Nova Scotia* (Montreal and Kingston: McGill-Queen's University Press 1994).

84 Toronto *Globe*, 21 Sept. 1860; New York *Herald*, 22 Sept. 1860; Woods, *Prince of Wales*, 261.

85 New York *Herald*, 22 Sept. 1860; Toronto *Globe*, 29 Aug. 1860.
86 Cornwallis, *Royalty in the New World*, 142.
87 Woods, *Prince of Wales*, 14, 34–7.
88 New York *Daily Tribune*, 7 Aug. 1860; Woods, *The Prince of Wales*, 21.
89 Ann Laura Stoler, 'Making Empire Respectable: The Politics of Race and Sexual Morality in 20th-Century Colonial Cultures,' *American Ethnologist* 16 (1989): 634–60, and 'Rethinking Colonial Categories: European Communities and the Boundaries of Rule,' *Comparative Studies in Society and History* 31 (1989): 134–61. See also Adele Perry, *On the Edge of Empire: Gender, Race, and the Making of British Columbia, 1849–1871* (Toronto: University of Toronto Press 2001), especially chapter 4.
90 Toronto *Globe* , 14 Sept. 1860; Hamilton *Spectator*, 20 Sept. 1860; Woods, *The Prince of Wales*, 153–5.
91 Robert J.C. Young, *Colonial Desire: Hybridity in Theory, Culture and Race* (London and New York: Routledge 1995).
92 Toronto *Leader*, 9 Aug. 1860.
93 Woods, *Prince of Wales*, 35–7.
94 For stimulating analyses of how the colonial 'Other' was used to construct English national identities, see Catherine Hall, ed., *White, Male and Middle Class: Explorations in Feminism and History* (New York: Routledge 1992), pt. 3, and *Civilising Subjects: Metropole and Colony in the English Imagination 1830–1867* (Chicago and London: University of Chicago Press 2002).
95 This is a tack taken in Phillips, 'First Nations Gifts for a Royal Prince.'
96 Henry, 'Imagining the Great White Mother'; MacDonnell, *Daylight upon Magic*, 131–2.

Chapter 7: Provincial Identities

1 Paul Connerton, *How Societies Remember* (Cambridge and New York: Cambridge University Press 1989); Geneviève Fabre, Jürgen Heideking, and Kai Dreisbach, ed., *Celebrating Ethnicity and Nation: American Festive Culture from the Revolution to the Early 20th Century* (New York: Berghahn Books 2001); Simon Peter Newman, *Parades and the Politics of the Street: Festive Culture in the Early American Republic* (Philadelphia: University of Pennsylvania Press 1997); David Waldstreicher, *In the Midst of Perpetual Fetes: The Making of American Nationalism, 1776–1820* (Chapel Hill: University of North Carolina Press and the Omohundro Institute 1997).
2 The addresses were widely reproduced; here I have used one convenient source: A British Canadian [Henry James Morgan,] *The Tour of H.R.H. the*

prince of Wales through British America and the United States (Montreal: John Lovell 1860).

3 Richard Williams, *The Contentious Crown: Public Discussion of the British Monarchy in the Reign of Queen Victoria* (Aldershot, U.K.: Ashgate 1997), 200.

4 Ibid., 192–204.

5 Ibid., 153–75.

6 Ibid., 174–82; John M. MacKenzie, *Propaganda and the Empire: The Manipulation of British Public Opinion, 1880–1960* (Manchester: Manchester University Press 1984).

7 Ian Ross Robertson, 'The 1850s: Maturity and Reform,' in Phillip A. Buckner and John G. Reid, eds., *The Atlantic Region to Confederation: A History* (Toronto: University of Toronto Press 1994), 359.

8 Fredericton *Reporter*, 3 Aug. 1860.

9 Saint John *Carleton Sentinel*, 18 Aug. 1860. See also Saint John *Morning News*, 17 Aug. 1860.

10 Ibid., 29 Aug. 1860.

11 Halifax *Constitutionalist*, 18 Aug. and 8 Sept. 1860.

12 Halifax *Acadian Recorder*, 8 Sept. 1860.

13 Saint John *Morning Freeman*, 13 Sept. 1860.

14 Saint John *Morning News*, 10 Sept. 1860.

15 Halifax *Acadian Recorder*, 8 Sept. 1860.

16 Woods, *Prince of Wales*, 14; article from *Harper's Weekly* reprinted in Halifax *Constitutionalist*, 30 Aug. 1860; article from *Edinburgh News*, headed 2 Aug. 1860, reprinted in Halifax *Constitutionalist*, 4 Oct. 1860.

17 Halifax *Constitutionalist*, 30 Aug. 1860.

18 Article from London *Times*, reprinted in *Acadian Recorder*, 3 Nov. 1860.

19 London *Times*, cited in Halifax *Constitutionalist*, 8 Sept. 1860.

20 London *Times*, cited in Saint John *Morning News*, 12 Sept. 1860.

21 New York *Times* article reprinted in *Morning News*, 17 Aug. 1860.

22 New York *Tribune*, 17 Aug. 1860.

23 Halifax *Constitutionalist*, 8 Sept. 1860.

24 Halifax *Morning Freeman*, 13 Sept. 1860. See also Fredericton *Reporter*, 17 Aug. 1860.

25 Charlottetown *Islander*, 24 Aug. 1860.

26 Saint John *Morning News*, 17 Aug. 1860.

27 Saint John *Morning News*, 10 Sept. 1860.

28 Halifax *Constitutionalist*, 23 Aug. and 8 Sept. 1860; Charlottetown *Examiner*, 23 Oct. 1860.

29 Editorial from *Nova Scotian*, reprinted in Fredericton *Reporter*, 14 Sept. 1860.

30 New York *Times*, 8 Aug. 1860.

31 Woods, *Prince of Wales*, 47.
32 Boston *Post*, 6 Aug. 1860.
33 Cornwallis, *Royalty in the New World*, 56, 61.
34 Philadelphia *Enquirer*, article reprinted in Fredericton *Head Quarters*, 22 Aug. 1860.
35 Fredericton *Head Quarters*, 22 Aug. 1860.
36 John F. McDevitt to the editor, 30 Aug. 1860, in Fredericton *Head Quarters*, 12 Sept. 1860.
37 Fredericton *Head Quarters*, 12 Sept. 1860.
38 Article in, for example, *Morning News*, 5 Sept. 1860.
39 *Le Courrier du Canada* [Quebec], letter-to-the-editor from Stanislas Drapeau, 20 July 1860.
40 Brian Young, *George-Étienne Cartier: Montreal Bourgeois* (Kingston and Montreal: McGill-Queen's University Press 1981), 53–76.
41 Jean-Paul Bernard, *Les rouges, liberalisme, nationalisme et anticlericalisme au milieu du XIXe siècle* (Montréal: Les Presses de l'Université du Québec 1971).
42 *Le Courrier du Canada* [Quebec], 5 Sept. 1860.
43 *L'Ordre* [Montreal], 15 Aug. 1860.
44 Ibid., 22 Aug. 1860.
45 Ibid., 28 July 1860.
46 *L'Ordre* [Montreal], 14 Sept. 1860. The tribute to the prince seems odd given that 'from 1850 to his death in 1871, Papineau ... remained the prophet of annexation and democracy.' See Fernand Ouellet, 'Papineau, Louis-Joseph,' *Dictionary of Canadian Biography*, vol. 10 (Toronto: University of Toronto Press 1972), 577).
47 *L'Ordre* [Montreal]. 5 Sept., 27 Aug. 1860.
48 Ibid., 15 Aug. 1860.
49 *Le Courrier du Canada* [Montreal], 20 Aug. 1860.
50 Frederick H. Armstrong, 'Rodier, Charles-Séraphin,' *Dictionary of Canadian Biography*, vol. 10 (Toronto: University of Toronto Press, 1972), 624–5.
51 *Le Canadien* [Quebec], 22 Aug. 1860.
52 *La Minerve* [Montreal], 27 Sept. 1860.
53 Jean-Paul Bernard, 'Guitté, P.-J.' *Dictionary of Canadian Biography*, vol. 9 (Toronto: University of Toronto Press 1976), 344–5. (The quotations are the translated ones that appear in Bernard's entry.)
54 Editorial from *La Minerve* (translation) in the *Globe*, 11 Aug. 1860.
55 Allan Gordon, *Making Public Pasts: The Contested Terrain of Montreal's Public Memories, 1891–1930* (Montreal and Kingston: McGill-Queen's University Press 2001), 82–3.
56 Toronto *Globe*, 13 Aug. 1860.

57 Saint John *Morning Freeman*, 8 Sept. 1860; Montreal *Gazette*, 17 Sept. 1860.
58 Cited in *La Minerve* [Montreal], 18 Sept. 1860.
59 *Le Canadien* [Quebec], 24 Sept. 1860; *La Minerve* [Montreal], 7 Aug. 1860.
60 *L'Ordre* [Montreal], 21 Sept. 1860. Allan Gordon reports that it took more than a decade for French Canadians to accept the name change to Victoria Square. By then, a square that had once been French Canadian had become a marker for an anglophone neighbourhood. Its associations with the queen were strongly reinforced in 1872, when the governor general, Lord Dufferin, inaugurated a monument to Queen Victoria in the square. (*Making Public Pasts*, 83.)
61 Toronto *Globe*, 24 and 28 Aug. 1860.
62 Halifax *Acadian Recorder*, 22 Sept. 1860; Fredericton *Head Quarters*, 19 Sept. 1860.
63 Articles in *L'Ordre* [Montreal], 21 Sept. 1860; *Le Courrier du Canada* [Quebec], 19 Sept. 1860.
64 Montreal *Gazette*, 17 Sept. 1860.
65 NA, MG 24 A34, Henry, Duke of Newcastle Papers, reel A-307, Newcastle to Lord Palmerston, 1 Sept. 1860.
66 Toronto *Globe*, 24 Aug. 1860.
67 *La Minerve* [Montreal], 27 Sept. 1860.
68 *L'Ordre* [Montreal], 22, 24, 27 Aug. 1860.
69 Three-colour banners had been flown by insurgents and criticized by authorities in the the 1837–8 rebellion; see Allan Greer, *The Patriots and the People: The Rebellion of 1837 in Rural Lower Canada* (Toronto: University of Toronto Press 1993), 196–7. The tricolour of France continued to be flown during public processions in late-nineteenth-century Quebec; see Craig Heron and Steve Penfold, 'The Craftmen's Spectacle: Labour Day Parades in Canada, the Early Years,' *Histoire sociale/Social History* 29 (1996): 368; Gordon, *Making Public Pasts*, 158.
70 *L'Ordre* [Montreal], 22 Aug. 1860.
71 Article from *Montreal Advertiser* reprinted in Quebec *Mercury*, 25 Aug. 1860.
72 *L'Ordre* [Montreal], 24 Aug. 1860.
73 NA, Newcastle Papers, reel A-307, Newcastle to Palmerston, 1 Sept. 1860. In this letter Newcastle reports that at Ottawa, 'the same circumstance occurred ... and with a similar result.'
74 *La Minerve* [Montreal], 13 Sept. 1860; Montreal *L'Ordre* [Montreal], 21 Sept. 1860.
75 P.M. Bardy (president of the Quebec chapter of the Société Saint-Jean Baptiste) to the editor of *Le Courrier du Canada* [Quebec], 29 Aug. 1860.

76 *Le Courrier du Canada* [Quebec], 15 Oct. 1860; see also 17 Sept., 1 Oct., and 31 Aug. 1860.
77 *Le Canadien* [Quebec], 27 Aug. 1860.
78 Quebec *Mercury* editorial reprinted in *Le Courrier du Canada* [Quebec], 1 Oct. 1860.
79 *L'Ordre* [Montreal], 19 Sept. 1860; *La Minerve* [Montreal], 27 Sept. 1860.
80 Toronto *Globe*, 29 June 1860. The Toronto *Leader* reported on the meeting, describing the large crowd and printing the resolutions, but it did not provide details about the speeches.
81 See Norman Knowles, *Inventing the Loyalist Past: The Ontario Loyalist Tradition and the Creation of Usable Pasts* (Toronto: University of Toronto Press 1997).
82 Toronto *Globe* and Toronto *Leader*, 22 Aug. 1860; newspaper reports on these developments were reprinted in pamphlet form and in J.H. Morris, 'The Origin of Our Maple Leaf Emblem,' *Papers and Records of the Ontario Historical Society* 5 (1904): 21–35.
83 James Henry Morris was a Toronto lawyer. (See Morris, 'Origin' 35.)
84 Toronto *Globe*, 18 Aug. 1860.
85 W.B. Jarvis to the editor, 22 Aug. 1860, in Toronto *Globe*, 23 Aug. 1860.
86 See John Higham, *Strangers in the Land: Patterns of American Nativism, 1860–1925* (New Brunswick, N.J.: Rutgers University Press 1955); Ray Allen Billington, *The Origins of Nativism in the United States, 1800–1844* (New York: Arno 1974); Tyler Anbinder, *Nativism and Slavery: The Northern Know Nothings and the Politics of the 1850s* (New York: Oxford University Press 1992).
87 'A German Resident' to the editor, 27 Aug. 1860, in the Toronto *Globe*, 1 Sept. 1860.
88 J.H. Morris to the editor, 23 Aug. 1860, in Toronto *Globe*, 24 Aug. 1860.
89 French-Canadian nationalists had claimed the maple leaf as a national symbol as early as 1836. See Gordon, *Making Public Pasts* 147–8.
90 Toronto *Globe*, 29 Aug. and 4 Sept. 1860.
91 New York *Times*, 12 Sept. 1860.

Chapter 8: Royal Tourist

1 Steve Clark, ed., *Travel Writing and Empire: Postcolonial Theory in Transit* (London: Zed Books 1999), 1.
2 John Urry maintains that tourist practices 'involve the notion of "departure,"' a limited breaking from the routines of everyday life and an engagement with 'a set of stimuli that contrast with the everyday and the mundane.' The tourist gaze is constructed in relationship to its opposite, to

the everyday. 'What makes a particular tourist gaze depends upon what it is contrasted with; what the forms of non-tourist experience happen to be.' See *The Tourist Gaze*, 2nd ed. (London: Sage Publications 2002), 2.

3 Gardner D. Engleheart, *Journal of the Progress of H.R.H. the Prince of Wales through British North America and His Visit to the United States* (London: privately printed 1860), 10.

4 Robert Cellem, *Visit of His Royal Highness, the Prince of Wales to the British North American Provinces and United States, in the Year 1860* (Toronto: Henry Rowsell 1861), 38–9; Kinahan Cornwallis, *Royalty in the New World; or the Prince of Wales in America* (New York: M. Doolady 1860), 29–30; Engleheart, *Journal*, 10.

5 Bruce Curtis, *The Politics of Population: State Formation, Statistics, and the Census of Canada, 1840–1875* (Toronto: University of Toronto Press 2000); M.J. Cullen, *The Statistical Movement in Early Victorian Britain: The Foundations of Empirical Research* (Hassocks (U.K.): Harvester Press 1975).

6 Toronto *Globe*, 9 Aug. 1860; New York *Tribune*, 7 Aug. 1860.

7 Royal Archives (RA), VIC/T 3/52, 'Bertie' [Prince of Wales] to 'Mama' [Queen Victoria], 24 July 1860; Oxford University, Bodleian Library, Acland Family Papers, MS Acland d.12, Henry Acland to Sarah Acland, 26 July 1860.

8 Nathaniel Augustus Woods, *The Prince of Wales in Canada and the United States* (London: Bradbury and Evans 1861), 41.

9 Montreal *Gazette* article reprinted in Halifax *Constitutionalist*, 28 Aug. 1860; New York *Times*, 18 Aug. 1860; Toronto *Globe*, 17 Aug. 1860; Cornwallis, *Royalty in the New World*, 61.

10 New York *Times*, 20 Aug. 1860.

11 Woods, *Prince of Wales*, 178; Cellem, *Visit of HRH*, 317.

12 A British Canadian [Henry James Morgan], *The Tour of H.R.H. the Prince of Wales through British America and the United States* (Montreal: John Lovell 1860), 185–6.

13 National Archives of Canada (NA), MG 40-Q40, Sir Henry Acland Fonds, C-12856.

14 Cellem, *Visit of HRH*, 134–5.

15 Acland Family Papers, Henry Acland to Sarah Acland, 20 Aug. 1860.

16 See Marjorie Hope Nicolson, *Mountain Gloom and Mountain Glory: The Development of the Aesthetics of the Infinite* (Ithaca, N.Y.: Cornell University Press 1959); Elizabeth McKinsey, *Niagara Falls: Icon of the American Sublime* (New York: Cambridge University Press 1985); Patricia Jasen, 'Romanticism, Modernity, and the Evolution of Tourism on the Niagara Frontier, 1790–1850,' *Canadian Historical Review*: 23 (1991): 283–318.

17 Woods, *Prince of Wales*, 39 and 60; New York *Times*, 7 Aug. 1860.

18 RA, VIC/Add A 3/17, 'Bertie' [Prince of Wales] to 'Mama' [Queen Victoria], 22 Aug. 1860; New York *Tribune*, 25 Aug. 1860; Woods, *Prince of Wales*, 95. On the gendering of waterfalls, see Karen Dubinsky, *The Second Greatest Disappointment: Honeymooning and Tourism at Niagara Falls* (Toronto: Between the Lines 1999), 38–53.
19 Ruth Phillips, *Trading Identities: The Souvenir in North American Art from the Northeast, 1700–1900* (Seattle and London: University of Washington Press 1998), 130.
20 *The Canadian Tourist* (1845), cited in ibid.
21 Woods, *Prince of Wales*, 103–4.
22 On the picturesque, see Alexander Ross, *The Imprint of the Picturesque on Nineteenth-Century British Fiction* (Waterloo: Wilfrid Laurier University Press 1986); Jasen, 'Romanticism, Modernity, and the Evolution of Tourism,' 287–91.
23 Toronto *Globe*, 13 Aug. 1860; New York *Tribune*, 9 Aug. 1860.
24 New York *Times*, 11 Aug. 1860; Woods, *Prince of Wales*, 50–2.
25 Woods, *Prince of Wales*, 137–9.
26 Patricia Jasen, *Wild Things: Nature, Culture, and Tourism in Ontario, 1790–1914* (Toronto: University of Toronto Press 1995).
27 Woods, *Prince of Wales*, 112; New York *Tribune*, 21 Aug. 1860; Cornwallis, *Royalty in the New World*.
28 Woods, *Prince of Wales*, 120–1; *New York Tribune*, 21 Aug. 1860.
29 Geoffrey Reaume, *Remembrance of Patients Past: Patient Life at the Toronto Hospital for the Insane, 1870–1940* (Don Mills, Ont.: Oxford University Press 2000). On touring institutions more generally, see Tina Loo and Carolyn Strange, '"Rock Prison of Liberation": Alcatraz and the American Imagination,' *Radical History Review* 78 (2000): 27–56; Carolyn Strange and Michael Kempa, 'Studies of Dark Tourism: Alcatraz and Robben Island,' *Annals in Tourism Research* (2003).
30 The Prince of Wales donated £100 to each of the educational institutions he visited, money intended to endow a student prize for academic achievement.
31 Acland Family Papers, Henry Acland to Sarah Acland, 11 Sept. 1860. The prince echoed the doctor's assessment of the University in a letter home: 'we went to the Provincial University, wh. is the Oxford & Cambridge of Canada. It is a very fine new building, and the Museums in progress will be very good I think.' See RA, VIC/Add A 3/19, 'Bertie' [Prince of Wales] to 'Mama' [Queen Victoria], 11 Sept. 1860).
32 On the Ottawa timber slide as tourist attraction, see Patricia Jason, *Wild Things*, 73–5.

33 Engleheart, *Journal*, 49. See also Robert Peter Gillis, 'Gilmour, Allan,' *Dictionary of Canadian Biography*, vol. 12 (Toronto: University of Toronto Press 1990), 366–8.
34 Toronto, *Globe*, 5 Sept. 1860; Woods, *Prince of Wales*, 165.
35 Acland Family Papers, Henry Acland to Sarah Acland, 3 Sept. 1860; NA, MG 29 E1,Thomas Wily Papers, Thomas Wily, 'A Reminiscence of the Visit of the Prince of Wales to Canada in 1860,' 218; Woods, *Prince of Wales*, 162–5.
36 Colleen Skidmore, '"All That Is Interesting in the Canadas": William Notman's Maple Box Portfolio of Stereographic Views, 1860,' *Journal of Canadian Studies* 32 (1998): 69–90.
37 David Edward Price was a son of the self-made timber baron, William Price, 'King of the Saguenay.' David Edward helped manage his father's firm, and he was a member of the assembly and later a legislative councillor. See Louise Dechêne, 'Price, William,' *Dictionary of Canadian Biography*, vol. 9 (Toronto: University of Toronto Press 1976), 642.
38 Cellem, *Visit of HRH*, 118.
39 Engleheart, *Journal*, 32; 'The Prince's Visit to the Rivers Saguenay and Ste Marguerite,' by a local correspondent for the Quebec *Mercury*, reprinted in Morgan, *Tour of H.R.H*, 54–5.
40 Acland Family Papers, Henry Acland to Willie [Acland], 18 Aug. 1860.
41 RA, Vic/Z 466/74, General Bruce to Prince Albert, 14 Aug. 1860.
42 Compare the accounts of 1860 with, for instance, passages from Charles Lanman, *A Tour of the River Saguenay in Lower Canada* (Philadelphia: Carey and Hart 1848), from B.J. Lossing, 'The Saguenay,' *Harper's New Monthly Magazine* 19 (July 1859), and from *Perham's Pictoral Voyage, Known as the Seven Mile Mirror to Canada ...* (New York: Baker, Godwin 1854), as cited in Skidmore, 'William Notman's Maple Box,' 77–81.
43 Fredericton *Head Quarters*, 29 Aug. 1860; Cornwallis, *Royalty in the New World*, 70.
44 Woods, *Prince of Wales*, 78–85.
45 See, for example, the discussion in the Ottawa *Citizen*, 25 Aug. 1860.
46 See the version of the story, complete with imagined dialogue, in the account of the special correspondent, in the Toronto *Globe*, 22 Aug. 1860; Engleheart downplays the event in his account, *Journal*, 32.
47 *Harper's Weekly*, 29 Sept. 1860.
48 Woods, *Prince of Wales*, 235.
49 The historical literature on tourism at Niagara Falls is extensive, but see especially Dubinsky, *Second Greatest Disappointment*; Patrick Vincent McGreevy, *Imagining Niagara: The Meaning and Making of Niagara Falls* (Amherst: University of Massachusetts Press 1994); William Irwin, *The New*

Niagara: Tourism, Technology and the Landscape of Niagara Falls, 1776–1917 (University Park: Pennsylvania State University Press 1996); Jasen, 'Romanticism, Modernity, and the Evolution of Tourism,' 283–318.

50 RA, Vic/Add A 3/20, 'Bertie' [the Prince of Wales] to 'Mama' [Queen Victoria], 16 Sept. 1860.

51 New York *Times*, 17 Sept. 1860.

52 Engleheart, *Journal*, 65.

53 Acland Family Papers, Henry Acland to Sarah Acland, 12 Sept. 1860; Engleheart, *Journal*, 63, 65.

54 Woods, *Prince of Wales*, 236.

55 Gordon Donaldson, 'Gravelet, Jean-François ["Charles Blondin"]' *Dictionary of Canadian Biography*, vol. 12 (Toronto University of Toronto Press 1996), 367–7.

56 Sir Sidney Lee, *King Edward VII: A Biography*, 2 vols. (London: Macmillan 1925), 1:95. On Blondin's rivalry with Farini, see Toronto *Globe*, 13 Aug. 1860.

57 RA, Vic/Add A 3/20, 'Bertie' [Prince of Wales] to 'Mama' [Queen Victoria], 16 Sept. 1860.

58 Cornwallis, *Royalty in the New World*, 151.

59 It is said that in 1861 the prince was responsible for bringing Blondin to London, where he performed 180 feet above the floor of the Crystal Palace. He continued to thrill audiences for decades. See Donaldson, 'Gravelet, Jean-François,' 367.

60 Engleheart, *Journal*, 35, 50, 65–6; RA, Vic/Add A 3/21, 'Bertie' [Prince of Wales] to 'Mama' [Queen Victoria], 23 Sept. 1860.

61 Montreal *Gazette* account reprinted in Halifax *British Colonist*, 28 Aug. 1860; *Daily Tribune* account reprinted in, for instance, the Toronto *Leader* 16 Aug. 1860.

62 Andrea Bear Nicholas, 'Acquin, Gabriel,' *Dictionary of Canadian Biography*, vol. 13 (Toronto: University of Toronto Press 1994), 3–4. Nicholas reports that Chief Gabriel, a celebrated hunter, befriended Governor Manners-Sutton's successor, Arthur Hamilton Gordon, who published a book about their trips together. It also records the chief's Maliseet stories. In 1883 Chief Gabriel visited London, England, where he renewed his acquaintance with royalty and was described as being 'the greatest social lion of the day.'

63 See Gillian Poulter, 'Representation as Colonial Rhetoric: The Image of "the Native" and "the *habitant*" in the Formation of Colonial Identities in Early Nineteenth-century Lower Canada,' *Journal of Canadian Art History* 16 (1994): 11–25.

64 Acland Family Papers, Henry Acland to Sarah Acland, 23 Aug., 1 and 12 Sept. 1860.
65 Ibid., 2 Sept. 1860.
66 Cellem, *Visit of HRH*, 40; Acland Family Papers, d.1 f.41–3, Albert Edward to Henry Acland, 16 May 1861, and appended note written by Acland's daughter, 26 Dec. 1925.
67 Skidmore, in 'William Notman's Maple Box,' examines, in part, the dispute between Notman and the commissioner of public works over the item's value and hence the amount of money due the photographer. She reports that the portfolio cannot now be located in the royal collections, although the Notman studio's (incomplete) copy is in the Archives at the McCord Museum of Canadian History in Montreal. The illustration in the *Illustrated London News* appears in the number for 22 June 1861. On Notman, see also Stanley Triggs, *The Stamp of a Studio* (Toronto: Coach House Press 1986); Robert G. Wilson, 'William Notman's Stereo Perspective: The Victoria Bridge,' *History of Photography* 20 (1996): 108–12.
68 Ruth Holmes Whitehead, 'Paul, Mary Christianne,' *Dictionary of Canadian Biography*, vol. 11 (Toronto: University of Toronto Press 1982), 679; R.H. Whitehead, 'Chistiana Morris: Micmac Artist and Artist's Model,' *Material History Bulletin* 3 (1977): 1–14.
69 Morgan, *Tour of H.R.H.*, 97; Stanley Triggs et al., *Victoria Bridge: The Vital Link* (Montreal: McCord Museum of Canadian History 1992), 83, 93.
70 *Cape Breton News*, in Halifax *British Colonist*, 9 Aug. 1860; 'Bertie' to 'Mama' in Lee, *King Edward VII*, 1: xx; Cellem, *Visit of HRH*, 104.
71 Acland letter cited in J.B. Atlay, *Sir Henry Wentworth Acland, Bart.* (London: Smith, Elder 1903), 285.
72 Woods, *Prince of Wales*, 26; Cellem, *Visit of HRH*, 206.
73 New York *Times*, 15 Oct. 1860.
74 St John's *Newfoundland Express*, 31 July 1860.
75 Frank Prochaska, *Royal Bounty: The Making of a Welfare Monarchy* (New Haven, Conn.: Yale University Press 1995).
76 Atlay, *Sir Henry Wentworth Acland*, 282; Wily, 'Reminiscence,' 210; New York *Times*, 19 Aug. 1860. See also New York *Times*, 23 Aug 1860.

Chapter 9: Renfrew in the Republic

1 Detroit *Daily Advertiser*, 21 Sept. 1860, reprinted in Washington *National Intelligencer*, 25 Sept. 1860; much of the report also appeared, for example, in the Toronto *Leader*, 25 Sept. 1860.
2 Ibid.

3 Ibid.; New York *Times*, 22 Sept. 1860.

4 Chicago *Press & Tribune*, 22 Sept. 1860; Detroit *Daily Advertiser*, 21 Sept. 1860; Toronto *Globe*, 25 Sept. 1860.

5 Toronto *Globe*, 25 Sept. 1860.

6 Toronto *Globe*, 25 Sept. 1860; Nathaniel Augustus Woods, *The Prince of Wales in Canada and the United States* (London: Bradbury and Evans 1861), 280; Detroit *Daily Advertiser*, 21 Sept. 1860.

7 Kinahan Cornwallis, *Royalty in the New World: or, the Prince of Wales in America* (New York: M. Doolady 1860), 167.

8 The party made overnight stays in Detroit, Chicago, Dwight (Ill.), St Louis, Cincinnati, Harrisburg, Washington, Richmond, Baltimore, Philadelphia, New York, West Point, Albany, Boston, and Portland (Me).

9 Royal Archives (RA), VIC/Z 466/22, Lord Lyons to the Duke of Newcastle, 14 May 1860 (copy).

10 In late September 1860, some prominent southerners petitioned for a visit to the south, so that the prince could see the cotton fields that supplied 'much of the wealth of the British Empire' and thus 'judge for himself our social condition.' The New York *Times*, on 21 Sept. 1860, printed the petition and vehemently insisted that the invitation be rejected on the grounds that the prince ought not to be 'called on to participate in our domestic broils.'

11 The contrast is with the kind of crowd activity discussed in Mary P. Ryan, *Civic Wars: Democracy and Public Life in the American City during the Nineteenth Century* (Berkeley: University of California Press 1997), and in David Waldstreicher, *In the Midst of Perpetual Fetes: The Making of American Nationalism, 1776–1820* (Chapel Hill: University of North Carolina Press and the Omohundro Institute 1997).

12 New York *Times*, 22 Sept. and 3 Oct. 1860; New York *Tribune*, 12 Oct. 1860; Cornwallis, *Royalty in the New World*, 205.

13 Woods, *Prince of Wales*, 279; Cornwallis, *Royalty in the New World*, 285; New York *Daily Tribune*, 12 Oct. 1860; Cornwallis, *Royalty in the New World*, 205.

14 New York *Evening Post*, 12 Oct. 1860; New York *Times*, 12 Oct. 1860.

15 New York *Times*, 5 Oct. 1860; Richmond *Whig*, 9 Oct. 1860; Cellem, *Visit of HRH*, 408; New York *Tribune*, 13 Oct. 1860; Cellem, *Visit of HRH*, 385.

16 Cornwallis, *Royalty in the New World*, 206; New York *Times*, 30 Oct. 1860; Cellem, *Visit of HRH*, 348.

17 Cellem, *Visit of HRH*, 337; Woods, *Prince of Wales*, 366; New York *Times*, 16 Oct. 1860.

18 New York *Tribune*, 20 Oct. 1860; New York *Evening Post*, 20 Oct. 1860.

19 Woods, *Prince of Wales*, 326; New York *Times*, 22 Sept. 1860; 'Hinch' to 'Papa'

[Earl of Sandwich], in Mrs [Beatrice] Steuart Erskine, *Memoirs of Edward, Earl of Sandwich, 1839–1916* (London: John Murray 1919), 46.

20 *Harper's Weekly*, 5 Oct. 1860; New York *Times*, 5 Oct. 1860. See also Cellem, *Visit of HRH*, 364–5; New York *Express*, cited in Washington *National Intelligencer*, 22 Oct. 1860; Oxford University, Bodleian Library, Acland Family Papers, MS d.12, Henry Acland to Sarah Acland, 3 Oct. 1860.

21 Woods, *Prince of Wales*, 338; New York *Daily Tribune*, 4 Oct. 1860.

22 Woods, *Prince of Wales*, 338.

23 Richmond *Whig*, 9 Oct. 1860; New York *Times*, 11 Oct. 1860.

24 Ibid.

25 New York *Times*, 11 Oct. 1860.

26 London *Times* editorial reprinted in New York *Times*, 6 Nov. 1860.

27 Woods, *Prince of Wales*, 359; Lyons's letter appears in the New York *Times*, 12 Oct. 1860.

28 New York *Times*, 29 Oct. 1860.

29 RA, VIC/Z 466/18, Lyons to Russell, 14 May 1860; Z 466/13, Lyons to Russell, 8 May 1860.

30 National Archives of Canada (NA), Colonial Office Records, CO42/625, Newcastle's jotting, 29 June 1860, on letter from 'Englishman' [of New York] to Newcastle, 10 June 1860; see also NA, MG 24 A34, Henry, Duke of Newcastle Papers, reel A-307, Newcastle to Lyons, 28 April 1860.

31 Philadelphia, *Public Ledger and Daily Transcript*, 28 Sept. 1860; London *Times* editorial reprinted in New York *Times*, 29 Oct. 1860.

32 New York *Irish-American*, 17 Nov. 1860; New York *Freeman's Journal and Catholic Register*, 20 Oct. 1860.

33 New York *Freeman's Journal*, 27 Oct. 1860; New York *Irish-American*, 17 Nov. 1860.

34 New York *Freeman's Journal*, 20 Oct. 1860; Bennett's role in the newspaper world of 1860 is covered in James L. Crouthamel, *Bennett's New York Herald and the Rise of the Popular Press* (Syracuse, N.Y.: Syracuse University Press 1989).

35 Robert Nugent, Lieutenant-Colonel of New York's 69th Militia Regiment, to the editor of the New York *Irish-American*, 3 Nov. 1860.

36 London *Times* editorial reprinted in New York *Times*, 29 Oct. 1860; New York *Times*, 11 Oct. 1860.

37 London *Spectator*, editorial reprinted in New York *Times*, 1 Aug. 1860; New York *Times*, 11 Oct. 1860; London *Times* editorial reprinted in New York *Times*, 29 Oct. 1860.

38 *The New England Tour of H.R.H. the Prince of Wales*, 3rd ed. (Boston: Bee Printing 1860), i & l. Neither the poet nor the author is identified in the publication.

39 London *Times* editorial reprinted in New York *Times*, 24 July 1860; New York *Times*, 22 Sept. 1860; *Frank Leslie's Illustrated Newspaper* [New York], 13 Oct. 1860.
40 New York *Times*, 1 Aug. 1860; *New York Tribune*, 12 Oct. 1860; Cornwallis, *Royalty in the New World*, 205.
41 Richard Williams, *The Contentious Crown: Public Discussion of the British Monarchy in the Reign of Queen Victoria* (Aldershot, U.K.: Ashgate 1997), 153–90.
42 *New England Tour*, 1; London *Times* editorial reprinted in New York *Times*, 29 Oct. 1860.
43 Chicago *Daily Evening Journal*, 26 Sept. 1860; Cornwallis, *Royalty in the New World*, 205, 219, 242. For context, see Reginald Horsman, *Race and Manifest Destiny: The Origins of American Racial Anglo-Saxonism* (Cambridge, Mass.: Harvard University Press 1981).
44 *Punch*, 20 Oct. 1860; *Frank Leslie's Illustrated Newspaper*, [New York], 20 Oct. 1860.
45 New York *Herald* clipping in Toronto *Leader*, 31 July 1860.
46 From 'Ode on the Departure of the Prince of Wales,' *Punch*, 21 July 1860.
47 *Harper's Weekly*, 13 Oct. 1860.
48 *Ibid.*, 15 Sept. 1860; Cellem, *Visit of HRH*, 372; New York *Tribune*, 12 Oct. 1860; New York *Times*, 5 Oct. 1860.
49 Cellem, *Visit of HRH*, 383–4.
50 Cornwallis, *Royalty in the New World*, 184.
51 Philadelphia *Public Ledger and Daily Transcript*, 12 Oct. 1860; *New England Tour*, 20; New York *Times*, 4 Oct. 1860; Cellem, *Visit of HRH*, 388.
52 Cellem, *Visit of HRH*, 416; New York *Evening Post*, 20 Oct. 1860; Boston *Courier* reprinted in New York *Times*, 16 Oct. 1860.
53 New York *Times*, 5 Oct. 1860.
54 Ryan, *Civic Wars*, 89.

Chapter 10: New York, New York

1 John Jacob Astor gave his imprimatur to the label, and its awkward abbreviation, in *The Upper Ten Thousand*, his 1852 account of life among the New York elite. See Edwin G. Burrows and Mike Wallace, *Gotham: A History of New York City to 1898* (New York: Oxford University Press 1999), 714.
2 The New York press of the mid-century is described in Burrows and Wallace, *Gotham*, 674–90.
3 Allan Nevins and Milton Halsey Thomas, ed., *The Diary of George Templeton*

Strong: The Civil War, 1860–1865, 4 vols. (New York: Macmillan 1952), 2: 34–52.

4 Fernando Wood to G.M. Dallas, 8 May 1860, in *Proceedings of the Board of Aldermen, City of New York*, vol. 79 (New York: Charles W. Babe 1860), 588–9.

5 Brooks McNamara, *Day of Jubilee: The Great Age of Public Celebrations in New York, 1788–1909* (New Brunswick, N.J.: Rutgers University Press 1997).

6 Royal Archives (RA), VIC/Z 466/22, Lord Lyons to the Duke of Newcastle, 14 May 1860; *Strong Diary*, 34.

7 Jerome Mushkat, *Fernando Wood: A Political Biography* (Kent, Ohio, and London: Kent State University Press 1990).

8 RA, Vic/Z 466/30, E.M. Archibald to Lord Lyons, 2 June 1860, enclosed in Z 466/29, Lord Lyons to Lord Russell, 5 June 1860; Z 466/22, Lord Lyons to the Duke of Newcastle, 14 May 1860.

9 The press interpreted the petition in this way; see New York *Herald* reprinted in Toronto *Globe*, 19 July 1860.

10 J. Russell to Fernando Wood, enclosed in G.M. Dallas to Lord Lyons, 22 June 1860, and printed in *A British Canadian* [Henry James Morgan], *The Tour of H.R.H. the Prince of Wales through British America and the United States* (Montreal: John Lovell 1860), 18–19.

11 Toronto *Globe*, 12 July 1860; New York *Daily Tribune*, 10 July 1860.

12 New York *Daily Tribune* and New York *Times*, 21 Aug. 1860; *Strong Diary*, 44.

13 New York Public Library, Manuscripts and Archives Division, Charles P. Daly Papers, 'Ball in Honor of H.R.H., The Prince of Wales' (printed minutes of meetings of ball committee, 1860).

14 New York *Times*, 24 and 27 Aug. 1860.

15 New York *Daily Tribune*, 15 Sept. 1860.

16 New York *Times*, 23 Aug. 1860. The advantages of various mansions, including Wood's, are assessed in New York *Herald*, 21 Aug. 1860.

17 New York *Daily Tribune*, 11 Oct. 1860.

18 Nathaniel Augustus Woods, *The Prince of Wales in Canada and the United States* (London: Bradbury and Evans 1861), 377; the same incident is covered in the New York *Evening Post*, New York *Times*, and New York *Daily Tribune*, 12 Oct. 1860.

19 *Proceedings of the Board of Aldermen of the City of New York, From October 1st, 1860 to January 4th, 1861* (New York: Edmond Jones 1861), 46, 54.

20 New York *Daily Tribune*, 12 Oct. 1860.

21 New York *Times* and New York *Daily Tribune*, 12 Oct. 1860.

22 RA, Vic/T 3/58, 'Bertie' [the Prince of Wales] to 'Papa' [Prince Albert], 14 Oct. 1860; Woods, *Prince of Wales*, 379–80; Cellem, *Visit of HRH*, 388.

23 Woods, *Prince of Wales*, 374.

24 Cornwallis, *Royalty in the New World*, 206; New York *Times* and New York *Daily Tribune*, 12 Oct. 1860; Toronto *Leader*, 13 Oct. 1860.
25 *Strong Diary*, 45.
26 Cellem, *Visit of HRH*, 389; Cornwallis, *Royalty in the New World*, 207; New York *Daily Tribune* and New York *Times*, 12 Oct. 1860.
27 RA, Vic/T 3/58, 'Bertie' [Prince of Wales] to 'Papa' [Prince Albert], 14 Oct. 1860.
28 Woods, *Prince of Wales*, 374; Cornwallis, *Royalty in the New World*, 205; New York *Times*, 12 Oct. 1860.
29 Rothschild letter cited by Douglas T. Miller, *Jacksonian Aristocracy: Class and Democracy in New York, 1830–1860* (New York: Oxford University Press 1967), 156; Strong *Diary*, 45; Oxford University, Bodleian Library, Acland Family Papers, MS Acland, d.13, Henry Acland to Sarah Acland, 15 Oct. 1860; NA, MG 24 A 34, Henry, Duke of Newcastle Papers, reel A-307, the Duke of Newcastle to the queen, 14 Oct. 1860; RA, Vic/T 3/58, 'Bertie' [Prince of Wales] to 'Papa' [Prince Albert], 14 Oct. 1860.
30 See Burrows and Wallace, *Gotham*, 735–60.
31 New York *Times*, 12 Oct. 1860.
32 *Harper's Weekly*, 6 Oct. 1860.
33 New York *Freeman's Journal and Catholic Register* [*Freeman's Journal*], 4 Aug. and 8 Sept. 1860.
34 New York *Irish-American*, 20 Aug. and 29 Sept. 1860.
35 Ibid., 25 Aug. 1860.
36 The complete poem appears in the New York *Irish-American*, 3 Nov. 1860. The poet is identified only as 'C.J.C.'
37 New York *Irish-American*, 15 Oct. 1860 (the article had been written before the event it discussed); New York *Times*, 12 Oct. 1860.
38 Edward K. Spann, 'Union Green: The Irish Community and the Civil War,' in Ronald H. Bayor and Timothy J. Meagher, ed., *The New York Irish* (Baltimore, Md.: Johns Hopkins University Press 1996).
39 New York *Irish-American*, 20 Oct. 1860 and 23 March 1861.
40 Ibid., 3 Nov. 1860.
41 Ibid., 1 and 22 Dec. 1860.
42 Ibid., 24 Nov. 1860.
43 See the summaries of the testimony that appeared in the New York *Irish-American*, 2 Feb. - 23 March 1861.
44 Ibid., 16 and 23 March 1861.
45 Ibid., 20 Oct. and 1 Dec. 1860, 26 Jan. 1861.
46 Spann, 'Union Green,' 194–6.

47 New York *Commercial Advertiser* article reprinted in Toronto *Leader,* 16 Oct. 1860.
48 Daly Papers, 'Ball in Honor of the Prince of Wales.'
49 New York *Daily Tribune,* 13 Oct. 1860.
50 Cornwallis, *Royalty in the New World,* 208.
51 *Commercial Advertiser* article reprinted in Toronto *Leader,* 16 Oct. 1860; New York *Daily Tribune,* 13 Oct. 1860; Douglas T. Miller, *Jacksonian Aristocracy,* 156–7.
52 RA, Vic/Z 467/56, Davis to Bates, 29 Sept. 1860, enclosed in Van der Veyer to Prince Albert, n.d.
53 On Brown, see Burrows and Wallace, *Gotham,* 717.
54 New York *Times,* 2 Oct. 1860.
55 RA, Vic/Z 467/56, Davis to Bates, 29 Sept. 1860, enclosed in Van der Veyer to Prince Albert, n.d.
56 New York *Times,* letter-to-the-editor, 1 Oct. 1860.
57 Ibid., 13 Oct. 1860.
58 Donna R. Gabaccia, *We Are What We Eat: Ethnic Food and the Making of Americans* (Cambridge, Mass., and London: Harvard University Press 1998), 95–6. See also Thomas Lately, *Delmonico's: A Century of Splendor* (Boston: Houghton Mifflin 1967).
59 New York *Post,* 13 Oct. 1860.
60 New York *Times,* 13 Oct. 1860.
61 *Mme Demorest's Mirror of Fashion,* 1st ed., 1860, cited by Ishbel Ross, *Crusades and Crinolines: the Life and Times of Ellen Curtis Demorest and William Jennings Demorest* (New York: Harper and Row 1963), 27; Burrows and Wallace, *Gotham,* 714.
62 *Strong Diary,* 43–4.
63 Ibid., 47.
64 New York *Daily Tribune* and New York *Times,* 13 Oct. 1860.
65 New York *Daily Tribune,* 13 Oct. 1860; *Strong Diary,* 47.
66 New York *Daily Tribune,* 13 Oct. 1860.
67 *Strong Diary,* 48.
68 Ibid.
69 Ibid. 49.
70 New York *Times,* 15 Oct. 1860.
71 Ibid.
72 New York *Evening Post,* 15 Oct. 1860.
73 The charge was made in the New York *Commercial Advertiser,* reprinted in the Toronto *Leader,* 16 Oct. 1860. The prince's letter to Queen Victoria is pre-

sented in Sir Sidney Lee, *King Edward the VII: A Biography*, 2 vols. (London: Macmillan 1925), 1:103. The committee's response appeared in the New York *Times*, 15 Oct. 1860, in a letter-to-the-editor from J. Harsen, chairman of the committee on police and carriages.

74 New York *Commercial Advertiser*, reprinted in Toronto *Leader*, 16 Oct. 1860; New York *Times*, 13 and 15 Oct. 1860.

75 Cornwallis, *Royalty in the New World*, 209; New York *Times*, 13 Oct. 1860.

76 New York *Times*, 15 Oct. 1860.

77 *Strong Diary*, 47; New York *Irish-American*, 20 Oct. 1860.

78 Boston *Courier* article reprinted in New York *Times*, 16 Oct. 1860; *Strong Diary*, 49; Newcastle cited by Lee, *King Edward the VII*, 1:105.

79 *Strong Diary*, 49; Frances Anne Kemble, *Further Records, 1848–1883: A Series of Letters by Frances Anne Kemble*, 2 vols. (London: Richard Bentley and Son 1890), 2:228. See also Dorothy Marshall, *Fanny Kemble* (London: Weidenfeld and Nicolson 1977), 233–4.

80 Citations from Lee, *King Edward VII*, 1:103–4.

81 London *Times*, 2 Dec. 1919, as cited by Lee, *King Edward VII*, 1:104; *Strong Diary*, 47.

Conclusion

1 The estimates of the number of deserters were debated in the press. See Toronto *Globe*, 2 Jan. 1861.

2 New York *Times*, 20 Oct. 1860.

3 Kinahan Cornwallis, *Royalty in the New World; or, the Prince of Wales in America* (New York: M. Doolady 1860), 240.

4 Nathaniel Augustus Woods, *The Prince of Wales in Canada and the United States* (London: Bradbury and Evans 1861), 429.

5 Mrs [Beatrice] Steuart Erskine, *Memoirs of Edward, Earl of Sandwich, 1839–1916* (London: John Murray 1919), 54.

6 Oxford University, Bodleian Library, Acland Family Papers, MS Acland. d.13, Henry Acland to Sarah Acland, 28 Oct., 7 Nov., 11 Nov. 1860.

7 Erskine, *Memoirs*, 54.

8 Lieutenant Thomas Bunbury Gough, *Boyish Reminiscences of His Majesty the King's Visit to Canada in 1860* (London: John Murray 1910), 209–15. In fact, the dowsing probably occurred on another occasion, during the outbound trip; but certainly there was a birthday dinner.

9 Acland Family Papers, Henry Acland to Sarah Acland, 11 Nov. 1860.

10 See the editorial in London *Times*, 13 Nov. 1860.

11 See also the news of 'Naval and Military Intelligence,' in London *Times*,

15 Nov. 1860, letters-to-the-editor of the *Times*, and an article from the London *Globe* on searches, 16 Nov. 1860.

12 Royal Archives (RA), Queen Victoria's Journal, 15 Nov. 1860.

13 Ibid. News of the prince's safe return did not reach North American for nearly two more weeks, by which time concern for his safety was considerable there too. See Toronto *Globe*, 29 Nov. 1860.

14 Cornwallis, *Royalty in the New World*, 242–3.

15 Cited by Sir Sidney Lee, *King Edward VII: A Biography*, 2 vols. (London: Macmillan 1925), 1:106.

16 RA, VIC/Z 467/62, Lord Lyons to Lord John Russell, 22 Oct. 1860.

17 Ibid., Z 467/39, General Bruce to Prince Albert, 20 Sept. 1860; Z 467/69, Lord John Russell to Queen Victoria, 27 Oct. 1860; Z 467/70, Lord Palmerston to Queen Victoria, 4 Nov. 1860.

18 Sir Theodore Martin, *Life of His Royal Highness the Prince Consort*, 5 vols. (London: Smith Elder 1880), 5:191.

19 Cited by Philip Magnus, *King Edward the Seventh* (John Murray: London 1964), 41.

20 NA, MG 29 E1 (F46), Thomas Wily Papers, Thomas Wily, 'A Reminiscence of the Visit of the Prince of Wales to Canada in 1860,' 238.

21 Ibid., 239.

22 Lord Lyons to Mr Griffith, 20 Nov. 1860, cited by Lord Newton, *Lord Lyons: A Record of British Diplomacy*, 2 vols. (London: Edward Arnold 1913), 1:28.

23 Toronto *Globe*, 20 Nov. 1860. On one side of the three-inch medal was the prince's crest, surrounded by a wreath of maple leaves and a scroll reading 'Welcome, Welcome'; on the other was the prince's portrait and the phrase, 'Visited Canada to inaugurate Victoria Bridge, 1860.'

24 Wily, 'Reminiscence,' 239.

25 NA, RG 11, Records of the Department of Public Works, vol. 771, T. Trudeau to Colonel T. Wily, 14 Jan. 1861.

26 Oliver Millar, *The Victorian Pictures in the Collection of Her Majesty the Queen* (Cambridge: Cambridge University Press 1992), 68.

27 John Plunkett, *Queen Victoria: First Media Monarch* (Oxford: Oxford University Press 2003), 229–31.

28 RA, VIC Z467/84, Queen Victoria to Lord Palmerston, 25 Nov. 1860. In the winter of 1860–1, on a visit to England, Head went to Windsor Castle where the queen and prince consort personally thanked and praised him for his assistance during the prince's tour. See a letter from Head cited by D.G.G. Kerr, *Sir Edmund Head: A Scholarly Governor* (Toronto: University of Toronto Press 1954), 215.

29 RA, VIC/Z 467/84, Queen Victoria to Lord Palmerston, 25 Nov. 1860;

Z 467/85 Lord Palmerston to Queen Victoria, 26 Nov. 1860; Lee, *King Edward VII*, 1: 110–11.

30 New York *Times*, 20 Oct. 1860.

31 Toronto, *Globe*, 20 Nov. 1860.

32 E.A. Heaman, *The Inglorious Arts of Peace: Exhibitions in Canadian Society during the Nineteenth Century* (Toronto: University of Toronto Press 1999), 91–2.

33 New York *Herald*, 15 Nov. 1860. On the auction of similar items in Saint John, see Toronto *Globe*, 2 Sept. 1860.

34 NA, RG 11, vol. 771.

35 NA, RG 7 G14, Office of the Governor General, Royal Visits, vol. 25, Commissioner John Rose to Sir Fenwick Williams, 10 Nov. 1860.

36 NA, RG 11, vol. 771, T. Trudeau to John Page, chief engineer, Public Works, Ottawa, 7 Dec. 1860. Overcharging by contractors working on the Ottawa buildings caused a public scandal; see Carolyn M. Young, *The Glory of Ottawa: Canada's First Parliament Buildings* (Montreal and Kingston: McGill-Queen's University Press 1995), 82–6.

37 NA, RG 11, vol. 771, T. Trudeau to I.M. Sanderson, 13 Nov. 1860; T. Trudeau to John P. Ryley and Company, proprietors, Royal Hotel, Hamilton, 29 Oct. 1860; Wily, 'Reminiscences,' 240. Protracted debates over compensation to William Notman, the Montreal photographer, are discussed in Colleen Skidmore, '"All that is interesting in the Canadas": William Notman's Maple Box Portfolio of Stereographic Views, 1860,' *Journal of Canadian Studies* 32 (1998): 69–90.

38 New York *Herald* editorial reprinted in the London *Times*, 15 Nov. 1860.

39 Palmerston's 14 November speech to the London Company of Salters was printed in the *Times* on 15 Nov. 1860; Newcastle's 7 December speech to the Masonic Order at Nottingham was printed in the *Times* on 8 December 1860 and is reproduced in Robert Cellem, *Visit of His Royal Highness, the Prince of Wales to the British North American Provinces and United States, in the Year 1860* (Toronto: Henry Rowsell 1861), 429–30; the *Times* editorial of 16 November is also reprinted in Cellem, *Visit of HRH*, 428.

40 New York *Times*, 20 Oct. 1860; Cornwallis, *Royalty in the New World*, 243; *New England Tour of H.R.H., the Prince of Wales*, 3rd ed. (Boston: privately printed 1860), 38.

41 Lyons to Lewis Cass, 8 Dec. 1860, and William Henry Trescott to Lyons, 11 Dec. 1860, in Cellem, *Visit of HRH*, 432–3.

42 Lee, *King Edward VII*, 1:110. George Ticknor Curtis, in *Life of James Buchanan, Fifteenth President of the United States*, 2 vols. (New York: Harper 1883), 1:234, makes the same point.

43 Brian Jenkins, *Britain and the War for the Union*, 2 vols. (Montreal and

Kingston McGill-Queen's University Press 1974), vol. 1; Gordon H. Warren, *Fountain of Discontent: The Trent Affair and the Freedom of the Seas* (Boston: Northeastern University Press 1981); W.L. Morton, 'British North America and a Continent in Dissolution, 1861–1871,' *History* 47 (1962): 139–56.

44 New York *Times,* 20 Oct. 1860.

45 London *Times,* 15 Nov. 1860; Cellem, *Visit of HRH,* 429.

46 Morgan, *Tour of H.R.H.,* 209; Toronto *Globe,* 29 Nov. 1860; Macdonald's speech is reproduced in full in Toronto *Globe,* 13 Nov. 1860.

47 Cornwallis, *Royalty in the New World,* 246–7; New York *Evening Post,* 16 Aug. 1860; New York *Times,* 21 Aug. 1860.

Bibliography of Primary Sources

Manuscript Sources

Archives of Ontario
Sarah Hill
Sir Allan McNabb
John Beverley Robinson

Archives of the Roman Catholic Archdiocese of Toronto
Bishop John Joseph Lynch

Bodelian Library, Oxford, England
Acland Family Papers

City of Toronto Archives
Toronto Board of Works, Minutes, 1860

National Archives of Canada
Henry, Duke of Newcastle
Henry Wentworth Acland
Brown Chamberlin
Joseph Howe
Sir John Alexander Macdonald
Sir Samuel Leonard Tilley
Thomas Wily

Canada State Books
Department of Indian Affairs

Department of Public Works
Office of the Governor General

France, Archives des Affaires Étrangères, Consulat de Québec
Great Britain, Colonial Office

New York Public Library
Charles P. Daly

Public Archives of Nova Scotia
George Hill

Royal Archives, Windsor, England
Victorian Archives
Queen Victoria's Journal

Toronto Reference Library, Baldwin Room
Larrett Smith Diaries

Newspapers (consulted for 1860–1)

St John's, Newfoundland
Newfoundland Express
Times
Halifax, Nova Scotia
Acadian Recorder
Constitutionalist
Morning Chronicle
Saint John, New Brunswick
Carleton Sentinel
Christian Visitor
Morning Freeman
Morning News
Fredericton, New Brunswick
Head Quarters
New Brunswick Reporter
Charlottetown, Prince Edward Island
Examiner
Islander
Quebec, Canada East
Le Canadien

Le Courier du Canada
Daily Mercury
Montreal, Canada East
La Minerve
L'Ordre
Pilot
Witness
Saint Hyacinthe, Canada East
Le Courrier de St Hyacinthe
Brockville, Canada West
Recorder
Ottawa, Canada West
Citizen
Union
Perth, Canada West
Courrier
Kingston, Canada West
British Whig
Daily News
Peterborough, Canada West
Examiner
Toronto, Canada West
Christian Guardian
Globe
Leader
Mackenzie's Weekly
Barrie, Canada West
Northern Advance
Hamilton, Canada West
Spectator
London, Canada West
Free Press
Sarnia, Canada West
Observer
London, England
News of the World
Nonconformist
Times
Weekly Chronicle and Register
Charleston, South Carolina
Mercury

Chicago, Illinois
Journal
Tribune
Detroit, Michigan
Free Press
New York, New York
Daily Tribune
Freeman's Journal and Catholic Register
Herald
Irish-American
Evening Post
Times
Philadelphia, Pennsylvania
Ledger and Transcript
Richmond, Virginia
Whig
Washington, D.C.
National Intelligencer

Periodicals and Illustrated Newspapers (consulted for 1860–1)

Toronto, Canada West
Journal of Education for Upper Canada
London, England
Illustrated London News
Illustrated Times
Punch
Westminster Review
New York, New York
Frank Leslie's Illustrated Newspaper
Harper's Weekly Journal of Civilization
New-York Illustrated News

Printed Materials

A British Canadian [Henry James Morgan]. *The Tour of H.R.H. the Prince of Wales through British America and the United States*. Montreal: John Lovell 1860.

Cellem, Robert. *Visit of His Royal Highness, the Prince of Wales to the British North American Provinces and United States, in the Year 1860*. Toronto: Henry Rowsell 1861.

Chaveau, Pierre-J., J. Lenoir-Rolland, J. Phelan. *The Visit of His Royal Highness, the Prince of Wales to America*. Montreal: Journal of Public Instruction for Lower Canada 1860.

Cornwallis, Kinahan. *Royalty in the New World; or, the Prince of Wales in America*. New York: M. Doolady 1860.

de Cordova, R.J. *The Prince's Visit: A Humorous Description*. New York: B. Fordham 1861.

Engleheart, Gardner D. *Journal of the Progress of H.R.H. the Prince of Wales through British North America and His Visit to the United States*. London: Privately printed 1860.

Erskine, Mrs Steuart, ed. *Memoirs of Edward, Earl of Sandwich, 1839-1916*. London: J. Murray 1919.

Fox, William Sherwood, ed. *Letters of William Davies, Toronto, 1854-1861*. Toronto: University of Toronto Press 1945.

Gough, Lieut. Thomas Bunbury. *Boyish Reminiscences of His Majesty the King's Visit to Canada in 1860*. London: John Murray 1910.

Kemble, Frances Anne. *Further Records, 1848–1883: A Series of Letters by Frances Anne Kemble*. London: Richard Bentley and Son 1890.

Minutes of the Council of the Corporation of the City of Toronto for 1860. Toronto 1861.

Nevins, Allan, and Milton Halsey Thomas, eds. *The Diary of George Templeton Strong: The Civil War Years, 1860–1865*. New York: Macmillan 1952.

The New England Tour of H.R.H. the Prince of Wales. 3rd ed. Boston: Bee Printing 1860.

Proceedings of the Board of Aldermen, City of New York. Vol. 79. New York: Charles W. Babe 1860.

Proceedings of the Board of Aldermen, City of New York, from October 1st 1860 to January 4th, 1861. New York: Edmond Jones 1861.

Shannon, William. *Narrative of the Proceedings of the Loyal Orangemen of Kingston and Belleville, on the 4th, 5th, and 6th of September, 1860 in Connection with the Visit of H.R.H. the Prince of Wales, to Central Canada*. Belleville: M. Bowell 1861.

Woods, Nathaniel Augustus. *The Prince of Wales in Canada and the United States*. London: Bradbury and Evans 1861.

Index

www.ingramcontent.com/pod-product-compliance
Lightning Source LLC
LaVergne TN
LVHW090758070826
844660LV00022B/1018

* 9 7 8 0 8 0 2 0 8 6 6 5 5 *